GLOBAL ECONOMIC STUDIES

GLOBAL ECONOMICS: CRISIS AND COOPERATION

GLOBAL ECONOMIC STUDIES

Additional books in this series can be found on Nova's website under the Series tab.

Additional E-books in this series can be found on Nova's website under the E-book tab.

GLOBAL RECESSION CAUSES, IMPACTS AND REMEDIES

Additional books in this series can be found on Nova's website under the Series tab.

Additional E-books in this series can be found on Nova's website under the E-book tab.

GLOBAL ECONOMIC STUDIES

GLOBAL ECONOMICS: CRISIS AND COOPERATION

JONATHAN P. CASTLE
EDITOR

Nova Science Publishers, Inc.
New York

Copyright © 2010 by Nova Science Publishers, Inc.

All rights reserved. No part of this book may be reproduced, stored in a retrieval system or transmitted in any form or by any means: electronic, electrostatic, magnetic, tape, mechanical photocopying, recording or otherwise without the written permission of the Publisher.

For permission to use material from this book please contact us:
Telephone 631-231-7269; Fax 631-231-8175
Web Site: http://www.novapublishers.com

NOTICE TO THE READER

The Publisher has taken reasonable care in the preparation of this book, but makes no expressed or implied warranty of any kind and assumes no responsibility for any errors or omissions. No liability is assumed for incidental or consequential damages in connection with or arising out of information contained in this book. The Publisher shall not be liable for any special, consequential, or exemplary damages resulting, in whole or in part, from the readers' use of, or reliance upon, this material. Any parts of this book based on government reports are so indicated and copyright is claimed for those parts to the extent applicable to compilations of such works.

Independent verification should be sought for any data, advice or recommendations contained in this book. In addition, no responsibility is assumed by the publisher for any injury and/or damage to persons or property arising from any methods, products, instructions, ideas or otherwise contained in this publication.

This publication is designed to provide accurate and authoritative information with regard to the subject matter covered herein. It is sold with the clear understanding that the Publisher is not engaged in rendering legal or any other professional services. If legal or any other expert assistance is required, the services of a competent person should be sought. FROM A DECLARATION OF PARTICIPANTS JOINTLY ADOPTED BY A COMMITTEE OF THE AMERICAN BAR ASSOCIATION AND A COMMITTEE OF PUBLISHERS.

Additional color graphics may be available in the e-book version of this book.

LIBRARY OF CONGRESS CATALOGING-IN-PUBLICATION DATA

Global economics : crisis and cooperation / editor, Jonathan P. Castle.
   p. cm.
  Includes index.
  ISBN 978-1-61761-114-8 (hbk.)
 1. Global Financial Crisis, 2008-2009. 2. Financial crises--Prevention--International cooperation. 3. Economic policy--International cooperation. I. Castle, Jonathan P.
  HB37172008 .G564 2009
  337--dc22
                        2010026727

Published by Nova Science Publishers, Inc. † New York

CONTENTS

Preface		vii
Chapter 1	The Global Financial Crisis: Analysis and Policy Implications *Dick K. Nanto*	1
Chapter 2	The G-20 and International Economic Cooperation: Background and Implications for Congress *Rebecca M. Nelson*	171
Chapter 3	Limiting Central Government Budget Deficits: International Experiences *James K. Jackson*	199
Chapter 4	The Global Economic Crisis: Impact on Sub-Saharan Africa and Global Policy Responses *Alexis Arieff, Martin A. Weiss and Vivian C. Jones*	217
Index		245

PREFACE

The world appears to be recovering from the global recession that has caused widespread business contraction, increases in unemployment, and shrinking government revenues. Although the industrialized economies have stopped contracting, for many, unemployment is still rising. The United States likely hit bottom in June 2009, but numerous small banks and households still face huge problems in restoring their balance sheets, and unemployment has combined with subprime loans to keep home foreclosures at a high rate. Nearly all industrialized countries and many emerging and developing nations avoided dropping into another "Great Depression" by implementing sizable economic stimulus and/or financial sector rescue packages. This book analyzes the crisis which has exposed fundamental weaknesses in financial systems worldwide, demonstrate how interconnected and interdependent economies are today, and has posed vexing policy dilemmas.

Chapter 1- The world appears to be recovering from the global recession that has caused widespread business contraction, increases in unemployment, and shrinking government revenues. Although the industrialized economies have stopped contracting, for many, unemployment is still rising. The United States likely hit bottom in June 2009, but numerous small banks and households still face huge problems in restoring their balance sheets, and unemployment has combined with sub- prime loans to keep home foreclosures at a high rate. Nearly all industrialized countries and many emerging and developing nations avoided dropping into another "Great Depression" by implementing sizable economic stimulus and/or financial sector rescue packages, such as the American Recovery and Reinvestment Act of 2009 (P.L. 111-5). Several countries have resorted to borrowing from the International Monetary Fund as a last resort. The crisis has exposed fundamental weaknesses in financial systems worldwide, demonstrated how interconnected and interdependent economies are today, and has posed vexing policy dilemmas.

The process for coping with the crisis by countries across the globe has been manifest in four basic phases. The first has been intervention to contain the contagion and restore confidence in the system. The second has been coping with the secondary effects of the crisis, particularly the global recession and flight of capital from countries in emerging markets and elsewhere that have been affected by the crisis. The third phase of this process is to make changes in the financial system to reduce risk and prevent future crises. In order to give these proposals political backing, world leaders have called for international meetings to address changes in policy, regulations, oversight, and enforcement. On September 24-25, 2009, heads of the G-20 nations met in Pittsburgh to address the global financial crisis. The fourth phase of the process is dealing with political, social, and security effects of the financial turmoil. One such effect is the strengthened role of China in financial markets.

Chapter 2- Governments discuss and coordinate economic policies using a mix of formal institutions, such as the World Trade Organization (WTO) and International Monetary Fund (IMF), and more informal economic forums, like the Group of Seven, or G-7, and the Group of 20, or G-20. This report focuses on informal economic forums, and, specifically, the role of the G-20 in coordinating governments' responses to the current economic crisis. The members of the G-7 are Canada, France, Germany, Italy, Japan, the United Kingdom, and the United States. The G-20 includes the G-7 members plus Argentina, Australia, Brazil, China, India, Indonesia, Mexico, Russia, Saudi Arabia, South Africa, South Korea, Turkey, and the European Union (EU).

Since the mid-1970s, leaders from the G-7, a small group of developed countries, have gathered annually to discuss and coordinate financial and economic policies. Large emerging-market economies such as China started to have more sway in financial markets in the 1 990s, and the Asian Financial Crisis in 1997-1998 showed that emerging markets were too important to exclude from international economic discussions. The G-20 was formed in 1999 as an opportunity for finance ministers and central bank governors from both developed and emerging-market countries to discuss financial issues. The G-20 remained a less prominent forum than the G-7, as it involved meetings among finance ministers while the G-7 sessions also involved summit meetings among heads of governments or heads of state.

With the onset of the current financial crisis, the G-7 leaders decided to convene the G-20 leaders for a meeting, or "summit," to discuss and coordinate policy responses to the crisis. To date, the G-20 leaders have held three summits to coordinate policy responses to the crisis: November 2008 in Washington, DC; April 2009 in London; and September 2009 in Pittsburgh. At the Pittsburgh summit, the G-20 leaders announced that the G-20 would henceforth be the premier forum for international economic coordination, supplanting the G-7's role as such.

Chapter 3- The global financial crisis and economic recession spurred national governments to boost fiscal expenditures to stimulate economic growth and to provide capital injections to support their financial sectors. Government measures included asset purchases, direct lending through national treasuries, and government-backed guarantees for financial sector liabilities. The severity and global nature of the economic recession raised the rate of unemployment, increased the cost of stabilizing the financial sector, and limited the number of policy options that were available to national leaders. In turn, the financial crisis negatively affected economic output and contributed to the severity of the economic recession. As a result, the surge in fiscal spending, combined with a loss of revenue, has caused government deficit spending to rise sharply when measured as a share of gross domestic product (GDP) and increased the overall level of public debt. Recent forecasts indicate that should the current economic rebound take hold, budget deficits on the whole likely will stabilize, but are not expected to fall appreciably for some time.

The sharp rise in deficit spending is prompting policymakers to assess various strategies for winding down their stimulus measures and to curtail capital injections without disrupting the nascent economic recovery. This report focuses on how major developed and emerging-market country governments, particularly the G-20 and Organization for Economic Cooperation and Development (OECD) countries, limit their fiscal deficits. Financial markets support government efforts to reduce deficit spending, because they are concerned over the long-term impact of the budget deficits. At the same time, they are concerned that the loss of spending will slow down the economic recovery and they doubt the conviction of some governments to impose austere budgets in the face of public opposition. Some central governments are examining such measures as budget rules, or fiscal consolidation, as a way to trim spending and reduce the overall size of their central government debt. Budget rules can be applied in a number of ways, including limiting central government budget deficits to a determined percentage of GDP. To the extent that fiscal consolidation lowers the market rate of interest, such efforts could improve a government's budget position by lowering borrowing costs and stimulating economic growth. Other strategies include authorizing independent public institutions to spearhead fiscal consolidation efforts and developing medium-term budgetary frameworks for fiscal planning. Fiscal consolidation efforts, however, generally require policymakers to weigh the effects of various policy trade-offs, including the trade-off between adopting stringent, but enforceable, rules-based programs, compared with more flexible, but less effective, principles-based programs that offer policymakers some discretion in applying punitive measures.

Chapter 4- Sub-Saharan Africa has been strongly affected by the global recession, despite initial optimism that the global financial system would have few spillover effects on the continent. The International Monetary Fund (IMF) estimated in 2009 that average economic growth in Africa would slow to 1%, from an annual average of over 6% to 1% over the previous five years, before rebounding to 4% in 2010. As a region, Africa is not thought to have undergone a recession in 2009. However, most African countries are thought to require high rates of economic growth in order to outpace population growth and make progress in alleviating poverty.

The mechanisms through which the crisis has affected Africa include a contraction in global trade and a related collapse in primary commodity exports, on which many countries are dependent. Foreign investment and migrant worker remittances are also expected to decrease significantly, and some analysts predict cuts in foreign aid in the medium term if the crisis persists. Africa's most powerful economies have proven particularly vulnerable to the downturn: South Africa has experienced a recession for the first time in nearly two decades, and Nigeria and Angola have reported revenue shortfalls due to the fall in global oil prices. Several countries seen as having solid macroeconomic governance, notably Botswana, have sought international financial assistance to cope with the impact of the crisis. At the same time, a number of low-income African countries are projected to experience relatively robust growth in 2009 and 2010, leading some economists to talk of Africa's underlying economic resilience.

In: Global Economics Crisis and Cooperation
Editor: Jonathan P. Castle

ISBN: 978-1-61761-114-8
© 2010 Nova Science Publishers, Inc.

Chapter 1

THE GLOBAL FINANCIAL CRISIS: ANALYSIS AND POLICY IMPLICATIONS

Dick K. Nanto

SUMMARY

The world appears to be recovering from the global recession that has caused widespread business contraction, increases in unemployment, and shrinking government revenues. Although the industrialized economies have stopped contracting, for many, unemployment is still rising. The United States likely hit bottom in June 2009, but numerous small banks and households still face huge problems in restoring their balance sheets, and unemployment has combined with sub- prime loans to keep home foreclosures at a high rate. Nearly all industrialized countries and many emerging and developing nations avoided dropping into another "Great Depression" by implementing sizable economic stimulus and/or financial sector rescue packages, such as the American Recovery and Reinvestment Act of 2009 (P.L. 111-5). Several countries have resorted to borrowing from the International Monetary Fund as a last resort. The crisis has exposed fundamental weaknesses in financial systems worldwide, demonstrated how interconnected and interdependent economies are today, and has posed vexing policy dilemmas.

The process for coping with the crisis by countries across the globe has been manifest in four basic phases. The first has been intervention to contain the contagion and restore confidence in the system. The second has been coping with the secondary effects of the crisis, particularly the global recession and flight of capital from countries in emerging markets and elsewhere that have been affected by the crisis. The third phase of this process is to make changes in the financial system to reduce risk and prevent future crises. In order to give these proposals political backing, world leaders have called for international meetings to address changes in policy, regulations, oversight, and enforcement. On September 24-25, 2009, heads of the G-20 nations met in Pittsburgh to address the global financial crisis. The fourth phase of the process is dealing with political, social, and security effects of the financial turmoil. One such effect is the strengthened role of China in financial markets.

The role for Congress in this financial crisis is multifaceted. While the recent focus has been on combating the recession, the ultimate issue perhaps is how to ensure the smooth and efficient functioning of financial markets to promote the general well-being of the country while protecting taxpayer interests and facilitating business operations without creating a moral hazard. In addition to preventing future crises through legislative, oversight, and domestic regulatory functions, On June 17, 2009, the Obama Administration presented a proposal for financial regulatory reform that focuses on five areas and includes establishing the Federal Reserve as a systemic risk regulator, creating a Council of Regulators, regulating all financial derivatives, creating a Consumer Financial Protection Agency, improving coordination and oversight of international financial markets, and other provisions. The reform agenda now has moved to Congress with legislation that addresses many of the issues in the Obama plan but also includes other financial issues. Among the numerous bills in Congress addressing the financial crisis, H.R. 4173 (Wall Street Reform and Consumer Protection Act of 2009, passed the House on December 1, 2009) addresses many of the concerns raised. Congress also plays a role in measures to reform and recapitalize the International Monetary Fund, the World Bank, and regional development banks.

This report provides a historical account and analysis of the crisis through January 2010. For information on current aspects of the crisis, see other CRS reports. This report will not be updated.

RECENT DEVELOPMENTS[1]

February 3. Federal Reserve Chairman Ben S. Bernanke begins second term.

February 2. Greece's prime minister, George Papandreou, makes appeal for unity over its worst financial crisis in decades. The European Commission endorses a fiscal rescue plan.

January 27. President Obama pledged to divert $30 billion of money repaid from the Troubled Asset Relief Program to smaller banks to help them make loans to small businesses.

January 21. President Obama proposed that a single bank be allowed to hold no more than 10% of total bank deposits and that banks no longer be allowed to operate hedge funds and private equity funds and to make riskier investments to reap a quick reward.

December 30. IHS Global Insight released its top-10 Global Economic Predictions for 2010: (1) The U.S. recovery will start slowly. (2) Europe and Japan will rebound even more slowly than the United States. (3) Most emerging markets—especially in Asia—will outpace the developed economies. (4) Interest rates will remain low—especially in the G7. (5) Fiscal stimulus will begin to ease. (6) Commodity prices will move sideways. (7) Inflation will (mostly) not be a problem. (8) After improving for a while, global imbalances will worsen again. (9) While the dollar may strengthen a little, it is on a downward path. (10) The risk of a double-dip growth profile is still uncomfortably high.

December 14. Abu Dhabi provided Dubai with an infusion of $10 billion that will enable Dubai to pay $4.1 billion to bondholders as well as bills from suppliers and contractors.

December 3. European Central Bank President Jean-Claude Trichet signaled that the bank's planned withdrawal of stimulus measures would proceed gradually.

November 14. Eurostat announced that the Euro Zone had officially emerged from recession during the third quarter 2009. The rebound was powered by Germany.

November 10. Senate Banking Committee Chairman Christopher Dodd released a draft of a financial regulation bill.

September 24-25. At the Group of 20 Summit held in Pittsburgh, world leaders agreed to make the G-20 the leading forum for coordinating global economic policy; not to withdraw stimulus measures until a durable recovery is in place; to co-ordinate their exit strategies from the stimulus measures; to harmonize macroeconomic policies to avoid imbalances (America's deficits and Asia's savings glut) that worsened the financial crisis; and to eliminate subsidies on fossil fuels (only in the medium term). In trade, there was only a weak commitment to get the Doha round of multilateral trade negotiations at the World Trade Organizations back on track by 2010, and for the International Monetary Fund, the leaders pledged to provide the "under-represented" mostly developing countries at least 5% more of the voting rights by 2011. The other large institutional change was the ascension of the Financial Stability Board, a group of central bankers and financial regulators, to take a lead role in coordinating and monitoring tougher financial regulations and serve, along with the International Monetary Fund, as an early-warning system for emerging risks.

THE GLOBAL FINANCIAL CRISIS AND U.S. INTERESTS[2]

Policymaking to deal with the global financial crisis and ensuing global recession has now moved from containing the contagion to specific actions aimed at promoting recovery and changing regulations to prevent a reoccurrence of the problem. Other issues, such as health care and the war in Afghanistan, also are competing for attention. Some have expressed concern that the improving economic and financial outlook may cause regulatory reform of the financial system to lose some traction in the crowded policy agenda. This report provides an overview of the global aspects of the financial crisis, how it developed, proposals for regulatory change, and a review of how the crisis is affecting other regions of the world.

According to Global Insight, an econometric forecasting firm, the global financial crisis, or Great Recession of 2007-2009, can now be viewed as a once-in-a-century disaster with more or less unique features. Super-aggressive liquidity injections and reflationary actions during the fourth quarter of 2008 and the early months of 2009 helped stabilize the situation. The global economy's rebound gathered considerable steam during the second half of 2009, when world GDP (gross domestic product) growth accelerated to well above 3.0%, from 1.7% in the second quarter, after having contracted at an alarming pace of 6.5% in the first quarter. Global Insight expects world GDP to be at a below-trend pace of about 2.8% in 2010, after having contracted by 2.0% in 2009 with the economies of Greater China and the United States leading the recovery.[3]

The role for Congress in this financial crisis is multifaceted. The overall issue seems to be how to ensure the smooth and efficient functioning of financial markets to promote the general wellbeing of the country while protecting taxpayer interests and facilitating business operations without creating a moral hazard.[4] The reality, however, is that financial interests are well entrenched, and the existing patchwork system of regulation (or non-regulation) has evolved over the past century largely in response to particular problems. If the United States were to "start from scratch" in designing an optimal regulatory system, it likely would not select the one it has, but making dramatic changes to the existing system invariably will result in someone's "ox being gored" and substantial bureaucratic inertia and lobbying activity.

Congress also has a role to play in preventing future crises through legislative, oversight, and domestic regulatory functions. In addition, Congress has been providing funds and ground rules for economic stabilization and rescue packages and informing the public through hearings and other means. Congress also plays a role in measures to reform the international financial system, in recapitalizing international financial institutions, such as the International Monetary Fund, in replenishing funds for poverty reduction arms of the World Bank (International Development Association) and regional development banks, and in providing economic and humanitarian assistance to countries in need.

The current crisis began as a bursting of the U.S. housing market bubble and a rise in foreclosures. As it ballooned into a global financial and economic crisis, some of the largest and most venerable banks, investment houses, and insurance companies have either declared bankruptcy or have had to be rescued financially. In October 2008, after the bankruptcy of Lehman Brothers, credit flows froze, lender confidence dropped, and one after another the economies of countries around the world dipped toward recession. The crisis exposed fundamental weaknesses in financial systems worldwide, and despite coordinated easing of monetary policy by governments, trillions of dollars in intervention by central banks and governments, and large fiscal stimulus packages, recovery appears to be just beginning.

This financial crisis which began in industrialized countries quickly spread to emerging market and developing economies. Investors pulled capital from countries, even those with small levels of perceived risk, and caused values of stocks and domestic currencies to plunge. Also, slumping exports and commodity prices have added to the woes and pushed economies world wide either into recession or into a period of slower economic growth.

For the United States, the financial turmoil touches on the fundamental national interest of protecting the economic security of Americans. It also is affecting the United States in achieving national foreign policy goals, such as maintaining political stability and cooperative relations with other nations and supporting a financial infrastructure that allows for the efficient functioning of the international economy. Reverberations from the financial crisis, moreover, are not only being felt on Wall Street and Main Street but are being manifest in world flows of exports and imports, rates of growth and unemployment, government revenues and expenditures, and in political risk in some countries. The simultaneous slowdown in economic activity around the globe indicates that emerging market and developing economies have not decoupled from industrialized countries and governments cannot depend on exports to pull them out of these recessionary conditions.

This global financial and economic crisis has brought to the public consciousness several arcane financial terms usually confined to the domain of regulators and Wall Street investors. These terms lie at the heart of both understanding and resolving this financial crisis and include:

- Systemic risk ("Too big to fail"): The risk that the failure of one or a set of market participants, such as core banks, will reverberate through a financial system and cause severe problems for participants in other sectors. Because of systemic risk, the scope of regulatory agencies may have to be expanded to cover a wider range of institutions and markets.[5]
- Deleveraging: The unwinding of debt. Companies borrow to buy assets that increase their growth potential or increase returns on investments. Deleveraging lowers the risk of default on debt and mitigates losses, but if it is done by selling assets at a discount, it may depress security and asset prices and lead to large losses. Hedge funds tend to be highly leveraged.
- Procyclicality: The tendency for market players to take actions over a business cycle that increase the boom-and-bust effects, e.g. borrowing extensively during upturns and deleveraging during downturns. Changing regulations to dampen procyclical effects would be extremely challenging.[6]
- Preferred equity: A cross between common stock and debt. It gives the holder a claim, prior to that of common stockholders, on earnings and on assets in the event of liquidation. Most preferred stock pays a fixed dividend. As a result of the stress tests in early 2009, some banks may increase their capital base by converting preferred equity to common stock.
- Collateralized debt obligations (CDOs): a type of structured asset-backed security whose value and payments are derived from a portfolio of fixed-income underlying assets. CDOs based on sub-prime mortgages have been at the heart of the global financial crisis. CDOs are assigned different risk classes or tranches, with "senior" tranches considered to be the safest. Since interest and principal payments are made in order of seniority, junior tranches offer higher coupon payments (and interest rates) or lower prices to compensate for additional default risk. Investors, pension funds, and insurance companies buy CDOs.
- Credit default swap (CDS): a credit derivative contract between two counterparties in which the buyer makes periodic payments to the seller and in return receives a sum of money if a certain credit event occurs (such as a default in an underlying financial instrument). Payoffs and collateral calls on CDSs issued on sub-prime mortgage CDOs have been a primary cause of the problems of AIG and other companies.

The global financial crisis has brought home an important point: the United States is still a major center of the financial world. Regional financial crises (such as the Asian financial crisis, Japan's banking crisis, or the Latin American debt crisis) can occur without seriously infecting the rest of the global financial system. But when the U.S. financial system stumbles, it may bring major parts of the rest of the world down with it.[7] The reason is that the United States is the main guarantor of the international financial system, the provider of dollars widely used as currency reserves and as an international medium of exchange, and a contributor to much of the financial capital that sloshes around the world seeking higher yields. The rest of the world may not appreciate it, but a financial crisis in the United States often takes on a global hue.

Policy and Legislation[8]

Early U.S. policy was aimed at containing the contagion and in dealing with the ensuing recession. The two largest legislative actions were the Troubled Asset Relief Program aimed at providing support for financial institutions[9] and the American Recovery and Reinvestment Act of 2009 aimed at providing stimulus to the economy.[10]

Policy proposals to change specific regulations as well as the structure of regulation and supervision at both the domestic and international levels have been coming forth through the legislative process, from the Administration, and from recommendations by international organizations such as the International Monetary Fund,[11] Bank for International Settlements,[12] and Financial Stability Board (Forum).[13] On June 17, 2009, the Obama administration announced its plan for regulatory reform of the U.S. financial system.[14] In Congress, numerous bills have been introduced that deal with issues such as establishing a commission/select committee to investigate causes of the financial crisis, provide oversight and greater accountability of Federal Reserve and Treasury lending activity, deal with problems in the housing and mortgage markets, provide funding for the International Monetary Fund, address problems with consumer credit cards, provide for improved oversight for financial and commodities markets, deal with the U.S. national debt, and establish a systemic risk monitor.

The United States, however, cannot be a regulatory island among competing nations of the world. In an international marketplace of multinational corporations, instant transfers of wealth, lightning fast communications, and globalized trading systems for equities and securities, if U.S. regulations are anomalous or significantly more "burdensome" than those in other industrialized nations, business and transactions could migrate toward other markets. Hence, many have emphasized the need to coordinate regulatory changes among nations. The vehicle for forming an international consensus on measures to be taken by individual countries is the G-20 along with the International Monetary Fund and new Financial Stability Board[15] (based in Switzerland), although some developing nations prefer the more inclusive G-30. The third G-20 Summit was held in Pittsburgh on September 24-25, 2009. World leaders there focused on tougher regulation of the financial sector, including limits on bonus payments for bankers, and attempted to decide what comes next, now that there are tentative signs of recovery. Among the issues that were on the U.S. agenda included measures to ease global economic trade imbalances, to prevent a repeat of financial crises through a process of regular consultations, and to have increased cooperation on policies that will ensure a rebalancing of world growth.

The April 2009 G-20 London Summit called for a greater role for the IMF and for it to collaborate with the new Financial Stability Board to provide early warning of macroeconomic and financial risks and actions needed to address them.[16] The leaders also agreed that national financial supervisors should establish Colleges of Supervisors consisting of national financial supervisory agencies that oversee globally active financial institutions. (See "G-20 Meetings" section of this report.) Still, work at the international level remains advisory.

At the April 2009 G-20 London Summit, a schism arose between the United States and the U.K., who were arguing for large and coordinated stimulus packages, and Germany and France, who considered their automatic stabilizers (increases in government expenditures for items such as unemployment insurance that are triggered any time the economy slows) plus existing stimulus programs as sufficient. In the communiqué, the G-20 leaders decided to add $1.1 trillion in resources to the international financial institutions, including $750 billion for the International Monetary Fund, $250 billion to boost global trade, and $100 billion for multilateral development banks. On June 24, 2009, President Obama signed H.R. 2346 into law (P.L. 111-32). This increased the U.S. quota in the International Monetary Fund by 4.5 billion SDRs ($7.69 billion), provided loans to the IMF of up to an additional 75 billion SDRs ($116.01 billion), and authorized the United States Executive Director of the IMF to vote to approve the sale of up to 12,965,649 ounces of the Fund's gold.[17]

On June 17, 2009, the Department of the Treasury presented the Obama Administration proposal for financial regulatory reform. This was followed by twelve titles of proposed legislation to implement the reforms. The proposals focus on five areas (and proposed legislation) as indicated below. Legislation in Congress also addresses these issues.

1. Promote robust supervision and regulation of financial firms.
    a. A new Financial Services Oversight Council to identify emerging systemic risks and improve interagency cooperation (chaired by Treasury and including the heads of the principal federal financial regulators as members).[18]
    b. New authority for the Federal Reserve to supervise all firms that could pose a threat to financial stability, even those that do not own banks.[19]
    c. Stronger capital and other prudential standards for all financial firms, and even higher standards for large, interconnected firms.[20]
    d. A new National Bank Supervisor (a single agency with separate status in Treasury to supervise all federally chartered banks).[21]
    e. Elimination of the federal thrift charter and other loopholes that allowed some depository institutions to avoid bank holding company regulation by the Federal Reserve.[22]
    f. The registration of advisers of hedge funds and other private pools of capital with the SEC.[23]
2. Establish comprehensive supervision of financial markets.
    a. Enhanced regulation of securitization markets, including new requirements for market transparency, stronger regulation of credit rating agencies, and a requirement that issuers and originators retain a financial interest in securitized loans.[24]
    b. Comprehensive regulation of all over-the-counter derivatives.[25]
    c. New authority for the Federal Reserve to oversee payment, clearing, and settlement systems.[26]
3. Protect consumers and investors from financial abuse.
    a. A new Consumer Financial Protection Agency (an independent entity) to protect consumers across the financial sector from unfair, deceptive, and abusive practices.[27]
    b. Stronger regulations to improve the transparency, fairness, and appropriateness of consumer and investor products and services.[28]
    c. A level playing field and higher standards for providers of consumer financial products and services, whether or not they are part of a bank.[29]
4. Provide the government with the tools it needs to manage financial crises.

a. A new regime to resolve nonbank financial institutions whose failure could have serious systemic effects.[30]
b. Revisions to the Federal Reserve's emergency lending authority to improve accountability.[31]
5. Raise international regulatory standards and improve international cooperation. Treasury proposed international reforms to support U.S. efforts, including strengthening the capital framework; improving oversight of global financial markets; coordinating supervision of internationally active firms; and enhancing crisis management tools.

Treasury also proposed the creation of an Office of National Insurance within the Department of the Treasury.[32]

In Congress, numerous bills have been introduced that address the above and other financial regulatory issues. In December 2009, the House passed **H.R. 4173**, The Wall Street Reform and Consumer Protection Act that addresses many of the issues raised by the financial crisis. (See Text Box below.) The following is a brief listing of the major regulatory issues that have been raised by selected regulatory bills in Congress. (**Appendix D** also provides a sketch of problems raised and possible policy options.)

H.R. 4173, THE WALL STREET REFORM AND CONSUMER PROTECTION ACT

(December 11, 2009, passed by the House;
January 20, 2010, referred to the Senate Banking Committee)

Includes the following major provisions:

- Creates the **Consumer Financial Protection** Agency;
- Creates the **Financial Stability Council** to identify and regulate financial firms that are so large, interconnected, or risky that their collapse would put the entire financial system at risk;
- Provides **Dissolution Authority** for dismantling large, failing financial institutions though an orderly process;
- Gives shareholders an advisory vote on **Executive Compensation** and golden parachutes;
- Strengthens the **Security and Exchange Commission's powers** in order to better protect investors and regulate the nation's securities markets;
- Regulates the **Over-the-counter Derivatives** marketplace.
- Provides for **Mortgage Reform** by outlawing many of the industry practices that marked the subprime lending boom;
- Reforms **Credit Rating Agencies** to reduce conflicts of interest and to impose a liability standard on the agencies;
- Requires almost all advisors to **Private Pools of Capital** (hedge funds and private equity) to register with the SEC and subjects them to systemic risk regulation by the Financial Stability regulator; and

- Creates a **Federal Insurance Office** to monitor all aspects of the insurance industry.

Systemic Risk Regulator. With respect to macro-prudential supervision and systemic risk, the Treasury Plan proposed that the U.S. Federal Reserve serve as a systemic regulator. In Congress, **H.R. 4173** and **H.R. 3996** would create a Financial Services Oversight Council to monitor systemic risk. **H.R. 1754/S. 664** would create a systemic risk monitor for the financial system of the United States, to oversee financial regulatory activities of the federal government, and for other purposes.[33] Among its provisions are to establish an independent Financial Stability Council, to require the Federal Reserve to promulgate rules to deal with systemic risk, and to transfer authorities and functions of the Office of Thrift Supervision to the Comptroller of the Currency. (The Treasury Plan would call this combined agency the National Bank Supervisor.)

Too Big to Fail (systemically significant financial companies). The question of what to do about financial firms that become so large that they cannot be allowed to become insolvent without putting the financial system and the economy at risk. It is related to the issue of systemic risk. Under **H.R. 4173** and **H.R. 3996** mentioned above, the Financial Services Oversight Council would identify financial companies and financial activities that should be subject to heightened prudential standards. **S. 2746,** Too Big to Fail, Too Big to Exist Act, would require the breakup of such companies. **H.R. 2897**, the Bank Accountability and Risk Assessment Act of 2009, would require premium assessments by the FDIC to reflect relative degrees of risk by banks.[34]

The Volker Rule. On January 21, 2010, President Obama proposed that a single bank be allowed to hold no more than 10% of total bank deposits and that banks no longer be allowed to operate hedge funds and private equity funds and to make riskier investments to reap a quick reward.[35] The latter proposal is referred to as the Volcker Rule. It would prevent commercial banks such as Bank of America and JPMorgan Chase from owning hedge funds and private equity funds, as well as bar them from speculative or proprietary trading. Banks have countered that it's impossible to unwind proprietary trading from critical market making operations and that it is "impossible to define so-called prop trading, anyway."[36] The problem as argued by former Federal Reserve Chairman Paul Volker is one of moral hazard and the existence of deposit insurance for banks. The United States has a long-established "safety net" undergirding the stability of commercial banks. After the recent bank rescue programs, however, the implication for the financial community is that really large, complex, and highly interconnected financial institutions can count on public support at critical times. This creates a moral hazard and may provide an incentive for such "too-big-to-fail" institutions to take even greater risks by engaging in speculative activities out of the regulatory purview of banking authorities.[37]

Credit Rating Agencies. In Congress, several bills deal with concerns over the perceived failures of credit rating agencies[38] in assigning ratings to derivatives and other financial products. **H.R. 4173** and **H.R. 3890,** the Accountability and Transparency in Rating Agencies Act would amend the Securities Exchange Act of 1934 to enhance oversight of nationally recognized statistical rating organizations. Other bills include **H.R. 74, H.R. 1181, H.R. 1445, S. 927,** and **S. 1073.**

Derivatives Regulation.[39] The issue of regulation of over-the-counter derivatives is addressed in several bills. These include **H.R. 4173, H.R. 3795**, reported out of both the House Financial Services (October 15, 2009) and House Agriculture (October 21, 2009) committees, **H.R. 977**, reported out of the House Agriculture Committee on February 12, 2009, and **H.R. 2454** (the capand-trade bill) that passed the House on June 26, 2009. Other derivatives bills include **H.R. 1754, H.R. 2448, H.R. 2869, H.R. 3145, H.R. 3153, H.R. 3300, S. 221, S. 272, S. 447, S. 664, S. 807, S. 961, S. 1225, S. 1399**, and **S. 1412**.

Investor Protection. **H.R. 4173** and **H.R. 3817**, The Investor Protection Act of 2009, would provide the Securities and Exchange Commission with additional authorities to protect investors from violations of the securities laws. **H.R. 3818**, Private Fund Investment Advisers Registration Act of 2009, would require advisers of certain unregistered investment companies (hedge funds) to register with and provide information to the Securities and Exchange Commission.

Commissions. Bills have been introduced that would provide for the establishment of commissions or special committees to study the causes of the financial crisis. **S. 386** (P.L. 111-21, Section 5) established a 10-member Financial Crisis Inquiry Commission in the legislative branch to examine the causes of the current U.S. financial and economic crisis, taking into account fraud and abuse in the financial sector and other specified factors. It authorized $5 million for the Commission and requires the Commission to submit a final report on its findings to the President and Congress on December 15, 2010, requires the Commission chairperson to appear before the House Committee on Financial Services and the Senate Committee on Banking, Housing, and Urban Affairs within 120 days after the submission of such report, and terminates the Commission 60 days after the submission of such report. It also requires Republican approval before the commission could issue subpoenas. Other bills related to commissions or special committees include **H.Res. 345/S.Res. 62, H.R. 74, H.R. 768, H.R. 2111, H.R. 2253/S. 298**, and S. 400.

Housing and Mortgages. Numerous bills have been introduced related to the housing market, mortgages, and foreclosures. They address issues such as: the Troubled Assets Relief Program and its operation[40] and foreclosure prevention initiatives. **S. 896,** Helping Families Save Their Homes Act of 2009, became P.L. 111-22 on May 20, 2009. It contained various measures intended to prevent mortgage foreclosures. **S. 386**, Fraud Enforcement and Recovery Act of 2009 or FERA became P.L. 111-21 on May 20, 2009. It amends the federal criminal code to include within the definition of "financial institution" a mortgage lending business or any person or entity that makes, in whole or in part, a federally related mortgage loan. For details on housing and mortgages, see the CRS reports cited in the footnote below.[41]

Consumer Protection. The protection of consumers from allegedly unscrupulous practices in mortgage, credit card, other financial markets also has risen as a priority issue with the Obama Administration. **H.R. 4173** and **H.R. 3126** would establish a Consumer Financial Protection Agency (CFPA).[42] Under **H.R. 4173**, this independent agency would have the mission of protecting consumers when they borrow money, make deposits, or obtain other financial products and services. CFPA's rules would cover all financial providers, including banks, thrifts, credit unions and non-bank financial institutions, such as subprime mortgage lenders. The bill, however, would exempt entities such as retailers, merchants, and sellers of primarily non-financial goods when providing a non-financial good or service directly to a consumer. It also would exempt accountants, income tax preparers, attorneys, real estate brokers and agents, doctors, automobile dealers and sellers, providers of retirement plans, and others when they are engaged in the normal activities of their respective businesses.

Oversight, Investigations, Reports. Several bills would provide for oversight, reports, or other investigations into activities related to the financial crisis. In the 110th Congress, **P.L. 110-343** (§125(b)(1)(B)) established the Congressional Oversight Panel and provides for monthly reports on the Troubled Asset Relief Program (TARP).[43] **H.R. 2424**, the Federal Reserve Credit Facility Review Act of 2009, would authorize reviews by the Comptroller General of the United States of any credit facility established by the Board of Governors of the Federal Reserve System or any federal reserve bank during the current financial crisis, and for other purposes. **H.R. 1207** would reform the manner in which the Board of Governors of the Federal Reserve System is audited by the Comptroller General of the United States and the manner in which such audits are reported. **S. 1223** would require congressional approval before any Troubled Asset Relief Program (TARP) funds are provided or obligated to any entity, on and after May 29, 2009, whose receipt of such funds would result in federal government acquisition of its common or preferred stock. **H.R. 4482/S. 1683** would require recaptured taxpayer investments under TARP be applied toward reducing the national debt.

Executive Compensation. The issue of compensation for executives of firms that have received government support during the financial crisis. The American Recovery and Reinvestment Act of 2009 (Title VII of **P.L. 111-5**) restricts the compensation of executives of companies during the period in which any obligation arising from financial assistance provided under the Troubled Assets Relief Program (TARP) remains outstanding and requires the Secretary of the Treasury to develop appropriate standards for executive compensation.[44] Some proposals, such as **H.R. 4173**, dubbed "say on pay," would give shareholders a greater voice in compensation and governance decisions. Among legislative initiatives, **S. 1074** would provide for greater influence by shareholders in selecting corporate officers and H.R. 3269 (passed the House on July 31, 2009) would authorize federal regulators of financial firms to prohibit incentive pay structures that are seen to encourage inappropriate risk-taking and require them to adopt say on pay.

Fiscal Stimulus and Monetary Policy. For legislation related to a fiscal stimulus and monetary policy, see CRS Report R40 104, *Economic Stimulus: Issues and Policies*, by Jane G. Gravelle, Thomas L. Hungerford, and Marc Labonte, and CRS Report RL34427, *Financial Turmoil: Federal Reserve Policy Responses*, by Marc Labonte.

Fannie Mae, Freddie Mac, and GSEs. For policy related to these issues, see CRS Report RS2 1663, *Government-Sponsored Enterprises (GSEs): An Institutional Overview*, by Kevin R. Kosar; CRS Report RS22950, *Fannie Mae and Freddie Mac in Conservatorship*, by

Mark Jickling; and CRS Report R40800, *Options To Restructure Fannie Mae and Freddie Mac*, by N. Eric Weiss.

International Monetary Fund. For policy related to the IMF, see CRS Report RS22976, *The Global Financial Crisis: The Role of the International Monetary Fund (IMF)*, by Martin A. Weiss and CRS Report R40578, *The Global Financial Crisis: Increasing IMF Resources and the Role of Congress*, by Jonathan E. Sanford and Martin A. Weiss.

Insurance Regulation. For policy discussion, see CRS Report R4077 1, *Insurance Regulation: Issues, Background, and Legislation in the 111th Congress*, by Baird Webel.

Senator Dodd's Draft Financial Regulation Bill

On November 10, 2009, Senate Banking Committee Chairman Christopher Dodd released a draft of a financial regulation bill.[45] The bill's provisions include:

- establishment of a Consumer Financial Protection Agency;
- ending "too big to fail;"
- establishment of a Financial Stability Agency to address systemic risks;
- creation of a single federal bank regulator, the Financial Institutions Regulatory Administration;
- providing corporate shareholders with a "say on pay;"
- resolution authority to unwind troubled financial firms;
- protecting investors through regulation of over-the-counter derivatives and registration of advisors for hedge funds; and creating an office within Treasury to monitor the insurance industry and an SEC Office of Credit Rating Agencies.

FOUR PHASES OF THE GLOBAL FINANCIAL CRISIS

The global financial crisis as it has played out in countries across the globe has been manifest in four overlapping phases. Although each phase has a policy focus, each phase of the crisis affects the others, and, until the crisis has passed, no phase seems to have a clear end point.

Contain the Contagion and Strengthen Financial Sectors

The first phase has been intervention to contain the contagion and strengthen financial sectors in countries.[46] On a macroeconomic level, this has included policy actions such as lowering interest rates, expanding the money supply, quantitative (monetary) easing, and actions to restart and restore confidence in credit markets. On a microeconomic level, this has entailed actions to resolve immediate problems and effects of the crisis including financial rescue packages for ailing firms, guaranteeing deposits at banks, injections of capital, disposing of toxic assets, and restructuring debt. This has involved decisive (and, in cases, unprecedented) measures both in scope, cost, and extent of government reach. Actions taken include the rescue of financial institutions considered to be "too big to fail" and government takeovers of certain financial institutions, government facilitation of mergers and acquisitions, and government purchases of problem financial assets. Nearly every industrialized country and many developing and emerging market countries have pursued some or all of these actions. Although the "panic" phase of containing the contagion has passed, operations still are continuing, and the ultimate cost of the actions are yet to be determined.

In the United States, traditional monetary policy almost has reached its limit as the Federal Reserve has lowered its discount rate to 0.5% and has a target rate for the federal funds rate of 0.0 to 0.25%. The Federal Reserve and Treasury, therefore, have turned toward quantitative monetary easing (buying government securities and injecting more money into the economy) and dealing directly with the toxic assets being held by banks.[47]

What has been learned from previous financial crises is that without a resolution of underlying problems with toxic assets and restoring health to the balance sheet of banks and other financial institutions, financial crises continue to drag on. This was particularly the case with Japan.[48] Even Sweden, often viewed as a successful model of how to cope with a financial crisis, had to take decisive action to deal with the nonperforming assets of its banking system.[49]

In the United States, the Treasury, Federal Reserve, Federal Deposit Insurance Corporation, Office of Thrift Supervision, and Comptroller of the Currency have worked together to contain the contagion. Under the $700 billion Troubled Asset Relief Program[50] (TARP, H.R. 1424/P.L. 110-343), the Treasury has invested in dozens of banks, General Motors, Chrysler and the insurer A.I.G. The investments are in the form of preferred stock that pays quarterly dividends. On March 23, 2009, The U.S. Treasury released the details of its $900 billion Public Private Partnership Investment Program to address the challenge of toxic (legacy) assets being carried by the financial system.[51]

The U.S. Federal Reserve also has conducted about $1.2 trillion in emergency commitments to stabilize the financial sector. Its interventions have included a safety net for commercial banks, the rescue of Bear Stearns, a lending facility for investment banks and brokerages, loans for money-market assets and commercial paper, and purchases of securitized loans and lending to businesses and consumers for purchases of asset-backed securities.[52]

Coping with Macroeconomic Effects

The second phase of this financial crisis is less uncommon except that the severity of the macroeconomic downturn confronting countries around the world is the worst since the Great Depression of the 1930s. The financial crisis soon spread to real sectors to negatively affect whole economies, production, firms, investors, and households. Many of these countries, particularly those with emerging and developing markets, have been pulled down by the ever widening flight of capital from their economies and by falling exports and commodity prices. In these cases, governments have turned to traditional monetary and fiscal policies to deal with recessionary economic conditions, declining tax revenues, and rising unemployment.

Figure 1 shows the effect of the financial crisis on economic growth rates (annualized changes in real GDP by quarter) in selected nations of the world. The figure shows the difference between the 2001 recession that was confined primarily to countries such as the United States, Mexico, and Japan and the current financial crisis that is pulling down growth rates in a variety of countries. The slowdown—recession for many countries—is global. The implication of this synchronous drop in growth rates is that the United States and other nations may not be able to export their way out of recession. Even China is experiencing a "growth recession." There is no major economy that can play the role of an economic engine to pull other countries out of their economic doldrums.

In July-August 2009, there was a growing consensus among forecasters that the world had seen the worst of the global recession and that economies would hit bottom in 2009 and begin a weak recovery as early as the second half of 2009. On June 24, the Organization for Economic Cooperation and Development revised its world economic outlook upwards for the first time in two years. Most of this improved outlook, however, was in higher growth in China (7.7%) and other developing countries and less negative growth in the United States (-2.8%) for 2009. The outlook for the Eurozone (-4.8%) and Japan (-6.8%) for 2009 was slightly worse. The OECD reported that housing prices were falling in all OECD countries except for Switzerland.[53] On November 14, 2009, Eurostat (the EU's statistics agency) reported that the euro area had officially emerged from recession during the third quarter of 2009.[54]

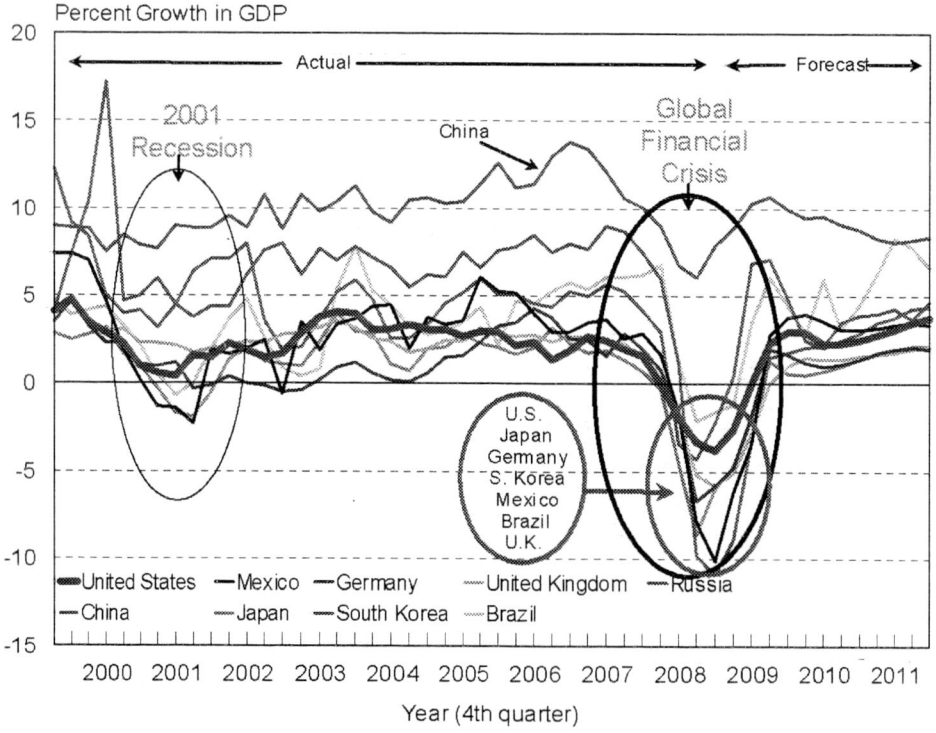

Source: Congressional Research Service. Data and forecasts (January 15, 2010) by IHS Global Insight.

Figure 1. Quarterly (Annualized) Economic Growth Rates for Selected Countries

In response to the recession or slowdown in economic growth, many countries have adopted fiscal stimulus packages designed to induce economic recovery or at least keep conditions from worsening. These are summarized in **Appendix B** and include packages by China ($586 billion), the European Union ($256 billion), Japan ($396 billion), Mexico ($54 billion), and South Korea ($52.5 billion).The global total for stimulus packages now exceeds $2 trillion, but some of the packages include measures that extend into subsequent years, so the total does not imply that the entire amount will translate into immediate government spending. The stimulus packages by definition are to be fiscal measures (government spending or tax cuts) but some packages include measures aimed at stabilizing banks and other financial institutions that usually are categorized as bank rescue or financial assistance packages. The $2 trillion total in stimulus packages amounts to approximately 3% of world gross domestic product, an amount that exceeds the call by the International Monetary Fund for fiscal stimulus totaling 2% of global GDP to counter worsening economic conditions world wide.[55] If only new fiscal stimulus measures to be done in 2009 are counted, however, the total and the percent of global GDP figures would be considerably lower. An analysis of the stimulus measures by the European Community for 2009 found that such measures amount to an estimated 1.32% of European Community GDP.[56] The IMF estimated that as of January 2009, the U.S. fiscal stimulus packages as a percent of GDP in 2009 would amount to 1.9%, for the euro area 0.9%, for Japan 1.4%, for Asia excluding Japan 1.5%, and for the rest of the G-20 countries 1.1%.[57]

At the G-20 London Summit, a schism arose between the United States and the U.K., who were arguing for large and coordinated stimulus packages, and Germany and France, who considered their automatic stabilizers (increases in government expenditures for items such as unemployment insurance that are triggered any time the economy slows) plus existing stimulus programs as sufficient. In their communiqué, the leaders noted that $5 trillion will have been devoted to fiscal expansion by the end of 2010 and committed themselves to "deliver the scale of sustained fiscal effort necessary to restore growth." In the communiqué, the G-20 leaders decided to add $1.1 trillion in resources to the international financial institutions, including $750 billion more for the International Monetary Fund, $250 billion to boost global trade, and $100 billion for multilateral development banks.

The additional lending by the international financial institutions would be in addition to national fiscal stimulus efforts and could be targeted to those countries most in need. Several countries have borrowed heavily in international markets and carry debt denominated in euros or dollars. As their currencies have depreciated, the local currency cost of this debt has skyrocketed. Other countries have banks with debt exposure almost as large as national GDP. Some observers have raised the possibility of a sovereign debt crisis[58] (countries defaulting on government guaranteed debt) or as in the case of Iceland having to nationalize its banks and assume liabilities greater than the size of the national economy.

Since November 1, 2008, the IMF, under its Stand-By Arrangement facility, has provided or is in the process of providing financial support packages for Iceland ($2.1 billion), Ukraine ($16.4 billion), Hungary ($25.1 billion), Pakistan ($7.6 billion), Belarus ($2.46 billion), Serbia ($530.3 million), Armenia ($540 million), El Salvador ($800 million), Latvia ($2.4 billion), Seychelles ($26.6 million), Mongolia ($229.2 million), Costa Rica ($735 million), Guatemala ($935 million), and Romania ($17.1 billion). The IMF also created a Flexible Credit Line for countries with strong fundamentals, policies, and track records of policy implementation. Once approved, these loans can be disbursed when the need arises rather than being conditioned on compliance with policy targets as in traditional IMF-supported programs. Under this facility, the IMF board has approved Mexico ($47 billion), Poland ($20.5 billion), and Columbia ($10.5 billion).[59]

REGULATORY AND FINANCIAL MARKET REFORM

The third phase of the global financial crisis—to decide what changes may be needed in the financial system—also is underway. (See "Policy and Legislation," above.) In order to coordinate reforms in national regulatory systems and give such proposals political backing, world leaders began a series of international meetings to address changes in policy, regulations, oversight, and enforcement. Some are characterizing these meetings as Bretton Woods II.[60] The G-20 leaders' Summit on Financial Markets and the World Economy that met on November 15, 2008, in Washington, DC, was the first of a series of summits to address these issues. The second was the G-20 Leader's Summit on April 2, 2009, in London,[61] and the third was the Pittsburgh Summit on September 24-25, 2009, with President Obama as the host.[62]

In this third phase, the immediate issues to be addressed by the United States and other nations center on "fixing the system" and preventing future crises from occurring. Much of this involves the technicalities of regulation and oversight of financial markets, derivatives, and hedging activity, as well as standards for capital adequacy and a schema for funding and conducting future financial interventions, if necessary. In the November 2008 G-20 Summit, the leaders approved an Action Plan that sets forth a comprehensive work plan.

The leaders instructed finance ministers to make specific recommendations in the following areas:

- Avoiding regulatory policies that exacerbate the ups and downs of the business cycle;
- Reviewing and aligning global accounting standards, particularly for complex securities in times of stress;
- Strengthening transparency of credit derivatives markets and reducing their systemic risks;
- Reviewing incentives for risk-taking and innovation reflected in compensation practices; and
- Reviewing the mandates, governance, and resource requirements of the International Financial Institutions.

Most of the technical details of this work plan have been referred to existing international standards setting organizations or the National Finance Ministers and Central Bank Governors. These organizations include the International Accounting Standards Board, the Financial Accounting Standards Board, Basel Committee on Banking Supervision, the International Organization of Securities Commissions, and the Financial Stability Forum (Board).

At the London Summit, the leaders addressed the issue of coordination and oversight of the international financial system by establishing a new Financial Stability Board (FSB) with a strengthened mandate as a successor to the Financial Stability Forum with membership to include all G-20 countries, Financial Stability Forum members, Spain, and the European Commission. The FSB is to collaborate with the IMF to provide early warning of macroeconomic and financial risks and the actions needed to address them. The Summit left it to individual countries to reshape regulatory systems to identify and take account of macro-prudential (systemic) risks, but agreed to regulate hedge funds and Credit Rating Agencies.[63] The results of the Pittsburgh Summit are summarized in the G-20 section of this report.

For the United States, the fundamental issues may be the degree to which U.S. laws and regulations are to be altered to conform to recommendations from the new Financial Stability Board and what authority the Board and IMF will have relative to member nations. Although the London Summit strengthened regulations and the IMF, it did not result in a "new international financial architecture." The question still is out as to whether the Bretton Woods system should be changed from one in which the United States is the buttress of the international financial architecture to one in which the United States remains the buttress but its financial markets are more "Europeanized" (more in accord with Europe's practices) and more constrained by the broader international financial order? Should the international financial architecture be merely strengthened or include more control, and if more control, then by whom?[64] What is the time frame for a new architecture that may take years to materialize?

For the United States, some of these issues are being addressed by the President's Working Group on Financial Markets (consisting of the U.S. Treasury Secretary, Chairs of the Federal Reserve Board, the Securities and Exchange Commission, and the Commodity Futures Trading Commission) in cooperation with international financial organizations. **Appendix C** lists the major regulatory reform proposals and indicates whether they have been put forward by various U.S. and international organizations. Those that have been proposed by both the U.S. Treasury and the G-20 include the following:

- **Systemic Risk**: All systemically important financial institutions should be subject to an appropriate degree of regulation. Use of stress testing by financial institutions should be more rigorous.
- **Capital Standards**: Large complex systemically-important financial institutions should be subject to more stringent capital regulation than other firms. Capital decisions by regulators and firms should make greater provision against liquidity risk.
- **Hedge Funds**: Hedge funds should be required to register with a national securities regulator. Systemically-important hedge funds should be subject to prudential regulation. Hedge funds should provide information on a confidential basis to regulators about their strategies and positions.
- **Over-the-Counter Derivatives**: Credit default swaps should be processed through a regulated centralized counterparty (CCP) or clearing house.
- **Tax Havens:** Minimum international standards—a regulatory floor—should apply in all countries, including tax havens and offshore banking centers.

Among the proposals put forward by the Treasury but not mentioned by the G-20 included creating a single regulator with responsibility over all systemically important financial institutions with power for prompt corrective action, strengthening regulation of critical payment systems, processing all standardized over-the-counter derivatives through a regulated clearing house and subjecting them to a strong regulatory regime, and providing authority for a government agency to take over a failing, systemically important non-bank institution and place it in conservatorship or receivership outside the bankruptcy system. (For the June 17, 2009, Obama Administration proposal for financial market regulation, see the "Policy" section of this report.)

Dealing with Political, Social, and Security Effects[65]

The fourth phase of the financial crisis is in dealing with **political, social, and security effects of the financial turmoil**. These are secondary impacts that relate to the role of the United States on the world stage, its leadership position relative to other countries, and the political and social impact within countries affected by the crisis. For example, on February 12, 2009, the U.S. Director of National Intelligence, Dennis Blair, told Congress that instability in countries around the world caused by the global economic crisis and its geopolitical implications, rather than terrorism, is the primary near-term security threat to the United States.[66]

Political Leadership and Regimes

The financial crisis works on political leadership and regimes within countries through two major mechanisms. The first is the discontent from citizens who are losing jobs, seeing businesses go bankrupt, losing wealth both in financial and real assets, and facing declining prices for their products. In democracies, this discontent often results in public opposition to the existing establishment or ruling regime. In some cases it can foment extremist movements, particularly in poorer countries where large numbers of unemployed young people may become susceptible to religious radicalism that demonizes Western industrialized society and encourages terrorist activity.

The precipitous drop in the price of oil holds important implications for countries, such as Russia, Mexico, Venezuela, Yemen, and other petroleum exporters, who were counting on oil revenues to continue to pour into their coffers to fund activities considered to be essential to their interests. While moderating oil prices may be a positive development for the U.S. consumer and for the U.S. balance of trade, it also may affect the political stability of certain petroleum exporting countries. The concomitant drop in prices of commodities such as rubber, copper ore, iron ore, beef, rice, coffee, and tea also carries dire consequences for exporter countries in Africa, Latin America, and Asia.[67]

In Pakistan, a particular security problem exacerbated by the financial crisis could be developing. The IMF has approved a $7.6 billion loan package for Pakistan, but the country faces serious economic problems at a time when it is dealing with challenges from suspected al Qaeda and Taliban sympathizers, when citizen objections are rising to U.S. missile strikes on suspected terrorist targets in Pakistan, and the country faces a budget shortfall that may curtail the ability of the government to continue its counterterror operations.[68]

The second way that the crisis works on ruling regimes is through the actions of existing governments both to stay in power and to deal with the adverse effects of the crisis. Any crisis generates centrifugal forces that tend to strengthen central government power. Most nations view the current financial crisis as having been created by the financial elite in New York and

London in cooperation with their increasingly laissez faire governments. By blaming the industrialized West, particularly the United States, for their economic woes, governments can stoke the fires of nationalism and seek support for themselves. As nationalist sentiments rise and economic conditions worsen, citizens look to governments as a rescuer of last resort. Political authorities can take actions, ostensibly to counter the effects of the crisis, but often with the result that it consolidates their power and preserves their own positions. Authoritarian regimes, in particular, can take even more dictatorial actions to deal with financial and economic challenges.

Economic Philosophy, Protectionism, and State Capitalism

In the basic economic philosophies that guide policy, expediency seems to be trumping free-market ideologies in many countries. The crisis may hasten the already declining economic neoliberalism that began with President Ronald Reagan and British Prime Minister Margaret Thatcher. Although the market-based structure of most of the world economies is likely to continue, the basic philosophy of deregulation, non-governmental intervention in the private sector, and free and open markets for goods, services, and capital, seems to be subsumed by the need to increase regulation of new financial products, increased government intervention, and some pull-back from further reductions in trade barriers. Emerging market countries, particularly those in Eastern Europe, moreover, may be questioning their shift toward the capitalist model away from the socialist model of their past.

State capitalism in which governments either nationalize or own shares of companies and intervene to direct parts of their operations is rising not only in countries such as Russia, where a history of command economics predisposes governments toward state ownership of the means of production, but in the United States, Europe, and Asia. Nationalization of banks, insurance companies, and other financial institutions, as well as government capital injections and loans to private corporations have become parts of rescue and stimulus packages and have brought politicians and bureaucrats directly into economic decision-making at the company level.

While state ownership of enterprises may affect the efficiency and profitability of the operation, it also raises questions of equity (government favoring one company over another) and the use of scarce government resources in oversight and management of companies. When taxpayer funds have been used to invest in a company, the public then has an interest in its operations, but protecting that interest takes time and resources. This has already been illustrated in the United States by the attention devoted to executive compensation and bonuses of companies receiving government loans or capital injections and by the threatened bankruptcy of Chrysler and General Motors. The ideological debate over the role of the government in the economy also has been manifest in public opposition to a larger government role in health care.[69]

In the G-20 and other meetings, world representatives have been vocal in calling for countries to avoid resorting to protectionism as they try to stimulate their own economies. Still, whether it be provisions to buy domestic products instead of imports, financial assistance to domestic producers, or export incentives, countries have been attempting to protect national companies often at the expense of those foreign. Overt attempts to restrict imports, promote exports, or impose restrictions on trade are limited by the rules of the World Trade Organization (WTO), but there is ample scope for increases in trade barriers that are consistent with the rules and obligations of the WTO. These include raising applied tariffs to higher bound levels as well as actions to impose countervailing duties or to take antidumping measures. Certain sectors also are excluded from trade agreements for national security or other reasons. Moreover, there are opportunities to favor domestic producers at the expense of foreign producers through industry- specific relief or subsidy programs, broad fiscal stimulus programs, buy-domestic provisions, or currency depreciation.

Several countries have imposed trade related measures that tend to protect or assist domestic industries. In July, 2009, the WTO reported that in the previous three-month period, there had been "further slippage towards more trade-restricting and distorting policies" but resort to high intensity protectionist measures had been contained overall. There also had been some trade- liberalizing and facilitating measures, but there had been no general indication of governments unwinding or removing the measures that were taken early on in the crisis. The WTO also noted that a variety of new trade-restricting and distorting measures had been introduced, including a further increase in the initiation of trade remedy investigations (anti-dumping and safeguards) and an increase in the number of new tariffs and new non-tariff measures (non-automatic licenses, reference prices, etc.) affecting merchandise trade. The WTO also compiled a list of new trade and trade-related policy measures that had been taken since September 2008. These included increases in steel tariffs by India, increases in tariffs on 940 imported products by Ecuador, restrictions on ports of entry for imports of certain consumer goods by Indonesia, imposition of non-automatic licensing requirements on products considered as sensitive by Argentina, increase in tariffs on imports of crude oil by South Korea, re-introduction of export subsidies for certain dairy products by the European Commission, and a rise in import duties on cars and trucks by Russia.[70]

According to the Centre for Economic Policy Research, an independent London think tank, between the G-20 Summit in November 2008 and November 2009, the governments of the world implemented 297 discriminatory trade measures, of which 184 were by the G-20 member states. The ratio of "blatantly discriminatory" measures to liberalizing measures over this period of time was nearly six to one. China was the most frequent target of protectionism under the financial crisis. They were hit with 146 protectionist measures from 58 trading partners. The European Union was the target of 140 measures, the United States 118 measures, and Japan 99 protectionist measures. The nations that have adopted the most protectionist measures are Russia, China, and Indonesia. The Centre, however, also emphasized that a repeat of the 1930s protectionism has—to date—been avoided.[71]

The China has announced a number of policy responses to deal with the crisis, including a pledge to spend $586 billion to boost domestic spending. However, China has also announced rebates of value added taxes for exports of certain products (such as steel, petrochemicals, information technology products, textiles, and clothing) and "Buy Chinese" for its stimulus package spending.[72] Also, despite calls to allow its currency to appreciate, in 2009, the Chinese government held its currency stable relative to the dollar even though the dollar, itself, was depreciating against major currencies.

In the United States, the Buy America provision in the February 2009 stimulus package[73] has been widely criticized. Even though the provision applies only to steel, iron, and manufactured goods used in government funded construction projects and language was included that the provision "shall be applied in a manner consistent with United States obligations under international agreements," many nations have protested the Buy America language as "protectionist"[74] and as possibly starting down a slippery slope that could lead to

WTO inconsistent protectionism by countries. The United States also imposed anti-dumping duties on imports of tires from China.

A concern also is rising among developing nations that a type of "financial protectionism" may arise. Governments may direct banks that have received capital injections to lend more domestically rather than overseas. Borrowing by the U.S. Treasury to finance the growing U.S. budget deficit also pulls in funds from around the world and could crowd out borrowers from countries also seeking to cover their deficits. Also of concern to countries such as Vietnam, China, and other exporters of foreign brand name exports is that private flows of investment capital may decline as producers face rising inventories and excess production capacity. Why build another factory when existing ones sit idle?

U.S. Leadership Position

Another issue raised by the global financial crisis has been the role of the United States on the world stage and the U.S. leadership position relative to other countries. The Obama Administration has placed more emphasis on diplomacy while still yielding a "big stick" in areas such as Afghanistan. The rest of the world seems to be expressing ambivalent feelings about the United States. On one hand, many blame the United States for the crisis and see it as yet another of the excesses of a country that had emerged as the sole superpower in a unipolar world following the end of the Cold War. Although not always explicit, their willingness to follow the U.S. lead appears to have diminished. On the other hand, countries recognize that the United States is still one of a scant few that can bring other nations along and induce them to take actions outside of their political comfort zone. In determining solutions to the financial crisis, the United States presence and leadership appears to be indispensible. The combination of U.S. military power, extensive economic and financial clout, its diplomatic clout, and its veto power in the IMF has put the United States at the center of any resolution to the global financial turmoil.

During the early phase of the crisis, European leaders (particularly British Prime Minister Gordon Brown, French President Nicolas Sarkozy, and German Chancellor Angela Merkel) played a major role and were influential in crafting international mechanisms and policies to deal with initial adverse effects of the crisis as well as proposing long-term solutions. Also, dealing with the financial crisis has enabled countries with rich currency reserves, such as China, Russia, and Japan, to assume higher political profiles in world financial circles. As China[75] helps to finance budget deficits in the United States[76] and as Beijing increasingly sees its economic and financial system as "superior" to that of the West, Washington appears to be losing leverage with China on issues such as climate change, human and labor rights, and product safety. Also, the inclusion of China, India, and Brazil in the G-20 Summits rather than just the G-7 or G-8 countries as originally proposed, reflects the growing influence of the non-industrialized nations in addressing global financial issues.[77]

However, as the crisis has played out and with rising approval of the Obama Administration abroad, it appears that the U.S. image is on the rise. According to a July 2009 Pew Research poll, the image of the United States (a key factor in the ability to sway world opinion) has improved markedly in most parts of the world. Improvements in the U.S. image were most pronounced in Western Europe, where favorable ratings for both the nation and the American people have soared, but opinions of America have also become more positive in key countries in Latin America, Africa, and Asia.[78]

International Financial Organizations

The financial crisis has brought international financial organizations and institutions into the spotlight. These include the International Monetary Fund, the Financial Stability Board (an enlarged Financial Stability Forum), the Group of Twenty (G-20), the Bank for International Settlements, the World Bank, the Group of 7 (G-7), and other organizations that play a role in coordinating policy among nations, provide early warning of impending crises, or assist countries as a lender of last resort. The precise architecture of any international financial structure and whether it is to have powers of oversight, regulatory, or supervisory authority is yet to be determined. However, the interconnectedness of global financial and economic markets has highlighted the need for stronger institutions to coordinate regulatory policy across nations, provide early warning of dangers caused by systemic, cyclical, or macroprudential risks[79] and induce corrective actions by national governments. A fundamental question in this process, however, rests on sovereignty: how much power and authority should an international organization wield relative to national authorities?

As a result of the global financial crisis, the IMF has expanded its activities along several dimensions.[80] The first is its role as lender of last resort for countries less able to access international capital markets. It also is attempting to become a lender of "not-last" resort by offering flexible credit lines for countries with strong economic fundamentals and a sustained track record of implementing sound economic policies. The second area of expansion by the IMF has been in oversight of the international economy and in monitoring systemic risk across borders. The IMF also tracks world economic and financial developments more closely and provides countries with the forecasts and analysis of developments in financial markets. It additionally provides policy advice to countries and regions and is assisting the G-20 with recommendations to reshape the system of international regulation and governance. Although the London Summit provided for more funding for the IMF and international development banks, some larger issues, such as governance of and reform of the IMF are now being determined. (For further discussion of the IMF, see sections below on "The Challenges" and "International Policy Issues."

On June 24, 2009. President Obama signed H.R. 2346 into law (P.L. 111-32). This increased the U.S. quota in the International Monetary Fund by 4.5 billion SDRs ($7.69 billion), provided loans to the IMF of up to an additional 75 billion SDRs ($116.01 billion), and authorized the United States Executive Director of the IMF to vote to approve the sale of up to 12,965,649 ounces of the Fund's gold. H.R. 2346 was the $105.9 billion war supplemental spending bill that mainly funds military operations in Iraq and Afghanistan but also included the IMF provisions. On June 26, the President released a signing statement that included:

> However, provisions of this bill within sections 1110 to 1112 of title XI, and sections 1403 and 1404 of title XIV, would interfere with my constitutional authority to conduct foreign relations by directing the Executive to take certain positions in negotiations or discussions with international organizations and foreign governments, or by requiring consultation with the Congress prior to such negotiations or discussions. I will not treat these provisions as limiting my ability to engage in foreign diplomacy or negotiations.[81]

This signing statement has been addressed in H.Amdt. 311 to H.R. 3081, the Fiscal 2010 State- Foreign Operations spending bill passed on July 7, 2009.

The Washington Action Plan from the G-20 Leader's Summit in November 2008 contained specific policy changes that were addressed in the April 2, 2009 Summit in London. The regulatory and other specific changes have been assigned to existing international organizations such as the Financial Stability Forum (now Financial Stability Board) and Bank for International Settlements, as well as international standard setting bodies such as the Basel Committee on Banking Supervision, International Accounting Standards Board, International Organization of Securities Commissions, and International Association of Insurance Supervisors.[82]

Effects on Poverty and Flows of Aid Resources

The global crisis is causing huge losses and dislocation in the industrialized countries of the world, but in many of the developing countries it is pushing people deep into poverty. The crisis is being transmitted to the poorer countries through declining exports, falling commodity prices, reverse migration, and shrinking remittances from citizens working overseas. This could have major effects in countries which provide large numbers of migrant workers, including Mexico, Guatemala, El Salvador, India, Bangladesh, and the Philippines.

The decline in tax revenues caused by the slowdown in economic activity also is increasing competition within countries for scarce budget funds and affecting decisions about the allocation of national resources. This budget constraint relates directly to the ability to finance official development assistance to poorer nations and other programs aimed at alleviating poverty.

In the United States, the economic downturn and the vast resources being committed to provide stimulus to the U.S. economy and rescue trouble financial institutions could clash with some policy priorities of the new Administration. In foreign policy, President Obama and top officials in his Administration—including Secretary of State Clinton and Secretary of Defense Gates— have pledged to increase the capacity of civilian foreign policy institutions and levels of U.S. foreign assistance. However, financial constraints could impose difficult choices between foreign policy priorities—for example, between boosting levels of non-military aid to Afghanistan and increasing global health programs–or changes to planned levels of increases across the board. The global reach of the economic downturn further complicates the resource problem, as it both limits what other countries can do to address common international challenges and potentially exacerbates the scale of need in conflict areas and the developing world.

NEW CHALLENGES AND POLICY IN MANAGING FINANCIAL RISK[83]

The Challenges

The actions of the United States and other nations in coping with the global financial crisis first aimed to contain the contagion, minimize losses to society, restore confidence in financial institutions and instruments, and lubricate the economic system in order for it to return to full operation. Attention now is focused on stimulating the economy and stemming the downturn in macroeconomic conditions that is increasing unemployment and forcing many companies into bankruptcy. As of early 2009, as much as 40% of the world's wealth may have been destroyed since the crisis began,[84] although equity markets have recovered somewhat since then. There still is uncertainty, however, over whether the nascent economic recovery will fade once the government stimulus measures end. It also is unknown whether the current crisis is an aberration that can be fixed by tweaking the system, or whether it reflects systemic problems that require major surgery. What has become evident is that entrenched interests are so strong that even relatively "small" changes in, for example, the structure of financial regulation in the United States, is difficult. The world now is working its way through the third phase of the crisis. The goal is to change the regulatory structure and regulations, the global financial architecture, and some of the imbalances in trade and capital flows to ensure that future crises do not occur or, at least, to mitigate their effects.

Judging from policy proposals to cope with the financial crisis in both the United States and in Europe, it appears that solutions are taking a multipronged approach. They are being aimed at the different levels in which financial markets operate: globally, nationally, and by specific financial sector.

On the global side, there exists no international architecture capable of coping with and preventing global crises from erupting. The financial space above nations basically is anarchic with no supranational authority with firm oversight, regulatory, and enforcement powers. Since financial crises occur even in relatively tightly regulated economies, the likelihood that a supranational authority could prevent an international crisis from occurring is questionable. International norms and guidelines for financial institutions exist, but most are voluntary, and countries are slow to incorporate them into domestic law.[85] As such, the system operates largely on trust and confidence and by hedging financial bets. The financial crisis has been a "wake-up call" for investors who had confidence in, for example, credit ratings placed on securities by credit rating agencies operating under what some have referred to as "perverse incentives and conflicts of interest." Between 2007 and November 2009, for example, the credit rating agency, Standard & Poor's, has downgraded nearly $1.5 trillion of U.S. residential-mortgage-backed bonds from AAA to junk.[86]

The financial crisis crossed national boundaries and spread from individual financial institutions to the wider economy. Not only did countries of the world not directly complicit in the original financial problems suffer "collateral damage," but the ensuing downturn in economic activity affected millions of "innocent bystanders" because of their being connected through trade, financial, and investment flows. To some extent, the International Monetary Fund, World Bank, or the Organization for Economic Cooperation and Development monitored the global economy, but they tended to focus on macroeconomic flows and not on macroprudential regulation. Since the onset of the crisis, the IMF has undertaken more programs to provide macroprudential oversight.

The global financial crisis resulted from a confluence of factors and processes at both the macro- financial level (across financial sectors) and at the micro-financial level (the behavior of individual institutions and the functioning of specific market segments). This joint influence of both macro and micro factors resulted in market excesses and the emergence of systemic risks of unprecedented magnitude and complexity.[87] In the United States, regulation tends to be by function. There has been no macroprudential or systemic regulation and oversight.[88] Separate regulatory agencies oversee each line of financial service: banking, insurance, securities, and futures. This is microprudential regulation under which no single regulator possesses all of the information and authority necessary to monitor systemic and synergistic risk or the potential that seemingly isolated events could lead to broad dislocation and a financial crisis so widespread that it affects the real economy.[89] Also no single regulator can take coordinated action throughout the financial system.

In a report on systemic regulation, the Council on Foreign Relations explained the problem as follows:

> One regulatory organization in each country should be responsible for overseeing the health and stability of the overall financial system. The role of the systemic regulator should include gathering, analyzing, and reporting information about significant interactions between and risks among financial institutions; designing and implementing systemically sensitive regulations, including capital requirements; and coordinating with the fiscal authorities and other government agencies in managing systemic crises. We argue below that the central bank should be charged with this important new responsibility.[90]

Analysis by the European Central Bank suggests three main considerations on the way in which systemic risks should be monitored and analyzed. First, macroprudential analysis needs to capture all components of financial systems and how they interact. This would include all intermediaries, markets, and infrastructures underpinning them. Second, macroprudential risk assessment should cover the interactions between the financial system and the economy at large. Third, financial markets are not static and are continuously evolving as a result of innovation and international integration. Several financial crises in history have resulted from financial liberalizations or innovations that were neither sufficiently understood nor managed.[91]

A related consideration in policymaking is that centers of financial activity, such as New York, London, and Tokyo, compete with each other, and multinational firms can choose where to conduct particular financial transactions. Unless the regulatory framework and the supervisory arrangements in the United States, Europe, and other large financial centers are broadly compatible with each other, business may flow from the United States to the area of minimal regulation and supervision. The interconnectedness of financial centers across the world also implies that systemic risk can be amplified because of actions occurring in different countries, often out of sight or reach of national regulators.

One challenge is that the world economy depends greatly on large financial (and other) institutions that may be deemed "too large to fail." If an institution is considered to be "too big to fail," its bankruptcy would pose a significant risk to the system as a whole. Yet, if there is an implicit promise of governmental support in case of failure, the government may create a moral hazard, which is the incentive for an entity to engage in risky behavior knowing that the government will rescue it if it fails. Another challenge is that innovative financial instruments may not be well understood or regulated. Some of the early proposals have been designed to bring hedge funds, off-balance sheet financial entities, and, perhaps, credit default swaps under regulatory authority.

A further challenge is that existing micro-prudential regulation, by and large, did not identify the nature and size of accumulating financial and systemic risks and impose appropriate remedial actions. Even though some analysts and institutions were sounding alarms before the crisis erupted, there were few regulatory tools available to cope with the accumulation of risk in the system as a whole or the risks being imposed by other firms either in the same or different sectors. There also seemed to be insufficient response to these risks either by market participants or by the authorities responsible for the oversight of individual financial institutions or specific market segments.

Under a free-enterprise system, a fundamental assumption is that markets will self-correct, and that individuals, in pursuing their own financial interests, like an "invisible hand," tend also to promote the good of the global community. If losses occur, investors and institutions naturally become more prudent in the future. A complex challenge remains to determine how much further regulation and oversight is necessary to moderate behavior by institutions that may be in their own financial interest but may pose excessive risk to the system as a whole. Also, how can supervisory authorities preclude a repeat of the same mistakes in the future as personnel and firms change and as memories of financial crises become distant? Also, how should the system be improved to fill gaps in information and technical expertise in order to compensate for faulty or incomplete methods of modeling risk or to provide more resilience in the system to offset human error?

For other nations of the world, what has become clear from the crisis is that U.S. financial ailments can be highly contagious. Foreign financial institutions are not immune to ill health in American banks, brokerage houses, and insurance companies. The financial services industry links together investors and financial institutions in disparate countries around the world. Investors seek higher risk-adjusted returns in any market. In financial markets, moreover, innovations in one market quickly spread to another, and sellers in one country often seek buyers in another. The revolution in communications, moreover, works both ways. It allows for instant access to information and remote access to market activity, but it also feeds the herd instinct and is susceptible to being used to spread biased or incomplete information.

The linking of economies also transcends financial networks.[92] Flows of international trade both in goods and services are affected directly by macroeconomic conditions in the countries involved. In the second phase of the financial crisis, markets all over the world have been experiencing historic declines. Precipitous drops in stock market values have been mirrored in currency and commodity markets.

Another issue is the mismatch between regulators and those being regulated. The policymakers can be divided between those of national governments and, to an extent, those of international institutions, but the resulting policy implementation, oversight, and regulation almost all rest in national governments (as well as sub-national governments such as states, e.g. New York, for insurance regulation). Yet many of the financial and other institutions that are the object of new oversight or regulatory activity may themselves be international in presence. They tend to operate in all major markets and congregate around world financial centers (i.e., London, New York, Zurich, Hong Kong, Singapore, Tokyo, and Shanghai) where client portfolios often are based and where institutions and qualified professionals exist to support their activities. The major market for derivatives, for example, is London, even though a sizable proportion of the derivatives, themselves, may be issued by U.S. companies based on U.S. assets.

A further issue is to what extent the U.S. government and Federal Reserve as "domestic lenders of last resort" should intervene in the day-to-day activities of corporations that have received federal support funds. Traditionally, financial regulations have been aimed at ensuring financial stability, transparency, and equity. Issues such as executive compensation and bonuses,[93] or, in the case of General Motors, whether executives travel by private jet, traditionally have not been subject to regulation. Yet once the government provides public support for companies, public pressure rises to intervene in such matters.

A fundamental issue deals with the nature of regulation and supervision. Banking regulation tends to be specific and detailed and places requirements and limits on bank behavior. Federal securities regulation, however, is based primarily on disclosure. Registration with the Securities and Exchange Commission is required, but that registration does not imply that an investment is safe, only that the risks have been fully disclosed. The SEC has no authority to prevent excessive risk taking.

ORIGINS, CONTAGION, AND RISK[94]

Financial crises of some kind occur sporadically virtually every decade and in various locations around the world. Financial meltdowns have occurred in countries ranging from Sweden to Argentina, from Russia to Korea, from the United Kingdom to Indonesia, and from Japan to the United States.[95] As one observer noted: as each crisis arrives, policy makers express ritual shock, then proceed to break every rule in the book. The alternative is unthinkable. When the worst is passed, participants renounce crisis apostasy and pledge to hold firm next time.[96]

Each financial crisis is unique, yet each bears some resemblance to others. In general, crises have been generated by factors such as an overshooting of markets, excessive leveraging of debt, credit booms, miscalculations of risk, rapid outflows of capital from a country, mismatches between asset types (e.g., short-term dollar debt used to fund long-term local currency loans), unsustainable macroeconomic policies, off-balance sheet operations by banks, inexperience with new financial instruments, and deregulation without sufficient market monitoring and oversight.

As shown in **Figure 2**, the current crisis harkens back to the 1997-98 Asian financial crisis in which Thailand, Indonesia, and South Korea had to borrow from the International Monetary Fund to service their short-term foreign debt and to cope with a dramatic drop in the values of their currency and deteriorating financial condition. Determined not to be caught with insufficient foreign exchange reserves, countries subsequently began to accumulate dollars, Euros, pounds, and yen in record amounts. This was facilitated by the U.S. trade (current account) deficit and by its low saving rate.[97] By mid-2008, world currency reserves by governments had reached $4.4 trillion with China's reserves alone approaching $2 trillion, Japan's nearly $1 trillion, Russia's more than $500 billion, and India, South Korea, and Brazil each with more than $200 billion.[98] The accumulation of hard currency assets was so great in some countries that they diverted some of their reserves into sovereign wealth funds that were to invest in higher yielding assets than U.S. Treasury and other government securities.[99]

Following the Asian financial crisis, much of the world's "hot money" began to flow into high technology stocks. The so-called "dot-com boom" ended in the spring of 2000 as the value of equities in many high-technology companies collapsed.

After the dot-com bust, more "hot investment capital" began to flow into housing markets—not only in the United States but in other countries of the world. At the same time, China and other countries invested much of their accumulations of foreign exchange into U.S. Treasury and other securities. While this helped to keep U.S. interest rates low, it also tended to keep mortgage interest rates at lower and attractive levels for prospective home buyers.[100] This housing boom coincided with greater popularity of the securitization of assets, particularly mortgage debt (including subprime mortgages), into collateralized debt obligations (CDOs).[101] A problem was that the mortgage originators often were mortgage finance companies whose main purpose was to write mortgages using funds provided by banks and other financial institutions or borrowed. They were paid for each mortgage originated but had no responsibility for loans gone bad. Of course, the incentive for them was to maximize the number of loans concluded. This coincided with political pressures to enable more Americans to buy homes, although it appears that Fannie Mae and Freddie Mac were not directly complicit in the loosening of lending standards and the rise of subprime mortgages.[102]

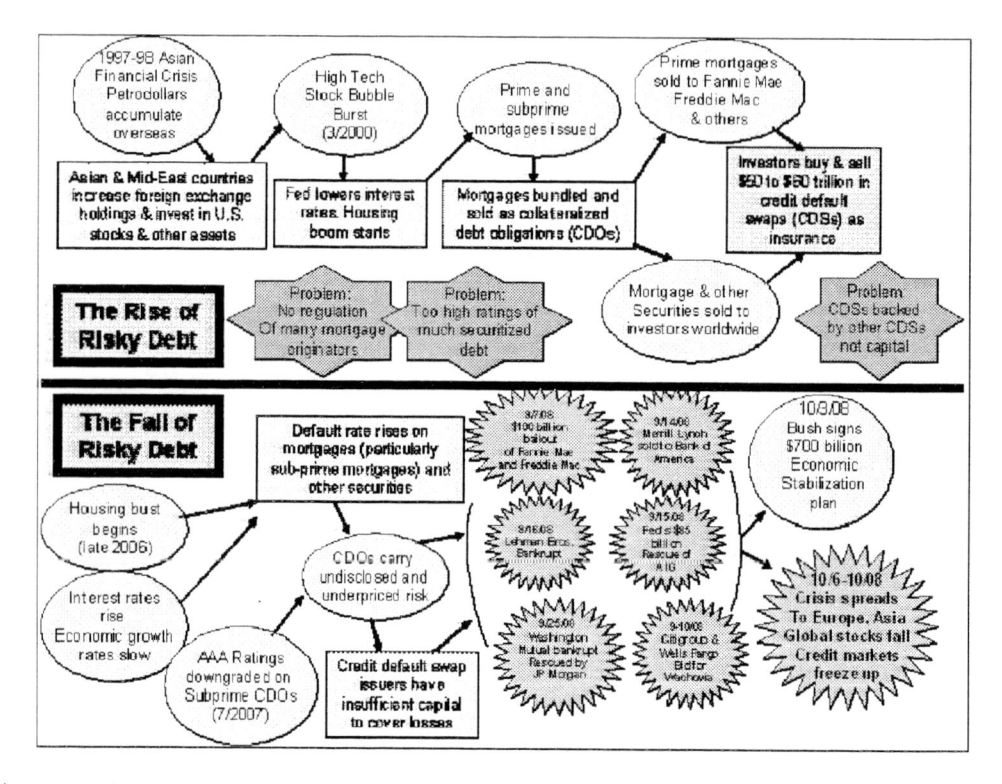

Figure 2. Origins of the Financial Crisis: The Rise and Fall of Risky Mortgage and Other Debt.

In order to cover the risk of defaults on mortgages, particularly subprime mortgages, the holders of CDOs purchased credit default swaps[103] (CDSs). These are a type of insurance contract (a financial derivative) that lenders purchase against the possibility of credit event (a default on a debt obligation, bankruptcy, restructuring, or credit rating downgrade) associated with debt, a borrowing institution, or other referenced entity. The purchaser of the CDS does not have to have a financial interest in the referenced entity, so CDSs quickly became more of a speculative asset than an insurance policy. As long as the credit events never occurred, issuers of CDSs could earn huge amounts in fees relative to their capital base (since these were technically not insurance, they did not fall under insurance regulations requiring sufficient capital to pay claims, although credit derivatives requiring collateral became more and more common in recent years). The sellers of the CDSs that protected against defaults often covered their risk by turning around and buying CDSs that paid in case of default. As the risk of defaults rose, the cost of the CDS protection rose. Investors, therefore, could arbitrage between the lower and higher risk CDSs and generate large income streams with what was perceived to be minimal risk.

In 2007, the notional value (face value of underlying assets) of credit default swaps had reached $62 trillion, more than the combined gross domestic product of the entire world ($54 trillion),[104] although the actual amount at risk was only a fraction of that amount (approximately 3.5%). By July 2008, the notional value of CDSs had declined to $54.6 trillion and by October 2008 to an estimated $46.95 trillion.[105] The system of CDSs generated large profits for the companies involved until the default rate, particularly on subprime mortgages, and the number of bankruptcies began to rise. Soon the leverage that generated outsized profits began to generate outsized losses, and in October 2008, the exposures became too great for companies such as AIG..

Risk

The origins of the financial crisis point toward three developments that increased risk in financial markets. The first was the originate-to-distribute model for mortgages. The originator of mortgages passed them on to the provider of funds or to a bundler who then securitized them and sold the collateralized debt obligation to investors. This recycled funds back to the mortgage market and made mortgages more available. However, the originator was not penalized, for example, for not ensuring that the borrower was actually qualified for the loan, and the buyer of the securitized debt had little detailed information about the underlying quality of the loans. Investors depended heavily on ratings by credit agencies.

The second development was a rise of perverse incentives and complexity for credit rating agencies. Credit rating firms received fees to rate securities based on information provided by the issuing firm using their models for determining risk. Credit raters, however, had little experience with credit default swaps at the "systemic failure" tail of the probability distribution. The models seemed to work under normal economic conditions but had not been tested in crisis conditions. Credit rating agencies also may have advised clients on how to structure securities in order to receive higher ratings. In addition, the large fees offered to credit rating firms for providing credit ratings were difficult for them to refuse in spite of doubts they might have had about the underlying quality of the securities. The perception existed that if one credit rating agency did not do it, another would.

The third development was the blurring of lines between issuers of credit default swaps and traditional insurers. In essence, financial entities were writing a type of insurance contract without regard for insurance regulations and requirements for capital adequacy (hence, the use of the term "credit default swaps" instead of "credit default insurance"). Much risk was hedged rather than backed by sufficient capital to pay claims in case of default. Under a systemic crisis, hedges also may fail. However, although the CDS market was largely unregulated by government, more than 850 institutions in 56 countries that deal in derivatives and swaps belong to the ISDA (International Swaps and Derivatives Association). The ISDA members subscribe to a master agreement and several protocols/amendments, some of which require that in certain circumstances companies purchasing CDSs require counterparties (sellers) to post collateral to back their exposures.[106] It was this requirement to post collateral that pushed some companies toward bankruptcy. The blurring of boundaries among banks, brokerage houses, and insurance agencies also made regulation and information gathering difficult. Regulation in the United States tends to be functional with separate government agencies regulating and overseeing banks, securities, insurance, and futures. There was no suprafinancial authority.

The Downward Slide

The plunge downward into the global financial crisis did not take long. It was triggered by the bursting of the housing bubble and the ensuing subprime mortgage crisis in the United States, but other conditions have contributed to the severity of the situation. Banks, investment houses, and consumers carried large amounts of leveraged debt. Certain countries incurred large deficits in international trade and current accounts (particularly the United States), while other countries accumulated large reserves of foreign exchange by running surpluses in those accounts. Investors deployed "hot money" in world markets seeking higher rates of return. These were joined by a huge run up in the price of commodities, rising interest rates to combat the threat of inflation, a general slowdown in world economic growth rates, and increased globalization that allowed for rapid communication, instant transfers of funds, and information networks that fed a herd instinct. This brought greater uncertainty and changed expectations in a world economy that for a half decade had been enjoying relative stability.

An immediate indicator of the rapidity and spread of the financial crisis has been in stock market values. As shown in **Figure 3**, as values on the U.S. market plunged, those in other countries were swept down in the undertow. By mid-October 2008, the stock indices for the United States, U.K., Japan, and Russia had fallen by nearly half or more relative to their levels on October 1, 2007. The downward slide reached a bottom in mid-March 2009, although there still is concern that the subsequent slow recovery in stock values has been a "bear market bounce" and that these stock markets may again go into sustained decline. the close tracking of the equities markets in the United States, Japan, and the U.K. provides further evidence of the global nature of capital markets and the rapidity of international capital flows.

Declines in stock market values reflected huge changes in expectations and the flight of capital from assets in countries deemed to have even small increases in risk. Many investors, who not too long ago had heeded financial advisors who were touting the long term returns from investing in the BRICs (Brazil, Russia, India, and China),[107] pulled their money out nearly as fast as they had put it in. Dramatic declines in stock values coincided with new accounting rules that required financial institutions holding stock as part of their capital base to value that stock according to market values (mark-to-market). Suddenly, the capital base of banks shrank and severely curtailed their ability to make more loans (counted as assets) and still remain within required capital-asset ratios. Insurance companies too found their capital reserves diminished right at the time they had to pay buyers of or post collateral for credit default swaps. The rescue (establishment of a conservatorship) for Fannie Mae and Freddie Mac in September 2008 potentially triggered credit default swap contracts with notional value exceeding $1.2 trillion.

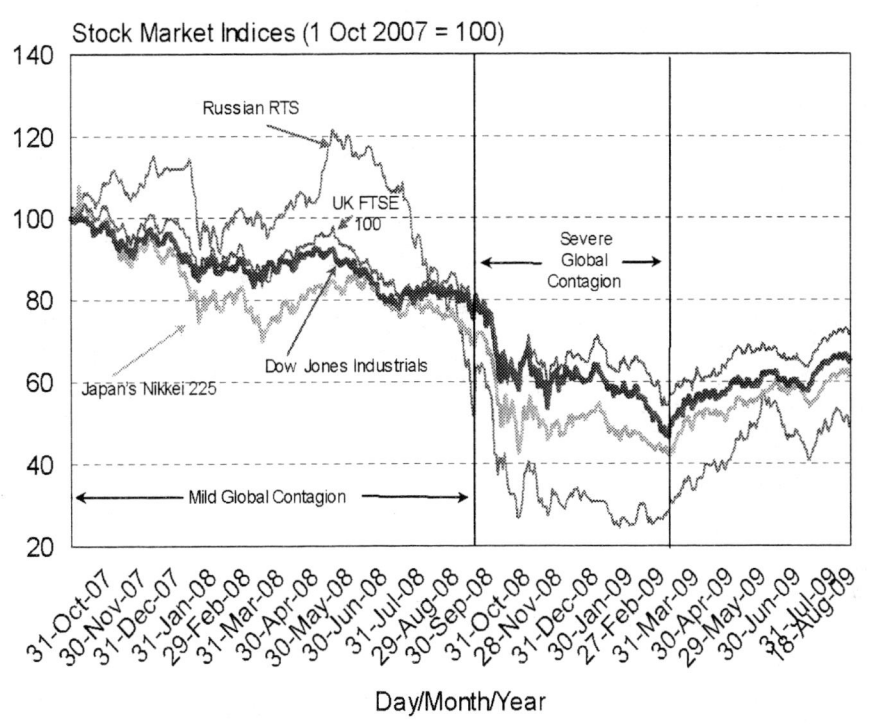

Figure 3. Selected Stock Market Indices for the United States, U.K., Japan, and Russia

In addition, the rising rate of defaults and bankruptcies created the prospect that equities would suddenly become valueless. The market price of stock in Freddie Mac plummeted from $63 on October 8, 2007 to $0.88 on October 28, 2008. Hedge funds, whose "rocket scientist" analysts claimed that they could make money whether markets rose or fell, lost vast sums of money. The prospect that even the most seemingly secure company could be bankrupt the next morning caused credit markets to freeze. Lending is based on trust and confidence. Trust and confidence evaporated as lenders reassessed lending practices and borrower risk.

One indicator of the trust among financial institutions is the Libor, the London Inter-Bank Offered Rate. This is the interest rate banks charge for short-term loans to each other. Although it is a composite of primarily European interest rates, it forms the basis for many financial contracts world wide including U.S. home mortgages and student loans. During the worst of the financial crisis in October 2008, this rate had doubled from 2.5% to 5.1%, and for a few days much interbank lending actually had stopped. The rise in the Libor came at a time when the U.S. monetary authorities were lowering interest rates to stimulate lending. The difference between interest on Treasury bills (three month) and on the Libor (three month) is called the "Ted spread." This spread averaged 0.25 percentage points from 2002 to 2006, but in October 2008 exceeded 4.5 percentage points. By the end of December, it had fallen to about 1.5%. The greater the spread, the greater the anxiety in the marketplace.[108]

As the crisis has moved to a global economic slowdown, many countries have pursued expansionary monetary policy to stimulate economic activity. This has included lowering interest rates and expanding the money supply.

Currency exchange rates serve both as a conduit of crisis conditions and an indicator of the severity of the crisis. As the financial crisis hit, investors fled stocks and debt instruments for the relative safety of cash—often held in the form of U.S. Treasury or other government securities. That increased demand for dollars, decreased the U.S. interest rate needed to attract investors, and caused a jump in inflows of liquid capital into the United States. For those countries deemed to be vulnerable to the effects of the financial crisis, however, the effect was precisely the opposite. Demand for their currencies fell and their interest rates rose.

Figure 4 shows indexes of the value of selected currencies relative to the dollar for selected countries. For much of 2007 and 2008, the Euro and other European currencies had been appreciating in value relative to the dollar; but the crisis pushed them down until the dollar began to decline. The Japanese yen continues to appreciate, while the Chinese RMB has risen slightly but, by and large, has been constant. Other currencies, such as the Korean won and Icelandic krona, had been steadily weakening over the previous year and experienced sharp declines as the crisis evolved. Recently, however, the won has recovered somewhat.

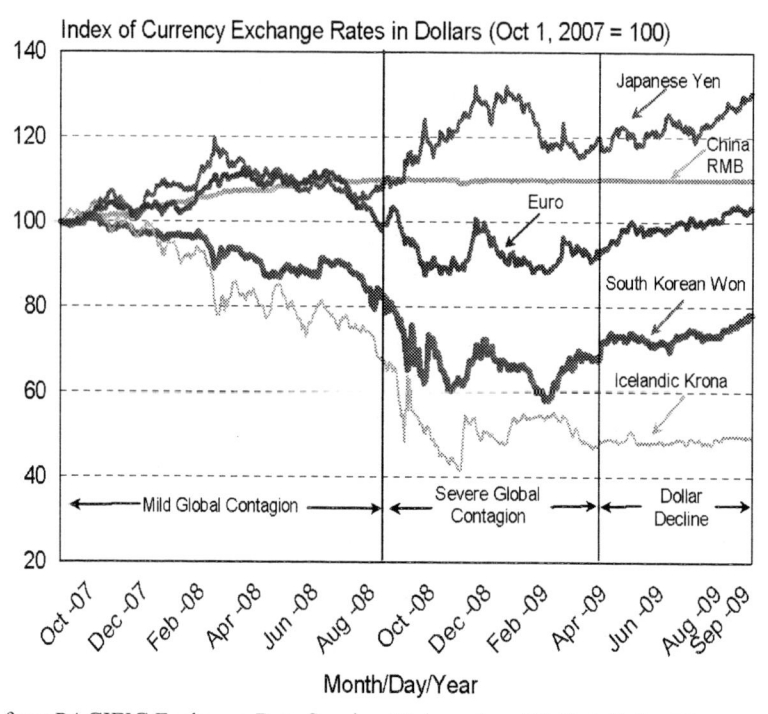

Source: Data from PACIFIC Exchange Rate Service, University of British Columbia.

Figure 4. Exchange Rate Values for Selected Currencies Relative to the U.S. Dollar

For a country in crisis, a weak currency increases the local currency equivalents of any debt denominated in dollars and exacerbates the difficulty of servicing that debt. The greater burden of debt servicing usually has combined with a weakening capital base of banks because of declines in stock market values to further add to the financial woes of countries. National governments have had little choice but to take fairly draconian measures to cope with the threat of financial collapse. As a last resort, some have turned to the International Monetary Fund for assistance.

Table 1. Stimulus Packages by Selected Countries

Date Announced	Country	$Billion	Status, Package Contents
17-Feb-09	United States	787.00	Infrastructure technology, tax cuts, education, transfers to states, energy, nutrition, health, unemployment benefits. Budget in deficit.
4-Feb-09	Canada	32.00	Two-year program. Infrastructure, tax relief, aid for sectors in peril. Government to run an estimated $1.1 billion budget deficit in 2008 and $52 billion deficit in 2009.
7-Jan-09	Mexico	54.00	Infrastructure, a freeze on gasoline prices, reducing electricity rates, help for poor families to replace old appliances, construction of low-income housing and an oil refinery, rural development, increase government purchases from small- and medium-sized companies. Paid for by taxes, oil revenues, and borrowing.
12-Dec-08	European Union	39.00	Total package of $256 billion called for states to increase budgets by $217 billion and for the EU to provide $39 billion to fund cross-border projects including clean energy and upgraded telecommunications architecture.
13-Jan-09	Germany	65.00	Infrastructure, tax cuts, child bonus, increase in some social benefits, $3,250 incentive for trading in cars more than nine years old for a new or slightly used car.
24-Nov-08	United Kingdom	29.60	Proposed plan includes a 2.5% cut in the value added tax for 13 months, a postponement of corporate tax increases, government guarantees for loans to small and midsize businesses, spending on public works, including public housing and energy efficiency. Plan includes an increase in income taxes on those making more than $225,000 and increase National Insurance contribution for all but the lowest income workers.
5-Nov-08	France	33.00	Public sector investments (road and rail construction, refurbishment and improving ports and river infrastructure, building and renovating universities, research centers, prisons, courts, and monuments) and loans for carmakers. Does not include the previously planned $15 billion in credits and tax breaks on investments by companies in 2009.
16-Nov-08	Italy	52.00	Three year program. Measures to spur consumer credit, provide loans to companies, and rebuild infrastructure.
		(3.56)	Feb. 6, 2009, $2.56 billion stimulus package that is part of the three-year program. Included payments of up to $1,950 for trading in an old car for a new, less polluting one and 20% tax deductions for purchases of appliances and furniture. Additional $1 billion allocated in March 2009 for building a bridge and increasing welfare aid.
20-Nov-08	Russia	20.00	Cut in the corporate profit tax rate, a new depreciation mechanism for businesses, to be funded by Russia's foreign exchange reserves and rainy day fund.
10-Nov-08	China	586.00	Low-income housing, electricity, water, rural infrastructure, projects aimed at environmental protection

Table 1. (Continued)

Date Announced	Country	$Billion	Status, Package Contents
			and technological innovation, tax deduction for capital spending by companies, and spending for health care and social welfare.
13-Dec-08 6-Apr-09	Japan Japan	250.00 146.00	Increase in government spending, funds to stabilize the financial system (prop up troubled banks and ease a credit crunch by purchasing commercial paper), tax cuts for homeowners and companies that build or purchase new factories and equipment, and grants to local government. The April 2009 package included increasing the safety net for non-regular workers, supporting small businesses, new car purchase subsidies, revitalizing regional economies, promoting solar power and nursing and medical services.
3-Nov-08	South Korea	14.64	$11 billion for infrastructure (including roads, universities, schools, and hospitals; funds for small- and medium-business, fishermen, and families with low income) and tax cuts. Includes an October 2008 stimulus package of $3.64 billion to provide support for the construction industry.
9-Feb-09	South Korea	37.87	The government announced its intention to invest $37.87 billion over the next four years in eco-friendly projects including the construction of dams; "green" transportation networks such as low-carbon emitting railways, bicycle roads, and other public transportation systems; and expand existing forest areas.
28-Nov-08	Taiwan	15.60	Shopping vouchers of $108 each for all citizens, construction projects to be carried out over four years include expanding metro systems, rebuilding bridges and classrooms, improving, railway and sewage systems, and renew urban areas.
26-Jan-09	Australia	35.2	$7 billion stimulus package in October 2008 was cash handouts to low income earners and pensioners. January's $28.2 billion package includes infrastructure, schools and housing, and cash payments to low- and middle-income earners. Budget is in deficit.
23-Dec-08	Brazil	5.00	Program established in 2007 to continue to 2010. Tax cuts (exempt capital goods producers from the industrial and welfare taxes, increase the value of personal computers exempted from taxes) and rebates. Funded by reducing the government's budget surplus.

Source: Congressional Research Service from various news articles and government press releases.
Notes: Currency conversions to U.S. dollars were either already done in the news articles or by CRS using current exchange rates.

As economies weakened, governments moved from shoring up their financial institutions to coping with rapidly developing recessionary economic conditions. While actions to assist banks, insurance companies, and securities firms recover or stave off bankruptcy continued, stimulus packages became policy priorities. In the fourth quarter of 2008, economic growth rates dropped in some countries at rates not seen in decades.(See **Figure 1**) China alone has estimated that 20 million workers have become unemployed. **Table 1** shows stimulus packages by selected major countries of the world. While the $787 billion package by the United States is the largest, China's $586 billion, the European Union's $256 billion, and Japan's $396 billion packages also are quite large.

EFFECTS ON EMERGING MARKETS[109]

The global credit crunch that began in August 2007 has led to a financial crisis in emerging market countries (**see box**) that is being viewed as greater in both scope and effect than the East Asian financial crisis of 1997-98 or the Latin American debt crisis of 2001-2002, although the impact on individual countries may have been greater in previous crises. Of the emerging market countries, those in Central and Eastern Europe appear, to date, to be the most impacted by the financial crisis.

The ability of emerging market countries to borrow from global capital markets has allowed many countries to experience incredibly high growth rates. For example, the Baltic countries of Latvia, Estonia, and Lithuania experienced annual economic growth of nearly 10% in recent years. However, since this economic expansion was predicated on the continued availability of access to foreign credit, they were highly vulnerable to a financial crisis when credit lines dried up.

WHAT ARE EMERGING MARKET COUNTRIES?

There is no uniform definition of the term "emerging markets." Originally conceived in the early 1980s, the term is used loosely to define a wide range of countries that have undergone rapid economic change over the past two decades. Broadly speaking, the term is used to distinguish these countries from the long-industrialized countries, on one hand, and less-developed countries (such as those in Sub-Saharan Africa), on the other. Emerging market countries are located primarily in Latin America, Central and Eastern Europe, and Asia.

Since 1999, the finance ministers of many of these emerging market countries began meeting with their peers from the industrialized countries under the aegis of the G-20, an informal forum to discuss policy issues related to global macroeconomic stability. The members of the G-20 are the European Union and 19 countries: Argentina, Australia, Brazil, Canada, China, France, Germany, India, Indonesia, Italy, Japan, Mexico, Russia, Saudi Arabia, South Africa, South Korea, Turkey, the United Kingdom and the United States.

For more information, see "When are Emerging Markets no Longer Emerging?, Knowledge@Wharton, available at
    http://knowledge.wharton.upenn.edu/article.cfm?articleid=1911.

Of all emerging market countries, Central and Eastern Europe appear to be the most vulnerable. On a wide variety of economic indicators, such as the total amount of debt in the economy, the size of current account deficits, dependence on foreign investment, and the level of indebtedness in the domestic banking sector, countries such as Hungary, Ukraine, Bulgaria, Kazakhstan, Kyrgyzstan, Latvia, Estonia, and Lithuania, rank among the highest of all emerging markets. Throughout the region, the average current account deficit increased from 2% of GDP in 2000 to 9% in 2008. In some countries, however, the current account deficit is much higher. Latvia's estimated 2008 current account deficit is 22.9% of GDP and Bulgaria's is 21.4%.[110] The average deficit for the region was greater than 6% in 2008 (**Figure 5**).

Due to the impact of the financial crisis, several Central and Eastern European countries have already sought emergency lending from the IMF to help finance their balance of payments. On October 24, the IMF announced an initial agreement on a $2.1 billion two-year loan with Iceland (approved on November 19). On October 26, the IMF announced a $16.5 billion agreement with Ukraine. On October 28, the IMF announced a $15.7 billion package for Hungary. On November 3, a staff-level agreement on an IMF loan was reached with Kyrgyzstan,[111] and on November 24, the IMF approved a $7.6 billion stand-by arrangement for Pakistan to support the country's economic stabilization.[112]

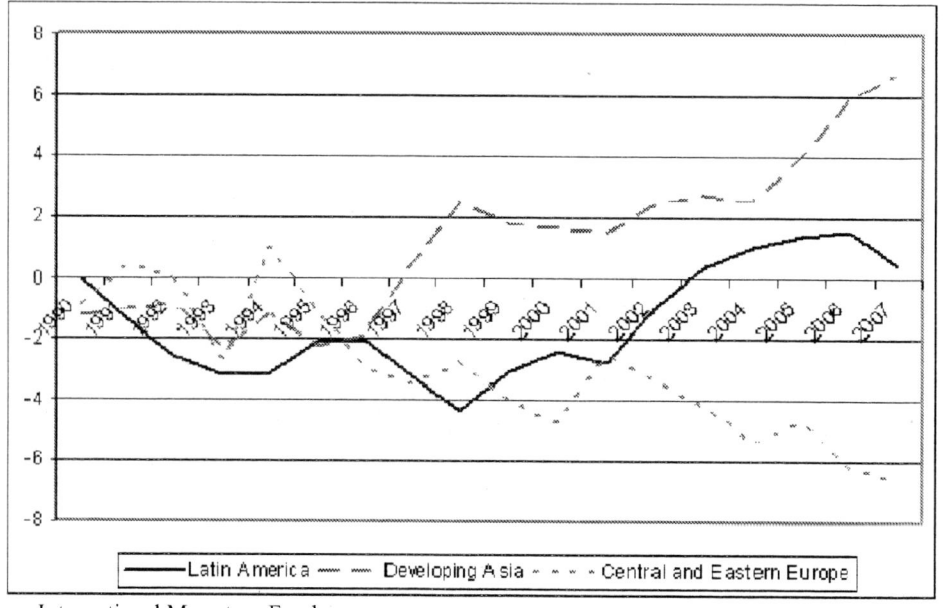

Source: International Monetary Fund.

Figure 5. Current Account Balances (as a percentage of GDP)

The quickness with which the crisis has impacted emerging market economies has taken many analysts by surprise. Since the Asian financial crisis, many Asian emerging market economies enacted a policy of foreign reserve accumulation as a form of self-insurance in case they once again faced a "sudden stop" of capital flows and the subsequent financial and balance of payments crises that result from a rapid tightening of international credit flows.[113] Two additional factors motivated emerging market reserve accumulation. First, several countries have pursued an export-led growth strategy targeted at the U.S. and other markets with which they have generated trade surpluses.[114] Second, a sharp rise in the price of commodities from 2004 to the first quarter of 2008 led many oil-exporting economies, and other commodity-based exporters, to report very large current account surpluses. **Figure 6** shows the rapid increase in foreign reserve accumulation among these countries. These reserves provided a sense of financial security to EM countries. Some countries, particularly China and certain oil exporters, also established sovereign wealth funds that invested the foreign exchange reserves in assets that promised higher yields.[115]

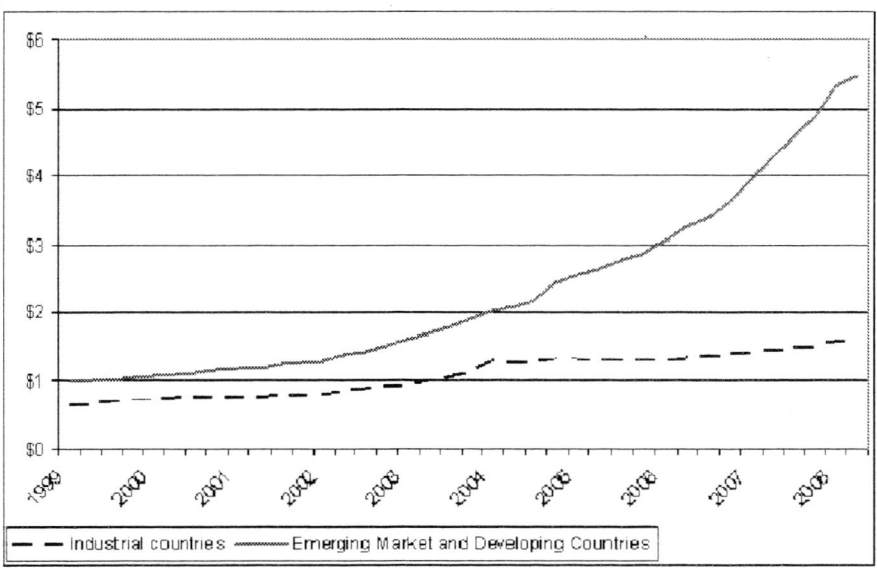

Source: IMF

Figure 6. Global Foreign Exchange Reserves ($ Trillion)

While global trade and finance linkages between the emerging markets and the industrialized countries have continued to deepen over the past decade, many analysts believed that emerging markets had successfully "decoupled" their growth prospects from those of industrialized countries. Proponents of the theory of decoupling argued that emerging market countries, especially in Eastern Europe and Asia, have successfully developed their own economies and intra-emerging market trade and finance to such an extent that a slowdown in the United States or Europe would not have as dramatic an impact as it did a decade ago. A report by two economists at the IMF found some evidence of this theory. The authors divided 105 countries into three groups: developed countries, emerging countries, and developing countries and studied how economic growth was correlated among the groups between 1960 and 2005. The authors found that while economic growth was highly synchronized between developed and developing countries, the impact of developed countries on emerging countries has decreased over time, especially during the past twenty years. According to the authors:

> In particular, [emerging market] countries have diversified their economies, attained high growth rates and increasingly become important players in the global economy. As a result, the nature of economic interactions between [industrialized and emerging market] countries has evolved from one of dependence to multidimensional interdependence.[116]

Despite efforts at self-insurance through reserve accumulation and evidence of economic decoupling, the U.S. financial crisis, and the sharp contraction of credit and global capital flows in October 2008 affected all emerging markets to a degree due to their continued dependence on foreign capital flows. According to the *Wall Street Journal*, in the month of October, Brazil, India, Mexico, and Russia drew down their reserves by more than $75 billion, in attempt to protect their currencies from depreciating further against a newly resurgent U.S. dollar.[117]

A key to understanding why emerging market countries have been so affected by the crisis (especially Central and Eastern Europe) is their high dependence on foreign capital flows to finance their economic growth (**Figures 7-8**). Even though several emerging markets have been able to reduce net capital inflows by investing overseas (through sovereign wealth funds) or by tightening the conditions for foreign investment, the large amount of gross foreign capital flows into emerging markets remained a key vulnerability for them. For countries such as those in Central and Eastern Europe which have both high gross and net capital flows, vulnerability to financial crisis is even higher.

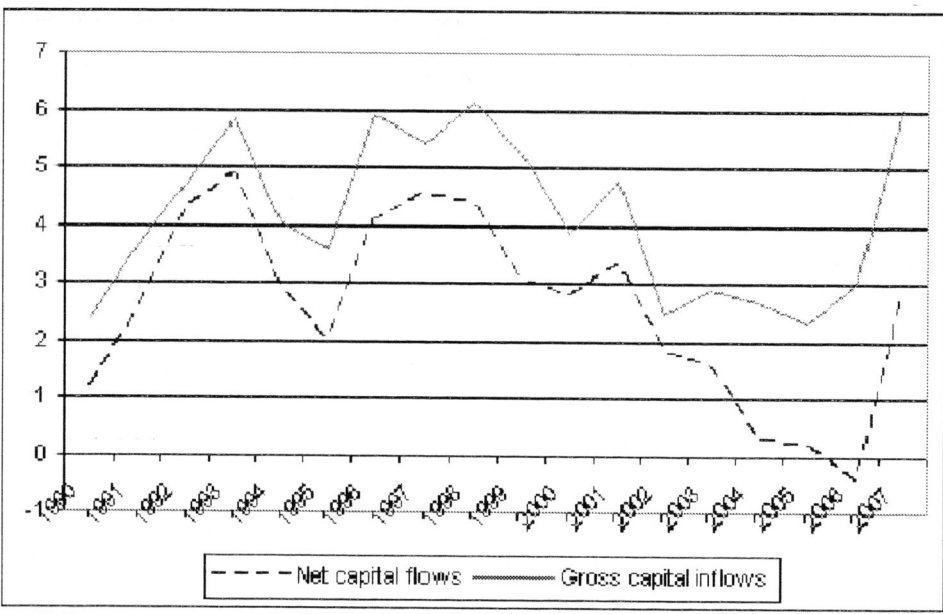

Source: IMF

Figure 7. Capital Flows to Latin America (in percent of GDP)

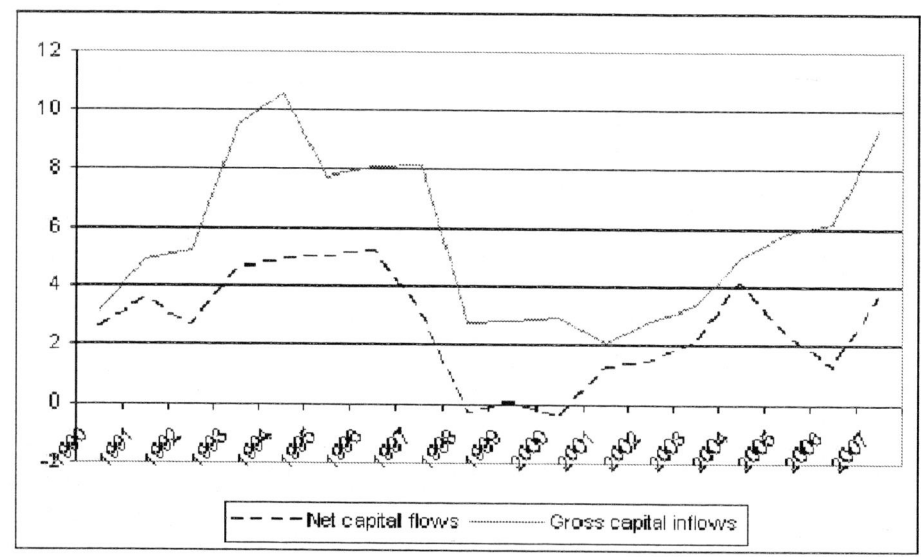

Source: IMF

Figure 8. Capital Flows to Developing Asia (in percent of GDP)

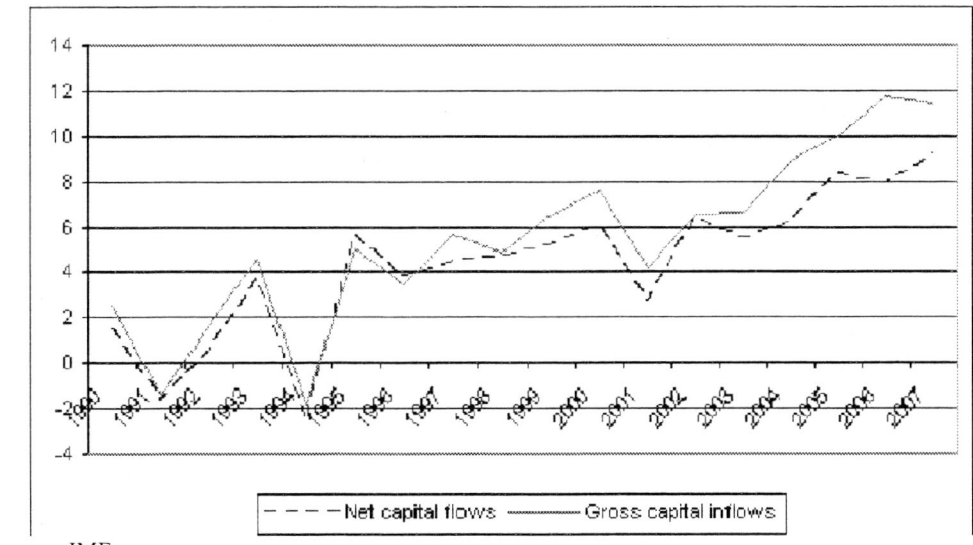

Source: IMF

Figure 9. Capital Flows to Central and Eastern Europe (in percent of GDP)

Once the crisis occurred, it became much more difficult for emerging market countries to continue to finance their foreign debt. According to Arvind Subramanian, an economist at the Peterson Institute for International Economics, and formerly an official at the IMF:

> If domestic banks or corporations fund themselves in foreign currency, they need to roll these over as the obligations related to gross flows fall due. In an environment of across-the-board deleveraging and flight to safety, rolling over is far from easy, and uncertainty about rolling over aggravates the loss in confidence.[118]

As emerging markets have grown, Western financial institutions have increased their investments in emerging markets. G-10[119] financial institutions have a total of $4.7 trillion of exposure to emerging markets with $1.6 trillion to Central and Eastern Europe, $1.5 trillion to emerging Asia, and $1.0 trillion to Latin America. While industrialized nation bank debt to emerging markets represents a relatively small percentage (13%) of total cross-border bank lending ($36.9 trillion as of September 2008), this figure is disproportionately high for European financial institutions and their lending to Central and Eastern Europe. For European and U.K. banks, cross-border lending to emerging markets, primarily Central and Eastern Europe accounts for between 21% and 24% of total lending. For U.S. and Japanese institutions, the figures are closer to 4% and 5%.[120] The heavy debt to Western financial institutions greatly increased central and Eastern Europe's vulnerability to contagion from the financial crisis.

In addition to the immediate impact on growth from the cessation of available credit, a downturn in industrialized countries will likely affect emerging market countries through several other channels. As industrial economies contract, demand for emerging market exports will slow down. This will have an impact on a range of emerging and developing countries. For example, growth in larger economies such as China and India will likely slow as their exports decrease. At the same time, demand in China and India for raw natural resources (copper, oil, etc) from other developing countries will also decrease, thus depressing growth in commodity-exporting countries.[121]

Slower economic growth in the industrialized countries may also impact less developed countries through lower future levels of bilateral foreign assistance. According to analysis by the Center for Global Development's David Roodman, foreign aid may drop precipitously over the next several years. His research finds that after the Nordic crisis of 1991, Norway's aid fell 10%, Sweden's 17%, and Finland's 62%. In Japan, foreign aid fell 44% between 1990 and 1996, and has never returned to pre-crisis assistance levels.[122]

Latin America[123]

Financial crises are not new to Latin America, but the current one has two unusual dimensions. First, as substantiated earlier in this report, it originated in the United States, with Latin America suffering shocks created by collapses in the U.S. housing and credit markets, despite minimal direct exposure to the "toxic" assets in question. Second, it spread to Latin America in spite of recent strong economic growth and policy improvements that have generally increased economic stability and reduced risk factors, particularly in the financial sector.[124] Repercussions from the global financial crisis have varied by country based in part on policy differences, but also on exposure to two major risks, the degree of reliance on the U.S. economy, and/or dependence on commodity exports. Investors, nonetheless, were initially very hard on the region as a whole, perhaps historically conditioned to be leery of its capacity to weather short-term financial contagion, let alone a protracted global recession.

A year after the crisis began, however, it appears that the financial and economic repercussions have stabilized, and that in many Latin American countries, a return to growth is evident. While the downturn was, and still is, very severe by many measures, relatively sound macroeconomic fundamentals and policy responses by many Latin American countries and international financial organizations may have ameliorated what could have been a deeper and longer regional decline. Nonetheless, it is still early in the recovery process to predict an unencumbered reversal of economic fortune and some countries face a steeper climb out of recession than others.

The economies of Latin America and the Caribbean grew at an average annual rate of nearly 5.5% for the five years 2004-2008, lending credence to the once prominent idea that they were "decoupling" from slower growing developed economies, particularly the United States.[125] Domestic policy reforms have been credited with achieving macroeconomic stability, stronger fiscal positions, sounder banking systems, and lower sovereign debt risk levels. Others note, however, that Latin America's growth trend is easily explained by international economic fundamentals, questioning the importance of the decoupling theory. The sharp rise in commodity prices, supportive external financing conditions, and high levels of remittances contributed greatly to the region's improved economic welfare, reflecting gains from a strong global economy. In addition, all three trends reversed even before the financial crisis began, suggesting that Latin America remains very much tied to world markets and trends.[126]

Latin America has experienced two levels of economic problems related to the crisis. First order effects from financial contagion were initially evident in the high volatility of financial market indicators. All major indicators fell sharply in the fourth quarter of 2008, as capital inflows reversed direction, seeking safe haven in less risky assets, many of them, ironically, dollar denominated. Regional stock indexes fell by over half from June to October 2008. Currencies followed suit in many Latin American countries. They depreciated suddenly from investor flight to the U.S. dollar reflecting a lack of confidence in local currencies, the rush to portfolio rebalancing, and the fall in commodity import revenue related to sharply declining prices and diminished global demand. In Mexico and Brazil, where firms took large speculative off-balance sheet derivative positions in the currency markets, currency losses were compounded to a degree requiring central bank intervention to ensure dollar availability. [127]

Debt markets followed in kind, as credit tightened and international lending contracted, even for short-term needs such as inventory and trade finance. Borrowing became more expensive, as seen in widening bond spreads. In 2008, bond spreads in the Emerging Market Bond Index (EMBI) and corporate bond index for Latin America jumped by some 600 basis points, half occurring in the fourth quarter. This trend suggests first, that Latin America was already beginning to experience a slowdown prior to the financial crisis, and second, that the crisis itself was a sudden subsequent shock to a deteriorating economic trend in the region. Some countries, including Brazil, Mexico, and Colombia, had continued access to international debt markets. Many others, however, have had to rely more heavily on domestic debt placements.

Signs of financial market stabilization appeared by the summer of 2009. Both regional stock and currency indexes recovered 60% of their losses by September 2009, indicating renewed interest and confidence in Latin America's ability to weather the downturn and perhaps emerge from it ahead of many developed economies, including the United States.[128] Overall, after spiking in the fall of 2008 at around 800 basis points, sovereign bond spreads have retreated to under 400 basis points, still off the 200 basis point level prior to the crisis, but a significant trend reversal. The exceptions are in Argentina, Ecuador, and Venezuela, all of which share a heavy dependence on commodity exports and weak economic policy frameworks. In each of these countries, bond spreads rose to over 1,500 basis points as the crisis unfolded, and although the spreads have narrowed to a range of 750 to 950 basis points, the difference still reflects a lack of confidence in their financials systems and their capacity to service debt.[129]

The more serious effects of the global crisis for Latin America appear in second order effects, which point to a deterioration of broader economic fundamentals. These will take much longer to recover than financial indicators. GDP growth for the region is expected to be a negative 2% in 2009, with an estimated growth of 3.4% in 20 10.[130] The fall in global demand, particularly for Latin America's commodity exports, has been a big factor, as seen in contracting export revenue. Latin American exports are expected to fall by 11% in 2009, the largest decline since 1937. Similarly, imports may fall by 14%, reflecting the decline in world demand in general. The trade account, along with rising unemployment, point to the most severe aspects of the crisis for Latin America.[131] Remittances have also fallen, ranging between 10% and 20% by country. Although still important financial inflows, the decline in remittances is expected to diminish family incomes and fiscal balances, contributing to the regional slowdown.[132] Public sector borrowing is expected to rise and budget constraints may threaten spending on social programs in some cases, with a predictably disproportional effect on the poor. Social effects are also seen in the rising unemployment throughout the region.

Policy responses have materialized from many quarters, including multilateral organizations, which have adopted programs to ameliorate the credit crisis and stimulate demand. The International Monetary Fund (IMF), World Bank, Inter-American Development Bank (IDB), Andean Development Corporation (CAF), and Latin American Reserve Fund (LARF) have all increased lending to the region, particularly on an expedited and short-term basis. The goal is to provide credit to the private sector and to support, in selective cases, bank recapitalization. Funds will also be made available for public sector spending (infrastructure and social programs) as a form of fiscal stimulus, primarily through the World Bank and IDB.

The United States took steps to provide dollar liquidity (reciprocal currency "swap" arrangement) on a temporary bilateral basis to many central banks of "systemically important" countries with sound banking systems. In Latin America, this group includes Mexico and Brazil, each of which had access to a $30 billion currency swap reserve with the U.S. Federal Reserve System, initially through April 30, 2009, but which was extended to February 1, 2010. The swap arrangement is intended to ensure dollar availability in support of the large trade and investment transactions conducted with the United States, and perhaps more importantly, reinforce confidence in the financial systems of the two largest Latin American economies. [133]

National governments are also relying on monetary, fiscal, and exchange rate policies to stimulate their economies. The capacity to undertake any of these options varies tremendously among the Latin American countries. Fiscal capacity is constrained in many countries by high debt levels, as well as the recession itself. Among the countries adopting a fiscal stimulus, estimates of their size range from 2.5% GDP in Mexico to 6.0% for Argentina and 8.5% for Brazil. Direct government spending is the primary vehicle for fiscal stimulus, but Brazil has devoted 20% to tax cuts or increased benefits (transfers).[134]

Many countries are also limited in their use of monetary policy to expand liquidity. In particular, reducing interest rates is difficult for those experiencing significant currency depreciations, which can increase inflationary pressures. Nonetheless, those countries with flexible exchange rates have relied on currency depreciations to shoulder much of the adjustment process, without experiencing severe financial instability.[135] There has been some concern that countries may eventually resort to nationalistic policies that will reduce the flows of goods, services, and capital, but these types of policies have generally been avoided, and the risk of their use likely diminishes as economies improve. The magnitude of the global economic downturn and adequacy of policy responses vary by country, as illustrated by three examples discussed below.

Mexico

The Mexican economy contracted for four consecutive quarters beginning in the fourth quarter of 2008, and the government forecasts an economic decline of 7%-8% for 2009. This would be the worst recession in six decades, making Mexico the hardest hit country in Latin America. Output fell in both industry and service sectors, with the 13% decline in industrial production over the past year the worst recorded since the 1995 "peso crisis." Remittances, which amounted to $25 billion in 2008, may fall by 15% in 2009. Mexico faces a number of problems: heavy reliance on the U.S. economy, falling foreign investment, and low (until recently) oil prices, and declining oil output, the largest source of national revenue. The

United States accounts for half of Mexico's imports, 80% of its exports, and most of its foreign investment and remittances income.[136]

A nascent recovery was measurable by the summer of 2009, signaling for many analysts the possibility of a solid turnaround in the downward trend. Analysts are forecasting a sharp increase in economic growth in the second half of 2009, with an annual expansion in economic activity of 3.3% for 2010. The sustainability of such a trend will depend heavily on recovery of the U.S. and global economies.[137]

The financial crisis hit Mexico hard and fast. At the outset, Mexico experienced a run on the peso, which caused its value to fall at one point by 40% from its August 2008 high (currently down by 20% from September 2008). The decline was unrelated to investments in U.S. mortgage-backed securities. Investor portfolio re-balancing away from emerging markets, the dramatic fall in commodity prices, and decline in U.S. demand for Mexican exports were the main causes. The peso also suffered from large private positions taken in the belief that the peso's strength would not be eroded by the U.S. financial crisis. Many firms had gone beyond hedging to taking large derivative positions in the peso. As the peso began to depreciate, companies had to unwind these off-balance-sheet positions quickly, accelerating its fall. One large firm had losses exceeding $1.4 billion and filed for bankruptcy, indicative of the severity of the problem. The Mexican government responded by selling billions of dollars of reserves and using a temporary currency swap arrangement with the U.S. Federal Reserve to assure dollar liquidity, but the peso remains the hardest hit of all emerging market currencies.[138]

In the non-financial sectors, industrial production was severely hit by the fall in U.S. demand for Mexican exports. The industrial sector, however, rebounded with 2.8% monthly growth in July 2009, and is expected to lead the recovery as it did the recession. Mexico's long-term economic prospects, however, hinge on recovery of U.S. aggregate demand. Because Mexico's trade is poorly diversified, the effects of the U.S. downturn were particularly noticeable, with Mexican exports to the United States on a monthly basis falling 37% from October 2008 to February 2009, hitting the lowest level since January 2005. U.S. imports from Mexico began to recover in June 2009, and are up nearly 15% from February 2009, but stand at only 70% of the peak reached in October 2007. The trade effect has been compounded by a nearly 20% annual decline in remittances from Mexican workers living in the United States. Employment figures for the formal economy at home are also registering large job losses.[139]

To date, the Mexican government has adopted supportive monetary and fiscal policies. The central government has increased liquidity in the banking system, including multiple cuts in the prime policy lending rate. It has also increased its credit lines with the World Bank, International Monetary Fund, and Inter-American Development Bank. Mexico's fiscal stimulus amounts to 2.5% of GDP and is targeted on infrastructure spending and subsidies for key goods of household budgets, particularly those reducing energy costs. Government programs to support small and medium-sized businesses, worker training, employment generation, and social safety nets have been maintained and expanded in some cases.[140]

The costs of these responses has placed additional strain on Mexico's public finances. The overall fiscal deficit is expected to reach 3.5% of GDP for 2009 and 2010, estimated to be near the maximum that Mexico can afford. Recent downward revisions of Mexico's credit rating (still investor grade) reflect growing concern over Mexico's financial position in light of weak economic fundamentals and Mexico's recovery relying so heavily on a U.S.

economic rebound. Mexico appears to have reached the financial limits of its fiscal and monetary responses, but some analysts speculate that at the margin, lagged effects of these policies may continue to support Mexico's nascent recovery.[141]

Brazil

Brazil entered the financial crisis from a position of relative macroeconomic and fiscal strength, and although it has not been immune to the global contraction, data suggest Brazil will experience only a two-quarter recession, with recovery solidly in place by in the second half of 2009. The economy grew by 5.1% in 2008 and is expected to contract by less than 1.0% over the full year 2009. Second quarter growth registered 1.9% on an annualized basis, indicating a technical end to recession. Commodity price rebound has contributed to growth in Brazilian output and exports, and industrial production has begun to rise as well. Still, a number of indicators in the real economy remain weak and fiscal pressures from the stimulus package present a short-term financial burden.[142]

Financial repercussions sparked the crisis and affected Brazil in ways similar to Mexico. Brazil's stock market index tumbled by half in 2008 as investors fled both equities and the Brazilian currency (the *real*). The Brazilian government sold billions of dollars to fight a rapidly depreciating currency, which fell at one point by over 35% from its August 2008 high. Brazil, like Mexico, also has a large currency derivatives market, where speculative trades contributed to the *real's* decline, although to a lesser degree than in Mexico. Brazil's central bank agreed to the temporary currency swap arrangement with the U.S. Federal Reserve. It also has some $200 billion in international reserves, which have served as an effective cushion against financial retreat from the financial markets. Brazil also has a sound and well-regulated banking system and experienced central bank leadership and staff that has helped maintain confidence in the financial system in the face of rising defaults and declining balance sheet quality.[143]

Financial indictors have all improved, reflecting a return to stability and portending a near-term broader economic recovery. Brazil's *real* has appreciated against the U.S. dollar, fully recovering any losses over the past year. The stock index has recovered 17% from January 2009 and the bond spreads on Brazilian debt are only 200 basis points above U.S. treasuries, reflecting confidence in Brazil's economic prospects. Brazilian government debt was upgraded from speculative to investment grade by the major ratings agencies in late September, lending further support for confidence in the country's financial and economic outlook.[144]

The real (nonfinancial) economy faces deeper challenges. Domestic demand is still weak and the unemployment rate has risen from 6.8% in December 2008 to an estimated 9.2%. July employment figures, however, showed a net job increase of 292,000 across all sectors, indicating the real economy is beginning to experience recovery as well. Although Brazil also experienced declines in exports, the recovery of commodity prices and strong demand from China, now the largest consumer of Brazil's exports, have helped improve Brazil's trade account. Capital inflows, which were strong in 2008, have also slowed, despite Brazil's recent solid macroeconomic performance and its investment grade rating. As with other countries, the extent to which global demand diminishes will ultimately affect all these variables. Brazil, however, has a large internal market and is well-positioned on the macroeconomic front, which has helped soften the effects of the global financial crisis.[145]

On the fiscal side, Brazil enacted a sizeable fiscal stimulus estimated at 8.5% of GDP. Tax cuts and direct government spending have been credited with ameliorating the effects of the global downturn. Brazil has maintained fiscal support for its social programs, expanded unemployment insurance, and made provisions for low-income housing and other support. To accommodate its increased fiscal commitments, it has reduced its primary fiscal surplus target from 3.8% to 2.5% of GDP, and will likely see its deficit and debt positions deteriorate in the short term. Observers, however, are beginning to raise concerns over Brazil's growing deficit, and have suggested that the government has reached the edge of its capacity for fiscal stimulus.[146]

In addition to a fiscal response, Brazil has emphasized enhancing financial sector liquidity through monetary policy. The Central Bank has injected billions of dollars into the banking system, lowered reserve requirements, and reduced the key short-term interest rate many times, from 13.75% to 8.75%. The Brazilian government has authorized state-owned banks to purchase private banks, approved stricter accounting rules for derivatives, extended credit directly to firms through the National Development Bank (BNDES) and the Central Bank, and exempted foreign investment firms from the financial transactions tax.[147] Unibanco, one of Brazil's largest banks, has also procured a $60 million credit extension from the World Bank's International Finance Corporation to support trade financing.

Argentina

Argentina, because of its shaky economic and financial position at the outset of the crisis, has been poorly positioned to deal with a protracted downturn compared to most other Latin American countries. Although until recently it has experienced dramatic economic growth since 2002, this trend reflects a rebound from the previous severe 2001-2002 financial crisis and rise in commodity prices that benefitted Argentina's large agricultural sector. This trend ended when Argentina experienced a contraction of -0.8% for the second quarter of 2009 (on an annualized basis). The collapse of commodity prices in late 2008 diminished export and fiscal revenues and Argentina is also experiencing declines in investment, domestic consumer demand, and industrial production. Installed capacity utilization fell from 79% in October 2008 to 67.4% in January 2009, recovering to 74.6% by August 2009. Particularly hard hit were motor vehicles, metallurgy, and textiles. Economists forecast the economy will contract by 2% to 4% in 2009 and recovery will be slow with unemployment still rising to nearly 9.0% in the summer of 2009.[148]

Argentina has been financially isolated from global markets since its 2001 crisis and is also hampered by a litany of questionable policy choices, which combined with the global recession and a prolonged draught, has further diminished confidence in its financial system. Although the banks remain liquid and solvent, the stock market fell at one point by 37% from last fall and the peso has depreciated by 18%. Among the highly questionable policies that have diminished confidence in the country is the 2002 historic sovereign debt default and failure to renegotiate with Paris Club countries and private creditor holdouts. Others include government interference in the supposedly independent government statistics office (particularly with respect to inflation reporting), price controls, high export taxes, and nationalization of private pension funds to bolster public finances.[149] These policies have isolated the economy from international capital markets despite the need to finance a growing debt burden and public and private sector investments. Price controls and export restrictions (quotas and taxes) have led to market distortions, protests over government policies, and declining consumer confidence.

Argentina's exports declined by 21% year-over-year in the first six months of 2009.[150] In response to falling demand for Argentine exports and the government's questionable financial policies and position, Argentina's currency has depreciated by 20% from September 2008, in spite of exchange rate intervention. In recognition that industrial production and exports fell rapidly and have stagnated until very recently, Argentina has also adopted administrative trade restrictions to limit imports, some of which it has reversed rather than face disputes in the World Trade Organization. These affected Brazilian goods in particular, including textiles and various machinery exports, raising tensions between the two major trade partners of the regional customs union, Mercosur.[151]

Risk assessment was swift and punishing. Bond ratings have fallen, yields on short-term public debt exceeded 30%, and the interest rate spread on Argentina's bonds rose to over 1,700 basis points, but have since settled around 750-800 basis points, nearly four times higher than Mexico's or Brazil's spreads. The interest rate spread on credit default swaps peaked at 4,500 basis points in December 2008, indicating the high cost required to insure against bond defaults. All these indicators point to a global perception of Argentina as a high-risk country, likely reinforcing its ostracism from international capital markets.[152]

Argentina has adopted a number of policies to address the domestic effects of the global economic crisis. The first initiative is a large fiscal stimulus equal to 9% of GDP focused almost entirely on public works spending, exasperating fiscal problems in the short run. Given Argentina's large expected public spending outlays for the coming year, the high and growing cost of its debt, falling revenues from imports, and its inability to access international credit markets, it had to take dramatic action to finance these programs. It did so by nationalizing, with the approval of the Congress, the private-sector pension system, effective January 1, 2009. The pension system provided $29 billion in assets immediately and access to an estimated $4.6 billion in annual pension contributions. In addition, Argentina has conducted two bond swaps (with 15.4% yields) for guaranteed loans maturing in 2009 to 2011.[153] Although these two moves have provided Argentina with increased fiscal capacity to meet short- and perhaps medium-term financing needs, the costs entail increased fiscal outlays in the future and heightened investor skepticism. Analysts estimate that Argentina has little room for additional fiscal expansion given its history of fiscal largesse over the past six years, which could temper a budding recovery.[154]

Russia and the Financial Crisis[155]

Russia tends to be in a category by itself. Although by some measures, it is an emerging market, it also is highly industrialized. As the case with most of the world's economies, the Russian economy has been hit hard by the global economic crisis. However, unlike the emerging economies of East Asia and some major developed economies, Russia's recovery from the crisis is proceeding slowly, reflecting fundamental structural problems, including a high dependence on production of oil and other commodities and a very weak banking system. The long-term challenge for Russian policymakers will be to address these problems once the immediate effects the global crisis have receded.

For about a decade (1999-2008) Russia experienced impressive growth rates and economic stability that allowed it to emerge from the chaos of the immediate post-Soviet period (1992- 1998) and to improve the standard of living of most Russian citizens. The growth was due in part to a rapid decline in the value of the ruble in the late 1990s that stimulated demand for and production of domestic goods and services as substitutes for imports. However, for most of the period, economic growth was rooted in the surge in world oil prices and resulting export revenues.

The economic growth came to an abrupt end with the global financial crisis and recession, which led to a decline in demand for energy and thus in world oil prices. Russia has also been adversely affected by the world-wide credit crunch. Because low interest credit was not available domestically, many Russian firms and banks depended on foreign loans to finance investments. As credit tightened, foreign loans became harder to obtain.

The economic downturn has been showing up in Russia's performance indicators. Although Russia's real GDP increased 5.6% in 2008, it increased more slowly than it did in 2007 (8.1%) and grew only 1.2% in the fourth quarter of 2008. Russia's GDP *declined* 9.8% during the first quarter of 2009 and 10.9% during the second quarter.[156] Declining revenues have forced the government to tighten fiscal policy but still incur budget deficits for the first time since 1999, a projected deficit of 8.0% of GDP by the end of 2009.[157] And for the first time since 1998, the government will likely have to obtain budget financing through the international debt market but the size of the bond issue will depend on world oil prices which have begun to rise.

The Russian government has responded to the crisis with various measures to prop up the stock market and the banks and to stimulate domestic demand. In mid-September 2008, the government made available $44 billion in funds to Russia's three largest state-owned banks to boost lending and another $16 billion to the next 25 largest banks. It also lowered taxes on oil exports to reduce costs to oil companies and made available $20 billion for the government to purchase stocks on the stock market. In late September 2008, the government announced that an additional $50 billion would be available to banks and Russian companies to pay off foreign debts coming due by the end of the year. On October 7, 2008, the government announced another package of $36.4 billion in credits to banks.[158] In 2009, the government changed strategies by focusing on macroeconomic measures rather than measures to assist specific industries or firms. For example, the government reduced the corporate tax rate from 24% to 20% and the tax rate on small companies to try to stimulate investment.[159] The government expects to rein in expenditures.[160]

While, on the one hand, cutting expenditures might be considered fiscally responsible, on the other hand, it could retard government investment in necessary items such as modernizing the infrastructure and in pensions and other social income transfers, contributing to a drag on the rest of the economy.

The IMF projects that Russia's real GDP will *decline* over 7.5% in 2009.[161] INS Global Insight, and the Economist Intelligence Unit (EIU), both private economic forecasting firms, project Russia's GDP to decline in 2009 by 7.5%-8.0% and 7.4%, respectively.[162] These forecasts are supported by data showing a continuing decline in both domestic and external demand (exports), among other things, although the rates of decline have slowed possibly indicating bottoming out, if not a full-fledged economic recovery. INS Global Insight, Inc. and the EIU each forecast modest recoveries in 2010 of 1.5% and 2.5%, respectively.

Russia remains highly dependent on oil and natural gas exports as a source of income. If world oil prices continue to be depressed or increase only modestly, the Russian economy would likely experience slow growth, if any. Many economists have argued that, in the long run, for Russia to achieve sustainable growth, it must reduce its dependence on exports of oil, natural gas, and other commodities and diversify into more stable production. In September 2009, President Medvedev published an article –"Russia, Forward"—in which he criticized Russia's failures to diversify and modernize its economy and pledged to change Russian economic policy in order to remedy the situation. He reiterated these views in his address to the state on November 12, 2009.[163] It is not clear if Prime Minister Putin, Medvedev's successor and presumptive holder of power in Russia, shares these views.

EFFECTS ON EUROPE AND THE EUROPEAN RESPONSE[164]

Some European countries[165] initially viewed the financial crisis as a purely American phenomenon. That view changed as economic activity Europe declined at a fast pace over a short period of time. Making matters worse, global trade declined sharply, eroding prospects for European exports providing a safety valve for domestic industries that are cutting output. In addition, public protests, sparked by rising rates of unemployment and concerns over the growing financial and economic turmoil, have increased the political stakes for European governments and their leaders. The global economic crisis is straining the ties that bind together the members of the European Union and has presented a significant challenge to the ideals of solidarity and common interests. In addition, the longer the economic downturn persists, the greater the prospects are that international pressure will mount against those governments that are perceived as not carrying their share of the responsibility for stimulating their economies to an extent that is commensurate with the size of their economy.

Since the start of the financial crisis, the European Union has taken a number of steps to improve supervision of financial markets. These actions include:

- Strengthened the Committee of European Securities Regulators. The Committee is an advisory body without any regulatory authority within the European Commission. The January 23, 2009 Directive strengthened the Committee's authority to mediate and coordinate securities regulations between EU members.
- Strengthened the Committee of European Banking Supervisors. The Committee is an advisory body without any regulatory authority that coordinates on banking supervision. The January 23, 2009 EU Directive broadened the role of the Committee to include supervision of financial conglomerates.
- Strengthened the Committee of European Insurance and Occupational Pensions Supervisors. The Committee is an advisory body without any regulatory authority within the European Commission in the areas of insurance, reinsurance, and occupational pensions fields. The January 23, 2009 Directive authorizes the Committee to coordinate policies among EU members and between the EU and other national governments and bodies.

- The European Parliament and the European Council approved on April 23, 2009, new regulations on credit rating agencies that are expected to improve the quality and transparency of the ratings agencies.
- Approved direct funding by the European Union to the International Accounting Standards Committee Foundation, the European Financial Reporting Advisory Group, and the Public Interest Oversight Body.
- The European Commission proposed a set of measures to register hedge fund managers and managers of alternative investment funds and measures to regulate executive compensation.
- Expressed support for a new European Systemic Risk Council and a European System of Financial Supervisors.

European countries have been concerned over the impact the financial crisis and the economic recession are having on the economies of East Europe and prospects for political instability[166] as well as future prospects for market reforms. Worsening economic conditions in East European countries are compounding the current problems facing financial institutions in the EU. Although mutual necessity may eventually dictate a more unified position among EU members and increased efforts to aid East European economies, some observers are concerned these actions may come too late to forestall another blow to the European economies and to the United States. Governments elsewhere in Europe, such as Iceland and Latvia, have collapsed as a result of public protests over the way their governments have handled their economies during the crisis.

The crisis has underscored the growing interdependence between financial markets and between the U.S. and European economies. As such, the synchronized nature of the current economic downturn probably means that neither the United States nor Europe is likely to emerge from the financial crisis or the economic downturn alone. The United States and Europe share a mutual interest in developing a sound financial architecture to improve supervision and regulation of individual institutions and of international markets. This issue includes developing the organization and structures within national economies that can provide oversight of the different segments of the highly complex financial system. This oversight is viewed by many as critical to the future of the financial system because financial markets generally are considered to play an indispensible role in allocating capital and facilitating economic activity.

Within Europe, national governments and private firms have taken noticeably varied responses to the crisis, reflecting the unequal effects by country. While some have preferred to address the crisis on a case-by-case basis, others have looked for a systemic approach that could alter the drive within Europe toward greater economic integration. Great Britain proposed a plan to rescue distressed banks by acquiring preferred stock temporarily. Iceland, on the other hand, had to take over three of its largest banks in an effort to save its financial sector and its economy from collapse. The Icelandic experience has raised important questions about how a nation can protect its depositors from financial crisis elsewhere and about the level of financial sector debt that is manageable without risking system-wide failure.

According to reports by the International Monetary Fund (IMF) and the European Central Bank (ECB), many of the factors that led to the financial crisis in the United States created a similar crisis in Europe.[167] Essentially low interest rates and an expansion of financial and investment opportunities that arose from aggressive credit expansion, growing complexity in mortgage securitization, and loosening in underwriting standards combined with expanded linkages among national financial centers to spur a broad expansion in credit and economic growth. This rapid rate of growth pushed up the values of equities, commodities, and real estate. Over time, the combination of higher commodity prices and rising housing costs pinched consumers' budgets, and they began reducing their expenditures. One consequence of this drop in consumer spending was a slowdown in economic activity and, eventually, a contraction in the prices of housing. In turn, the decline in the prices of housing led to a large-scale downgrade in the ratings of subprime mortgage-backed securities and the closing of a number of hedge funds with subprime exposure. Concerns over the pricing of risk in the market for subprime mortgage-backed securities spread to other financial markets, including to structured securities more generally and the interbank money market. Problems spread quickly throughout the financial sector to include financial guarantors as the markets turned increasingly dysfunctional over fears of under-valued assets.

As creditworthiness problems in the United States began surfacing in the subprime mortgage market in July 2007, the risk perception in European credit markets followed. The financial turmoil quickly spread to Europe, although European mortgages initially remained unaffected by the collapse in mortgage prices in the United States. Another factor in the spread of the financial turmoil to Europe has been the linkages that have been formed between national credit markets and the role played by international investors who react to economic or financial shocks by rebalancing their portfolios in assets and markets that otherwise would seem to be unrelated. The rise in uncertainty and the drop in confidence that arose from this rebalancing action undermined the confidence in major European banks and disrupted the interbank market, with money center banks becoming unable to finance large securities portfolios in wholesale markets. The increased international linkages between financial institutions and the spread of complex financial instruments has meant that financial institutions in Europe and elsewhere have come to rely more on short-term liquidity lines, such as the interbank lending facility, for their day-to-day operations. This has made them especially vulnerable to any drawback in the interbank market.[168]

Estimates developed by the International Monetary Fund in January 2009 provide a rough indicator of the impact the financial crisis and an economic recession are having on the performance of major advanced countries. Economic growth in Europe is expected to slow by nearly 2% in 2009 to post a 0.2% drop in the rate of economic growth, while the threat of inflation is expected to lessen. Economic growth, as represented by gross domestic product (GDP), is expected to register a negative 1.6% rate for the United States in 2009, while the euro area countries could experience a combined negative rate of 2.0%, down from a projected rate of growth of 1.2% in 2008. The drop in the prices of oil and other commodities from the highs reached in summer 2008 may have helped improve the rate of economic growth, but the length and depth of the economic downturn has challenged the ability of the IMF projections to accurately estimate projected rates of economic growth. In mid-February, the European Union announced that the rate of economic growth in the EU in the fourth quarter of 2008 had slowed to an annual rate of negative 6%.[169] By mid-summer 2009, the pace of economic growth had picked up in both France and Germany.

Central banks in the United States, the Euro zone, the United Kingdom, Canada, Sweden, and Switzerland staged a coordinated cut in interest rates on October 8, 2008, and announced they had agreed on a plan of action to address the ever-widening financial crisis.[170] The actions, however, did little to stem the wide-spread concerns that were driving financial markets. Many Europeans were surprised at the speed with which the financial crisis spread across national borders and the extent to which it threatened to weaken economic growth in Europe. This crisis did not just involve U.S. institutions. It has demonstrated the global economic and financial linkages that tie national economies together in a way that may not have been imagined even a decade ago. At the time, much of the substance of the European plan was provided by the British Prime Minister Gordon Brown,[171] who announced a plan to provide guarantees and capital to shore up banks. Eventually, the basic approach devised by the British arguably would influence actions taken by other governments, including that of the United States.

On October 10, 2008, the G-7 finance ministers and central bankers,[172] met in Washington, DC, to provide a more coordinated approach to the crisis. At the Euro area summit on October 12, 2008, Euro area countries along with the United Kingdom urged all European governments to adopt a common set of principles to address the financial crisis.[173] The measures the nations supported are largely in line with those adopted by the U.K. and include:

- Recapitalization: governments promised to provide funds to banks that might be struggling to raise capital and pledged to pursue wide-ranging restructuring of the leadership of those banks that are turning to the government for capital.
- State ownership: governments indicated that they will buy shares in the banks that are seeking recapitalization.
- Government debt guarantees: guarantees offered for any new debts, including inter-bank loans, issued by the banks in the Euro zone area.
- Improved regulations: the governments agreed to encourage regulations to permit assets to be valued on their risk of default instead of their current market price.

In addition to these measures, EU leaders agreed on October 16, 2008, to set up a crisis unit and they agreed to a monthly meeting to improve financial oversight.[174] Jose Manuel Barroso, President of the European Commission, urged EU members to develop a "fully integrated solution" to address the global financial crisis, consistent with France's support for a strong international organization to oversee the financial markets. The EU members expressed their support for the current approach within the EU, which makes each EU member responsible for developing and implementing its own national regulations regarding supervision over financial institutions. The European Council stressed the need to strengthen the supervision of the European financial sector. As a result, the EU statement urged the EU members to develop a "coordinated supervision system at the European level."[175] This approach likely will be tested as a result of failed talks with the credit derivatives industry in Europe. In early January 2009, an EUsponsored working group reported that it had failed to get a commitment from the credit derivatives industry to use a central clearing house for credit default swaps. As an alternative, the European Commission reportedly is considering adopting a set of rules for EU members that would require banks and other users of the CDS markets to use a central clearing house within the EU as a way of reducing risk.[176]

The "European Framework for Action"

On October 29, 2008, the European Commission released a "European Framework for Action" as a way to coordinate the actions of the 27 member states of the European Union to address the financial crisis.[177] The EU also announced that on November 16, 2008, the Commission will propose a more detailed plan that will bring together short-term goals to address the current economic downturn with the longer-term goals on growth and jobs in the Lisbon Strategy.[178] The short-term plan revolves around a three-part approach to an overall EU recovery action plan/framework. The three parts to the EU framework are:

A new financial market architecture at the EU level. The basis of this architecture involves implementing measures that member states have announced as well as providing for (1) continued support for the financial system from the European Central Bank and other central banks; (2) rapid and consistent implementation of the bank rescue plan that has been established by the member states; and (3) decisive measures that are designed to contain the crisis from spreading to all of the member states.

Dealing with the impact on the real economy. The policy instruments member states can use to address the expected rise in unemployment and decline in economic growth as a second-round effect of the financial crisis are in the hands of the individual member states. The EU can assist by adding short-term actions to its structural reform agenda, while investing in the future through: (1) increasing investment in R&D innovation and education; (2) promoting flexicurity[179] to protect and equip people rather than specific jobs; (3) freeing up businesses to build markets at home and internationally; and (4) enhancing competitiveness by promoting green technology, overcoming energy security constraints, and achieving environmental goals. In addition, the Commission will explore a wide range of ways in which EU members can increase their rate of economic growth.

A global response to the financial crisis. The financial crisis has demonstrated the growing interaction between the financial sector and the goods-and services-producing sectors of economies. As a result, the crisis has raised questions concerning global governance not only relative to the financial sector, but the need to maintain open trade markets. The EU would like to use the November 15, 2008 multi-nation G-20 economic summit in Washington, DC, to promote a series of measures to reform the global financial architecture. The Commission argues that the measures should include (1) strengthening international regulatory standards; (2) strengthen international coordination among financial supervisors; (3) strengthening measures to monitor and coordinate macroeconomic policies; and (4) developing the capacity to address financial crises at the national regional and multilateral levels. Also, a financial architecture plan should include three key principles: (1) efficiency; (2) transparency and accountability; and (3) the inclusion of representation of key emerging economies.

European leaders, meeting prior to the November 15, 2008 G-20 economic summit in Washington, DC, agreed that the task of preventing future financial crisis should fall to the International Monetary Fund, but they could not agree on precisely what that role should be.[180] The leaders set a 100-day deadline to draw up reforms for the international financial system. British Prime Minister Gordon Brown reportedly urged other European leaders to back fiscal stimulus measure to support the November 6, 2008 interest rate cuts by the European Central Bank, the Bank of England, and other central banks. Reportedly, French Prime Minister Nicolas Sarkozy argued that the role of the IMF and the World Bank needed to be rethought. French and German officials have argued that the IMF should assume a larger role in financial market regulation, acting as a global supervisor of regulators. Prime Minister Sarkozy also argued that the IMF should "assess" the work of such international bodies as the Bank of International Settlements. Other G-20 leaders, however, reportedly have disagreed with this proposal, agreeing instead to make the IMF "the pivot of a renewed international system," working alongside other bodies. Other Ministers also were apparently not enthusiastic toward a French proposal that Europe should agree to a more formalized coordination of economic policy.

In an effort to confront worsening economic conditions, German Chancellor Angela Merkel proposed a package of stimulus measures, including spending for large-scale infrastructure projects, ranging from schools to communications. The stimulus package represents the second multi-billion euro fiscal stimulus package Germany has adopted in less than three months. The plan, announced on January 13, 2009, reportedly was doubled from initial estimates to reach more than 60 billion Euros[181] (approximately $80 billion) over two years. The plan reportedly includes a pledge by Germany's largest companies to avoid mass job cuts in return for an increase in government subsidies for employees placed temporarily on short work weeks or on lower wages.[182] Other reports indicate that Germany is considering an emergency fund of up to 100 billion Euros in state-backed loans or guarantees to aid companies having problems getting credit.[183]

Overall, Germany's response to the economic downturn changed markedly between December 2008 and January 2009 as economic conditions continued to worsen. In a December 2008 article, German Finance Minister Peer Steinbruck defended Germany's approach at the time. According to Steinbruck, Germany disagreed with the EU plan to provide a broad economic stimulus plan, because it favored an approach that is more closely tailored to the German economy. He argued that Germany is providing a counter-cyclical stimulus program even though it is contrary to its long-term goal of reducing its government budget deficit. Important to this program, however, are such "automatic stabilizers" as unemployment benefits that automatically increase without government action since such benefits play a larger role in the German economy than in other economies. Steinbruck argued that, "our experience since the 1970s has shown that ... stimulus programs fail to achieve the desired effect.... It is more likely that such large-scale stimulus programs—and tax cuts as well—would not have any effects in real time. It is unclear whether general tax cuts can significantly encourage consumption during a recession, when many consumers are worried about losing their jobs. The history of the savings rate in Germany points to the opposite."[184]

France, which has been leading efforts to develop a coordinated European response to the financial crisis, has proposed a package of measures estimated to cost over $500 billion. The French government is creating two state agencies that will provide funds to sectors where they are needed. One entity will issue up to $480 billion in guarantees on inter-bank lending issued before December 31, 2009, and would be valid for five years. The other entity will use a $60 billion fund to recapitalize struggling companies by allowing the government to buy stakes in the firms. On January 16, 2009, President Sarkozy announced that the French government would take a tougher stance toward French banks that seek state aid. Up to that point, France had injected $15 billion in the French banking system. In order to get additional aid, banks would be required to suspend dividend payments to shareholders and bonuses to top management and to increase credit lines to such clients as exporters. France reportedly was preparing to inject more money into the banking system.[185]

On December 4, 2008, President Sarkozy announced a $33 billion (26 billion euros) package of stimulus measures to accelerate planned public investments.[186] The package is focused primarily on infrastructure projects and investments by state-controlled firms, including a canal north of Paris, renovation of university buildings, new metro cars, and construction of 70,000 new homes, in addition to 30,000 unfinished homes the government has committed to buy in 2009. The plan also includes a 200 Euro payment to low-income households. On December 15, 2008, France agreed to provide the finance division of Renault and Peugeot $1.2 billion in credit guarantees and an additional $250 million to support the car manufacturers' consumer finance division.[187] In an interview on French TV on January 14, 2009, French Prime Minister Francois Fillon indicated that the French government is considering an increase in aid to the French auto industry, including Renault and Peugeot.[188] The auto industry and its suppliers reportedly employ about 10% of France's labor force.

The de Larosiere Report and the European Plan for Recovery

When the European Union released its "Framework for Action" in response to the immediate needs of the financial crisis, it was moving to address the long-term requirements of the financial system. As a key component of this approach, the EU commissioned a group within the EU to assess the weaknesses of the existing EU financial architecture. It also charged this group with developing proposals that could guide the EU in fashioning a system that would provide early warning of areas of financial weakness and chart a way forward in erecting a stronger financial system. As part of this way forward, the European Union issued two reports in the first quarter of 2009 that address the issue of supervision of financial markets. The first report,[189] issued on February 25, 2009 and commissioned by the European Union, was prepared by a High-Level Group on financial supervision headed by former IMF Managing Director and ex-Bank of France Governor Jacques de Larosiere and, therefore, is known as the de Larosiere Report. The second report[190] was published by the European Commission to chart the course ahead for the members of the EU to reform the international financial governance system.

The de Larosiere Report

The de Larosiere Report focuses on four main issues: (1) causes of the financial crisis; (2) organizing the supervision of financial institutions and markets in the EU; (3) strengthening European cooperation on financial stability, oversight, early warning, and crisis mechanisms; and (4) organizing EU supervisors to cooperate globally. The Report also proposes 31 recommendations on regulation and supervision of financial markets.

As the financial crisis unfolded, the de Larosiere Report concludes, the regulatory response by the European Union and its members was weakened by, "an inadequate crisis management infrastructure in the EU." Furthermore, the Report emphasizes that an inconsistent set of rules across the EU as a result of the closely guarded sovereignty of national financial regulators led to a wide diversity of national regulations reflecting local traditions, legislation, and practices. While micro-prudential supervision focused on limiting the distress of individual financial institutions in order to protect the depositors, it neglected the broader objective of macro- prudential supervision, which is aimed at limiting distress to the financial system as a whole in order to protect the economy from significant losses in real output. In order to remedy this obstacle, the Report offers a two-level approach to reforming financial market supervision in the EU. This new approach would center around new oversight of broad, system-wide risks and a higher-level of coordination among national supervisors involved in day-to-day oversight.

The de Larosiere Report recommends that the EU create a new macro-prudential level of supervision called the European Systemic Risk Council (ESRC) chaired by the President of the European Central Bank. A driving force behind creating the ESRC is that it would bring together the central banks of all of the EU members with a clear mandate to preserve financial stability by collectively forming judgments and making recommendations on macro-prudential policy. The ESRC would also gather information on all macro-prudential risks in the EU, decide on macro- prudential policy, provide early risk warning to EU supervisors, compare observations on macroeconomic and prudential developments, and give direction on the aforementioned issues.

Next, the Report recommends that the EU create a new European System of Financial Supervision (ESFS) to transform a group of EU committees known as L3 Committees[191] into EU Authorities. The three L3 Committees are: the Committee of European Securities Regulators (CESR); the Committee of European Banking Supervisors (CEBS); and the Committee of European Insurance and Occupational Pensions Supervisors (CEIOPS). The ESFS would maintain the decentralized structure that characterizes the current system of national supervisors, while the ESFS would coordinate the actions of the national authorities to maintain common high level supervisory standards, guarantee strong cooperation with other supervisors, and guarantee that the interests of the host supervisors are safeguarded.

The main tasks of the ESFS authorities would be to: provide legally binding mediation between national supervisors; adopt binding supervisory standards; adopt binding technical decisions that apply to individual institutions; provide oversight and coordination of colleges of supervisors; license and supervise specific EU-wide institutions; provide binding cooperation with the ESRC to ensure that there is adequate macro-prudential supervision; and assume a strong coordinating role in crisis situations. The main mission of the national supervisors would be to oversee the day-to-day operation of firms.

Driving European Recovery

"Driving European Recovery," issued by the European Commission, presents a slightly different approach to financial supervision and recovery than that proposed by the de Larosiere group, although it accepts many of the recommendations offered by the group. The recommendations in the report were intended to complement the economic stimulus measures that were adopted by the EU on November 27, 2008, under the $256 billion Economic Recovery Plan[192] that funds cross- border projects, including investments in clean energy and upgraded telecommunications infrastructure. The plan is meant to ensure that, "all relevant actors and all types of financial investments are subject to appropriate regulation and oversight." In particular, the EC plan notes that nation-based financial supervisory models are lagging behind the market reality of a large number of financial institutions that operate across national borders.

The European Commission praised the de Larosiere report for contributing "to a growing consensus about where changes are needed." Of particular interest to the EC were the recommendations to develop a harmonized core set of standards that can be applied throughout the EU. The EC also supported the concept of a new European body similar to the proposed European Systemic Risk Council to gather and assess information on all risks to the financial sector as a whole, and it supported the concept of reforming the current system of EU Committees that oversee the financial sector. The EU plan, however, would accelerate the plan proposed by the de Larosiere group by combining the two phases outlined in the report. Using the de Larosiere report as a basis, the EC is attempting to establish a new European financial supervision system. These efforts to reform the EC's financial supervision system would be based on five key objectives:

- First, provide the EU with a supervisory framework that detects potential risks early, deals with them effectively before they have an impact, and meets the challenge of complex international financial markets. At the end of May 2009 the EC presented a European financial supervision package to the European Council for its consideration. The package included two elements: measures to establish a European supervision body to oversee the macro-prudential stability of the financial system as a whole; and proposals on the architecture of a European financial supervision system to undertake micro-prudential supervision.
- Second, the EC will move to reform those areas where European or national regulation is insufficient or incomplete by proposing: a comprehensive legislative instrument that establishes regulatory and supervisory standards for hedge funds, private equity and other systemically important market players; a White Paper on the necessary tools for early intervention to prevent a similar crisis; measures to increase transparency and ensure financial stability in the area of derivatives and other complex structured products; legislative proposals to increase the quality and quantity of prudential capital for trading book activities, complex securitization, and to address liquidity risk and excessive leverage; and a program of actions to establish a more consistent set of supervisory rules.
- Third, to ensure European investors, consumers, and small and medium-size enterprises can be confident about their savings, their access to credit and their rights, the EC will: advance a Communication on retail investment products to strengthen the effectiveness of marketing safeguards; provide additional measures to reinforce the protection of bank depositors, investors, and insurance policy holders; and provide measures on responsible lending and borrowing.
- Fourth, in order to improve risk management in financial firms and align pay incentives with sustainable performance, the EC intends to strengthen the 2004 Recommendation on the remuneration of directors; and bring forward a new Recommendation on remuneration in the financial services sector followed by legislative proposals to include remuneration schemes within the scope of prudential oversight.

- Fifth, to ensure more effective sanctions against market wrongdoing, the EC intends to: review the Market Abuse Directive[193] and make proposals on how sanctions could be strengthened in a harmonized manner and better enforced.

The British Rescue Plan

On October 8, 2008, the British Government announced a $850 billion multi-part plan to rescue its banking sector from the current financial crisis. Details of this plan are presented here to illustrate the varied nature of the plan. The Stability and Reconstruction Plan followed a day when British banks lost £17 billion on the London Stock Exchange. The biggest loser was the Royal Bank of Scotland, whose shares fell 39%, or £10 billion, of its value. In the downturn, other British banks lost substantial amounts of their value, including the Halifax Bank of Scotland which was in the process of being acquired by Lloyds TSB.

The British plan included four parts:

- A coordinated cut in key interest rates of 50 basis, or one-half of one percent (0.5) between the Bank of England, the Federal Reserve, and the European Central Bank.
- An announcement of an investment facility of $87 billion implemented in two stages to acquire the Tier 1 capital, or preferred stock, in "eligible" banks and building societies (financial institutions that specialize on mortgage financing) in order to recapitalize the firms. To qualify for the recapitalization plan, an institution must be incorporated in the UK (including UK subsidiaries of foreign institutions, which have a substantial business in the UK and building societies). Tier 1 capital often is used as measure of the asset strength of a financial institution.
- The British Government agreed to make available to those institutions participating in the recapitalization scheme up to $436 billion in guarantees on new short- and medium-term debt to assist in refinancing maturing funding obligations as they fall due for terms up to three years.
- The British Government announced that it would make available $352 billion through the Special Liquidity Scheme to improve liquidity in the banking industry. The Special Liquidity Scheme was launched by the Bank of England on April 21, 2008 to allow banks to temporarily swap their high-quality mortgage- backed and other securities for UK Treasury bills.[194]

On November 24, 2008, Britain's majority Labor party presented a plan to Parliament to stimulate the nation's slowing economy by providing a range of tax cuts and government spending projects totaling 20 billion pounds (about $30 billion). [195] The stimulus package includes a 2.5% cut in the value added tax (VAT), or sales tax, for 13 months, a postponement of corporate tax increases, and government guarantees for loans to small and midsize businesses. The plan also includes government plans to spend 4.5 billion pounds on public works, such as public housing and energy efficiency. Some estimates indicate that the additional spending required by the plan will push Britain's government budget deficit in 2009 to an amount equivalent to 8% of GDP. To pay for the plan, the government would increase income taxes on those making more than 150,000 pounds (about $225,000) from 40% to 45% starting in April 2011. In addition, the British plan would increase the National Insurance contributions for all but the lowest income workers.[196]

On January 14, 2009, British Business Secretary Lord Mandelson unveiled an additional package of measures by the Labor government to provide credit to small and medium businesses that have been hard pressed for credit as foreign financial firms have reduced their level of activity in the UK. The three measures are: (1) a 10 billion pound (approximately $14 billion) Capital Working Scheme to provide banks with guarantees to cover 50% of the risk on existing and new working capital loans on condition that the banks must use money freed up by the guarantee to make new loans; (2) a one billion pound Enterprise Finance Guarantee Scheme to assist small, credit-worthy companies by providing guarantees to banks of up to 75% of loans to small businesses; and (3) a 75 million pound Capital for Enterprise Fund to convert debt to equity for small businesses.[197] In an effort to address the prospect that large banks or financial firms may become insolvent or fail and thereby cause a major disruption to the financial system, the British Parliament in February 2009 passed the Banking Act of 2009. The act makes permanent a set of procedures the U.K. government had developed to deal with troubled banks before they become insolvent or collapse. Such procedures are being considered by other EU governments and others as they amend their respective supervisory frameworks.

Collapse of Iceland's Banking Sector

The failure of Iceland's banks has raised some questions about bank supervision and crisis management for governments in Europe and the United States. As Icelandic banks began to default, Britain used an anti-terrorism law to seize the deposits of the banks to prevent the banks from shifting funds from Britain to Iceland.[198] This incident raised questions about how national governments should address the issue of supervising foreign financial firms that are operating within their borders and whether they can prevent foreign-owned firms from withdrawing deposits in one market to offset losses in another. In addition, the case of Iceland raises questions about the cost and benefits of branch banking across national borders where banks can grow to be so large that disruptions in the financial market can cause defaults that outstrip the resources of national central banks to address.

On November 19, 2008, Iceland and the International Monetary Fund (IMF) finalized an agreement on an economic stabilization program supported by a $2.1 billion two-year standby arrangement from the IMF.[199] Upon approval of the IMF's Executive board, the IMF released $827 million immediately to Iceland with the remainder to be paid in eight equal installments, subject to quarterly reviews. As part of the agreement, Iceland has proposed a plan to restore confidence in its banking system, to stabilize the exchange rate, and to improve the nation's fiscal position. Also as part of the plan, Iceland's central bank raised its key interest rate by six percentage points to 18% on October 29, 2008, to attract foreign investors and to shore up its sagging currency.[200] The IMF's Executive Board had postponed its decision on a loan to Iceland three times, reportedly to give IMF officials more time to confirm loans made by other nations. Other observers argued, however, that the delay reflected objections by British, Dutch, and German officials over the disposition of deposit accounts operated by Icelandic banks in their countries. Iceland reportedly smoothed the way by agreeing in principle to cover the deposits, although the details had not be finalized. In a joint statement, Germany, Britain, and the Netherlands said on November 20, 2008, that they would "work constructively in the continuing discussions" to reach an agreement.[201] Following the decision of IMF 's Executive Board, Denmark, Finland, Norway, and Sweden agreed to provide an additional $2.5 billion in loans to Iceland.

Between October 7 and 9, 2008, Iceland's Financial Supervisory Authority (FSA), an independent state authority with responsibilities to regulate and supervise Iceland's credit, insurance, securities, and pension markets took control, without actually nationalizing them, of three of Iceland's largest banks: Landsbanki, Glitnir Banki, and Kaupthing Bank prior to a scheduled vote by shareholders to accept a government plan to purchase the shares of the banks in order to head off the collapse of the banks. At the same time, Iceland suspended trading on its stock exchange for two days.[202] In part, the takeover also attempted to quell a sharp depreciation in the exchange value of the Icelandic krona.

The demise of Iceland's three largest banks is attributed to an array of events, but primarily stems from decisions by the banks themselves. Some observers argued that the collapse of Lehman Brothers set in motion the events that finally led to the collapse of the banks,[203] but this conclusion is controversial. Some have argued that at the heart of Iceland's banking crisis is a flawed banking model that is based on an internationally active banking sector that is large relative to the size of the home country's GDP and to the fiscal capacity of the central bank.[204] As a result, a disruption in liquidity threatens the viability of the banks and overwhelms the ability of the central bank to act as the lender of last resort, which undermines the solvency of the banking system.

On October 15, 2008, the Central Bank of Iceland set up a temporary system of daily currency auctions to facilitate international trade. Attempts by Iceland's central bank to support the value of the krona are at the heart of Iceland's problems. Without a viable currency, there was no way to support the banks, which have done the bulk of their business in foreign markets. The financial crisis has also created problems with Great Britain because hundreds of thousands of Britons hold accounts in online branches of the Icelandic banks, and they fear those accounts will default. The government of British Prime minister Gordon Brown has used powers granted under antiterrorism laws to freeze British assets of Landsbanki until the situation is resolved.

IMPACT ON ASIA AND THE ASIAN RESPONSE[205]

Many Asian economies have been through wrenching financial crises in the past 10-15 years. Although most observers say the region's economic fundamentals have improved greatly in the past decade, this crisis has provided a worrying sense of *deja vu*, and an illustration that Asian policy changes in recent years—including Japan's slow but comprehensive banking reforms, Korea's opening of its financial markets, China's dramatic economic transformation, and the enormous buildup of sovereign reserves across the region— have not fully insulated Asian economies from global contagion.

However, in the second quarter of 2009, there were signs that many Asian economies were rebounding sharply from the slowdowns and contractions they suffered in the previous months. Many observers have attributed this recovery to the rapid implementation of large fiscal and monetary stimulus programs that were possible because of the comparatively strong fiscal positions that most Asian governments were in, and the fact that many Asian banking systems are considered healthy. Still, Asian governments remain deeply concerned about the state of their economies, and those in countries whose economies depend heavily on exports worry about the sustainability of their recoveries if the United States and other developed economies recover more slowly. This has been reflected in bilateral relations between the United States and some, including China, whose officials are seen as increasingly assertive in their discussions with U.S. economic officials on policies the United States should follow to emerge from the recession.

In the early months of the crisis, Asian nations did not have to deal with outright bankruptcies or rescues of major financial institutions, as Western governments did. With only a few exceptions— most notably in South Korea—leverage within Asian financial systems was comparatively low and bank balance sheets were comparatively healthy at the outset of the crisis. Nearly all East Asian nations run current account surpluses, a reversal from their state during the Asian financial crisis of the late 1 990s. These surpluses have been one reason for the buildup of enormous government reserves in the region, including China's $2.1 trillion and Japan's $996 billion—the two largest reserve stockpiles in the world. Such reserves have given Asian governments resources to provide fiscal stimulus, inject capital into their financial systems, and provide backstop guarantees for private financial transactions where needed. So overall, Asian economies were much healthier at the outset of the current crisis than they were before the Asian Financial Crisis of 1997-1998, when several Asian countries burned through their limited reserves quickly trying to defend currencies from speculative selling.

The initial stage of the crisis, which centered around losses directly from subprime assets in the United States, gave way to a broader global crisis marked by slowing economies and dried-up liquidity. Asia and the United States are deeply linked in many ways, including trade (primarily Asian exports to the United States), U.S. investments in the region, and financial linkages that entwine Asian banks, companies and governments with U.S. markets and financial institutions. As a result, even though Asian banks disclosed relatively low direct exposures to failed institutions and toxic assets in the United States and Europe, Asian economies were caught in a second phase of the crisis. With Western economies slowing and global investors short of cash and pulling back from any markets deemed risky, many Asian economies suffered sharp slowdowns or dipped into recession in the fourth quarter of 2008 or the first quarter of 2009.

However, several Asian countries—including China, Japan, South Korea, Thailand, Malaysia, Taiwan and Singapore—implemented large fiscal stimulus programs that have shown signs of stimulating domestic investment and consumption. Japan announced several stimulus packages that amounted to 5% of the nation's GDP, while China implemented a package worth 12% of GDP. China also mandated an easing of lending by its state banks, opening up credit lines that had been frozen in the crisis's early stages. By early August, China, Indonesia, South Korea and Singapore had each reported second quarter GDP growth of at least 2.5% over the previous quarter.[206] China's rebound has been particularly striking. The country's industrial production in the January-July period was up 11% from the same period a year earlier.[207] Stock markets around the region are up, most by amounts larger than in the United States. Between January and July, markets in China, Hong Kong, Taiwan, South Korea, Singapore, and Indonesia were each up by more than 40%.

Still, in Asia, a belief that held sway in recent years that Asian economies were starting to "decouple" from the United States and Europe, generating growth that didn't depend on the rest of the world, has given way to a realization that a crisis that originated in the West can sweep up the region as well. Most Asian economies are showing signs of recovery, some of it based on purely domestic conditions or trade within the region, but Asian officials continue to stress that the strength of their economies is highly dependent on recoveries in the United States and Western Europe.

One worrying development is that Pakistan, already coping with severe political instability, has been forced to seek emergency loans from the IMF because of dwindling government reserves. This points to the limits of bilateral solutions to the crisis: For much of October and early November, Pakistan reportedly sought support from China, Saudi Arabia and other Middle Eastern states before being forced to the IMF.[208] On November 13, well into discussions with the IMF, Pakistan officials announced they had received a $500 million aid package from Beijing, far short of the $10 billion-$15 billion that Pakistani leaders say they need over the next two years.[209] Then on November 15, Pakistani and IMF officials confirmed that Pakistan would receive $7.6 billion in emergency loans, including $4 billion immediately to avoid sovereign default. But this remains short of what Pakistan says it needs.[210]

Asian Reserves and Their Impact

Some analysts argue that substantial Asian reserves could be one source of relief for the global economy.[211] Japan has contributed funding for the IMF support package of Iceland, and on November 14, 2008, Prime Minister Taro Aso said Japan would lend the IMF $100 billion to support further packages that might be needed before the IMF increases its capital in 2009.[212] Many wonder if China and other reserve-rich developing nations will find ways to use those reserves to support financially-strapped governments. As noted previously, Pakistan reportedly approached China and several Gulf states for such support.

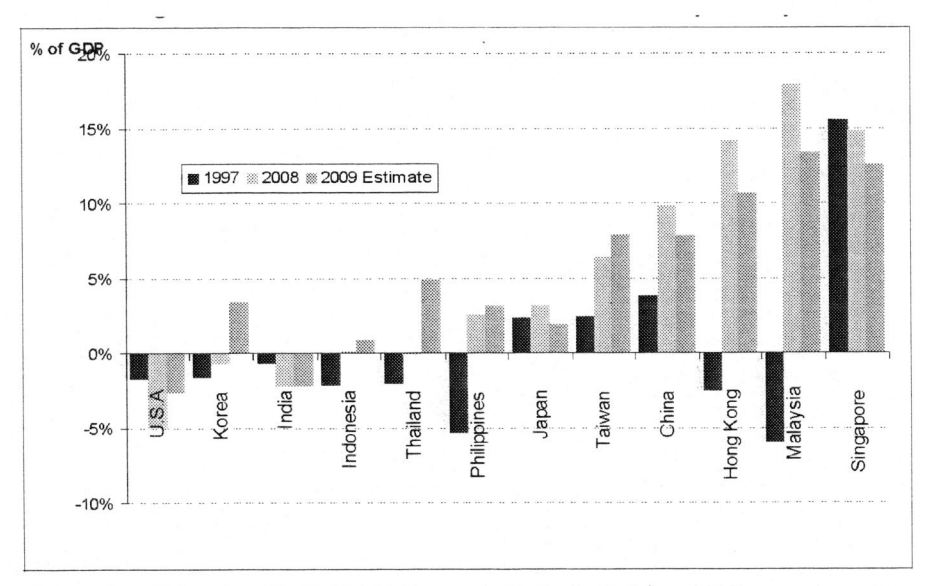

Source: International Monetary Fund. World Economic Outlook, October, 2009.

Figure 10. Asian Current Account Balances are Mostly Healthy

One key question is whether Asian countries will seek to play a larger role in setting multilateral moves to shore up regulation, and international support for troubled countries. Five Asian countries—Japan, China, South Korea, India and Indonesia, were present at the G-20 summit. But Asian approaches to multilateral regulation are still unclear. At an October 25-26 meeting of the Asia Europe Forum (ASEM), Chinese Premier Wen Jiabao said China generally agrees with many European governments which seek an expansion of multilateral regulations. "We need financial innovation, but we need financial oversight even more," Wen reportedly told a press conference.[213] In late January, speaking at an annual gathering of economic and political leaders in Davos, Switzerland, Wen blamed the crisis on an "excessive expansion of financial institutions in blind pursuit of profit," a failure of government supervision in the financial sector, and an "unsustainable model of development, characterized by prolonged low savings and high consumption."[214] Many analysts saw this as a criticism of the United States, which has much lower savings and higher consumption rates than China.

Previous Asian attempts to play a leadership role have been unsuccessful. In 1998, in the midst of the Asian Financial Crisis, Japan and the Asian Development Bank proposed the creation of an "Asian Monetary Fund" through which wealthier Asian governments could support economies in financial distress. The proposal was successfully opposed by the U.S. Treasury Department, which argued that it could be a way for countries to bypass the conditions that the IMF demands of its borrowers and go straight to "easier" sources of credit.

Two years later, in 2000, Finance Ministers from the ASEAN+3 nations (the 10 members of the Association of Southeast Asian Nations[215], plus Japan, South Korea and China) announced the Chiang Mai Initiative (CMI), whose primary measure was to provide a swap mechanism that countries could tap to cover shortfalls of foreign reserves. This was a less aggressive proposal than the Asian Monetary Fund. Although a small portion of the swap lines could be tapped in an emergency, most would likely be subject to IMF conditions for recipients.[216]

On October 26, Japan, China, South Korea, and ASEAN members agreed to start an $80 billion multilateral swap arrangement in 2009, which would allow countries with substantial balance of payments problems to tap the reserves of larger economies. There remains, however, disagreement within the region about whether the IMF should play an active role in setting conditions for countries that use these swap lines.

Asian leaders have sought to start other regional discussions. On October 22, a Japanese government official floated the idea of a pan-Asian financial stability forum, modeled after the Financial Stability Forum at the BIS, which was discussed in May at a meeting of Finance Ministers from Japan, South Korea and China.[217] On December 13, the leaders of Japan, China, and South Korea held a trilateral summit in Fukuoka, Japan, agreeing on bilateral swap lines between South Korea and the two others – a new renminbi-won swap line worth the equivalent of $28 billion and an expansion of an existing yen-won swap line to the equivalent of $20 billion.[218]

Beyond this measure of support for South Korea, however, the summit did not provide broader multilateral initiatives.

National Responses

So far, the national-level responses among Asian governments include the following:

Japan

Japan was part of the early moves among major economies to flood markets with liquidity, in the "crisis containment" part of the global response, and the Bank of Japan has continued its aggressive monetary stimulus in the months since. Alongside other major central banks, the Bank of Japan pumped tens of billions of dollars into financial markets in late September and early October. It followed these moves with an announcement on October 14 that it would offer an unlimited amount of dollars to institutions operating in Japan, to ensure that Japanese interbank credit markets continued to function. The BOJ did not lower interest rates in the crisis's early stages, but on October 31, it joined other global central banks, including the U.S. Federal Reserve, by cutting a key short-term interest rate to 0.3%, from 0.5%, and on December 19 it cut the rate to 0.1%.

For a time, Japan was considered relatively insulated, because of its well capitalized banks, substantial reserves and current account surplus. Japan spent nearly $440 billion between 1998 and 2003 to assist and recapitalize its banking system, and most observers say Japan's financial system emerged from the experience fairly sound. Healthy capital positions helped Mitsubishi UFG Group, Japan's largest bank, and Nomura, the country's largest brokerage, to buy pieces of distressed U.S. investment banks as the crisis was deepening in October. Mitsubishi UFG bought 21% of Morgan Stanley for $9 billion, and Nomura purchased the Asian, European and Middle Eastern operations of Lehman Brothers.

But as Western economies began to slow, Japan's financial insulation thinned. The Japanese economy is highly exposed to slowdowns in export markets, particularly in the U.S. and Europe. The U.S. accounted for 20.1% of Japan's exports in 2007. Japan has sought to provide fiscal stimulus: The government unveiled a $107 billion stimulus package in August, and on January 27, the Japanese parliament passed a second package, valued at $54 billion. The package—and, more broadly, Prime Minister Taro Aso's response to the crisis—has been the subject of severe infighting within Aso's ruling Liberal Democratic Party. Aso's government currently faces extremely low support ratings of around 20%, and he now faces an August 30 Parliamentary election in which the LDP could lose its hold on power, which it has held almost continuously since the 1950s.[219]

China[220]

Despite China's large-scale holdings of U.S. securities, its exposure to the fallout from the U.S. sub-prime mortgage crisis is believed to have been relatively small. China's numerous restrictions on capital flows to and from China limit the ability of individual Chinese citizens and many firms to invest their savings overseas. Most of Chinese investment flows are controlled by government entities, such as state-owned banks, State Administration of Foreign Exchange (which administers China's foreign exchange reserves), and the China Investment Corporation (a $200 billion sovereign wealth fund created in 2007),[221] and state-owned enterprises. Such entities have maintained relatively conservative investment strategies.

The Chinese government generally does not release detailed information on the holdings of its financial entities, although some of its banks have reported on their supposed level of exposure to sub-prime U.S. mortgage securities. Such entities have generally reported that their exposure to troubled sub-prime U.S. mortgages has been minor relative to their total investments, that they have liquidated such assets or have written off losses, and that they continue to earn high profit margins.[222]

However, China's economy has not been immune to the effects of the global financial crisis, given its heavy reliance on trade and foreign direct investment (FDI) for its economic growth. Numerous sectors have been hard hit.[223] To illustrate:

- The real estate market in several Chinese cities exhibited signs of a bursting bubble, including a slowdown in construction, falling prices and growing levels of unoccupied buildings.
- China's trade plummeted. Both exports and imports declined each month from November 2008 to October 2009 on a year-on-year basis (see **Figure 11**). The 26.4% decline in exports (year-on-year basis) in May 2009 was the biggest monthly decline ever recorded (since such data were collected).
- The level of FDI flows to China fell for 10 straight months from October 2008 to August 2009 on a year-on-year basis. For example, FDI flows to China dropped by nearly a third in January 2009).
- Numerous Chinese press reports in 2008 and early 2009 indicated sharp reductions of production and employment in China. The Chinese government in January 2009 estimated that 20 million migrant workers had lost their jobs in 2008 because of the global economic slowdown.

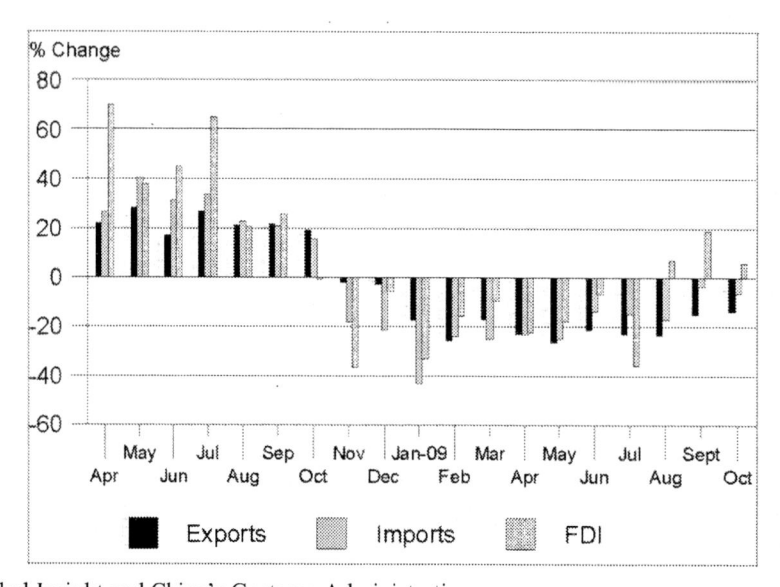

Source: Global Insight and China's Customs Administration.

Figure 11. Monthly Change in Chinese FDI and Trade: April 2008-October 2009 year-on-year basis

China responded to the crisis on a number of fronts. On September 27, 2008, Chinese Premier Wen Jiabao reportedly stated in a speech that "What we can do now is to maintain the steady and fast growth of the national economy and ensure that no major fluctuations will happen. That will be our greatest contribution to the world economy under the current circumstances." [224] On October 8, 2008, China's central bank announced plans to cut interest rates and the reserve- requirement ratio in order to help stimulate the economy. The announcement coincided with announcements by the U.S. Federal Reserve and other central banks of major economies around the world to lower their benchmark interest rates, although, neither China's central bank or the media stated that these measures were taken in conjunction with the other major central banks. On October 21, 2008, China's State Council announced it was considering implementing a new economic stimulus package, which would include an acceleration of construction projects, new export tax rebates, a reduction in the housing transaction tax, increased agriculture subsidies, and expanding lending to small and medium enterprises.[225]

On November 9, 2008 the Chinese government announced it would implement a two-year $586 billion stimulus package, mainly dedicated to infrastructure projects. The package would finance programs in 10 major areas, including affordable housing, rural infrastructure, water, electricity, transport, the environment, technological innovation and rebuilding areas hit by disasters (especially, areas that were hit by the May 12, 2998 earthquake).[226] **Table 2** provides a breakdown of China's stimulus program spending priorities. In addition, the government directed banks to loosen credit requirements, which resulted in sharp increase in bank lending. It is estimated that Chinese banks made $1.27 trillion in new loans during the first nine months of 2009.[227]

Table 2. China's Central Government November 2008 Domestic Stimulus Package

	In Chinese Yuan (billions)	In U.S. Dollars (billions)	As a Percent of Total Stimulus Package	As a Percent of China's 2008 GDP
Transport infrastructure investment	1,500	220	37.5	5.0
Post-earthquake reconstruction	1,000	146	25.0	3.3
Public housing	400	59	10.0	1.3
Rural infrastructure	370	54	9.3	1.2
Research and development and structural change	370	54	9.3	1.2
Environmental development	210	31	5.3	0.7
Healthcare and education	150	22	3.8	0.5
Totals	4,000	586	100.0	13.3

Source: Global Insight.
Notes: Ranked according to planned spending levels.

China's stimulus package and easy monetary policies appear to have produced positive results for China's economy. For example:

- China's real quarterly GDP on a year-on-year basis, which rose by only 6.1% in the first quarter of 2009, increased by 7.9% in the 2nd quarter, 8.9% in the 3rd quarter of 2009, and is projected by the IMF to grow by 10.1% in the 4th quarter.
- China's monthly FDI flows on a year on year basis, showed positive growth for three straight months (August-October 2009).
- During the first 10 months of 2009, investment in real estate development was up 18.9% on a year-on-year basis.
- Although China's trade in 2009 has not rebounded to 2008 growth levels, it has shown gradual growth since around February 2009.

The IMF in October 2009 projected China's real GDP would rise by 8.5% in 2009 (and by 9.0% in 2010), a level significantly higher than most of the other major world economies (see **Figure 12**).

Despite these positive growth projections, some economies warn that long-term economic growth will depend largely on the ability of the government to rebalance the economy away from trade and fixed investment to domestic consumption. Many have also raised concerns that easy money policies could lead to overcapacity n some industries, create asset bubbles in certain sectors, such as in real estate and the stock market, and result in a sharp increase in the amount of nonperforming loans held by China's banks. For example, in June 2009, a Chinese government agency estimated that 20% of new bank credit was going into China's stock markets. Some analysts contend that China's refusal to appreciate its currency against the dollar could result in growing trade frictions with the United States.

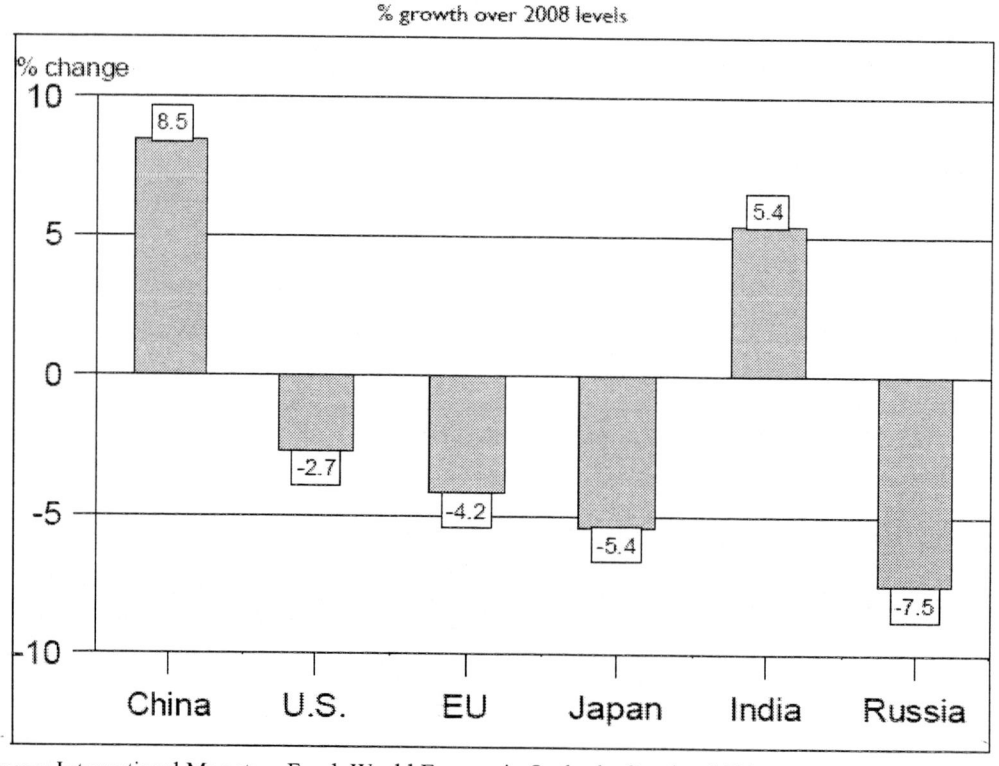

% growth over 2008 levels

Country	% change
China	8.5
U.S.	-2.7
EU	-4.2
Japan	-5.4
India	5.4
Russia	-7.5

Source: International Monetary Fund, World Economic Outlook, October 2009.

Figure 12. IMF's Projected Real GDP of Major Economies in 2009

South Korea

South Korea, Asia's fourth largest economy, was deeply affected by the crisis, with both the South Korean stock market and the won tumbling throughout the months, sometimes precipitously. On October 28, the won reached its lowest point since 1998, when South Korea was in the middle of its IMF support package. Oxford Analytica estimates that foreign investors withdrew a net $25 billion from the Korean stock market between January and late September.[228] Experts say South Korean banks have large dollar-denominated debts, and therefore need to protect their holdings of dollars. This has contributed to the won's fall, and in early October, President Lee Myung-bak invoked patriotism to encourage Korean banks to stop hoarding dollars and buy won.[229]

South Korea has announced several packages to stimulate the economy and shore up the domestic banking industry. The government announced a broad economic rescue package on October 19, 2008, promising to guarantee $100 billion in South Korean banks' foreign-currency debt and provide another $30 billion to directly support South Korean banks. (The total amount was equivalent to 14% of the country's GDP.) Struggling with its plunging stock market and currency, President Lee's government has also announced policies to spend up to $9.2 billion to support real-estate developers struggling with unsold apartments, and to provide further financial support to small businesses. On October 27, Korea's central bank cut its prime interest rate by 0.75 percentage points to 4.25%, the largest cut it has made since it began setting base interest rates in 1999. The rate has since been cut two more times, to 3%. On December 17, the government said it would launch a $15 billion fund to boost the capital of Korean banks.

South Korea has been an enormous economic success, and has bounced back strongly from the Asian Financial Crisis that forced it to turn to the IMF for a $58 billion support package in December 2007. After contracting by 6.9% in 1998, South Korea's GDP bounced back by 9.5% and 8.5% in the ensuing two years. Since 2002, GDP growth has been in the 3%-6% range. However, President Lee has said the current situation is more severe than the 1997 crisis. Economically, South Korea is an outlier within Asia. It is one of the few Asian countries that is running a current account deficit ($12.6 billion in January-August 2008). Its banks are unusually leveraged, with loan-deposit ratios of more than 130%, higher than that in the United States and the EU, and the only East Asian country over 100%.[230]

Pakistan

Pakistan's economy went into a steady decline in 2008. After several years of strong and comparatively stable growth, Pakistan quickly slid into a severe economic crisis in 2008.[231] Growth in real GDP declined sharply from about 8% to 3-4%; inflation rose to nearly 24%; and Pakistan's rupee depreciated by over 23% against the U.S. dollar. Pakistan's unemployment rate rose, and the United Nations reported that 10 million Pakistanis were undernourished. In the words of Pakistan President Asif Ali Zardari, "The greatest challenge this government faces is an economic one."[232]

Rising trade and current account deficits generated a "capital crisis" in the autumn of 2008. Pakistan's foreign reserves slid from $14.2 billion in October 2007 to $4.1 billion at the end of October 2008. According to President Zardari's chief economic advisor, Shaukat Tarin, Pakistan needed $4 to $5 billion by the end of November 2008 to avoid defaulting on maturing sovereign debt obligations. In addition, even if Pakistan does secure the money it needs by the end of November, Tarin stated that Pakistan requires $10 to $15 billion in assistance over the next two to three years to continue to service its account deficits and outstanding debt.[233]

Several factors, in addition to the current global financial crisis, are contributing to the recent downturn in Pakistan's economy. Pakistan's continuing struggle against Islamist militancy in its tribal areas along the border with Afghanistan has led to high federal deficits and uncertainty about the stability of the Pakistan government. A recent escalation of bombings and violence in Pakistan has raised the risk for and scared off many foreign investors and businesses. This has worsened the nation's capital shortage. In addition, the flight from risk that has followed the U.S. financial crisis has apparently contributed to some capital flight from Pakistan, especially among overseas Pakistanis and investors from the Middle East.

Pakistan has sought the required assistance from several countries (including China, Saudi Arabia, and the United States), international financial institutions (including the Asian Development Bank (ADB), the International Monetary Fund (IMF), the Islamic Development Bank (IDB), and the World Bank), and an informal group of nations called the "Friends of Pakistan." Although the ADB, the World Bank and others did offer some support, the total amount was insufficient to avoid the default risk. As a consequence, Pakistan reluctantly began negotiating a loan with the IMF. On November 15, Tarin announced that Pakistan had reached a tentative agreement with the IMF to borrow $7.6 billion over the next 23 months.[234] The first installment of the loan—up to $4 billion—was expected by the end of November; Pakistan is to repay the loan by 2016.[235]

Assuming Pakistan and the IMF formally conclude the agreement, the $7.6 billion loan is well short of the estimated $10 billion to $15 billion Pakistan says it needs over the next two years to avoid a financial crisis. Some observers speculate that the IMF agreement will spur help from other potential donors, such as China, Saudi Arabia, and the United States. However, given the continuing economic problems of the potential donor nations, Pakistan may not be able to secure the full amount of assistance it says it needs. As a result, the IMF loan may end up being only a short-term patch to a long-term economic problem.

In the meantime, Pakistan has announced some changes in economic policy designed to alleviate their capital crisis. On September 19, 2008, acting finance minister Naveed Qamar released new economic policies designed to bring about macroeconomic stability and avoid seeking IMF assistance that included the elimination of fuel, electricity and food subsidies, and a reduction in the government deficit.[236] On November 3, 2008, Tarin announced reforms of Pakistan's tax system, including the politically sensitive taxation of large landowners, to reduce the incidence of tax evasion.[237] There has also been talk of cutting Pakistan's defense budget.

According to some analysts, the new economic policies may foster popular discontent and threaten political stability. The elimination of fuel, electricity and food subsidies may cause significant harm to Pakistan's poor, many of whom are already undernourished. The tax on large landowners may undermine support for Zardari's Pakistan People's Party among its party members and its coalition partners. A cut in Pakistan's defense budget also could harm its military efforts against Islamist militants and weaken the military's political support for the current coalition government.

International Policy Issues

In making policy changes, Congress faces several fundamental issues. First is whether any longterm policies should be designed to restore confidence and induce return to the normal functioning of a self-correcting system or whether the policies should be directed at changing a system that may have become inherently unstable, a system that every decade or so creates bubbles and then lurches into crisis. [238] For example, in Congressional testimony on October 23, 2008, former Federal Reserve Chairman Alan Greenspan stated that a "once-in-a-century credit tsunami"' had engulfed financial markets, and he conceded that his free-market ideology shunning regulation was flawed.[239] In a recent book, the financier George Soros stated that the currently prevailing paradigm, that financial markets tend towards equilibrium, is both false and misleading. He asserted that the world's current financial troubles can be largely attributed to the fact that the international financial system has been developed on the basis of that flawed paradigm.[240] Could this crisis mark the beginning of the end of "free market capitalism?" On the other hand, the International Monetary Fund has observed that market discipline still works and that the focus of new regulations should not be on eliminating risk but on improving market discipline and addressing the tendency of market participants to underestimate the systemic effects of their collective actions.[241]

A second question deals with what level any new regulatory authority should reside. Should it primarily be at the state, national, or international level? If the authority is kept at the national level, how much power should an international authority have? Should the major role of the IMF, for example, be informational, advisory, and technical, or should it have enforcement authority? Should enforcement be done through a dispute resolution process similar to that in the World Trade Organization, or should the IMF or other international institution be ceded oversight and regulatory authority by national governments?

As of mid-2009, the primary role of the IMF in the financial crisis appears to be twofold. The first is of lender of last resort, and the second is to provide analysis and advice to member countries. The IMF has been tracking economic and financial developments worldwide in order to provide policymakers with forecasts and analysis of developments in financial markets. It also is providing policy advice to countries and regions and is assisting the Group of 20 and other international organizations with recommendations to reshape the system of international regulation and governance.

The June 17 Treasury proposal for financial regulation cedes no sovereignty to the IMF. It calls for international reforms to support U.S. efforts. Even the IMF recognizes that its authority over countries comes primarily through its advisory capacity and through the conditions it places on loans to borrowing countries.

Bretton Woods II

The second question above is central for those calling for a new Bretton Woods conference. U.K. Prime Minister Gordon Brown called for such a conference to have the specific objective of remaking the international financial architecture.[242] In the declaration of the G-20 Summit on Financial Markets and the World Economy, world leaders stated:

We underscored that the Bretton Woods Institutions must be comprehensively reformed so that they can more adequately reflect changing economic weights in the world economy and be more responsive to future challenges. Emerging and developing economies should have greater voice and representation in these institutions.

G-20 Meetings

The G-20 is an informal forum that promotes open and constructive discussion between industrial and emerging-market countries on key issues related to global economic stability. The members include the finance ministers and central bankers from the member nations. A G-20 leaders' summit is a new development.

On September 24-25, 2009, a **G-20 Summit** was held in **Pittsburgh**. At the summit, the G-20 members agreed to support six broad policy goals:

1. The new G-20 "Framework for Strong, Sustainable and Balanced Growth" will launch by November 2009. This framework promotes shifting from public to private sources of demand, establishing a pattern of growth that is sustainable and balanced, avoiding destabilizing booms and busts in asset and credit prices, and adopting macroeconomic policies that are consistent with stable prices. In order to achieve this framework, the G-20 members agreed to implement a "cooperative process of mutual assessment." This cooperative process is comprised of: shared policy objectives; a medium-term policy framework and an assessment of the impact national policies have on global economic growth and financial stability; and actions to meet common objectives. Within this framework, the G-20 members agreed to:
   - implement responsible fiscal policies, attentive to short-term flexibility considerations and longer-run sustainability requirements;
   - strengthen financial supervision to prevent the re-emergence in the financial system of excess credit growth and excess leverage and undertake macro prudential and regulatory policies to help prevent credit and asset price cycles from becoming forces of destabilization;
   - promote more balanced current accounts and support open trade and investment to advance global prosperity and growth sustainability, while actively rejecting protectionist measures;
   - undertake monetary policies consistent with price stability in the context of market oriented exchange rates that reflect underlying economic fundamentals;
   - undertake structural reforms to increase potential growth rates and, where needed, to improve social safety nets; and
   - promote balanced and sustainable economic development in order to narrow development imbalances and reduce poverty.

2. To strengthen the regulatory system for banks and other financial firms by raising capital standards, implementing strong international compensation standards, improving the over-the- counter derivatives market, and holding large global firms accountable for their risks. As components of this process, the G-20 agree to: building high quality bank capital and mitigating procyclical actions; reforming compensation practices to strengthen financial stability; improving over-the-counter derivatives markets; and addressing cross-border resolutions and systemically important financial institutions. In addition, the G-20 leaders indicated their support for efforts to improve the financial system by taking actions against non-cooperative

jurisdictions, including using "countermeasures against tax havens," and by tasking the Financial Action Task Force (FATF) to issue a list of high risk jurisdictions by February 2010.
3. To modernize the global architecture by designating the G-20 as the premier forum for international economic cooperation, by establishing the Financial Stability Board (F SB), by having the FSB include major emerging economies, and by having the FSB coordinate and monitor progress in strengthening financial regulation. Also, the G-20 agreed to shift the IMF quota share to dynamic emerging markets and developing countries of at least 5%, using the current IMF quota formula. The change in quotas is keyed to the IMF 's quota review that is scheduled to be completed by January 2010. In addition to reviewing the quotas, the G-20 indicated its support for reviewing the size of any increase in IMF quotas, the size and composition of the Executive Board, ways of enhancing the Board's effectiveness, the Fund Governors' involvement in the strategic oversight of the IMF, and the diversity of IMF staff, and the appointment of department heads and senior leadership through an open, transparent and merit-based process. The G-20 countries also agreed to contribute over $500 billion to a renewed and expanded New Arrangements to Borrow facility in the IMF. Additional IMF funding will also be available through gold sales and through additional Special Drawing Rights (SDRs). The G-20 also called for reforming the mission, mandate, and governance of the development banks, including the IMF, which the G-20 indicated must play a "critical role in promoting global financial stability and rebalancing growth." They also called on the World Bank to play a leading role in responding to problems whose nature requires globally coordinated action, such as climate change and green technology, food security, human development, and private-sector led growth.
4. To take new steps to increase access to food, fuel, and finance among the world's poorest economies, while clamping down on illicit outflows. The G-20 also agreed to improve energy market transparency and stability, and to improve regulatory oversight of energy markets.
5. To phase out and rationalize over the medium term inefficient fossil fuel subsidies while providing targeted support for the poorest. Agreed to stimulate investment in clean and in renewable energy and in energy efficiency, and to take steps to diffuse and transfer clean energy technology.
6. To maintain openness and move toward greener, more sustainable growth.

In addition, the G-20 countries are addressing a number of issues related to correcting abuses in the financial markets, particularly those involving non-bank financial institutions and complex financial instruments. Analysts and policymakers generally agree that the lack of regulation of new non-bank financial institutions, such as hedge funds and private equity firms, and the lack of transparency of new complex financial instruments, such as derivatives, were key factors in the current financial crisis.

The G-20 leaders also called for common principles for reforming financial markets. These principles include: strengthening the transparency and accountability of firms and financial products, extending regulation to all financial market institutions, promoting the integrity of financial markets (such as bolstering consumer protection) and consistent regulations across national borders, and reforming international financial institutions to better monitor the health of the financial system. The G-20 London Summit reiterated the need for financial supervision, regulation, and transparency of financial products.[243]

The role of the G-20 in dealing with the global financial crisis began on November 15, 2008, with the G-20 Summit on Financial Markets and the World Economy that was held in Washington, DC. This was billed as the first in a series of meetings to deal with the financial crisis, discuss efforts to strengthen economic growth, and to lay the foundation to prevent future crises from occurring. This summit included emerging market economies rather than the usual G-7 or G-8 nations that periodically meet to discuss economic issues. It was not apparent that the agenda of the emerging market economies differed greatly from that of Europe, the United States, or Japan.

The G-20 Washington Declaration to address the current financial crisis was both a laundry list of objectives and steps to be taken and a convergence of attitudes by national leaders that concrete measures had to be implemented both to stabilize national economies and to reform financial markets. The declaration established an Action Plan that included high priority actions to be completed prior to March 31, 2009. Details are to be worked out by the G-20 finance ministers. The declaration also called for a second G-20 summit that was held in London on April 2, 2009. Since the attendees now include the Association for Southeast Asian Nations, the G-20 no longer refers to just 20 nations.

At the April 2009 **G-20 London Summit**, leaders agreed on establishing a new Financial Stability Board (incorporating the Financial Stability Forum) to work with the IMF to ensure cooperation across borders; closer regulation of banks, hedge funds, and credit rating agencies; and a crackdown on tax havens. The leaders could not agree on the need for additional stimulus packages by nations, but they considered the additional funding for the IMF and multilateral development banks as key stimulus directed at developing and emerging market economies. The leaders reiterated their commitment to resist protectionism and promote global trade and investment.[244]

At the November G-20 summit, the leaders agreed on common principles to guide financial market reform:

- Strengthening transparency and accountability by enhancing required disclosure on complex financial products; ensuring complete and accurate disclosure by firms of their financial condition; and aligning incentives to avoid excessive risk-taking.
- Enhancing sound regulation by ensuring strong oversight of credit rating agencies; prudent risk management; and oversight or regulation of all financial markets, products, and participants as appropriate to their circumstances.
- Promoting integrity in financial markets by preventing market manipulation and fraud, helping avoid conflicts of interest, and protecting against use of the financial system to support terrorism, drug trafficking, or other illegal activities.
- Reinforcing international cooperation by making national laws and regulations more consistent and encouraging regulators to enhance their coordination and cooperation across all segments of financial markets.
- Reforming international financial institutions (IFIs) by modernizing their governance and membership so that emerging market economies and developing countries have greater voice and representation, by working together to better identify vulnerabilities and anticipate stresses, and by acting swiftly to play a key role in crisis response.

At the London Summit, the leaders reviewed progress on the November G-20 Action Plan that set forth a comprehensive work plan to implement the above principles. The Plan included immediate actions to:

- Address weaknesses in accounting and disclosure standards for off-balance sheet vehicles;
- Ensure that credit rating agencies meet the highest standards and avoid conflicts of interest, provide greater disclosure to investors, and differentiate ratings for complex products;
- Ensure that firms maintain adequate capital, and set out strengthened capital requirements for banks' structured credit and securitization activities;
- Develop enhanced guidance to strengthen banks' risk management practices, and ensure that firms develop processes that look at whether they are accumulating too much risk;
- Establish processes whereby national supervisors who oversee globally active financial institutions meet together and share information; and
- Expand the Financial Stability Forum to include a broader membership of emerging economies.

The leaders instructed finance ministers to make specific recommendations in the following areas:

- Avoiding regulatory policies that exacerbate the ups and downs of the business cycle;
- Reviewing and aligning global accounting standards, particularly for complex securities in times of stress;
- Strengthening transparency of credit derivatives markets and reducing their systemic risks;
- Reviewing incentives for risk-taking and innovation reflected in compensation practices; and
- Reviewing the mandates, governance, and resource requirements of the International Financial Institutions.

The leaders agreed that needed reforms will be successful only if they are grounded in a commitment to free market principles, including the rule of law, respect for private property, open trade and investment, competitive markets, and efficient, effectively-regulated financial systems. The leaders further agreed to:

- Reject protectionism, which exacerbates rather than mitigates financial and economic challenges;
- Strive to reach an agreement this year on modalities that leads to an ambitious outcome to the Doha Round of World Trade Organization negotiations;
- Refrain from imposing any new trade or investment barriers for the next 12 months; and
- Reaffirm development assistance commitments and urge both developed and emerging economies to undertake commitments consistent with their capacities and roles in the global economy.

The International Monetary Fund[245]

Policy proposals for changes in the international financial architecture have included a major role for the IMF. As a lender of last resort, coordinator of financial assistance packages for countries, monitor of macroeconomic conditions worldwide and within countries, and provider of technical assistance, the IMF has played an important role during financial crises whether international or confined to one member country.

The financial crisis has shown that the world could use a better early warning system that can detect and do something about stresses and systemic problems developing in world financial markets. It also may need some system of what is being called a macro-prudential framework for assessing risks and promoting sound policies. This would not only include the regulation and supervision of financial instruments and institutions but also would incorporate cyclical and other macroeconomic considerations as well as vulnerabilities from increased banking concentration and inter-linkages between different parts of the financial system.[246] In short, some institution could be charged with monitoring synergistic conditions that arise because of interactions among individual financial institutions or their macroeconomic setting.

However, the IMF's current system of macroeconomic monitoring tends to focus on the risks to currency stability, employment, inflation, government budgets, and other macroeconomic variables. The IMF, jointly with the Financial Stability Board, has recently stepped up its work on financial markets, macro-financial linkages, and spillovers across countries with the aim of strengthening early warning systems. The IMF has not, however, traditionally pressed countries to counter specific risks such as how macroeconomic variables, potential synergisms and blurring of boundaries among regulated entities, and new investment vehicles affect prudential risk for insurance, banking, and brokerage houses. The Bank for International Settlements makes recommendations to countries on measures to be undertaken (such as Basel II) to ensure banking stability and capital adequacy, but the financial crisis has shown that the focus on capital adequacy has been insufficient to ensure stability when a financial crisis becomes systemic and involves brokerage houses and insurance companies as well as banks.

THE INTERNATIONAL MONETARY FUND

The IMF was conceived in July 1944, when representatives of 45 governments meeting in the town of Bretton Woods, New Hampshire, agreed on a framework for international economic cooperation. The IMF came into existence in December 1945 and now has membership of 185 countries.

The IMF performs three main activities:

- monitoring national, global, and regional economic and financial developments and advising member countries on their economic policies (surveillance);
- lending members hard currencies to support policy programs designed to correct balance of payments problems; and
- offering technical assistance in its areas of expertise, as well as training for government and central bank officials.

The financial crisis has created an opportunity for the IMF to reinvigorate itself and possibly play a constructive role in resolving, or at the least mitigating, the effects of the global downturn. It has been operating on two fronts: (1) through immediate crisis management, primarily balance of payments support to emerging-market and less-developed countries, and (2) contributing to longterm systemic reform of the international financial system.[247] The IMF also has a wealth of information and expertise available to help in resolving financial crises and has been providing policy advice to member countries around the world.

IMF rules stipulate that countries are allowed to borrow up to three times their quota[248] over a three-year period, although this requirement has been breached on several occasions in which the IMF has lent at much higher multiples of quota. In response to the current financial crisis, the IMF has activated its Emergency Financing Mechanism to speed the normal process for loans to crisis-afflicted countries. The emergency mechanism enables rapid approval (usually within 48- 72 hours) of IMF lending once an agreement has been reached between the IMF and the national government.

As of April 2009, the IMF, under its Stand-By Arrangement facility, has provided or is in the process of providing financial support packages for Iceland ($2.1 billion), Ukraine ($16.4 billion), Hungary ($25.1 billion), Pakistan ($7.6 billion), Belarus ($2.46 billion), Serbia ($530.3 million), Armenia ($540 million), El Salvador ($800 million), Latvia ($2.4 billion), and Seychelles ($26.6 million). The IMF also created a Flexible Credit Line for countries with strong fundamentals, policies, and track records of policy implementation. Once approved, these loans can be disbursed when the need arises rather than being conditioned on compliance with policy targets as in traditional IMF-supported programs. The IMF board has approved Mexico for $47 billion under this facility. Poland has requested a credit line of $20.5 billion.

The IMF also may use its Exogenous Shocks Facility (ESF) to provide assistance to certain member countries. The ESF provides policy support and financial assistance to low-income countries facing *exogenous shocks*, events that are completely out of the national government's control. These could include commodity price changes (including oil and food), natural disasters, and conflicts and crises in neighboring countries that disrupt trade. The ESF was modified in 2008 to further increase the speed and flexibility of the IMF's response. Through the ESF, a country can immediately access up to 25% of its quota for each exogenous shock and an additional 75% of quota in phased disbursements over one to two years.

The increasing severity of the crisis has led world leaders to conclude that the IMF needs additional resources. At the 2009 February G-7 finance ministers summit, the government of Japan lent the IMF $100 billion dollars.[249] At the April 2009 London G-20 summit leaders of the world's major economies agreed to increase resources of the IMF and international development banks by $1.1 trillion including $750 billion more for the International Monetary Fund, $250 billion to boost global trade, and $100 billion for multilateral development banks. For the additional IMF resources, $250 billion was to be made available immediately through bilateral arrangements between the IMF and individual countries, while an additional $250 billion would become available as additional countries pledged their participation. The increased resources include the $100 billion loan from Japan, and the members of the European Union had agreed to provide an additional $100 billion. Subsequently, Canada ($10 billion), South Korea ($10 billion), Norway ($4.5 billion), and

Switzerland ($10 billion) agreed to subscribe additional funds. The Obama Administration has asked Congress to approve a U.S. subscription of $100 billion to the IMF's New Arrangements to Borrow. China reportedly has said it is willing to provide $40 billion through possible purchases of IMF bonds.[250] The sources for the remaining $145.5 billion of the planned increase in the NAB have not been announced.

The IMF reportedly is considering issuing bonds, something it has never done in its 60-year history.[251] These would be sold to central banks and government agencies and not to the general public. According to economist and former IMF chief economist Michael Mussa, the United States and Europe previously blocked attempts by the IMF to issue bonds since it could potentially make the IMF less dependent on them for financial resources and thus less willing to take policy direction from them.[252] However, several other multilateral institutions such as the World Bank and the regional development banks routinely issue bonds to help finance their lending.

The IMF is not alone in making available financial assistance to crisis-afflicted countries. The International Finance Corporation (IFC), the private-sector lending arm of the World Bank, has announced that it will launch a $3 billion fund to capitalize small banks in poor countries that are battered by the financial crisis. The Inter-American Development Bank (IDB) announced on October 10, 2008 that it will offer a new $6 billion credit line to member governments as an increase to its traditional lending activities. In addition to the IDB, the Andean Development Corporation (CAF) announced a liquidity facility of $1.5 billion and the Latin American Fund of Reserves (FLAR) has offered to make available $4.5 billion in contingency lines. While these amounts may be insufficient should Brazil, Argentina, or any other large Latin American country need a rescue package, they could be very helpful for smaller countries such as those in the Caribbean and Central America that are heavily dependent on tourism and property investments.

APPENDIX A. MAJOR RECENT ACTIONS AND EVENTS OF THE GLOBAL FINANCIAL CRISIS[253]

2010

February 17. The global crisis made many **banks dependent on government support**. This succeeded in averting financial catastrophe, but aggravated the problem of moral hazard: banks have an incentive to take risks if they believe that losses will ultimately be borne by the taxpayer. Some progress has been made in the policy debate to design a more resilient financial system. Proposals seek to ensure that the costs of bank failure fall on the banking industry rather than on the taxpayer. Former Federal Reserve chairman Paul Volcker has proposed a separation between commercial and investment banking. This approach has been adopted by the Obama administration. A separation between deposit taking and risky trading might have prevented the failure of RBS, which had to be bailed out by the UK government. However, it would not have prevented the failure of investment banks, such as Lehman Brothers, which filed for bankruptcy in September 2008 If approved by Congress, the U.S. scheme would restrict the ability of deposit banks to engage in proprietary trading on their own account and participate in other risky activities, such hedge funds and private equity. An international levy is an attractive idea, but practical changes are more likely to be implemented at the country level. Oxford Analytica.

February 17. Net capital flows to developing countries fell to $780 billion in 2008, reversing an upward trend that began in 2003 and peaked at $1,222 billion in 2007, according to a new report from the World Bank, Global Development Finance 2010: External Debt of Developing Countries. Particularly hard hit were private capital flows, which fell by almost 40%. All developing regions were affected, with emerging market economies in Europe and Central Asia experiencing the sharpest downturn. Some trends and developments from the report follow:

- Official creditors stepped in to offset the decline in private capital flows, increasing their support to low- and middle-income countries. The net inflow of medium- and long-term financing from official creditors, including grants, rose by 54% in 2008 to $114 billion. Almost 75% of these funds took the form of grants.
- Foreign direct investment (FDI) rose moderately in 2008 to $594 billion. But it remained concentrated: the top ten recipient countries received 70% of FDI inflows, with China alone commanding one quarter of the total.
- Increased concessional financing in 2008, including $6.7 billion from the International Development Association (IDA), helped support low-income countries with limited or no access to market-based financing. Official grants (excluding technical cooperation grants) from bilateral and multilateral sources rose by 13%. In addition, bilateral creditors restructured claims of $3.1 billion with six low-income countries, canceling more than half of them.
- External debt indicators improved. Since 2000 the rate of growth in developing countries outpaced the accumulation of new external obligations. Developing countries registered a ratio of outstanding external debt to export earnings of 57.8% in 2008, down from 122.2% in 2000. The ratio of debt to gross national income (GNI) fell to 22.1%, compared to 37.2% at the start of the decade. The debt service to exports ratio was 9.5% in 2008, half the 2000 level. World Bank: Global Development Finance 2010.

February 16. To mark the one year **anniversary** of the signing into law of the **American Recovery and Reinvestment Act (ARRA)**, the Committee for a Responsible Federal Budget released a review of the ARRA. The ARRA was enacted as the fiscal centerpiece of a set of wide-ranging policy efforts designed to stabilize the financial sector and the macro-economy; these efforts also included stimulus from the Economic Stimulus Act of 2008 and Troubled Asset Relief Program, among other initiatives. Originally projected to provide $787 billion in stimulus, the Congressional Budget Office (CBO) now puts the ten-year costs of the ARRA at $862 billion. Read the report at http://crfb.org/sites/default/files/ARRA_One_Year_Later.pdf. Committee for a Responsible Federal Budget.

February 16. Greek fiscal difficulties provoke concerns over Eurozone fiscal stability despite EU's Pledge to Greece. Deep economic recession has exposed serious fault lines within the Eurozone that will require major corrective action over both the short and longer term. Failure to take such action would threaten the very existence of the Eurozone in its current make-up, and there is growing talk that one or more countries may end up leaving the single currency altogether.

- The trigger for the current tensions within the Eurozone has been the plight of Greece, following revelations that its fiscal deficit is substantially higher than previously reported.
- Meanwhile, markets have fundamentally reappraised risk as central banks have looked to start unwinding the various emergency measures that were introduced when the recession was at its deepest and financial market dislocation was compounding problems.
- Consequently, markets have come to the conclusion that the risk spreads of the "Club Med" countries (Spain, Portugal, Greece, and Italy) and Ireland had converged far more with German bunds than was justified by economic fundamentals.
- Despite the brinkmanship of Germany, in particular, and concerns over "moral hazard," it is now evident that the European Union (EU) will eventually do whatever is necessary to save Greece. The implicit indication that a Eurozone country will not be left to default on its debt will ease market pressure on Spain, Portugal, Ireland, and Italy.
- If Greece were to leave the Eurozone, a precedent would be set and attention would immediately focus on the next candidate. This would be massively destabilizing for the single currency area.
- Support for Greece does not guarantee that it will be able to get its finances in order. There remains great uncertainty as to how the government will proceed and overcome major public unrest, even if opinion polls suggest that there is broad acceptance that difficult decisions are required.
- Even if the EU's pledge to support Greece leads to a near-term easing of pressures on it, as well as on Spain, Portugal, Ireland, and Italy, the Eurozone will be prone to persistent tensions until structural problems are properly addressed and tighter fiscal coordination is achieved. IHS Global Insight.

January 29. In the fourth quarter of 2009 **American Gross Domestic Product (GDP)** grew by a 5.7%, annual rate, the best quarterly performance since 2003. Expansion was driven by growth in private inventories and an increase in exports. For all of 2009 output declined by 2.4%. Government economic support will fade during 2010. Mark Zandi, an economist with Moody's Economy.com, estimates that the federal stimulus contributed about two percentage points of growth in the fourth quarter. That will drop below one percentage point by mid-year and fall to nothing thereafter. State budget cuts will also be a drain on output, as they have been for most of the recession. Drops in state-government spending subtracted 0.1% from output for all of 2009. Economist.

January 27. U.S. lawmakers in a **hearing** before the U.S. House of Representatives **Oversight** Committee challenged Treasury Secretary Timothy Geithner's credibility after he said he was not involved with **AIG**'s decision to withhold details on $62 billion the bailed-out insurer paid to banks. Geithner insisted the government-funded rescue which cost more than

$180 billion had been necessary to avert an economic collapse. Lawmakers questioned why a better deal for taxpayers could not have been negotiated when money was being poured into the stricken insurer.

Geithner maintained that he had withdrawn from decisions by the New York Fed after he was nominated to the Treasury post in late 2008. Defending his role in helping rescue American International Group Geithner stated, "For the first time since the Great Depression you were seeing a full-scale run on the financial system." Reuters.

January 26. GM signed a deal to sell Saab to Spyker Cars NV for $74 million in cash plus $326 million worth of preferred shares in Saab. The deal hinges on a $550 million loan from the European Investment Bank, which the Swedish government on Tuesday committed to guaranteeing. The sale is a coup for Spyker, which is based in Zeewolde, Netherlands, and a lifeline for Saab, which has lost money ever since GM bought a 50% stake and management control for $600 million in 1989. The Detroit automaker gained full ownership in 2000 for $125 million more. Saab employs around 3,500 people in Sweden and was within days of liquidation as part of GM's restructuring. GM will continue providing vehicles and parts to the new company, to be called Saab Spyker Automobiles NV. Associated Press.

January 26. In its latest World Economic Outlook, the IMF reported the global economy, battered by two years of crisis, is recovering faster than previously anticipated, with world growth bouncing back from negative territory in 2009 to a forecast 3.9 % this year and 4.3% in 2011. Major findings include: the world economy bouncing back, but advanced economies drag; global recovery from recession is led by emerging markets; and countries should maintain stimulus measures while recovery is not yet well established. Highlights below. IMF.

2009

December 14. Abu Dhabi has sprung to the **rescue** of its heavily indebted fellow emirate with a timely cash infusion of US$10 billion. This will enable **Dubai** to pay off US$4.1 billion to Nakheel bondholders as well as unpaid bills from suppliers and contractors. There are no obvious strings attached, but Dubai has been obliged to bring forward legislation that would allow Dubai World to be declared insolvent. Dubai has striven over the past 15 months to sustain the fiction that it could deal with the debts of its government-related entities through a combination of refinancing and streamlining, until its November 25th request for a standstill on US$26 billion of debts owed by Dubai World and its two real estate affiliates, Nakheel and Limitless. The Abu Dhabi government has agreed to provide US$10 billion to the Dubai Financial Support Fund to pay the Nakheel sukuk-holders, and other accounts. The Dubai government said that Dubai World must satisfy the condition of negotiating a standstill on the remaining US$22 billion of debts declared as being subject to restructuring. The support fund has now received US$25 billion in total. That appears insufficient to cover Nakheel's sukuk redemption, and other payments already or soon to be in arrears. At the same time as it announced the Abu Dhabi funding, the Dubai government issued a decree setting up a tribunal under the jurisdiction of the Dubai International Finance Centre (DIFC) to decide on disputes related to financial obligations of Dubai World and its subsidiaries. This move implicitly acknowledges the possibility that Dubai World may need to declare bankruptcy to obtain protection from its creditors. Abu Dhabi has stepped in at the last minute in order to safeguard the reputation and credit status of the UAE as a whole. There will undoubtedly be a price to pay, whether in the form of the transfer of assets to Abu Dhabi or through subjecting Dubai to closer administrative and political control by the federal government in the capital. Economist/Global business Portfolio.

Latest IMF projections

(year over year percent change)

	2008	2009	Projections 2010	Projections 2011	Difference from October 2009 WEO projections 2010	Difference from October 2009 WEO projections 2011
World output	3.0	-0.8	3.9	4.3	0.8	0.1
Advanced economies	0.5	-3.2	2.1	2.4	0.8	-0.1
United States	0.4	-2.5	2.7	2.4	1.2	-0.4
Euro area	0.6	-3.9	1.0	1.6	0.7	0.3
Germany	1.2	-4.8	1.5	1.9	1.2	0.4
France	0.3	-2.3	1.4	1.7	0.5	-0.1
Italy	-1.0	-4.8	1.0	1.3	0.8	0.6
Spain	0.9	-3.6	-0.6	0.9	0.1	0.0
Japan	-1.2	-5.3	1.7	2.2	0.0	-0.2
United Kingdom	0.5	-4.8	1.3	2.7	0.4	0.2
Canada	0.4	-2.6	2.6	3.6	0.5	0.0
Other advanced economies	1.7	-1.3	3.3	3.6	0.7	-0.1
Newly industrialized Asian economies	1.7	-1.2	4.8	4.7	1.2	0.0
Emerging market and developing economies	6.1	2.1	6.0	6.3	0.9	0.2
Africa	5.2	1.9	4.3	5.3	0.3	0.1
Sub-Saharan Africa	5.6	1.6	4.3	5.5	0.2	0.0
Central and eastern Europe	3.1	-4.3	2.0	3.7	0.2	-0.1
Commonwealth of Independent States	5.5	-7.5	3.8	4.0	1.7	0.4
Russia	5.6	-9.0	3.6	3.4	2.1	0.4
Excluding Russia	5.3	-3.9	4.3	5.1	0.7	0.1
Developing Asia	7.9	6.5	8.4	8.4	1.1	0.3
China	9.6	8.7	10.0	9.7	1.0	0.0
India	7.3	5.6	7.7	7.8	1.3	0.5
ASEAN-5[1]	4.7	1.3	4.7	5.3	0.7	0.6
Middle East	5.3	2.2	4.5	4.8	0.3	0.2
Western Hemisphere	4.2	-2.3	3.7	3.8	0.8	0.1
Brazil	5.1	-0.4	4.7	3.7	1.2	0.2
Mexico	1.3	-6.8	4.0	4.7	0.7	-0.2

Source: IMF, World Economic Outlook Update, January 2010.
[1] Indonesia, Malaysia, the Philippines, Thailand, and Vietnam.

December 8. U.S. **President** Barack **Obama called for a major new burst of federal spending** to jolt the wobbly economy into a stronger recovery and reduce painfully persistent double-digit unemployment. Obama said the U.S. must continue to "spend our way out of this recession" as long as so many people are out of work. More than 7 million Americans have lost their jobs since the recession began two years ago, and the jobless rate stands at 10%, a statistic Obama called "staggering." Congressional approval would be required for the new spending, the amount unspecified but sure to be at least tens of billions of dollars. "We avoided the depression many feared," Obama said in a speech at the Brookings Institution, a Washington think tank. But, he added, "Our work is far from done." Obama proposed new spending for highway and bridge construction, for small business tax cuts and for retrofitting millions of homes to make them more energy-efficient. He said he wanted to extend economic stimulus programs to keep unemployment insurance from expiring for millions of out-of-work Americans and to help laid- off workers keep their health insurance. He proposed an additional $250 apiece in stimulus spending for seniors and veterans and aid to state and local governments to discourage them from laying off teachers, police officers and firefighters. Proposals in Congress that cover much the same ground would add up to $170 billion or more. Administration aides suggested the infrastructure proposals alone being weighed by the president could cost about $50 billion. Reuters.

December 7. Kuwait's sovereign wealth fund said on Sunday it had **sold its stake in Citigroup** Inc. for a profit of $1.1 billion, becoming the latest Gulf investor to sell foreign shares as markets improve. Kuwait Investment Authority (KIA) transferred the preferred stock it owned in Citigroup to common shares and sold all of them for $4.1 billion, KIA said in a statement. KIA said it made a 37 % return on its initial January 2008 investment of $3 billion in Citigroup's preferred stock. It did not disclose the number of shares it had sold or what it planned to do with proceeds from the sale. Citigroup's stock closed at $4.12 on the New York Stock Exchange on Friday. KIA follows Singapore's wealth fund, GIC, which halved its stake in Citigroup in September, cashing in on a market rally for a profit of $1.6 billion. Reuters.

December 7. Efforts by **Japanese** officials to boost the world's second-biggest economy and a U.S. jobs report led to the **currency's biggest weekly decline in a decade**. Japan's currency plunged 2.5% against the dollar and 1.3% versus the euro on December 4 after the U.S. Labor Department said employers cut the fewest jobs since the recession began. The yen rose against the dollar today, after sinking last week by the most since February 1999, extending a retreat from a 14-year high. Traders sold yen and bought dollars on speculation U.S. interest rates will increase before June. This is causing options traders to become less bullish on the yen. Options showed declining bets the yen will rise. The odds for a gain to 84.5 yen per dollar by the end of March from 90.56 last week fell to 38% from 80% on November 30, data compiled by Bloomberg show. Chances of a decline to 92 versus the dollar by December 31 reached 63%. Bloomberg.

December 7. The Obama administration, buoyed by a resurgent Wall Street, plans to cut the projected **long-term cost of the Troubled Asset Relief Program** by more than $200 billion, in a move that could smooth the way for the introduction of a new jobs program. The White House and leaders in Congress are debating whether to use any of the remaining TARP funds for other domestic efforts, such as a jobs bill. Congress authorized $700 billion for the program during the height of the financial crisis. The Treasury now estimates that over the next 10 years TARP will cost $141 billion at most, down from the $341 billion the White

House projected in August. The reduction stems in large part from faster-than-expected repayments by some of the nation's largest banks, as well as less spending on programs to help shore up the financial sector. The government's efforts appear to have helped stabilize the financial sector, and banks have already repaid the Treasury about $70 billion. Wall Street Journal.

December 4. Federal Reserve Chairman Ben S. Bernanke made the case for a strong, independent central bank during a hearing on his nomination to a second four-year term. Some senators urged him to do more to resuscitate the economy while others pressed him to roll back efforts before they provoke vicious inflation. Senators noted the highest unemployment rate in a generation and continuing reluctance of banks to stimulate economic activity by lending to businesses. But as he faced sometimes hostile questions about the Fed's recent actions, he also acknowledged its failure to spot problems in the financial system before they exploded into a crisis last year, and he vowed that it would not happen again. **Testifying before the Senate Banking, Housing and Urban Affairs Committee**, Bernanke repeatedly steered the conversation toward what he considers the potential dangers of financial regulation proposals moving through Congress. Two issues dominated his testimony—a proposal by Banking Chairman Christopher J. Dodd, D-Conn., to strip the Fed of its authority to regulate the banking system and one from Rep. Ron Paul, R-Texas, that would give the government expanded audit authority over Fed decision-making. Bernanke has argued that the measures would hinder the central bank's ability to carry out monetary policy and subject it to undue political pressure. When Utah Republican Robert F. Bennett spoke of his experience as a business owner in the inflation-ravaged late 1970s, Bernanke used the opportunity to address then-Fed Chairman Paul A. Volcker 's politically unpopular—but highly successful—efforts to whip inflation by substantially raising interest rates. Despite intense pressure from Congress to ease rates, support for Volcker 's policies from presidents Jimmy Carter and Ronald Reagan "let him do what he had to do," Bernanke said, and that "was the reason inflation was conquered." CQ Today, Washington Post.

December 4. The **U.S. unemployment rate edged down to 10.0% in November**, from 10.2% in October 2009, the Bureau of Labor Statistics reported. Nonfarm payroll employment was essentially unchanged, with a loss of 11,000 jobs. In the prior three months, payroll job losses had averaged 135,000 a month. In November, employment fell in construction, manufacturing, and information, while temporary help services and health care added jobs. In November, both the number of unemployed persons, at 15.4 million, and the unemployment rate, at 10.0%, edged down. At the start of the recession in December 2007, the number of unemployed persons was 7.5 million, and the jobless rate was 4.9%. BLS press release.

December 4. Bank of America Corp., the largest U.S. lender, **raised $19.3 billion** selling securities at $15 apiece in the biggest sale of stock or preferred shares by a U.S. public company since at least 2000. In May, Bank of America raised $13.5 billion issuing 1.25 billion common shares at $10.77 each in response to government stress tests. The bank, which plans to repay $45 billion of U.S. rescue funds, sold 1.286 billion so-called common equivalent securities, according to Bloomberg data. The security is made up of one depositary share and one warrant and is convertible into one common share, subject to stockholder approval, according to a regulatory filing by the Charlotte, North Carolina-based bank. Bank of America plans to use the proceeds to free itself from government restrictions after accepting funds from the Troubled Asset Relief Program. Banks, brokerages and insurers have raised $1.5 trillion to shore up capital after the biggest financial crisis since the Great Depression spurred more than $1.7 trillion in writedowns and credit losses globally. Bloomberg.com

December 4. General Motors has reached an agreement to **sell about half of its India operations** and a small stake in its China business to its main joint-venture partner in China, people with a detailed knowledge of the transaction said on Thursday evening. G.M.'s main partner in China, the Shanghai Automotive Industry Corporation, better known as S.A.I.C., suspended trading in its shares on the Shanghai stock market on Thursday pending an announcement, but declined to release details. G.M. said in a statement that it was constantly in discussions with S.A.I.C. on various issues, but also did not disclose any details. G.M.'s international operations have been in a quiet but intense search for cash this autumn to cover losses incurred when its South Korean subsidiary, Daewoo, lost $2 billion last year on a bad bet on financial derivatives based on the Korean won and then burned through its remaining lines of credit during the recent global downturn. New York Times.

December 4. The **Nile Delta** is one of the regions most at **risk** from the anticipated rise in **sea levels** associated with global warming. One of Egypt's most accomplished hydraulic engineers has made a thorough study of the dimensions of the potential problems, and has drawn up proposals for preserving the Delta. Agricultural land will not be the only loss. Roads, railways, schools, hospitals, offices, and factories will be damaged beyond use. Especially devastating will be the loss of housing, particularly in the heavily populated rural and urban areas with a high concentration of the very poor, and of several hundred thousand jobs. It is estimated that if the sea rise occurred today, an estimated 3.5 million inhabitants would become "climate refugees," unless the government of Egypt takes action to protect the Delta. At current prices, the cost of constructing the proposed scheme would be in the range of €5 billion/US $7.5 billion; the time needed to construct the protective system would be between eight and ten years. This cost is in addition to that required to raise the embankment along the 1 60-km length of the Suez Canal. The question this poses is who should pay the price—the victims or those who induced the suffering? Economist/Global business Portfolio.

December 4. Mexico's recession, the steepest in the Western Hemisphere and among the worst in the world, has yet to hit bottom in some sectors of the economy, even as some other regional economies began growing steadily months ago. Besides having a lagging recovery, Mexico's growth prospects in 2010-2011 will be very modest. Poor labor market indicators are also fuelling concerns about longer-term growth prospects. Given the very poor performance of the economy for most of the year, the Economist Intelligence Unit estimates that GDP will contract by at least 7% in full-year 2009. We do not expect real GDP to return to 2008 levels until the end of 2011, reflecting both continuing dependence on the US and internal structural weaknesses. We project growth of 3% in 2010, with a fallback to 2.7% in 2011 in line with trends in the United States. Economist/Global business Portfolio.

December 4. Azerbaijan will be the **fastest-growing economy during 2009** according to the Economist Intelligence Unit. For this, Azerbaijan can thank its international oil consortium, the government's wage policies and the country's free-spending consumers. Azerbaijan's GDP will grow by nearly 13% this year, according to the government. The Economist Intelligence Unit estimates that, Azerbaijan aside, the fastest-growing economies in 2009 will be China at 8.2%, Zambia at 8.3%, and Malawi at 7.6%. The oil sector accounts for over 50% of Azerbaijan's GDP. The increase in international oil prices in the second and third quarters of 2009 has been supportive of real GDP growth. So too has been a sharp rise in output from the BP-operated Azeri-Chirag-Guneshli (ACG) oil complex in the Caspian Sea. Economist/Global business Portfolio.

December 4. Dubai symbolizes the arrival of the **financial crisis in the Middle East**, in a unique economy. No other country built a ski resort in a desert. No other country constructed an archipelago of 300 artificial islands, complete with a man-made reef colonized by parrot fish. But even if Dubai is a gaudy outlier—a sort of Donald Trump of a nation—the bankruptcy of its flagship investment company, Dubai World, holds a warning for others. The nonchalance with which global financial markets have reacted is not reassuring in the least. The lack of alarm is alarming. Start with the size of the Dubai bankruptcy. Most analysts reckon the emirate will end up defaulting on more than $30 billion. That's up from the $26 billion advertised at Dubai World but perhaps less than half of the city-state's accumulated $80 billion debt. Dubai's bust will be larger than South Korea's 1998 debt restructuring, which involved $22 billion worth of loans, and not much smaller than Russia's default that year (which affected loans worth $40 billion). The South Korean and Russian traumas spread panic around the world. Nowadays, investors yawn at losses that don't run into the hundreds of billions. This is a touch complacent. Washington Post.

December 3. By a vote of 421-0, the **U.S. House of Representatives** on December 2 passed a bill aimed at bolstering **oversight of the government's 2008 financial industry bailout**, which has become increasingly unpopular with lawmakers from both parties. Sponsored by New York Democrat Carolyn B. Maloney, the measure, 111th Congress H.R. 1242, would broaden government oversight of the bailout law, P.L. 110-343, known as the Troubled Asset Relief Program (TARP). The bill would require the Treasury Department, which administers the program, to provide continuous data on money spent under the bailout to the TARP special inspector general, the comptroller general, and the Congressional Oversight Panel. The Treasury Department would have to present the funding updates through a standardized electronic database. CQ Today.

December 3. U.S. nonfarm business sector **labor productivity increased at an 8.1% annual rate** during the third quarter of 2009, as unit labor costs fell 2.5%, the U.S. Bureau of Labor Statistics reported. This was the largest gain in productivity since the third quarter of 2003, and reflects a 2.9% increase in output and a 4.8% decline in hours worked. BLS press release.

December 3. President Obama's invited 130 business leaders, union chiefs, economists and others to a **jobs summit** aimed at producing ideas to battle a surging unemployment problem. The event highlighted the tough dilemma he confronts: jobs versus funding. Obama says he does not have the money for the plan many liberal supporters say packs the biggest employment punch— direct federal investment in job creation. Instead, he came close to embracing a to-do list for the private sector: weatherization, small-business incentives, regulatory and other help for exporters, and tax credits for employers who hire new workers. The President said the proposals could create jobs immediately, while providing long-term benefit at a relatively small expense to the federal government. "Overall, we generated a lot of important ideas," he said. "Some of them, I think, can translate immediately into administration plans and, potentially, legislation." Washington Post.

December 3. European Central Bank (ECB) President Jean-Claude Trichet signaled that the bank's planned withdrawal of stimulus measures would proceed gradually, as signs emerged of a split within the ECB's governing council over the timing of the move. "The improved conditions in financial markets have indicated that not all our liquidity measures are needed to the same extent as in the past," Mr. Trichet said. He stressed the bank would "gradually phase out" the programs. The ECB said it would hold its **main policy rate steady at 1%**, as expected. The ECB also stated that its upcoming one-year refinancing operation on December 16 will be the last of its kind. The six-month tender will end March 31, 2010. Regarding the terms of allotment, the ECB specifies that the interest rate on the last 12-month long term refinancing operation (LTRO) "will be fixed at the average minimum bid rate of the main refinancing operations (MROs) over the life of this operation." This is a departure from the previous two one-year LTROs where the interest rate was fixed at 1.0% with full allotment. Wall Street Journal, Roubini Global Economics.

December 3. After nearly nine months of negotiations, **Comcast**, the nation's largest cable operator, announced an agreement to **acquire NBC Universal from the General Electric Company**. The deal valued NBC Universal at about $30 billion. The agreement will create a joint venture, with Comcast owning 51% and G.E. owning 49%. Comcast will contribute to the joint venture its stable of cable channels, which includes Versus, the Golf Channel and E Entertainment, worth about $7.25 billion, and will pay G.E. about $6.5 billion in cash, for a total of $13.75 billion. For now, the network will remain NBC Universal, but ultimately Comcast could decide to change the name. Almost immediately, the transaction reshapes the nation's entertainment industry, giving a cable provider a huge portfolio of new content, even as it raises the sector's anxieties about the future. New York Times.

December 2. The House Financial Services Committee voted for a bill that creates a council of regulators to **monitor systemic risk**, shifts costs of a failure to the financial industry, and gives regulators the power to break up even healthy firms, an amendment demanded by Rep. Paul Kanjorski (D-PA). The bill also includes a provision first recommended by Sheila Bair that would require secured creditors to bear losses of as much as 20% to cover costs to unwind a failed systemically important firm. The industry is lobbying hard to remove the latter provision and Chairman Frank said that it may still be revised. The Senate Finance Committee similarly voted for a measure to break up any institutions that may pose a systemic risk. Chairman Frank said the House Finance Committee will vote on a measure to police the $605 trillion over-the-counter **derivatives market** when it takes up broader legislation giving regulators more authority to police financial companies that pose a risk to the U.S. economy.

December 2. Government-owned **Dubai World** spearheaded the emirate's rapid growth for decades, then disclosed its debt woes. On November 25, the government of Dubai announced the restructuring of Dubai World, one of the emirate's three state-owned investment giants, which would "ask all providers of financing to Dubai World and Nakheel to 'stand still' and extend maturities until at least 30 May 2010." Dubai World's overall liabilities total almost $60 billion, including those of units not part of its restructuring. Banks from Britain are the most exposed to the conglomerate. Banks Standard Chartered, HSBC, Lloyds and Royal Bank of Scotland, along with local lenders Emirates NBD and Abu Dhabi Commercial Bank are on the creditors' panel. Dubai World will meet its main creditors next week to discuss payment delay on $26 billion in debt. The most urgent question is the fate of Nakheel's $3.52 billion Islamic bond, which matures on December 14. Foreign banks had lent to Dubai government-linked firms on the implicit understanding that they were backed by the UAE—the world's third largest oil exporter flush with cash from a six-year boom in oil prices. "Something that has irritated international investors is that the government distanced itself from Dubai World, which legally speaking is true, but morally speaking, they had gone out of their way before to make that tie," one investor said. Moody's estimated the Dubai government and its related entities have debt of $100 billion— higher than the market estimate of around $80 billion. Dubai now has the tallest building in the world, and 11 skyscrapers that are taller than any European building. Edward Glaeser/Economix, Reuters.

December 2. Last week, state-owned **Dubai World requested** a six-month **standstill on its debts**, calling into question the emirate's ability and willingness to service the debt of its state-owned enterprises. This followed months of the emirate reassuring creditors and issuing over US$15 billion in sovereign debt. The debt standstill suggests the emirate had run out of options for a preemptive comprehensive bail-out from the well-resourced region. While the debt in question, including a US$3.5 billion bond issued by a property development subsidiary, was not sovereign-guaranteed, investors had treated it as such, relying on the fact that the size of Dubai World and the profile of the underlying projects would imply a government rescue. Uncertainty was heightened by illiquidity and poor price action from the holiday period while the lack of information and communication at the time of the request added to concerns about the complete scale of Dubai's implicit and explicit obligations—with on and off balance sheet debts by some estimates as high as $200 billion, or over 400% of GDP. Capital support makes an outright default of Dubai World's debt unlikely. Dubai World's restructuring implies that the creditors will take a share of the pain for the most distressed assets in the holding company's portfolio. The Dubai property development model will need to be reassessed in a lower-leverage world. Beyond the UAE, the reassessment of government support could draw further attention to other countries where state support is murkier. Attention has returned to sovereign credit risk, particularly in the Eurozone and its periphery, where weaker countries, like Greece and the more indebted of the Central and Eastern European countries, are under pressure. While Dubai World's financing issues are not a surprise and are relatively small given global credit losses, they are a reminder that the vulnerabilities and imbalances that contributed to the credit crunch have not disappeared. A fundamental message from Dubai World's problems is that investors should never assume implicit government support. Credit ratings for Dubai-owned companies now reflect this lesson, based on a fundamental credit outlook, not an implicit government backstop. Roubini Global Economics.

December 1. After Dubai, many wonder where the **next debt bomb** will be found. Even in rich nations like the United States and Japan, which are increasing government spending to shore up slack economies, mounting budget deficits are raising concern about governments' ability to shoulder their debts, especially once interest rates start to rise again. In Germany, long the bastion of fiscal rectitude in Europe, government debt outstanding is expected to increase to the equivalent of 77% of the nation's economic output next year, from 60% in 2002. In Britain, that figure is expected to more than double over the same period, to more than 80%. Public debt in Ireland is expected to soar to 83% of gross domestic product next year, from just 25% in 2007. Latvian borrowings will reach the equivalent of nearly half the economy next year, up from 9% a mere two years ago. Lithuania, Estonia, Bulgaria and Hungary all carry foreign debt that exceeds 100% of their GDPs, said Ivan Tchakarov, chief economist for Russia and the former Soviet states at Nomura bank. External debt is often held in a foreign currency, which means governments cannot use devaluation of their own currencies as a tool to reduce their debt when they run into trouble. Dubai's refusal to guarantee the debts of its investment arm, Dubai World, may set a precedent for other indebted governments to abandon companies that investors had in the past assumed enjoyed full state backing. Harvard economist Kenneth Rogoff said he expected a wave of defaults about two years from now, when the countries now serving as implicit guarantors turn their focus to economic problems at home. Some governments have taken on **increasingly short-term debt**. In the United States, for example, Treasury debt maturing within one year has risen from around 33% of total debt two years ago to around 44% this summer, while falling slightly since then, according to Wrightson ICAP. The United States will soon have debt problems of its own. "In another couple years as industrialized countries' own debts—in places like Germany, Japan and the United States—get worse, they will become more reluctant to open up their wallets to spendthrift emerging markets, or at least countries they view that way," Mr. Rogoff said. This might spell trouble for struggling nations. Facing a need to roll over their maturing debts, emerging markets may have to borrow around $65 billion in 2010 alone, according to Gary N. Kleiman of Kleiman International. But while government debt may be a problem, corporate debt may set off a crisis that is already unfolding. Corporate borrowing surged over the last five years. According to Mr. Kleiman, $200 billion of corporate debt is coming due this year or next year. He estimates that companies in Russia and the United Arab Emirates account for about half of that borrowing. New York Times.

December 1. The U.S. government promised **tougher scrutiny of lenders** participating in its marquee foreclosure-prevention effort and threatened to penalize companies that don't do enough to help struggling homeowners. The move is aimed at breaking a bottleneck in the Making Home Affordable program, which was launched in March but has been slow to reach many borrowers. Most of the 650,000 homeowners enrolled in the program are stuck in its initial phase and still must prove that they qualify for reduced mortgage payments. Moving those borrowers from trial modifications into permanent ones is a key test of the effort's effectiveness. Treasury Department officials would not say Monday how many loans have been permanently modified. But a recent report by the Congressional Oversight Panel, which is monitoring the government's Troubled Assets Relief Program, found that only about 1% of borrowers had moved from a trial modification into a permanent one. Washington Post.

December 1. U.S. manufacturing expanded in November for a fourth consecutive month, propelled by gains in orders and exports that signal growth will be sustained. The Institute for Supply Management's manufacturing index fell to 53.6, lower than forecast, from October's three-year high of 55.7, according to the Tempe, Arizona-based group. Readings above 50 signal expansion. Another report showed home sales will probably rise further. A report showing factory output in China rose at the fastest pace in five years, lifted earnings prospects at U.S. exporters including Caterpillar Inc. Growing demand from overseas and lean inventories may keep American assembly lines running into 2010, when government stimulus efforts begin to wane. Bloomberg.com.

December 1. Bread for the World published its latest annual report, the 2010 Hunger Report, titled A Just and Sustainable Recovery. It chronicles the **U.S. socioeconomic effects** of the worst recession in 75 years. A lot remains unclear as to how recovery will unfold, whether it will be just or sustainable. "Business as usual" would be neither. How the country recovers will be a de facto verdict on many of the actions that made this recession worse than it had to be. In the long run, the greatest threat to a sustainable recovery may come from a looming crisis: global climate change. The actions that drove the economy into recession are in a sense magnified by the exploitation of this one, irreplaceable natural resource. "We created a way of raising standards of living that we can't possibly pass on to our children," remarked one analyst. Continuing the reckless consumption of fossil fuels mirrors the actions of speculators who wrecked the economy by creating an unsustainable asset bubble. Climate change is both a huge challenge—and a huge economic opportunity. The 2010 Hunger Report embraces the job-creating potential of greening the economy, thereby creating the potential to reduce poverty. A green economy may mean different things to different people, but in this report we mean the transformation of the nation's energy infrastructure from today's heavy reliance on carbon-intensive fossil fuels to a much stronger embrace of clean, renewable forms of energy such as solar, wind, and geothermal. Creating a green economy also means investing in cost-effective strategies to boost energy efficiency, such as weatherizing homes and office buildings. In fact, this is the quickest way to reduce the greenhouse gas emissions that are causing climate change. Clean energy and energy efficiency can engage a sizeable share of the U.S. workforce for at least a generation and probably several. Public and private investments in greening the economy will ensure that the recovery is sustainable for years to come. A family's path out of poverty has several key elements. A job is still the best anti-poverty program there is. On the Internet: http://www.hungerreport.org/ 2010/.

November 29. The Obama Administration asked Congress to pass legislation requiring SEC **registration of advisers to hedge funds** and other private pools of capital, including private equity funds and venture capital funds, with assets under management over a certain threshold. The Administration's proposal is broadly in line with proposals advanced by the G-20, which recommended the adoption of a confidential reporting regime pursuant to which hedge funds would be required to register and provide a regulator with information relevant to the assessment of systemic risk. Because many hedge funds fall within certain exemptions of the Investment Company Act and the Investment Advisers Act, those hedge fund are required neither to register with the SEC nor to disclose publicly all their investment positions. The exemption has enabled private funds to operate largely outside the framework of the financial regulatory system even as they have become increasingly interwoven with the financial markets. As a result, there is no data on the number and nature of these firms or ability to calculate the risks they pose to the broader markets and the economy. Thus, hedge funds and other private funds are not currently subject to the same set of standards and regulations as banks and mutual funds, reflecting the traditional view that their investors are more sophisticated and therefore require less protection. Jim Hamilton's World of Securities Regulation. On the Internet: http://jimhamiltonblog.blogspot.com/ 2009/1 1/acting-on-obama-proposal-house.html.

November 25. General Motors cast around for fresh options for Sweden's loss-making Saab after the collapse of its sale added a fresh complication to GM's attempts to restructure Opel. On November 24, GM's deal to sell Saab to niche luxury carmaker Koenigsegg, backed by China's BAIC, collapsed after the buyer walked away. Trolhattan, Sweden-based Saab, which has not made a profit since 2001, was facing uncertainty on Wednesday. Joran Hagglund, state secretary at Sweden's Industry Ministry, said GM appeared to still harbor hope of being able to sell Saab. The Swedish government had effectively ruled out a state bailout of the 60-year-old auto brand, saying on Tuesday that a private buyer was the only option for Saab. Earlier this month the U.S. automaker backtracked on months of talks to sell a majority stake in Opel to a consortium led by Canada's Magna International, opting to keep and revamp the business itself. GM was due to present Opel labor leaders with a restructuring plan. GM had said that the group would cut between 9,000 and 9,500 jobs out of the 50,000 strong workforce at Opel in Germany and in Belgium and British sister brand Vauxhall as part of the 3.3 billion euro/US$4.92 billion plan. GM said the turmoil unleashed by the failure of the Saab deal would not affect Opel. Some analysts say the European market in which Opel and Saab operate is burdened with as much as 20% too much production capacity. Reuters.

November 25. The **global economy** is recovering, helped by massive **fiscal stimulus** in many countries. Now attention is turning to what will happen after such programs are withdrawn. Most governments cannot afford to keep the economy on life support indefinitely, but the more effective stimulus is now, the greater the slowdown will be when it inevitably comes to an end. Although the global crisis originated in the rich world, developed and developing countries alike have primed the pumps. In the **OECD fiscal stimulus** has been worth about **2% of GDP in 2009**, and is expected to dip only moderately to 1.6% in 2010. Among OECD economies, **South Korea** has had the **most aggressive stimulus**, but the United States and Japan have been close behind. The OECD estimates that **U.S. stimulus** measures between 2008 and 2010 will be the equivalent of **5.6% of GDP**. Germany is also spending substantially in an effort to boost the economy, but some European countries are less enthusiastic. The stimulus in France is worth only 0.7% of GDP, and in Italy there is no stimulus. Many non-OECD countries have also implemented large stimuli. **China's** is the most prominent, with the country's direct **fiscal measures** amounting to **8% of GDP**, according to Economist Intelligence Unit estimates. The boost to the economy has been amplified by the fact that Chinese banks, under government guidance, have increased lending to the private sector by a staggering US$1.4 trillion since the start of 2009, according to end-September data. Some of the loans would have been made anyway, but the amount of the increase is equivalent to 29% of GDP and almost double the previous record for a full year. The high costs of stimulus have polarized political opinion in several countries—most notably in the United States, where there is a fierce ideological debate about the effectiveness of state intervention. Despite such concerns, it seems clear that fiscal measures have contributed substantially to economic recovery in most countries, including the United States. For an indication of what might have happened without such support, U.S. housing starts fell by nearly 11% at an annualized rate in October because tax credits for new home-buyers were due to expire at the end of November (even though the government ultimately extended it to April 2010). Similarly, in Japan government incentives encouraged spending on durable consumer goods in the second and third quarters of 2009, but areas of consumer spending that did not benefit from fiscal support continued to languish. What is likely to happen as governments start to unwind stimulus programs? In most countries, the amounts being spent are already peaking or will do so in the first half of 2010, before gradually declining in the second half of that year and in 2011. The time lag between the disbursement of stimulus funds and their impact on the economy means that GDP growth in many countries in 2010 will still be inflated by government support. But the reversal will be fierce in 2011. This is why we expect U.S. GDP growth to fall from 2.5% in 2010 to just 1.3% in 2011. Economist.

November 23. Dominique Strauss-Kahn, Managing Director, **International Monetary Fund**, said in a **speech** in London, "the global economy remains very much in a holding pattern—stable, and getting better, but still highly vulnerable. The major advanced country areas in particular remain fragile, still dependent on policy support. Financial conditions have improved, but are far from normal. Signs show confidence returning, but banking systems in many advanced economies remain undercapitalized, weighed down by leaden legacy assets and, increasingly, non-performing loans. On the household side, weak financial positions and high unemployment will damp down on consumption for some time. And large public deficits add to vulnerabilities. So then, if we are to have sustained global growth, somebody else needs to step into the breach. The leading candidates are the surplus countries. And we can see some shifts in the right direction. China and other emerging Asian economies are shifting from exports toward domestic demand, aided by expansionary fiscal policy. But they have some way to go. This shift would be helped by stronger social security systems and higher spending on health and education, as well as reforms to boost access to credit. An appreciation of China's exchange rate, along with some other Asian currencies, will also need to be part of the package." IMF press release.

November 23. Japan's public debt is approaching 200% of GDP, by far the highest in the OECD, as the global economic crisis has increased pressure on the government's fragile finances. Investors are concerned that the country's fiscal position is unsustainable, as a recent spike in Japanese government bond (JGB) yields uncomfortably suggested. But the Economist Intelligence Unit believes that Japan is not in imminent danger of crossing a "tipping point," beyond which the government's debt would be unmanageable. As in many other rich countries, the downturn has battered the Japanese government's finances. The contraction in the economy has hit tax revenues, while stimulus measures have pushed up government spending. We expect the fiscal deficit to rise sharply, to around 8% of GDP in both 2009 and 2010. Where Japan differs is that its public finances were already in bad shape—much worse than in other rich countries— when the crisis began. Public debt has been on a steady upward trend since the bursting of Japan's asset-price bubble in the late 1980s and early 1990s. Gross public debt was equal to 65% of GDP in 1990 but has risen to an estimated 192%. We think the ratio will continue to rise, exceeding 200% within the next two years. In the past, ill-conceived public-works spending in the "bridges to nowhere" mould has contributed to the problem. The fiscal accounts have run a deficit every year since 1993. But a greater factor has been the stagnation of nominal GDP as Japan became mired in a deflationary cycle. All this has increased the real burden of the country's debt. The new government of the Democratic Party of Japan (DPJ) has social-spending proposals for the fiscal year starting next April; these are expected to cost some ¥7 trillion (US$79 billion). The DPJ claims, somewhat dubiously, that it can find the requisite funds internally. There is clearly no prospect of an improvement any time soon. Economist.

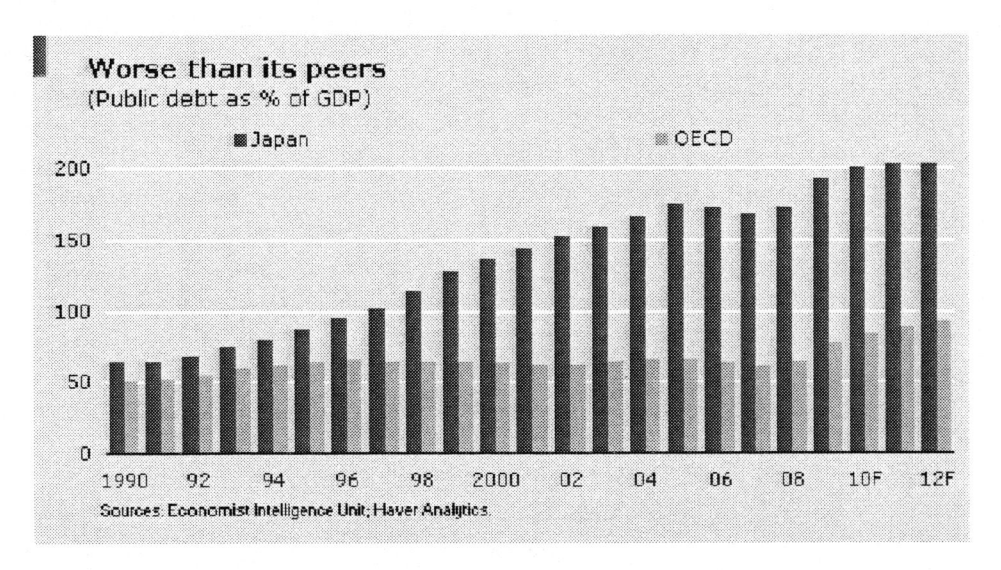

Worse than its peers
(Public debt as % of GDP)
Japan / OECD
Sources: Economist Intelligence Unit; Haver Analytics.

November 19. Treasury Secretary Timothy F. Geithner testified before the Joint Economic Committee regarding the economic collapse of 2008 and the subsequent bailout of Wall Street firms by TARP (P.L. 110-343). Rep. Peter A. DeFazio, D-Ore., previously, and Rep. Kevin Brady, R-Texas, at the hearing, expressed lack of confidence in Treasury actions and Geithner. The Treasury Secretary replied that regulators simply had no other choice, given the panic and near meltdown of the financial system that started with the failure of Lehman Brothers Holdings Inc. "The judgment made at the time was that we had the ability to prevent that, and that was the necessary and prudent thing to do," he said. "In acting that way, we were going to save the economy from even greater devastation than you saw in the wake of Lehman's collapse." CQ Today.

November 19. Federal Reserve auditing provision added to U.S. systemic risk bill. The House Financial Services Committee approved a series of amendments designed to enhance oversight of the Federal Reserve Board and create a government fund to pay for the failure of systemic institutions. The Committee voted to broaden the ability of the Government Accountability Office (GAO) to audit the Federal Reserve, despite concerns from the central bank that such scrutiny might lead investors to believe that its decisions on interest rates and other monetary policy would now be subject to political interference. This is due to Committee approval of a measure proposed by Representative Ron Paul of Texas that would allow Congress to order audits of all the Fed's lending programs as well as of its basic decisions to set monetary policy by raising or lowering interest rates. Rep. Paul has proposed this legislation before to no effect. The panel added these provision to a bill, H.R. 3996, designed to stem economic risks posed by the failure of major financial institutions and create an orderly process for restructuring such institutions. It also approved by voice vote an amendment that would cap the Fed's emergency lending authority at $4 trillion. The Committee approved several amendments which would give the Federal Reserve Board oversight of systemically crucial companies and let the Federal Deposit Insurance Corp. resolve them. American Banker, New York Times, CQ Today.

November 18. Parent banks reaffirm **commitment to Romania**, European Commission and IMF say. The parent banks of the nine largest banks operating in Romania reaffirmed their commitment to maintain their exposure to the country and ensure adequate capital levels over 10% for their affiliates. The nine parent banks with subsidiaries in Romania are: Erste Group Bank, Raiffeisen International, Eurobank EFG, National Bank of Greece, UniCredit Group, Société Générale, Alpha Bank, Volksbank, and Piraeus These banks emphasized the need for the availability of appropriate investment instruments. All parent banks complied with their commitments to provide additional capital needs for 2009 as of end-September 2009, thus ensuring the capital-adequacy ratio of their affiliates to remain above 10%. IMF press release.

November 12. Foreclosure filings were down 3% in October, the third consecutive monthover-month dip, according to RealtyTrac, the online seller of foreclosed homes. Foreclosure rates are still up 18% compared with October 2008. But the month-over-month decrease followed a 4% drop in filings during September and a 1% fall in August. James Saccacio, RealtyTrac's CEO, said "The fundamental forces driving foreclosure activity in this housing downturn—high-risk mortgages, negative equity, and unemployment—continue to loom over any nascent recovery." Broad economic distress, such as the rising unemployment rate, has RealtyTrac spokesman Rick Sharga thinking that declining foreclosures may be artificial rather than a real trend. "Processing delays and legislative actions are slowing down foreclosures," not actual improvement in the market, he said. The slowdowns include banks taking time to judge whether some loans are eligible for the Making Home Affordable program, President Obama's foreclosure-prevention initiative that was passed last spring. New state-level regulations have also lowered foreclosure statistics. Those factors may have especially delayed bank repossessions. RealtyTrac reported 77,077 REOs in October, down 12.2% compared to September, when nearly 88,000 homes were lost. For the year, there have been a total of 700,929 properties taken back by banks.Foreclosures require a double trigger, said Sharga. The first is that mortgage borrowers must have experienced a financial setback, such as medical bills, divorce, unemployment, and the like. The second trigger is owing more on the mortgage than the home is worth. Millions of borrowers are in that position: More than 20% of borrowers are underwater, according to Zillow. Most will continue to pay off their mortgages. However, if a family member loses their job or someone gets sick or the loan resets to a much higher interest rate, that's when the home may be lost. The "sand states," Nevada, California, Florida, and Arizona, continued to suffer the worst foreclosure problems. Nevada had the highest foreclosure rate in the nation, one filing for every 80 housing units. In second place was California, where filings dipped 1% to one filing for every 156 households. The state, by far the most heavily populated, had more filings, 85,420, than any other. Florida, with 51,911 filings, had the third highest foreclosure rate, one for every 168 households. Arizona was fourth with one for every 200. Las Vegas is still the worst hit metro area. More than one in every 68 households received a filing during October, five times the national average. CNNMoney.com

November 12. The **American dollar** is in the midst of a large fall in its **value**, or depreciation, as measured against other major currencies. The decline has been steady since 2002 and our currency is down about 35% from that peak. After strengthening slightly more than 10% during the global financial crisis of the past 18 months, the dollar is again falling back toward its pre- crisis lows, representing its weakest international value since 1967. There is a definite possibility that the dollar could soon decline further or faster. In addition to a financial crisis, we also have a large current-account deficit, meaning that we buy more from the world than we sell. The deficit was $100 billion in the latest available (second quarter) data, which is around 3% of gross domestic product, and we finance that with capital inflows from abroad. (The current-account deficit is down from around 6%, but two-thirds of the decline is due to the lower price of oil.) In the past, many of those inflows have been private investments of various kinds, but as investors around the world question whether U.S. government debt, and its dollars, are really worth the paper, it is increasingly difficult for us to finance our deficit with the outside world. The 1980s classic, Stephen Marris's "Deficits and the Dollar: The World Economy at Risk," stresses that a rapidly falling dollar would push up United States inflation, resulting in higher interest rates and a deep recession (pp. lx-lxi). Writing in the latest edition of Foreign Affairs, Fred Bergsten emphasizes that such outcomes are still possible today. A weakening dollar will cause inflation fears, so yields on long-term government bonds will rise to compensate investors for inflation, and we will need to pay more and more to finance our large debts. The idea that the American dollar might follow emerging markets such as Russia in 1998 and Argentina in 2002, or Britain in the 1970s—and so depreciate by 50% or more in a relatively short time—is certainly implausible now. But such a "doom scenario" is not unrealistic in the future without change. In this context, the American government needs to control its budget deficit to keep this adjustment on track, and to stop confidence in the dollar from falling further. Our government collects far too little in taxes for what it spends. There is no choice but to raise taxes soon and rein in spending. Peter Boone and Simon Johnson, New York Times/Economix

November 12. Wen Jiabao, **China's** premier, **pledged** U.S.$ 10 billion in cheap **loans to Africa** over the next three years, and refuted claims that the Asian powerhouse is only looking to exploit Africa's resources. The loan pledge for Africa was double a U.S.$5 billion commitment made in 2006. Wen said eight new Chinese policy measures aimed at strengthening relations with Africa were "more focused on improving people's livelihoods," underlining what he called Beijing's "selfless" engagement in Africa, the *Washington Post* reported. He said China will construct 100 new clean-energy projects on the continent and gradually lower customs duties on 95% of products from African states with which it has diplomatic ties. The IMF has expressed concern about African governments taking on too much debt from Chinese lenders. But Wen said China would write off some loans it had made to the poorest and most heavily indebted countries. African heads of state, including Zimbabwe's Robert Mugabe and Sudan's Omar Hassan alBashir, lauded China's support. But others said African nations needed to devise their own development plans to take full advantage of Chinese finance. Last year, European Union lawmakers assailed China for courting "oppressive" African governments, such as Sudan, to satisfy its soaring demand for oil and raw materials. "China is very stung by criticism from so- called Western quarters in recent years," Martyn Davies, CEO of Frontier Advisory, a Johannesburg-based research and strategy consulting company, told Bloomberg news. China is trying "to have a softer approach" in an effort to rebut the notion that its interest in Africa is "extractionist in nature." The pattern of trade—raw materials going to China and Chinese finished goods flooding Africa—has angered some Africans. "We are sick and tired of the old model, where China comes to Africa and extracts raw materials and goes back to China," Zimbabwean Deputy PM Arthur Mutambara said in the *Zimbabwe Times* in September. "We are not now interested in that." Source: Global Development Briefing.

November 12. Senegal has hailed **the completion of an assembly plant for Chinese buses** in its western city of Thies, Agence France-Presse (AFP) reports. The construction of the plant was funded by a loan of 11 billion CFA francs/U.S. $24.7 million from China, and spearheaded by Chinese company King Long. The Chinese buses to be assembled at the plant are part of a partnership with Senegalese company Senbus, which supplies the public transport system in Dakar. AFP reports that King Long's operations in Senegal are replacing those of India's Tata Motors, which assembled more than 500 minibuses over 2005–2008 for public transport. The significance of this project is that Senegal continues to benefit from its diplomatic ties to China. Since 2005, when it changed its position on Taiwan to favor China's "One China" policy, Senegal has been the recipient of numerous aid and loan packages. IHS Global Insight.

November 11. Strong data from **China** released November 11, especially in factory output and retail sales, underscored the speed of the giant **economy's rebound**, thanks to extensive government stimulus measures that have put the economy on track to grow more than 8% in 2009. Industrial output and retail sales for October jumped 16.1% and 16.2%, respectively, from a year earlier. The increases also were higher than in September, showing that the pace of recovery was continuing to increase. Separately, the customs office said exports in October had been 13.8% below the level of a year earlier, while imports had fallen 6.4%, more than expected. China's trade surplus for the month swelled to $24 billion, nearly double the level in September. The data confirmed a picture that has been emerging over the past few months: buoyed by a huge stimulus package announced a year ago, as well as by lower interest rates and greatly increased lending by state-owned banks, China has recovered much more forcefully than other leading economies. The World Bank and the International Monetary Fund upgraded their growth forecasts for the country—to 8.4% and 8.5% for this year. Data also out Wednesday, showed that bank lending had slowed to 253 billion yuan, or $37 billion, in October, from 516.7 billion yuan in September. China said Wednesday that it would consider major currencies in guiding the yuan, suggesting a departure from an effective peg to the dollar that has been in place since the middle of last year, Reuters reported from Beijing. It was the first time since a revaluation and establishing of exchange rate changes in July 2005 that the People's Bank of China had strayed from the language of keeping the yuan "basically stable at a reasonable and balanced level" in quarterly reports. The comments came before a visit to China next week by President Barack Obama and amid growing pressure from other countries for Beijing to be more flexible in handling the yuan in the face of dollar weakness. New York Times

November 11. The relationship between **AIG** and some of its U.S. government paymasters has come close to breaking point over compensation at the stricken company. Tensions between the new board of AIG, and Kenneth Feinberg, the administration's special master on pay, came out into the open during a three-hour meeting in New York last week. AIG's directors, led by chief executive Robert Benmosche, told Mr. Feinberg his recent decision to slash salaries for 12 of its top executives by more than 90% was triggering high-level departures, upsetting employees' morale and reducing the chances the company will repay federal aid. Mr. Feinberg replied that AIG "did not get" the fact it has been bailed out with billions of dollars in taxpayers' funds and had to show restraint on compensation. Financial Times

November 10. The U.S. government lost the first major criminal trial spawned by the financial crisis as two former **Bear Stearns** hedge-fund managers were **acquitted of securities fraud**. Wall Street Journal

October 7. A U.S. House of Representatives' plan to impose **rules on** the enormous and largely unregulated **financial derivatives market** is getting a cautious thumbs up from industry groups, who had worried that the bill could cripple some businesses. House Financial Services Committee Chairman Barney Frank, D-MA, released draft legislative text late last week that would apply federal scrutiny to specially tailored financial instruments that are used by companies from airlines to manufacturers to insure against unanticipated costs and other risks. Currently, much of the $580 trillion market in so-called over-the-counter derivatives operates outside of government oversight. Congressional lawmakers, along with the Obama administration, are looking to change that after some companies, notably insurance giant American International Group Inc., took huge losses on bad derivatives bets during the financial crisis. Frank's proposal would give broad authority to regulators to require that a third-party clearinghouse approve such derivative contracts and guarantee that both parties to these contracts will fulfill their terms. The goal is to limit threats to the broader financial system. If a clearinghouse accepts the particulars of a derivative contract, it will cover any losses if one of the parties defaults. For companies that are big participants in this market, the bill would encourage the use of clearinghouses by imposing higher amounts of collateral be held in reserve for trades that aren't cleared. When setting the rules for what derivatives need to be cleared, the bill requires regulators to consider trading liquidity, total exposure, and questions of systemic risk. Congressional Quarterly. CQ Today.

October 7. The idea of a **tax credit for companies that create new jobs**, something the federal government has not tried since the 1970s, is gaining support among economists and Washington officials grappling with the highest unemployment in a generation. The proposal has some bipartisan appeal among politicians eager both to help their unemployed constituents and to encourage small-business development. Legislators on Capitol Hill and President Obama's economic team have been quietly researching the policy for several weeks. "There is a lot of traction for this kind of idea," said Representative Eric Cantor of Virginia, the Republican whip. "If the White House will take the lead on this, I'm fairly positive it would be welcomed in a bipartisan fashion." In addition to the economists working on the proposal, some heavyweights support the concept, including the Nobel laureate Edmund S. Phelps, Dani Rodrik of Harvard, and former Labor Secretary Robert B. Reich. New York Times.

October 7. A U.S. Federal Reserve report found that **U.S. banks** are slow to take **losses on their commercial real estate loans** that have been hit by slumping property values and rental payments, the *Wall Street Journal* said. Citing a September 29 presentation made by Fed analyst K.C. Conway to banking regulators, the paper said the report's remarks suggested that regulators were preparing for a rerun of housing-related losses that plagued many banks after the residential property bubble burst. Conway is a senior real estate analyst at the Federal Reserve Bank of Atlanta. The Journal said a Fed official had confirmed the authenticity of the document, but added it did not represent the central bank's formal opinion. Conway's report predicted that commercial real-estate losses would reach roughly 45% next year, the *Journal* said. CNBC.com/Reuters.

October 6. The Reserve Bank of **Australia** (RBA) emerged as the trend-setter among the G-20 with its decision to **increase the official cash rate** from 3% to 3.25%. Australia's economy stared down recession and it was the only developed nation to grow in the first half of 2009, despite the global economic downturn, with the help of massive counter-cyclical macroeconomic stimulus. At the start of the rate-cutting cycle the official cash rate (OCR) stood at 7.25%, then between September 2008 and April 2009, the OCR was reduced 425 basis points to the 49-year low of 3.00%. Monetary policy was then supported by an aggressively expansionary fiscal stance implementing two major stimulus packages worth a cumulative A$50 billion/U.S.$41 .2 billion, and an expansionary fiscal year 2009/10 budget. The combination of monetary and fiscal stimulus fuelled private consumption and business investment and allowed the Australian economy to grow by 0.6% quarter on quarter in the three months to June. Beyond macroeconomic stimulus, growth has also been driven by continued strong demand from China for commodities exports such as coal and iron ore. Following a string of better-than-expected data releases the RBA moved to a neutral policy bias at its August meeting. IHS Global Insight.

October 6. The **U.S. dollar's** value plunged on October 6, while the **price of gold** simultaneously hit a record high ($1,045 per ounce). The near-term causes of the latest round of dollar decline are obvious. Australia's central bank raised interest rates slightly on October 6. By itself, this would not be an exciting development, but it comes fast on the heels of the G-20 Pittsburgh summit in which all participants (including Australia) seemed to imply that "tightening monetary policy" (i.e., raising rates) was some way off. So if Australia begins to tighten—an implication that its economy is picking up—market participants reckon that more commodity producers and other parts of the Pacific Rim will soon feel the need to do likewise. At the same time, the United States has signaled that interest rates here will remain low for the foreseeable future. If you can borrow in dollars and buy Australian (or Korean or Chinese, etc) government debt, you are in what is known as a positive "carry trade"—because of low interest rates here, you pay close to zero to borrow the dollars and you can invest in Australia at more than 3% interest (or you can plunge into speculative Chinese automotive stocks). The United States could counteract all of this by making warning noises about potential intervention in the currency market: If you borrow heavily in dollars to lend in

Chinese renminbi, you can be easily rattled by the prospect that G-7 industrialized nations will intervene in a coordinated manner to strengthen the dollar. But the G-7 met this weekend and made no statement about the dollar—despite what must have been considerable pressure from Japan, France, Germany, and Italy, all of which are always worried about a rapid weakening of the dollar because they are so dependent on exports. The U.S. officials can continue to allow the dollar to float because ... we're not currently afraid of inflation. Simon Johnson, The Daily Beast.

October 6. IMF Managing Director Dominique Strauss-Kahn told policymakers from 186 countries gathered for the IMF-World Bank Annual Meetings in Istanbul that **global cooperation had saved the world from a far worse crisis** and leaders should now seize the opportunity to shape a post-crisis world. A year ago, people feared the worst. But after concerted action to combat the crisis, the world had pulled back from the brink. "Even if it is much too early to declare victory, we have at least stepped onto the road to recovery." Strauss-Kahn told the world's economic and monetary policymakers they have an historic opportunity to create the conditions necessary for "a virtuous cycle of peace and prosperity" if they continue to work together and with the IMF on key policy measures. Strauss-Kahn noted the "profound change" that formal and informal cooperation among nations had brought, adding that "in the face of crisis, countries came together to face common challenges with common solutions, focusing on the global common good." The IMF chief pointed to fiscal stimulus amounting to nearly 2% of world gross domestic product in the past year as a critical factor in staunching the crisis, and he stated that countries are moving to address key weaknesses in their financial sectors, which will further underpin recovery if they stay the course on these reforms. He asked the Fund to address four key reform areas—the IMF's mandate, its financing role, multilateral surveillance, and governance. These "**Istanbul Decisions**," he said, will be a focal point of IMF activities for the coming year. The four decisions comprise: (1) a review of the mandate of the IMF, through all macroeconomic and financial sector policies that affect global stability; (2) assessing how to build on the success of the Flexible Credit Line (FCL) and provide insurance to more countries as the lender of last resort and reduce the need for countries to self-insure against crisis by building up large reserves; (3) endorsement of the G-20 proposal for the IMF to help with their mutual assessment of policies. This represents a new kind of multilateral surveillance for the IMF; and endorsement of IMF governance reform agreed by the G-20. This would shift quota shares toward dynamic emerging markets and developing countries by at least 5% from over-represented to underrepresented countries, by January 2011. IMF press release.

October 6. The **General Motors** path out of bankruptcy isn't proving to be as smooth as its quick trip through it. In the past week, the company's plans to sell its Saturn brand to auto retailer Penske Auto Group fell through, forcing GM to start winding down a network of about 350 dealerships. Then, its plans to sell Hummer to a Chinese industrial company missed a target date of closing by Sept. 30. CNN.

October 6. The Obama administration's pay czar is planning to **clamp down on compensation** at firms receiving large sums of government aid by cutting annual cash salaries for many of the top employees under his authority, according to people familiar with the matter. Instead of awarding large cash salaries, Kenneth Feinberg is planning to shift a chunk of an employee's annual salary into stock that cannot be touched for several years. This move would mark the government's first effort to curb the take-home pay of managers from auto executives to financial traders. Mr. Feinberg is expected to issue by mid-October his determination on compensation packages for 175 of the most-highly compensated executives and employees at the seven firms he oversees. The companies are: American International Group Inc., Bank of America Corp., Citigroup Inc., General Motors Co., GMAC Financial Services Inc., Chrysler LLC and Chrysler Financial. Wall Street Journal.

October 2. American nonfarm payroll **employment** continued to decline in September, losing 263,000 jobs, and the unemployment rate rose from 9.4% in July to 9.7% in August, and now to 9.8% in September, the U.S. Bureau of Labor Statistics reported. The largest job losses were in construction, manufacturing, retail trade, and government. Since the start of the recession in December 2007, the number of unemployed persons has increased by 7.6 million to 15.1 million, and the unemployment rate has doubled to 9.8%. Though the job market continued to worsen, the pace of deterioration remained markedly slower than earlier in the year, when roughly 700,000 jobs a month were disappearing. U.S. Bureau of Labor Statistics, New York Times.

October 1. International Monetary Fund (IMF) releases its World Economic Outlook (WEO). Key WEO projections include: World growth. After contracting by about 1% in 2009, global activity is forecast to expand by about 3% in 2010 (see table). Advanced economies are projected to expand sluggishly through much of 2010. Average annual growth in 2010 will be only modestly positive at about 11/4, following a contraction of 31/2% during 2009. Emerging and developing economies. Real GDP growth is forecast to reach 5 percent in 2010, up from 13/4% in 2009. The rebound is driven by China, India, and a number of other emerging Asian countries. Economies in Africa and the Middle East are also expected to post solid growth of close to 4%, helped by recovering commodity prices.

September 28. According to an **IMF staff study** of 15 emerging market countries with IMF- supported programs, recent IMF programs in these countries are delivering the support needed to help these countries weather the worst of the global financial crisis, through increased resources, supportive policies, and more focused conditionality. "What this study tells us is that, with IMF support, many of the severe disruptions characteristic of past crises have so far been either avoided or sharply reduced," IMF Managing Director Dominique Strauss-Kahn said. The study finds that support from the IMF has enabled countries to lessen the effects of the crisis by avoiding currency overshooting and bank runs—traits of past crises. At a time when capital flows were severely curtailed, the IMF provided large-scale financial assistance to countries in need. The IMF has sharply increased the resources it has available to lend, from about $250 billion to $750 billion, following pledges made by the Group of Twenty leading emerging and advanced economies after the London Summit in April 2008. As part of its efforts to support countries during the global economic crisis, the IMF also conducted a major overhaul of how it lends money by offering higher loan amounts and tailoring loan terms to countries' circumstances. The IMF has been instrumental in bringing down borrowing costs for emerging markets that had spiked following the bankruptcy of Lehman Brothers.

Latest IMF projections

(year over year percent change)

	2007	2008	Projections 2009	2010	Difference from July 2009 WEO projections 2009	2010
World output	5.2	3.0	-1.1	3.1	0.3	0.6
Advanced economies	2.7	0.6	-3.4	1.3	0.4	0.7
United States	2.1	0.4	-2.7	1.5	-0.1	0.7
Euro area	2.7	0.7	-4.2	0.3	0.6	0.6
Germany	2.5	1.2	-5.3	0.3	0.9	0.9
France	2.3	0.3	-2.4	0.9	0.6	0.5
Italy	1.6	-1.0	-5.1	0.2	0.0	0.3
Spain	3.6	0.9	-3.8	-0.7	0.2	0.1
Japan	2.3	-0.7	-5.4	1.7	0.6	0.0
United Kingdom	2.6	0.7	-4.4	0.9	-0.2	0.7
Canada	2.5	0.4	-2.5	2.1	-0.2	0.5
Other advanced economies	4.7	1.6	-2.1	2.6	1.8	1.6
Newly industrialized Asian economies	5.7	1.5	-2.4	3.6	2.8	2.2
Emerging market and developing economies	8.3	6.0	1.7	5.1	0.2	0.4
Africa	6.3	5.2	1.7	4.0	-0.1	-0.1
Sub-Saharan Africa	7.0	5.5	1.3	4.1	-0.2	0.0
Central and eastern Europe	5.5	3.0	-5.0	1.8	0.0	0.8
Commonwealth of Independent States	8.6	5.5	-6.7	2.1	-0.9	0.1
Russia	8.1	5.6	-7.5	1.5	-1.0	0.0
Excluding Russia	9.9	5.4	-4.7	3.6	-0.8	0.4
Developing Asia	10.6	7.6	6.2	7.3	0.7	0.3
China	13.0	9.0	8.5	9.0	1.0	0.5
India	9.4	7.3	5.4	6.4	0.0	-0.1
ASEAN-5¹	6.3	4.8	0.7	4.0	1.0	0.3
Middle East	6.2	5.4	2.0	4.2	0.0	0.5
Western Hemisphere	5.7	4.2	-2.5	2.9	0.1	0.6
Brazil	5.7	5.1	-0.7	3.5	0.6	1.0
Mexico	3.3	1.3	-7.3	3.3	0.0	0.3

Visit the World Economic Outlook on the internet at http://www.imf.org/external/pubs/ft/weo/2009/02/index.htm.

September 28. World Trade Organization, WTO, Director-General Pascal Lamy, in his address to the WTO Public Forum, said the **G20 must now "walk the talk" on Doha** (multilateral trade negotiations). He stated that G20 leaders at their Pittsburgh Summit agreed that "their negotiators now embark on the work programs that we have established for the next three months, and that they then assess our collective ability to achieve our 2010 target". World Trade Organization.

September 24-25. G20 Pittsburgh summit. The leaders of the Group of Twenty (G20) met in Pittsburgh to "turn a page on the era of irresponsibility" by adopting reforms to "meet the needs of the 21st century economy." The final communiqué pledged

- not to withdraw stimulus measures until a durable recovery is in place;
- to co-ordinate their exit strategies, while also acknowledging that timing will vary from country to country depending on the forcefulness of measures in place;
- for macroeconomic policies to be harmonized to avoid imbalances—America's spendthrift ways and deficits; Asia's savings glut—that made the financial crisis so much worse;

- for the G20 to replace the narrower, Western-dominated G8 as the primary global economic facilitator, providing China, India and Brazil a permanent seat at the table. In return, it is hoped that they will be more flexible in other areas, such as climate change and trade;
- for the G20 to eliminate subsidies on fossil fuels, but only "in the medium term"; and
- for trade, a weak commitment to get the Doha round back on track by next year.

The governance structure of the rejuvenated IMF also is to change with "under-represented," mostly developing, countries getting at least 5% more of the voting rights by 2011. The **Financial Stability Board (FSB)**, a group of central bankers and financial regulators, also was broadened to include the big developing countries, and from now on it is to take a lead role in coordinating and monitoring tougher financial regulations and serve, along with the IMF, as an early-warning system for emerging risks. The FSB is to help ensure that the rules governing big banks are commensurate with the cost of their failure. The main tool for this could be higher capital requirements. All agree that banks need more capital and that a greater share of it should be pure equity, the strongest buffer against loss. The G20 communiqué also supported forcing banks to hold especially high levels of capital in good times so they are better prepared to ride out the bad—though it did not endorse an American proposal for big banks to hold more than smaller ones. The G20 has set a deadline of the end of 2012 for new standards to be adopted, with exact figures to be decided by the end of 2010.

France and Germany had pushed hard for firm numerical limits on bonuses as a proportion of revenues or capital. The communiqué was closer to the Americans' position to tie bankers' pay more closely to long-term value creation—more paid in restricted shares, with employers able to claw back a portion if trades lead to big losses and multi-year bonus guarantees to be avoided. The Economist.

September 25. Why did **hedge funds**, supposedly the bad boys of the financial world, come through last year's crisis in relatively **good shape**? HedgeFund Intelligence data shows that U.S.- based funds suffered an average loss of 12.7% in 2008. That's nothing like the 38.5% decline for the Standard & Poor's 500. Losses for banks were much higher still. Some hedge funds got pounded because they made bad bets or because investors decided to pull out their money. Nearly 500 funds disappeared last year, according to HedgeFund Intelligence, but that's out of a universe of roughly 7,000. The salvation of the hedge fund industry was that its existential crisis came 10 years earlier, with the 1998 implosion of Long-Term Capital Management. After that fund went down, the hedge funds' lenders got nervous and tightened their standards. As a result, in the past decade the supposedly go-go hedge funds were actually less leveraged than many banks.

To see how the borrowing mania hit banking, look at confidential numbers for big Swiss banks, once renowned for their caution. Debt ratios at the two largest banks rose in the past dozen years from 90% to 97%—meaning that they had 97 Swiss francs of borrowed money for every three francs of capital. In the banks' trading accounts, the use of borrowed money was even greater. One study calculated that by 2006, the traders at big Swiss banks were borrowing 400 times their capital—which was about 100 times as high as the leverage ratio of a typical hedge fund. Washington Post.

September 24. The Shared National Credit Program (SNC) 2009 Review, an annual inter-agency report, stated that **U.S. credit quality deteriorated** to record levels with respect to large loans and loan commitments. The report says that the level of losses from syndicated loans facing banks and other financial institutions tripled to $53 billion in 2009, due to poor underwriting standards and the continuing weakness in economic conditions. According to the report, classified assets rated 'special mention', 'substandard', 'doubtful' and 'loss', touched $642 billion, representing 22.3% of the SNC portfolio, compared with 13.4% a year ago. The report also said foreign banks held about 38% of the $2.9 trillion in loans, while hedge funds, pension funds, insurance companies and other entities held about 21%. The report also said that non-banks continued to hold a "disproportionate share" of classified assets compared with their total share of the SNC portfolio. They hold 47% of loans seen as 'substandard', 'doubtful' and 'loss'. The SNC review is prepared by the Federal Reserve Board of Governors, Federal Deposit Insurance Corp (FDIC), Office of the Comptroller of the Currency (OCC), and the Office of Thrift Supervision (OTS). Reuters.

September 24. The U.S. National Association of Realtors reported **sales of existing U.S. homes fell** a seasonally adjusted 2.7% **in August** following four months of increasing sales. Economists said it was too soon to say whether the drop represented a hiccup in the market or a sign of deeper problems for the housing market. In August, median home prices across the country fell by nearly $4,000, to $177,700, and were down 12.5% from a year earlier. New York Times.

September 24. Former Federal Reserve chairman **Paul Volcker** testified before the House Financial Services Committee that the Obama administration's proposed overhaul of financial rules would preserve the policy of "too big to fail" and could lead to future banking bailouts. He endorsed a **stricter separation between banks that hold deposits and investment banks**. He said the "safety net" should be limited clearly to commercial banks, while investment banks should be excluded. He urged lawmakers to make clear that nonbank companies would not be saved with federal money. Mr. Volcker said he did not differ with the administration on most of its proposals and that he took "as a given" that banks would be bailed out in times of crisis. But he said he opposed bailouts of insurance companies like the American International Group, the automakers' finance arms and others. "The safety net has been extended outside the banking system," Mr. Volcker said. "That's what I want to change." New York Times.

September 24. China has been an essential player in **fostering global economic recovery**. As one of the first countries to announce a massive stimulus package last November, China brought increased stability to markets when it was needed. Today's conventional wisdom holds that in order to ensure a stable global recovery, Chinese consumers must increase their consumption patterns to fill the economic void left by their battered American counterparts. In regards to stimulating domestic consumption, assertions that the Chinese aren't spending enough may be overblown. For example, Morgan Stanley released a report last week arguing that China's under-consumption is over-stated, and that Chinese consumption is likely to increase. This week, China took two steps towards assuming a greater international leadership role in putting the global economy back on its feet. First, Hu Xiaolian, deputy governor of China's central bank, proposed the formation of a multinational sovereign wealth fund to assist developing countries gain access to capital. Second, in a speech to the U.N. yesterday, Chinese president Hu Jintao announced that China will take an active role in providing assistance to the developed economies most hit by the crisis. The English-language China Daily reports: that China will increase support for those hit hard by the global financial crisis, earnestly implement relevant capital increase and financing plans, intensify trade and investment cooperation and help raise their capacity for risk-resistance and sustainable development. Crisis Talk (World Bank).

September 24. The McKinsey Global Institute in its sixth annual survey of the world's capital markets says that the **mature financial markets** of North America, Europe and Japan may have reached an "inflection point," beyond which their **growth** will be much slower than the breakneck expansion of the past two decades. In emerging markets, though, they still see plenty of room to grow. The report estimates that the total value of global financial assets—including stocks, bonds, government debt and bank deposits—fell by $16 trillion in 2008, the largest setback since at least 1990. Financial globalization also took a big hit, as total global capital flows fell to $1.9 trillion in 2008, down 82% from 2007. Among developed nations, the shrinkage of financial markets was particularly pronounced. The total value of U.S. financial assets declined $5.5 trillion in 2008 to $54.9 trillion, putting an end to a two-decade run during which the value of the U.S. financial markets, expressed as a percentage of the country's annual economic output, grew more than twice as much as it did in the previous 80 years.

In Russia, the total value of financial assets stood at only 68% of gross domestic product as of the end of 2008, compared to nearly 4 times GDP in the U.S. The ratio of financial assets to GDP for all of Eastern Europe was 99%, for Latin America 119%, for India 162%, and for emerging Asia 232%. Wall Street Journal. Real Time Economics.

September 24. In preparation for the Pittsburgh G20 meeting, U.S. negotiators propose to press Group-of-20 world leaders to raise the stakes in the Doha Development Agenda negotiations by directing their negotiators to start identifying the "gaps" in the still incomplete modalities texts in agriculture, nonagricultural market access and services. The fate of the Doha agreement would largely depend on two major players—the United States and China, commented one envoy. He argued that if there is an agreement between the two members, others—including India, Brazil, and South Africa—will follow.

Brazil is considering hosting another Group-of-20 trade ministerial summit November 28 and 29 near Geneva for what trade diplomats describe as a crucial final attempt to increase pressure on key members to enter into hard bargaining on the few issues left in Doha negotiations on agriculture and market-opening for industrial goods. The ministerial reportedly will take place just before the scheduled biennial meeting of the World Trade Organization on November 30. Washington Trade Daily.

September 23. Representative Barney Frank, of Massachusetts announced a plan that preserved the core of the White House's proposal for a new **U.S. consumer financial protection agency**, while jettisoning a smaller though symbolically significant provision. The agency's core mission would be to protect consumers from deceptive or abusive credit cards, mortgages and other loans. Mr. Frank also announced an ambitious schedule to complete the

House's work on the legislation over the next two months. The Obama administration embraced the changes. New York Times.

September 23. Switzerland and the United States have signed a treaty to increase the amount of **tax information** they share to help crack down on tax evasion, Swiss officials said Wednesday. The agreement follows a model set out by the Paris-based Organization for Economic Cooperation and Development, OECD, designed to make it harder for taxpayers to hide money in offshore tax havens. U.S. tax authorities will be able to request information on Americans suspected of concealing Swiss bank accounts, the Swiss Finance Ministry said. Associated Press.

September 23. The United Steelworkers union filed a new **petition asking for U.S. duties on coated paper from both China and Indonesia.** The steelworkers union is joined in its latest trade case by paper manufacturers NewPage Corp of Miamisburg, Ohio; Appleton Coated LLC of Kimberly, Wisconsin; and Sappi Fine Paper North America of Boston, Massachusetts, which together employ about 6,000 union workers at paper mills in nine states. "Neither the companies nor the union will tolerate being obliterated without asking our government to investigate and enforce the rules of fair trade," Steelworkers President Leo Gerard said in a statement. Reuters.

September 22. The United States wants world leaders to agree this week to launch a major rethink of the world economy in November as they try to strengthen the global economy after its near meltdown, Reuters news service reported. Documents outlining the **U.S. position** ahead of the September 24-25 Pittsburgh **summit of Group of 20, G20,** leaders said exporters, which include China, Germany and Japan, should consume more, while debtors like the United States must boost savings.

"The world will face anemic growth if adjustments in one part of the global economy are not matched by offsetting adjustments in other parts of the global economy," said the document obtained by Reuters.

President Obama, cutting through the coded diplomatic courtesies, made the case more bluntly for a change in business as usual. "We can't go back to the era where the Chinese or Germans or other countries just are selling everything to us, we're taking out a bunch of credit card debt or home equity loans, but we're not selling anything to them," he said on September 20.

European Central Bank President Jean-Claude Trichet said on September 21 that persuading Europe, the United States and China to accept International Monetary Fund advice on economic polices may be difficult. G7 sources told Reuters there was a renewed determination to act to stem the global imbalances because the crisis had underlined the interconnectedness of the financial system and how joint action could be more effective.

China has long been the target of calls from the West to get its massive population to spend more. It may be reluctant to offer a significant change in economic policy when Chinese President Hu Jintao meets Obama this week. Washington Trade Daily.

September 16. Reports on industrial production and consumer prices today showed the **U.S. economy** is emerging from the economic slump without spurring inflation. Output at factories, mines, and utilities climbed 0.8% last month, exceeding the median estimate of economists surveyed by Bloomberg News, data from the Federal Reserve in Washington showed. The Fed revised July's increase up to 1% from the previously reported 0.5%. The back-to- back gain was the biggest since late 2005. The Labor Department said the cost of living climbed 0.4%, and was down 1.5% from August 2008. Another report today showed an index of homebuilder confidence climbed in September for a third consecutive month. The National Association of Home Builders/Wells Fargo's measure climbed to 19, the highest level since May 2008, from 18 in August, the Washington-based group said. A reading below 50 means most respondents view conditions as poor. Bloomberg.com.

September 16. **Japan**'s parliament named **Yukio Hatoyama** as the country's **new Prime Minister**, a move that formalizes the first change of government by a political party with a solid majority for over half a century. Mr. Hatoyama is president of the center-left Democratic Party of Japan, DPJ. He told a news conference after his appointment, "History has not changed yet. Whether history will really change will hinge on our future works." The DPJ's rise to power marks the end of the Liberal Democratic Party's, LDP 's, almost unbroken rule since 1955. Although the LDP helped to engineer Japan's economic revival in the post-war era, the party has not had the same success in reviving the country's economy following the bursting of an asset bubble in the early 1990s. The LDP also become mired in a number of financial scandals that chipped away at voter trust. The DPJ hopes to steer the economy back to prosperity while restoring trust in politics. Hatoyama's coalition government, with its two junior partners the Social Democratic Party and the People's New Party, is expected to try to boost domestic demand by giving money to families with children, cutting highway tolls and gasoline taxes and offering increased aid to the unemployed. Wall Street Journal.

September 16. New York Attorney General Andrew **Cuomo subpoenaed** five members of **Bank of America** Corp.'s board of directors amid a probe of the bank's purchase of Merrill Lynch & Co., said a person close to the investigation. The board members will be asked to testify under oath, the person said. The Wall Street Journal reported on its website today the five directors are Thomas May, chief executive officer of NStar; William Barnet III, a Spartanburg, South Carolina, developer; retired Morehouse College President Walter Massey; Boston investment firm owner John Collins; and retired Army General Tommy Franks. The bank will "cooperate with the attorney general's office as we maintain that there is no basis for charges against either the company or individual members of the management team," according to a statement by the Charlotte, North Carolina-based Bank of America. The subpoenas reflect continuing pressure on bank Chief Executive Officer Kenneth Lewis after U.S. District Judge Jed Rakoff in New York this week refused to accept a settlement between the bank and the Securities and Exchange Commission. The $33 million agreement would have resolved the SEC's claim that the bank deceived investors in November about bonuses to be paid to executives at Merrill Lynch & Co. Bank of America bought Merrill in January. Bloomberg.com.

September 16. Investors turned the most bearish on the **U.S. dollar** in 18 months as signs of a recovery in the global economy reduced demand for the currency as a refuge, a survey of Bloomberg users showed. The world's main reserve currency will fall and Treasury yields will rise over the next six months, according to 1,851 respondents in the Bloomberg

Professional Global Confidence Index. Sentiment toward the greenback fell to 30.8 in September, from 38.8 in August, according to the survey. The reading is the lowest since it dropped to 30.3 in March 2008, and has tumbled from a high of 68.86 a year ago. The measure is a diffusion index, meaning a reading below 50 indicates Bloomberg users expect the dollar to weaken. Bloomberg.com.

September 16. When the U.S. Congress passed an $8,000 **tax credit for first-time home buyers** last winter, it was intended as shock therapy during a crisis. Now the question is becoming whether the housing market can function without it. As many as 40% of all home buyers this year will qualify for the credit. It is on track to cost the government $15 billion, more than twice the amount that was projected when Congress passed the stimulus bill in February. New York Times.

September 15. The heads of the Organization for Economic Cooperation and Development, OECD, the United Nations Conference on Trade and Development, UNCTAD, and the World Trade Organization, WTO, have drafted a **joint report to G-20 leaders** meeting in Pittsburgh later this month concerning **protectionist acts** by G-20 nations. The report states that G-20 and advanced developing countries have refrained from extensive use of restrictive trade and investment measures in recent months but have continued – "in a limited way" – to apply tariffs and non-tariff instruments that have hindered trade flows. The report also said that trade rules and investment agreements have prevented wide-scale protectionist policies. But tariffs, nontariff measures, subsidies and burdensome administrative procedures regarding imports have been applied in recent months and have acted as "sand in the gears of international trade that may retard the global recovery," the report said. "It is urgent that governments start planning a coordinated exit strategy that will eliminate these elements as soon as possible," the statement continued. Washington Trade Daily.

September 15. One year ago, Lehman Brothers filed for bankruptcy, triggering the most acute phase of the financial crisis. The precipitating cause of Lehman's demise was a decision—by Treasury Secretary Henry Paulson, Federal Chairman Ben Bernanke and New York Fed President Timothy Geithner—to send a message. Paulson is quoted in David Wessel's "In Fed We Trust" as saying: "I'm being called Mr. Bailout. I can't do it again." Geithner, for his part, was more circumspect, saying, "There is no political will for a **federal bailout**." This made sense on the surface. Not only is it questionable public policy to use taxpayer money to bail out private companies, but, more important, it creates a **moral hazard**: the incentive for those companies to take excessive risks with the knowledge that the government will save them should things go wrong. The plan backfired. The chaos that ensued forced the government to step in to protect almost every financial instrument involved in the credit markets, from money market funds to commercial paper to asset-backed securities, and to ride to the rescue of some of America's largest banks. In the process, the government created moral hazard on an epic scale, transforming a vague expectation that certain financial institutions were "too big to fail" into a virtual government guarantee. Moral hazard had at least three aspects:

Bank employees and managers had asymmetric compensation structures. In good years, they stood to make huge amounts of money; in bad years, even if the bank lost money, they would still make healthy sums. This gave employees the incentive to take excessive risks because they could shift their potential losses to shareholders.

Shareholders had the same payoff structure. Banks are highly leveraged institutions; every dollar contributed by shareholders is magnified by 10 to 30 dollars from creditors. This meant that in good years, shareholders benefited from profits magnified by leverage, but should things go wrong, they could shift their potential losses to creditors. As a result, paying bank executives in stock did not mitigate their behavior; in fact, the most senior executives at both Bear Stearns and Lehman had and lost enormous amounts of money tied up in their companies.

Creditors had only limited incentives to watch over major banks. Ordinarily, creditors should demand high interest rates on loans to highly leveraged institutions. However, the expectation that large banks would not be allowed to fail made creditors more willing to lend to them. Washington Post.

September 14. President Obama sternly admonished the financial industry and lawmakers to accept his proposals to reshape **financial regulation** to protect the nation from a repeat of the excesses that drove Lehman Brothers into bankruptcy and wreaked havoc on the global economy last year. But with the markets slowly healing, Mr. Obama's plan to revamp financial rules faces a diminishing political imperative. Disenchantment by many Americans with big government, along with growing obstacles from financial industry lobbyists pressing Congress not to do anything drastic, have also helped to stall his proposals. Big institutions and community banks have unified against a central provision of the plan to create a **new consumer finance protection agency**. Lawmakers, particularly in the Senate but also in the House, have been skeptical of a second major plank that would give the **Federal Reserve more explicit authority** to monitor the markets for systemwide problems. Opponents prefer an enlarged role for a council of regulators. The Obama plan creates such a council, but makes the Fed the first among equals and acknowledges, as the Treasury secretary, Timothy F. Geithner, has said, that you cannot put out a fire by committee. New York Times.

September 14. Euro zone industrial output fell in July and **employment** dropped again in the second quarter, pointing to continued weakness in the economy despite signs that euro zone recession may be ending. Industrial output in the 16 countries using the euro fell 0.3% month on month in July for a 15.9% year-on-year fall, the European Union's statistics office Eurostat said on Monday. The annual numbers showed clearly the contractions in output are becoming smaller. In June, production was 16.7% lower than a year earlier and in May it was 17.6%, better than the 21.3% in April. Eurostat also said employment in the euro zone fell 0.5% in the second quarter against the previous three months, and was 1.8% lower than the year before. This points to continued weakness of the labor market, as companies scale down production capacity because of weak demand. Economists say that more people without jobs mean less demand in the economy and therefore a slower recovery. Reuters.

September 14. U.S. President Barack Obama announced on September 11 that he will impose **duties** of 35% on $1.8 billion of **automobile tires from China**. Then on September 14 the President defended his decision, saying he was simply enforcing a trade agreement and not resorting to protectionism. His decision sparked a complaint by China to the World Trade

Organization. China also said it will begin dumping and subsidy probes of chicken and auto products from the United States. Bloomberg.com, Washington Trade Daily.

September 11. U.S. poverty increased, **median household income** fell, and the percentage of Americans with **employer-based health coverage** continued to decline in 2008, according to Census data for 2008 issued today. The figures reflect the initial effects of the recession. Median household income declined 3.6% in 2008 after adjusting for inflation, the largest single-year decline on record, and reached its lowest point since 1997. The poverty rate rose to 13.2%, its highest level since 1997. The number of people in poverty hit 39.8 million, the highest level since 1960. These data include only the early months of the recession. Poverty is expected to rise more in 2009 but would be worse without the Recovery Act. Though the increases in poverty in 2009 are likely to be large, they would have been much greater without the economic recovery legislation. A Center analysis issued on September 9 that examines the effects of seven Recovery Act provisions finds those provisions will keep an estimated 6.2 million Americans—including 2.4 million children—from falling into poverty and will reduce the severity of poverty for 33 million others. Economist's View.

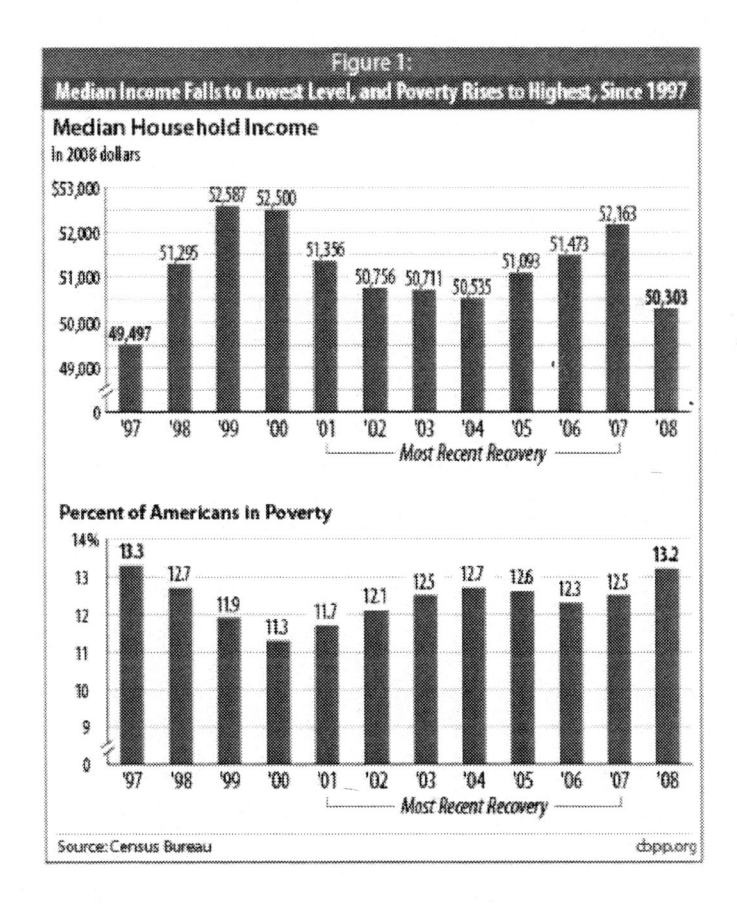

Figure 1:
Median Income Falls to Lowest Level, and Poverty Rises to Highest, Since 1997

Median Household Income
In 2008 dollars

Year	Income
'97	49,497
'98	51,295
'99	52,587
'00	52,500
'01	51,356
'02	50,756
'03	50,711
'04	50,535
'05	51,093
'06	51,473
'07	52,163
'08	50,303

Most Recent Recovery

Percent of Americans in Poverty

Year	Percent
'97	13.3
'98	12.7
'99	11.9
'00	11.3
'01	11.7
'02	12.1
'03	12.5
'04	12.7
'05	12.6
'06	12.3
'07	12.5
'08	13.2

Most Recent Recovery

Source: Census Bureau   cbpp.org

September 11. The U.S. government is concerned about overall **demand for U.S. Treasury securities**, not appetite from individual countries, said David Dollar, the U.S. Treasury Department's economic and financial emissary to China. "The interest rate on long-term treasury bonds is at a very low level by historical standards," Dollar said. "That says that the market has confidence the U.S. will get the fiscal problem under control." Chinese Premier Wen Jiabao said in March that the Asian nation was "worried" about the safety of its investment in U.S. debt, as a weakening dollar erodes the value of its record U.S. $2.1 trillion of foreign-exchange reserves.

President Barack Obama is relying on China to sustain buying of Treasuries amid record amounts of debt sales to fund a $787 billion stimulus spending package. Treasuries of all maturities have lost 2.8% so far this year, after returning 14% in 2008, indexes from Merrill Lynch & Co. show. The Dollar Index, which tracks the greenback against the currencies of six major U.S. trading partners, fell September 11 to its lowest level since September, 2008. Chinese investors have doubled their holdings of U.S. government bonds in the past three years to $776 billion as of June, according to Treasury data. Diversification of currency reserves by China "makes some sense" due to their huge scale, said Dollar, who was formerly the World Bank's country director for China and Mongolia and was named emissary to China in June. "It is healthy to have a variety of different reserve-type of currencies," he said. Bloomberg.com.

September 11. General Motors is hoping to jump-start its revitalization by guaranteeing car buyers that if they don't like their new Chevrolet, GMC, Buick or Cadillac, they have 60 days to bring it back for a **full refund**. Associated Press.

September 11. The People's Republic of **China** announced that it has developed its own large- body **jetliner**. The government-owned Commercial Aircraft Corp. of China, or Comac, unveiled a model of the C9 19, whose fuel efficiency will challenge Boeing Co. and EADS Co.'s Airbus. Analysts say it's unlikely any of the world's airlines—including China's own domestic carriers— will ever want to buy one. This project began in 2007, when the State Council, China's Cabinet, first outlined plans to build a 150 seat regional jet to lessen the nation's dependence on Airbus and Boeing. The creation of Comac was approved in February 2007, and the new firm was given an initial investment of 19 billion yuan/U.S. $2.7 billion. Comac produced the C9 19, a narrow- body, single-aisle regional jet that will seat as many 200 passengers. A prototype is planned to take off five years from now. MarketWatch.

September 10. The U.S. is starting **to pare back its emergency support for banks** and financial markets, Treasury Secretary Tim Geithner declared, saying that the financial system no longer needed extensive government props. Almost a year since the collapse of Lehman Brothers triggered a financial panic that tipped the world into a deep recession, Secretary Geithner said it was time to move from crisis response to recovery. Banks have repaid more than $70 billion in emergency bail-out funds and Secretary Geithner said "we now estimate that banks will repay another $50 billion over the next 12 to 18 months." He also said, "we must continue reinforcing recovery until it is self-sustaining and led by private demand." Financial Times.

September 10. General Motors is expected to sell its **Saab** Co. subsidiary to Swedish sports car maker Koenigsegg Automotive AB and Beijing Automotive Industry Holdings Co. Ltd., China's fastest-growing carmaker. Beijing Automotive will take a minority stake in the team bidding for Saab and help the unprofitable GM division find opportunities to expand in China, the group said. Bloomberg.

September 9. China National Petroleum Corp., parent of the state-run oil and natural gas giant **PetroChina**, announced that it had received a low-interest $30 billion loan to finance overseas acquisitions—the latest sign that Beijing was deploying its vast cash reserves to ensure that its economy had the resources it needed to keep growing. The five-year loan from the China Development Bank, a state-run lender, serves a long-term strategy to protect growth and stability. This year, China has spent $12 billion on overseas oil and refining assets alone. The deals include the one that Athabasca Oil Sands announced late last month, in which PetroChina will acquire 60% in two oil sands projects in northeastern Alberta for $1.7 billion, with further plans to build a pipeline to the coast to transport crude to China. China's strategy has an eye on Australia.

On September 8, China Railway Materials closed deals to buy stakes in FerrAus and United Minerals, two miners of iron ore in Australia, while China Guangdong Nuclear Power agreed to acquire Energy Metals, a uranium explorer in the country. Half of Australia's iron ore exports are already exported to China's steel mills, and more than half its wool is exported to the mainland as well. New York Times.

September 9. China is stepping up efforts to internationalize its parochial currency, the **yuan or renminbi**. That's prompted concern about the future of the U.S. dollar, the dominant global currency for trade and investment. But just how far can China push others to use the yuan? One precedent for what China is doing with its currency is Japan, which also tried to broaden international use of the yen in earlier decades as its economy took on greater global heft. Tomo Kinoshita, an economist for Nomura, says Japan's experience with the yen could help predict how far China will get with the yuan, since the two economies are of similar size and share a heavy focus on exports. Japanese companies had definite success in convincing many of their trading partners to do business in the yen rather than the dollar – something that China is also now starting to look at. But the use of yen in trade eventually hit an upper limit: according to Nomura's figures, the share of Japan's exports that are settled in yen has been roughly stable for the past two decades, at 35% to 40% of the total. Similarly, Japan has paid for about 20% to 25% of its imports in yen for the last decade or so. Chinese exporters adjust their prices to match prevailing levels in their target markets—what's called pricing-to-market – to a similar degree as exporters from Japan and the Czech Republic. That level is typically associated with 20% to 30% of exports being priced in the exporter's currency, they say, based on comparative figures from other countries. So in the near term, an "upper bound" for the use of yuan in China's exports is likely to be about a third of total exports, the Hong Kong Monetary Authority paper concludes. Wall Street Journal. Real Time Economics.

September 9. The **World Bank** issued its annual ***Doing Business*** report, which ranks 183 economies on the ease of doing business by comparing quantitative measures of regulations of the life cycle of a small or medium-size enterprise. Regulations related to registering property, employing workers, dealing with construction permits, and paying taxes are measured. Getting electricity and worker protection were added to this year's metrics. In 2008-2009 more governments implemented regulatory reforms aimed at making it easier to do business than in any year since 2004, when *Doing Business* started to track reforms through its indicators. *Doing Business* recorded 287 such reforms in 131 economies between June 2008 and May 2009, 20% more than in the year before. The top slots are occupied by the usual suspects: Singapore, New Zealand, Hong Kong, United States, United Kingdom, and

Denmark are the easiest places to do business. Each country was in the top six last year. Indonesia is the top reformer of business regulations in the East Asia and Pacific region, but judicial reform is urgently needed to attract new investment. Reuters/Forbes and World Bank Crisis Talk.

September 8. Gold bullion surged as high as $1,009.70 in New York, within 3% of the record of $1,033.90 set in March 2008. Silver climbed to a 13-month high as a weaker dollar and concern that inflation may accelerate boosted the appeal of precious metals. Gold is headed for a ninth annual gain. Crude oil and all six industrial metals on the London Metal Exchange rallied as the U.S. Dollar Index fell as much as 1.2% to an 11-month low. Raw materials typically rise when the greenback falls. Equity indexes climbed from Tokyo to London and New York.

"The market thinks inflation is coming," Leonard Kaplan, the president of Prospector Asset Management in Evanston, Illinois, said by telephone. He has been trading gold for more than 30 years and believes gold won't stay above $1,000 for long. "With interest rates so low, money is chasing money and the dollar is getting murdered." Bloomberg.

September 8. Lawyers and tax advisers from London to Hong Kong have had a surge in inquiries from expatriate Americans worried about whether they have correctly declared **offshore assets** ahead of the September 23 deadline. Concerns have been fuelled by the Swiss government's decision to reveal the names of 4,450 wealthy Americans who hold offshore accounts at UBS, the country's biggest bank. Financial Times.

September 2. The U.S. Institute for Supply Management's survey of factories and industry had been edging higher this spring, as the blistering pace of economic declines began to level off. In August, the group's manufacturing index turned positive, rising to 52.9, from 48.9 in July. A reading above 50 indicates expansion and growth; a number below 50 means economic contraction. Four industry groups said their payrolls were growing while nine reported decreases. Manufacturing jobs have been devastated by the recession, with some two million positions lost since the downturn's official beginning in December 2007. New York Times.

September 2. European Union finance ministers will press for clearly defined restrictions on **bonus pay for bankers** when they hold talks with their U.S. and other G20 counterparts this month. "The bankers are partying like it's 1999, and it's 2009," said Anders Borg, finance minister of Sweden, which holds the EU's rotating presidency. "Obviously, there's a need for stronger muscles and sharper teeth. It won't be satisfactory for Europe to end up with broad principles and guidelines." Financial Times.

September 2. Senior **International Monetary Fund and World Bank** economists at a Washington panel discussion on Tuesday said the **world recovery** was starting to gain momentum, though a number of challenges remain. The IMF now expected the global economy to expand at slightly less than 3% in 2010, said Jörg Decressin, an IMF forecaster, a upward revision from the IMF's July estimate of 2.5%. "The recovery is for real but it is very heavily policy dependent," he said at a session at the Carnegie Endowment for International Peace. At some point, he said, private demand would have to replace the boost to the global economy from government monetary and fiscal expansion. Hans Timmer, a World Bank forecaster, didn't give an estimate, but said the strength of the recovery depends "on how sustainable the rebound in developing countries is." He especially cited the role of China in boosting global demand. Wall Street Journal's Real time Economics.

September 1. Nine of 10 **U.S. cities** are forced to **cut spending** as sales and income taxes decline reports the National League of Cities. Future prospects look grim with property taxes expected to drop in 2010 and 2011. To combat declining revenues, 62% of cities are delaying or canceling infrastructure projects, the study found. CNNMoney.com.

August 31. India's gross domestic product accelerated to 6.1% from a year earlier in the April- June quarter from 5.8% in the previous quarter as government spending helped to overcome the worst of the global downturn but drought threatens to stall the recovery. The worst effects of the global financial crisis may have passed for Asia's third-largest economy. India's relatively low dependence on exports meant that it weathered the global economic storm better than other countries. Associated Press.

August 31. The **Chinese** government has been struggling to find enough infrastructure projects to **finance in Sub-Saharan Africa**, according to the *Business Day*. The China-Africa Development Fund was founded in June 2007 after the 2006 Beijing Summit of the Forum on China-Africa Cooperation and established offices for the Southern African Development Community in Johannesburg, South Africa in March 2009. However, the fund is finding it increasingly challenging to fund infrastructure programs in most African states because of the "lack of essential facilities like sound telecommunications systems." IHS Global Insight.

August 31. Mauritius, Seychelles, Zimbabwe and Madagascar have signed an interim trade agreement with the **European Union** (EU). These **south-east African** economies have had full access to the European consumer market since 2008 (except for rice and sugar, with trade barriers being gradually removed). The countries have agreed to phase out tariffs on all European imported goods over the next 15 years. The agreement excludes trade on certain agricultural products, such as milk, meat, vegetables, textiles, footwear and clothing. Zambia and the Comoros have agreed to sign an interim agreement with the EU at a later date. The EU imports mostly textiles, clothes, sugar, fish products and copper from Eastern and Southern Africa, while European exports to the region consist mostly of mechanical and electrical machinery and vehicles. IHS Global Insight.

August 31. The **Croatia**n central budget in January–May 2009 posted a deficit of 4.5 53 billion kuna/U.S. $810 million. The gap was a sharp, negative turnaround from the same period of 2008, when the budget had been in surplus by 3.936 billion kuna/U.S. $824 million. Over the first five months of 2009, budgetary revenues declined 8.6% year on year, undermined by a sharp decline in economic activity, which caused tax revenues to fall 17.8% year on year. Meanwhile, government expenditures grew at an annual rate of increase of 9.3%. Croatia remains on track to post a deficit for the year as a whole of less than 4% of GDP, quite manageable in comparison to other economies of the region in 2009. IHS Global Insight.

August 28. The **International Monetary Fund** implemented a **general allocation** of Special Drawing Rights, **SDRs**, equivalent to about U.S. $250 billion. This was the allocation initially requested at the G-20 meeting this spring in London. It was formally approved by the IMF's Board of Governors on August 7, and is designed to provide more global liquidity to the world economy by supplementing IMF members' foreign exchange reserves. It represents a quick multilateral response to the world financial crisis. Nearly $100 billion of this $250 billion will go to emerging markets and developing countries, and over $18 billion to low-income countries. This general allocation is made in proportion to members' existing quotas and will count immediately toward their reserves. Member nations can either hold them in their reserves or sell all or part of their allocations to others in order to finance immediate hard currency imports. It is also possible to buy SDRs from another member. Separately, the IMF will implement, on September 9, a special, one-time allocation of 21.5 billion SDRs, about U.S. $33 billion. This allocation, which is sometimes called the Fourth Amendment Allocation because it required an amendment to the Fund's Articles of Agreement, will mean that every member country has an SDR allocation. IMF Press Briefing.

August 28. The **IMF** Executive Board completed the first review of the **Latvia**n program. This enabled immediate disbursement of about €195.2 million/U.S. $278.5 million, bringing the level of total disbursements from the IMF under the stand-by arrangement to €780.7 million/U.S. $1.2 billion. IMF support for Latvia is part of a coordinated package together with the European Union, the World Bank, Nordic countries and other program partners. The program was originally approved in December 2008. Latvia's economic strategy is centered around keeping the exchange rate peg and achieving euro adoption as soon as possible. The very dramatic economic downturn over the last few months required program revision. The most important is that the fiscal deficit ceiling has been revised upward to up to 13% from the original target of 5%. This allows for 1% of GDP in additional resources for social safety nets. IMF.

August 28. Toyota will shut down the joint venture it operated with **General Motors** in Fremont, California, in March 2010, eliminating 4,700 jobs. The plant, which makes Corolla compact cars and Tacoma pickups for Toyota and, until last week, Pontiac Vibe hatchbacks for GM, was the Japanese company's only U.S. auto plant with a union workforce. Sagging sales and GM's bankruptcy are blamed. Los Angeles Times.

August 28. The inspector general of the **U.S. Securities and Exchange Commission** said in a report that the SEC has "historically been slow to act" in regulating the nation's credit ratings agencies before the financial crisis and recommended a broad range of improvements to the SEC's oversight. The report also called for further evaluation of several controversial policies, such as the ability of debt issuers to shop among different rating agencies for the highest possible rating. The financial crisis raised serious questions about the rating agencies, including Moody's, Fitch and Standard and Poor's, which often gave top ratings to mortgage-backed securities that now may be worthless. The audit report found that the commission delayed adopting rules on the rating agencies, and sometimes failed to follow the rules that existed.

August 28. Iceland decided Friday to repay Britain and the Netherlands the $5.7 billion it borrowed to compensate savers in those countries who lost money in the collapse of an Icelandic Internet bank last year. The Icelandic government overcame heavy opposition to the compensation plan, securing backing from a majority of lawmakers by pledging to link the pace of debt repayment to the rate of growth in the island nation. Iceland will begin repaying £2.3 billion (U.S. $3.8 billion) to Britain and 1.3 billion euros ($1.9 billion) to the Netherlands from 2016, with payments spread over nine years. Iceland must settle the claims arising from the collapse of the Icesave online bank before it can draw on $4.6 billion in promised bailout funds from the International Monetary Fund and Nordic countries. Iceland was an early victim of the credit crunch, which sent its debt-fueled economy into a tailspin. Landsbanki collapsed in October, as did Glitnir and Kaupthing, the country's two other leading banks. New York Times.

August 27. U.S. Gross Domestic Product shrank at a seasonally adjusted 1% annual rate from April through June, unrevised from an estimate on second-quarter GDP a month ago. This was far less than the 6.4% decline experienced in the first quarter of 2009. Wall Street economists expected the second quarter revision to be a decline of 1.5%. Corporate earnings rose by the most in four years, the department also said. This means that the U.S. economy took a first step toward recovering from the worst recession since the 1930s in the second quarter as companies reduced inventories, spending started to climb and profits grew. Bloomberg, Wall Street Journal.

August 27. The Federal Deposit Insurance Corporation, FDIC, revealed that the number of **U.S. banks at risk** of failing reached 416 during the second quarter. The numbers were published as part of a broader survey on the nation's banking system. The number of institutions on the government's so-called "problem bank" list surpassed 400 in the latest quarter, climbing to its highest level in 15 years, since June 1994. The FDIC, which insures bank deposits, has been hit by a wave of relatively large and costly failures recently, prompting concerns about the size of the agency's insurance fund. The FDIC reported that the fund decreased by $2.6 billion, or 20%, during the quarter to $10.4 billion. The number of banks under scrutiny by regulators has moved steadily higher since the recession began in late 2007. A year ago, the number of banks on the FDIC's watch list was 117. At the end of this year's first quarter, the number stood at 305. CNNMoney.com.

August 27. The **U.S. banking system** will lose some 1,000 institutions over the next two years, said John Kanas, whose private equity firm bought BankUnited of Florida in May. "We've already lost 81 this year," Kanas told CNBC. "The numbers are climbing every day. Many of these institutions nobody's ever heard of. They're smaller companies." Failed banks tend to be smaller and private, which exacerbates the problem for small business borrowers, said Kanas, the former chairman and CEO of North Fork bank. "Government money has propped up the very large institutions as a result of the stimulus package," he said. "There's really very little lifeline available for the small institutions that are suffering." CNBC.com.

August 27. European companies are objecting against proposed reforms of the **derivatives** markets, saying that new rules requiring contracts to be routed through clearing houses could impose a huge drain on corporate cash. U.S. companies ranging from Caterpillar and Boeing to 3M – which use derivatives contracts to hedge interest rate, currency and commodity price risks – have been lobbying lawmakers to highlight the potential higher costs of a proposed overhaul of rules on derivatives. Financial Times.

August 26. Toyota Motor Corp, the world's largest automaker, said it would halt a production line in Japan as it cuts excess capacity to return to profitability amid an industrywide sales slump. Car plants around the world are idle or running below capacity as the industry copes with a slide in sales that sent General Motors Co and Chrysler Group LLC into bankruptcy and has Toyota headed for a record loss this year. Total cuts could reach 700,000 cars, or 7% of Toyota's global capacity. *Nikkei* business daily reported that Toyota planned to reduce its global capacity by 10%, or 1 million vehicles, as early as the current financial year to March 2010. Reuters.

August 26. Eighteen of the 20 cities tracked by Standard & Poor's Case-Shiller **U.S. Home Price Index** showed improvement in June, up from eight in May, four in April and only one in March. In a convincing sign that the worst housing slump of modern times is coming to an end, prices are starting to rise in nearly all of the nation's large cities. The trend, displayed in newly released data for June, is both pronounced and wide-ranging. It is affecting the high-priced coastal cities, with a 3.8% jump for the month in San Francisco and a 2.6% rise in Boston; the industrial Midwest, with Cleveland prices up 4.2%; and even the epicenter of the crash, the Sun Belt, with Phoenix homes up 1.1%. New York Times.

August 25. The White House Office of Management and Budget (OMB) now forecasts a $9 trillion **U.S. federal deficit** from 2010-1019. The Congressional Budget Office (CBO) in its *Budget and Economic Outlook: An Update*, http://www.cbo.org/ftpdocs/105xx/doc10521/08-25- BudgetUpdate.pdf, is more optimistic, projecting a 10-year budget deficit of $7.14 trillion. The Congressional Budget Office (CBO) estimates that the federal budget deficit for 2009 will total $1.6 trillion, which, at 11.2% of gross domestic product (GDP), will be the highest since World War II. That deficit figure results from a combination of weak revenues and elevated spending associated with the economic downturn and financial turmoil. The deficit has been boosted by various federal policies implemented in response, including the stimulus legislation and aid for the financial, housing, and automotive sectors. New American Foundation says the U.S. needs renewed economic growth—not austerity. That is the true lesson to be drawn from new government projections of long-term federal budget deficits. Congressional Budget Office, New American Foundation.

August 18. Israel emerges from recession with GDP growth of 1% in Q2, after two quarters of negative growth. Seasonally adjusted GDP rose at a 1% annual rate. The second quarter's growth was driven in large part by an increase in exports of goods and services which rose at a 5.8% annual rate. Excluding diamonds and start-up companies, exports rose at an even higher rate of 7.1%. IHS Global Insight.

August 18. U.S. industrial production increased by 0.5% in July, while manufacturing output rose by 1.0%. The industrial production report was good for the first time in almost a year and a half, with no hidden causes for concern. Total output of mines, utilities, and factories rose 0.5%, and would have been much better if electric utilities did not have to dial back output because of the milder-than-normal summer, pushing utility output down 2.4%. The motor vehicle industry provided the biggest upward push to output, and boosted the manufacturing sector to a 1.0% gain. The good showings were not confined to vehicles. Core manufacturing (excluding high technology and motor vehicles) recorded an output gain of 0.1%. While that seems tepid, this was only the second increase since March 2008; the other was a feeble bounce-back last October, when refining and chemicals were recovering from hurricane outages. The output gains lifted total capacity utilization to 68.5%, and the manufacturing operating rate to 65.4%. Both readings were noticeable improvements over June, but still 11–12 percentage points below a year ago. IHS Global Insight.

August 17. Demand for **U.S. Treasuries** grew in June, despite sales by China. Foreign investors bought $90.7 billion more in long-term U.S. securities than they sold in June. In May, foreign investors sold $19.4 billion more securities than they bought. China, the largest U.S. creditor, reduced its June U.S. Treasury holdings by $25.1 billion or 3.1% to $776.4 billion from May's $801.5 billion. China Daily reported the 3.1% decrease was the largest percentage cut in nine years. China's June holdings were still larger than April's $763.5 billion and $767.9 billion in March. Japan, the second largest holder of U.S. Treasuries, increased its holdings to $711.8 billion, up $34.6 billion from May. Britain, the third largest holder, held $214 billion in June, up $50.2 billion from May. UPI.com and Wall Street Journal's Real Time Economics.

August 17. Economists typically say every recession is different in its own way, but recoveries are all alike, driven by the **housing sector and consumer spending**. If so, this recovery may be on very shaky ground. Consumer spending, roughly 70% of economic activity, and housing, about 20% of GDP, have been hit with the equivalent of 100-year storms. "Is the consumer back in the game? No, not yet," says John J. Castellani, chief economist and president of the business roundtable. "When we look at our members who are tied to the housing market, they are nowhere near a recovery, while our [consumer products] companies are still moving to downscale." Between June 2007 and December 2008, for instance, inflation-adjusted personal wealth fell by 22.8%—the most since the Federal Reserve began collecting data almost 60 years ago. Some $6 trillion in housing wealth alone was lost in 2008. Consumer spending shrank for two consecutive quarters for the first time in half a century. "Consumers simply have to retrench, save more, spend less," says David Jones of DMJ Advisors. "That in itself will give us a much slower, longer and uneven recovery." CNBC.com.

August 17. Japan returned to growth in the second quarter, as gross domestic product expanded a seasonally adjusted 0.9% quarter on quarter between April and June. This follows a year of contraction, and is its first rise since the first quarter of 2008 and the equivalent of 3.7% growth on an annual basis. Economists warned that the recovery remained vulnerable to any faltering in export demand or tightening of the government's fiscal stimulus. Financial Times.

August 17. U.S. Banks and other financial institutions are lobbying against **fair-value accounting** for their asset holdings. They claim many of their assets are not impaired, that they intend to hold them to maturity anyway and that recent transaction prices reflect distressed sales into an illiquid market, not what the assets are actually worth. Legislatures and regulators support these arguments, preferring to conceal depressed asset prices rather than deal with the consequences of insolvent banks. This is not the way forward. While regulators and legislators are keen to find simple solutions to complex problems, allowing financial institutions to ignore market transactions is a bad idea. Financial Times.

August 17. Being in debt is about to get a lot more expensive for millions of Americans. Credit card issuers have been rushing to raise rates in advance of August 20, when the first provisions of the **U.S. Credit Card** Accountability Responsibility and Disclosure Act (CARD) will go into effect, with other protections starting in February 2010. Starting this week, card issuers need to give you more time to pay your bills. Also, instead of mailing bills 14 days before the due date, issuers must send bills 21 days in advance of the payment date. That will mean fewer people will get hit with late fees because of postal delays. Another provision effective this week requires card issuers to give you 45 days' notice when they plan to raise your rate, instead of the current 15-day advance notice. That's behind the rash of notifications sent in recent weeks, advising you that no matter what your credit history, you'll be paying higher rates. Next year's requirements include a ban on marketing to students or anyone under age 21. They'll be required to have a parent or guardian as a co-signer. Individual bankruptcies are up 36% for the first half of this year, compared with last year. And that translates into more defaults on card balances. Bank of America, the largest bank in the country, reported its default rate jumped to 13.8% in June from 12.5% in May. Other issuers such as JPMorgan Chase, Citigroup, Capitol One, Discover and American Express have reported default rates around the 10% level. Chicago Sun Times.

August 17. China attracted foreign direct investment of $5.36 billion in July, a 35.7% decline from a year earlier, according to data released Monday by the Ministry of Commerce. July's figures marked the tenth straight monthly decline, and far outpaced June's one-year drop of 6.8%. In the January-July period, foreign direct investment totaled $48.3 billion, a decrease of 20.3% from that period a year earlier. Dow Jones Newswires.

August 16. Nearly three years into the deepest **U.S.** housing slump in generations, lenders are modifying only a small number of **problem mortgages**, and rising foreclosures are restraining the economy's recovery. The Obama administration has stepped up pressure on lenders and their mortgage servicers, who act as bill collectors on behalf of investors who own mortgage bonds. The administration on August 4 unveiled the first of what will be monthly "name and shame" exercises, publishing data on the loan-modification efforts of about three dozen companies. The administration thinks that about 2.7 million U.S. homeowners are at least two months behind on their mortgage payments, roughly equal to the population of Kansas. Yet only 9% of eligible borrowers had been offered trial loan modifications through June. Borrowers from across the nation say they were encouraged, directly or indirectly, by their lenders to fall behind on their mortgage payments in order to qualify for loan modifications. The modifications never came. For example, 47% of South Florida homeowners are behind on mortgages. The U.S. mortgage lending industry reports in June 2009 it helped about 10% of eligible homeowners complete "workout plans" to stay in their homes. Of 3.1 million eligible homeowners, with loans 60 days or more past due,

310,000 completed plans. Of the 3.1 million eligible homeowners, 96,000, or 3%, received loan modifications. McClatchy Washington Bureau.

August 14. German GDP expanded 0.3% in the second quarter, the first increase since the first quarter of 2008. This represents a clear reversal from the 3.5% contraction in the first quarter, which was a post-reunification record low. Net exports boosted activity as imports fell more rapidly than exports, while consumer spending and housing investment also provided positive growth impulses. IHS Global Insight.

August 14. Hong Kong's economy grew by 3.3% on a seasonally adjusted quarter-to-quarter basis in the second quarter of 2009. The territory benefited from strong growth in mainland China and better conditions in the West, the government said Friday. Higher demand for Hong Kong's exports, particularly from mainland China, where massive stimulus spending and relaxed monetary policy is driving growth, helped explain the turnaround. Exports dropped 12.4% in the second quarter compared to the same period last year. Washington Post.

August 3. America's manufacturing base has not entirely vanished. Americans continue to make things. Manufacturing employment has shrunk considerably since peaking in the late 1970s, but this has largely been a product of productivity growth. America remains the world's largest manufacturer, responsible for 20% of global manufacturing. China's share is currently around 12%. This ratio has been moving steadily in favor of China, and it seems fairly clear that within a decade China's share will overtake America's. America, with 5% of the world's population, produces 20% of the world's manufactures; China, with 20% of the world's population produces 12% of the world manufactures. Developed nations tend to devote between 20% and 30% of employment to industry; China as a developing nation employs 50% of workers to industry. Free Exchange Economist.com.

July 31. China is spearheading the recovery in both the auto market and the global economy. Car sales in China accelerated to a 48% year on year surge in June, lifting purchases above an annualized 7.0 million units for the first time on record, and well above the 5.9 million unit peak reached in March 2008 prior to the sharp global economic downturn. Noteworthy, our data only include cars. If trucks and buses are included, vehicle purchases in China are on the way to exceed 10.5 million units this year and surpass the United States as the world's largest vehicle market.... Auto sales in China have been increasing rapidly since 2001, and this pace is expected to continue well into the next decade. General Motors might be well positioned to take advantage of this growth. GM—the top-selling brand in China—padded its lead this year, with first-half sales soaring 38% to 814,000 units—a level fast approaching the 948,000 vehicles it sold in the United States. As recently as 2004, GM sold roughly 10 vehicles in the United States for each model sold in China. Highlighting the importance of China in GM's revival strategy, the company expects to double its sales to 2 million units over the next five years, and plans to launch more than 30 new models in the country. Other automakers, including Nissan and Honda, also continue to expand their assembly facilities in China. Scotiabank. Global Auto Report.

July 31. French recession less severe but recovery tepid, IMF reports. The IMF projects French real GDP to drop by 3% in 2009, followed by a gradual recovery starting in 2010. France has been shielded from the worst effects of the crisis by its generous social safety net, which has protected domestic demand, and the country's limited reliance on exports, which has shielded it from the worst effects of falling global demand. Relatively rigid labor markets and high social protection are likely to slow the pace of recovery. Credit default swap spreads of French banks have increased considerably, but somewhat less than for other European banks. The relative resilience of French banks can be partly attributed to their conservative lending practices and to the consistent supervision of all lending institutions. The authorities also undertook a number of measures to recapitalize banks and support liquidity. This has resulted in no French bank coming under majority state ownership. Strong automatic stabilizers and appropriate fiscal stimulus measures have helped cushion the downturn in France. A fiscal stimulus package—worth more than 1 1/2 percent of GDP for 2009–10—contains measures that are mostly front loaded and relatively well diversified, with an emphasis on temporary investment expenditures and various tax breaks. IMF Survey Magazine, by Erik De Vrijer and Boriana Yontcheva.

July 31. U.S. real Gross Domestic Product declined 1.0% in the second quarter, much shallower than the 6.4% decline in the first quarter. These figures are consistent with a return to modest growth in the second half of 2009. However, revised historical data show that the recession has been deeper than previously thought and weak positive growth in the second half may not be sufficient to prevent employment from continuing to fall.

Major factors for U.S. second quarter GDP growth include:

- Business fixed investment and exports declined much less steeply than in the first quarter.
- Government spending bounced higher, probably in part due to the stimulus package, although the biggest contributor was a sharp rise in defense spending, often volatile.
- Inventories fell more sharply than in the first quarter, but were a smaller drag on growth.
- Foreign trade boosted growth as imports fell faster than exports. Some of the import decline reflects the big drop in inventories.
- Consumer spending fell 1.2%, after a small 0.6% increase in the first quarter.
- Inflation was near zero. The GDP price index rose 0.2%.

Historical revision reveals this recession to be deeper than previously thought. The decline in real GDP from its peak in the second quarter of 2008 stands at 3.9%, which is the most severe drop in postwar history. Real GDP rose just 0.4% in calendar 2008, rather than rising 1.1% as previously announced. Consumer spending declined 0.2% in calendar 2008, instead of rising 0.2% as previously announced. The saving rate in 2008 was 2.7%, rather than 1.8%. Previous years were also revised up. However, the saving rate for the first half of 2009 is lower than previously reported because personal incomes decreased more than previously thought, not good for future spending prospects. IHS Global Insight.

July 31. U.S. Treasury Secretary Timothy Geithner issued a stern warning to U.S. regulators to end turf battles and support President Obama's plan to overhaul financial regulation. Geithner told Federal Reserve Chairman Ben Bernanke, Securities and Exchange Commission Chairman Mary Schapiro, and Federal Deposit Insurance Corp. Chairman Sheila Bair to end public criticism and stop airing concerns over their potential loss of authority. A Treasury Department spokesman said the message to regulators was to work together to get reform done. Reuters.

July 8-10. The G8 Summit in Italy included a dialogue with five developing countries (Brazil, China, India, Mexico, and South Africa). The summit resulted in declarations or statements dealing with Responsible leadership for a sustainable future, Non Proliferation, Counter Terrorism, Promoting the global agenda, Energy and Climate, G8-Africa Partnership on Water and Sanitation, and Global Food Security. During the summit, on **July 9,** China pressed for new international exchange rules. China criticized the dominant role of the U.S. dollar as a global reserve currency and urged diversification of the reserve currency system aiming at relatively stable exchange rates among leading currencies. Chinese state councilor Dai Bingguo's remarks caused concern among western leaders, some of whom fear that even discussion of long-term currency issues could unsettle markets and undercut economic recovery. (G-8 Chair's Summary and *Financial Times*)

July 10. A **new General Motors** emerged from bankruptcy protection (filed for bankruptcy on June 1) as a leaner automaker and with 60.8% government ownership. The new company will include the Chevrolet, Cadillac, Buick, and GMC Brands, with its overseas operations. About 4,100 of its 6,000 U.S. dealerships will remain with the new company, while other dealerships will be shed over the next 14 months. The company will have only a fraction of the $54 billion in unsecured debt it previously held. Other holdings, contracts and liabilities that GM needed to divest as part of the bankruptcy process will be held by the old company, to be known as Motors Liquidation Co. (GMGMQ). The process of disposing of those assets and liabilities could take two to three years. These holdings include about 16 U.S. plants and facilities that employ about 20,000 workers. Some of the plants will stay open through 2012. The federal government will initially hold 60.8% of the stock in the new company, with a union-controlled health care trust fund owning 17.5%, the Canadian and Ontario governments owning 11.7% and bondholders of the old GM eventually getting about 10%. (CNNMoney.com)

July 10. Treasury Secretary Timothy Geithner **urged Congress** to **rein in** the $592 trillion **derivatives market** with new U.S. laws that are "difficult to evade." The complexity of over-the-counter derivatives contracts and industry growth let corporations take on excessive risk and caused a "very damaging wave of deleveraging" that exacerbated the global credit crisis, Geithner said in prepared testimony at a joint hearing of the House Agriculture and Financial Services committees. Geithner repeated the President's call to force "standardized" contracts onto exchanges or regulated trading platforms, and regulate all dealers. Contracts would be subject to new disclosure rules, and "conservative" capital and margin requirements, as well as business-conduct standards, would be imposed on market participants. The market, which grew almost seven-fold since 2000, complicated government efforts throughout the credit crisis to assess potential losses at U.S. banks and corporations because regulators lacked adequate data to measure their risk, Geithner said. (Bloomberg)

July 9. The **U.S. House of Representatives passed 111th Congress bill H.R. 3081** that contained H.Amdt. 311, a provision designed to overrule the President with respect to his signing statement of June 24, 2009. That Presidential statement rejected certain congressional conditions on the funding for the International Monetary Fund contained in 111th Congress bill H.R. 2346, The Supplemental Appropriations Act, 2009, P.L. 111-32. (CQ Today)

July 9. A report from the McKinsey Global Institute (MGI) found that big oil investors and Asia's central banks and sovereign wealth funds are poised to grow twice as fast as other institutional investors, underscoring how financial power is continuing to shift away from the West. According to MGI, petrodollar investors—including central banks, sovereign wealth funds, and individual magnates based mostly in the Middle East and Russia—will see the value of their foreign assets soar to at least $9 trillion by 2013, up from an estimated $5 trillion at the end of 2008. Similarly, foreign financial assets held by Asia's sovereign investors will collectively swell to $7.5 trillion by 2013, up from $4.8 trillion in 2008. The projected rate of growth between 2009 and 2013 will be the slowest since 2000, but, "impressive" nonetheless.

What explains these two group's ability to sail right through financial turmoil that wrecked some of the West's biggest and boldest investors? Mostly, it's the nature of the assets they hold. As the economy rebounds, oil prices will go up responding to growing demand for gasoline products tied to greater economic activity. Likewise, when global trade picks up again, Asian reserves will resume building up, reflecting those countries' ample trade surpluses. In other words, both petrodollar and Asian investors have a hedge over other institutional investors not so much because of the investment decisions they'll make but because their existing portfolios will benefit from "structural flows that will bring money in," as the world economy heads toward recovery.

At least some of these structural advantages may wind down in the long run –China, for example, is slowly steering its economy more towards satisfying domestic demand—but in the short-term, they'll help tick the financial power balance increasingly toward the economic power centers in the developing world. One risk connected to continued growth in petrodollars and Asian sovereign investment assets is that so much idle money will end up, again, feeding assets bubbles around the world as it did in the run-up to the current recession, warns the MGI report. (*Wall Street Journal—Real Time Economics*)

July 8. The **International Monetary Fund (IMF) and Canada** have signed an agreement to provide the Fund with up to the equivalent of US$10 billion/about SDR 6.5 billion. The Fund can now add these resources to those already available from borrowing agreements with Japan and Norway to provide balance of payments assistance to its members in the current crisis. (IMF)

July 6. The **world's top wealth management firms** were reported by Reuters from a survey of 14,000 private bankers and 7,000 wealthy individuals by Scorpio Partnership. Private wealth managed by banks and investment managers around the world dropped nearly 17% to $14.5 trillion in 2008 from 2007. (CNBC.com)

July 6. U.S. manufacturing output from factories has **contracted** for four consecutive quarters and analysts now expect manufacturing output to fall as much as 12% this year, the worst contraction since 1946. Nearly 1.7 million manufacturing workers—or one in eight— have lost their jobs in the last 18 months alone. (Reuters)

July 5. A bankruptcy judge said late Sunday, July 5, that **General Motors Corporation (GM)** can sell the bulk of its assets to a new government-backed company, clearing the way for the automaker to quickly emerge from bankruptcy protection. GM and the government are reportedly preparing to complete the sale transaction within this week. Chrysler's assets were recently sold to a new company led by Italian automaker Fiat. If GM is able to execute its sale this week, both automakers would have completed their trips through bankruptcy in about 40 days—an unusually speedy process. The government and GM have argued that a quick sale was critical to preserve the automaker's value. (AP and *Washington Post*)

July 2. The **American economy lost 467,000 jobs** in June and the unemployment rate edged up to 9.5% in a sobering indication that the most painful downturn since the Great Depression continues. The number of unemployed persons, 14.7 million and the unemployment rate (9.5%) were little changed in June. Since the start of the recession in December 2007, the number of unemployed persons has increased by 7.2 million, and the unemployment rate has risen by 4.6 percentage points. "The numbers are indicative of a continued, very severe recession," said Stuart G. Hoffman, chief economist at PNC Financial Services Group in Pittsburgh. (U.S. Bureau of Labor Statistics and *New York Times*)

July 2. **Eurozone unemployment rose** above 15 million in May; unemployment rate at 10 year high of 9.5%, the highest level since February 1999. The number of jobless across the Eurozone spiked up by a further 273,000 in May. This followed increases of 398,000 in April and 423,000 in March. May witnessed the 14th successive monthly rise in unemployment. This took the number of Eurozone jobless up to 15.0 million, the highest level since the bloc's inception in January 1999. It was also up by 3.95 million from the five-and-a-half-year low of 11.063 million seen in March 2008. (IHS Global Insight)

July 2. The **Federal Deposit Insurance Corporation (FDIC)** plans to issue **new rules** that could make it slightly easier for private equity firms to buy failed banks. Under a new directive the agency is expected to demand that investment firms like the Carlyle Group or Kohlberg Kravis Roberts provide support to the banks they acquire if the banks get into more trouble and need additional capital. The new rules represent a balancing act for the F.D.I.C, which is responsible for protecting depositors from losses. Government officials have been eager to recruit private investors to stretch out Congressional bail-outs. Bank regulators remain concerned about permitting comparatively high-risk investor groups take control of banks with billions of dollars in government-guaranteed deposits. The agency has seized 45 failing banks this year, and more than 60 since last fall. (*New York Times*)

July 2. China's tax administration reports that the total value-added tax **(VAT) refund for exporting goods** rose 23.4% year on year during the first five months, hitting 290 billion yuan/U.S.$42.5 billion, as a result of progressive rebate rate increases since last year. China has introduced seven consecutive export tax rebate hikes since the second half of last year to rein in the freefall of the country's exports. (IHS Global Insight)

Top 10 Wealth Managers

Rank	Bank	Assets in Million $
1	Bank of America	1,501
2	UBS	1,393
3	Citi	1,320
4	Wells Fargo	1,000
5	Credit Suisse	612
6	JPMorgan	552
7	Morgan Stanley	522
8	HSBC	352
9	Deutsche Bank	231
10	Goldman Sachs	215

Source: Scorpio Partnership via Reuters via CNBC.com

July 1. Planned job cuts announced by U.S. employers totaled 74,393 in June, down 33% from 111,182 in May, according to a report released on Wednesday by global outplacement firm Challenger, Gray & Christmas, Inc. June marked the fifth consecutive month of declining planned layoffs at U.S. firms, hitting the lowest level since March 2008 and providing another hopeful sign that the U.S. economy is attempting to end its worst recession in decades. (Reuters)

July 1. The **contraction in euro zone manufacturing** output moderated for the fourth consecutive month in June, a fresh sign that the severe economic downturn in the currency block is gradually bottoming out, final data from Markit Economics showed. However, there were marked differences in the pace of recovery in the region's largest economies, with Germany, Spain, and Italy still suffering sharp downturns in manufacturing, while France and the Netherlands moved closer to stabilization. (Wall Street Journal)

July 1. Asian economic data from Japan, China and South Korea indicate possible **stabilization**, or a hesitant steps with a considerable distance to full recovery. In Japan, the Tankan survey of big manufacturers, conducted quarterly by the Bank of Japan, bounced back from a record low it hit in March, recording minus 48 in its June survey. Below 50 indicates economic recession, while above 50 indicates growth. In China, an important official purchasing managers' index, rose for the fourth month in a row in June. And South Korea reported that exports in June were 11.3% lower than a year earlier, up from a 28.5% fall recorded in May. (New York Times)

July 1. Home prices in 20 major U.S. metropolitan areas **fell** in April at a slower pace than forecast, the S&P/Case-Shiller home- price index showed today. Today's Case-Shiller numbers are the latest sign that that the worst of the housing slump may be passing. Sales of existing homes posted gains in April and May, while housing starts jumped in May from a record low. Home prices saw a "striking improvement in the rate of decline" in April and trading in funds launched today indicates investors believe the U.S. housing slump is nearing a bottom, said Yale University economist Robert Shiller. "At this point, people are thinking the fall is over," Shiller, co-founder of the home price index that bears his name, said in a Bloomberg Radio interview today. "The market is predicting the declines are over." (Bloomberg)

July 1. California's lawmakers failed to agree on a **balanced budget** by the start of its new fiscal year, clearing the way to suspend payments owed to the state's vendors and local agencies, who instead will get "IOU" notes promising payment. The notes will mark the first time in 17 years the most populous U.S. state's government will have to resort to the unusual and dramatic measure. Democrats who control the legislature could not convince Republicans late Tuesday night to back their plans to tackle a $24.3 billion budget shortfall or a stopgap effort to ward off the IOUs. The two sides agree on the need for spending cuts but are split over whether to raise taxes. Democrats have pushed for new revenues while Republican lawmakers and Governor Arnold Schwarzenegger, also a Republican, have ruled out tax increases. (CNBC)

July 1. The **Turkish economy declined** by 13.8% year on year in the first quarter of 2009. The drop was the largest ever recorded for the country. This follows a 6.2% year on year fourth- quarter decline, placing the Turkish economy officially in recession. This deep contraction is among the steepest in the region, surpassed by only Estonia and Latvia. (IHS Global Insight)

July 1. Ukraine's GDP dropped by 20.3% in the first quarter, following a decline by 7.9% in the final quarter 2008. The first quarter's decline was the steepest since 1994, when the economy slumped by 22.3% for the year as a whole. The key driving force for the downturn was gross fixed capital formation, which fell -48.7% year on year. (IHS Global Insight)

July 1. China granted a U.S. $950 million **credit line to Zimbabwe**. According to Agence France-Presse, the loan will be used primarily in assisting the Zimbabwean government to rebuild its shattered economy, which is expected to cost around US$10 billion in the near term. The Zimbabwean prime minister also received pledges of US$500 million from Europe and the United States. (IHS Global Insight)

June 30. The **United Kingdom's** first quarter **GDP contraction** was deeper than previously reported at 2.4% quarter on quarter and 4.9% year on year. These statistics represent the sharpest decline since the second quarter of 1958 and the deepest since quarterly records began in 1948.
Consumer spending, investment, exports, and imports all fell substantially and inventories were slashed. The revised data show that the recession began in the second quarter of 2008 rather than the third, and has been deeper than previously thought. Problems unique to the United Kingdom included the sharp housing-market downturn, high levels of consumer debt, and the relative importance of the financial sector.

June 30. In the first quarter of 2009, **Croatian GDP shrank** by 6.7% year-on-year, its greatest economic contraction in over 16 years. This represents its most severe economic downturn since its post-Yugoslav violence in 1992. The Croatian economy was undermined by severe downturns in household consumption and fixed capital formation. Exports of goods and services dropped 14.2% year on year. Imports of goods and services fell an even sharper 20.9% year on year. The Croatian kuna depreciated by 1.8% over this period. Lack of export orders forced manufacturers to begin laying off thousands of workers.

June 30. The **International Monetary Fund (IMF)** approved an increase of 40% in financial assistance for **Belarus**, bringing total support to some US$3.5 billion. The increase in financial support of US$679 million will supply Belarus with vital liquidity relief. This increase signals the IMF's trust in Belarus's ability and willingness to pursue responsible macroeconomic policy and further structural reforms. In the longer term, challenges remain extensive and economic and financial risks high.

June 30. Iran was reported to plan to scrap **domestic gasoline subsidies** for private vehicles. No time frame for implementation was given. It was announced that the government would still provide gasoline subsidies for fishing vessels and domestic trucks. Iranians currently purchase up to 20 gallons per month at the subsidized price of US$0.40 per gallon, and unlimited quantities at $1.60 per gallon. Iran's gasoline imports of 130,000 barrels per day and profitable crude oil exports are considered to be potential sanctions targets over Iran's nuclear program.

June 29. Kosovo formally **joined the IMF and World Bank**. This gives Kosovo increased international legitimacy, which is important since support for its 2008 unilateral declaration of independence has been questioned by some. It is hoped that membership in the international financial institutions will bring new investment to the country, the poorest in Europe. It suffers widespread corruption and massive infrastructure problems. Kosovo has an unemployment rate near 60%, and a massive trade deficit. Almost half its population lives in poverty.

June 26. United States real GDP declined a revised 5.5% in the first quarter. Profits from current production increased US$48.1 billion, or increased 3.8% quarter on quarter. It is the first quarterly increase since the second quarter of 2007. All profits came from the financial sector. Earnings in other industries declined.

June 26. The French gross domestic product contracted by 1.2% quarter on quarter during the first three months of 2009. This follows a revised contraction of 1.4% during the final quarter of 2008, and falls of 0.2% and 0.4% during the third and second quarters of last year. Investment and exports continued to perform particularly badly during the first quarter.

June 26. New Zealand's gross domestic product contracted 0.7% quarter-on-quarter in the three months through March and by 2.2% for the year, marking it as the deepest recession on record. In March growth contracted for the fifth consecutive quarter. A slump in domestic demand despite positive net exports has driven New Zealand's economic drop.

June 25. American International Group (AIG) announced that it has reached a deal to reduce its debt to the Federal Reserve Bank of New York by $25 billion. AIG said that it would give the New York Fed preferred stakes in Asian-based American International Assurance (AIA) and American Life Insurance Company (Alico), which operates in more than 50 countries. Under the agreement, AIG will split off AIA and Alico into separate company-owned entities called "special purpose vehicles," or SPVs. The New York Fed will receive preferred shares now valued at $25 billion—$16 billion in AIA and $9 billion in Alico—and in exchange will forgive an equal amount of AIG debt. The Fed is now in the insurance business.

June 24. H.R. 2346 (P.L. 111-32) established a $1 billion program to provide $3,500 to $4,500 rebates for the purchase of new, fuel-efficient vehicles, provided the trade-in vehicles are scrapped (Cash for Clunkers program). On August 7, H.R. 3435 (P.L. 111-47) increased the amount by $2 billion, tapping funds from the economic recovery act (American Recovery and Reinvestment Act (P.L. 111-5)).

June 24. H.R. 2346 was signed to become P.L. 111-32, increasing the U.S. quota in the International Monetary Fund by 4.5 billion SDRs ($7.69 billion), providing loans to the IMF of up to an additional 75 billion SDRs ($116.01 billion), and authorizing the United States Executive Director of the Fund to vote to approve the sale of up to 12,965,649 ounces of the Fund's gold. On June 18, Congress had cleared H.R. 2346, the $105.9 billion war supplemental spending bill, that mainly funds military operations in Iraq and Afghanistan through September but also included the IMF provisions. The President's signing statement rejected certain congressional conditions on the funding, but a provision in H.R. 3081 that passed the house on July 9, 2009, was designed to overrule the President on this issue.

June 24. The United States and the European Union lodged a complaint in the World Trade Organization (WTO) against China, accusing Beijing of unfairly helping their domestic steel, aluminum, and chemical industries by limiting overseas exports of raw materials. The United States and the EU allege that while Chinese companies get primary access low priced raw materials from domestic producers, non-Chinese companies must buy the products in the open market, where prices are higher due to the lack of Chinese output restricting supplies. EU Trade Commissioner Catherine Ashton said that the Chinese restrictions on raw materials "distort competition and increase global prices." China responded that the curbs were put in place to protect the environment, and retaliated with a request for the WTO to investigate U.S. restrictions on the import of Chinese poultry products. The case represents the first trade action taken by the United States against China, or any country, under President Barack Obama. The U.S. president is aware that China is the largest creditor to the United States. Washington frequently complains about China flooding the world market with cheap exports, rather than holding them back.

June 24. The International Monetary Fund (IMF) approved an increase in assistance to Armenia. Armenia may now immediately withdraw an additional U.S. $103 million under its stand-by program approved in March.

June 23. The Chinese Ministry of Commerce (MofCOM) reported new measures to promote domestic consumption. The government plans to subsidize consumer durable trade-ins, reduce electricity prices for commercial enterprises, and promote credit cards. The trade-in of home appliances and automobiles will be emphasized.

June 23. The IMF froze Bosnia and Herzegovina's 1.2 billion euro/U.S. $1.66 billion stand-by arrangement when the country failed to implement agreed fiscal tightening. The IMF suspended the loan following the Bosnian government agreement with protests by war veterans and invalids to reverse planned cuts in benefits and pensions. The situation may be reviewed by the IMF in September.

June 23. Airbus displayed the first A320 aircraft made outside Europe at a factory in Tianjin, China. It was delivered to Dragon Aviation Leasing and will be used by Sichuan Airlines, a regional Chinese airline. Airbus began assembling the A320 in Tianjin in September, shipping components from Europe to China. The company has invested nearly U.S. $1.47 billion in the plant, a joint venture that is 51% owned by Airbus and 49% owned by a Chinese aviation consortium. Another 10 aircraft will be assembled this year in China, with Airbus planning to assemble four planes per month by the end of 2011. Airbus decided to construct the China plant based on predictions the country will purchase up to 2,800 passenger and transport planes over the next twenty years. Passenger travel is expected to expand five-fold during the next 20 years. The company's target is to gain more than 50% market share from now until 2012, a significant increase from its 39% market share in 1995.

June 23. The World Bank approved an U.S. $8 million grant for Guinea-Bissau's poverty reduction and reform program. The grant will be provided under the country's Interim Strategy Note (ISN), for the 2009-2010 period. The grant aims to improve economic management, foster economic growth and strengthen the delivery of basic services. It also seeks to support the government's reform agenda, targeting greater efficiency, transparency, and accountability in the management of public finances. Guinea-Bissau continues to be one of the most fragile states in sub-Saharan Africa, trapped in a cycle of political instability, weak institutional capacity and poor economic growth since the 1998-1999 civil war. The World Bank's grant is part of a broader initiative to support the country's stabilization and recovery.

June 18. Congress cleared H.R. 2346, the U.S. $105.9 billion war supplemental spending bill, sending it to the President's desk. House leaders advanced the measure on June 16, on a 226-202 vote. The Senate voted, 91-5, on June 18 to adopt the report, clearing the bill. The legislation mainly funds military operations in Iraq and Afghanistan through September. It includes $5 billion in borrowing authority for the International Monetary Fund (IMF).

June 17. The U.S. Treasury released a white paper containing proposals to reorganize the financial regulatory system. Key areas of reform include systemic risk, securitization, derivatives, and consumer protection. Visit the full document at http://www.financialstability.gov/docs/regs/ FinalReport_web.pdf.

June 1. General Motors Corp. declares bankruptcy, filing for chapter 11. By asset value, GM was the second largest industrial bankruptcy in history, after WorldCom in 2002. Costs to the U.S. government to save GM Corp. and Chrysler LLC now exceed $62 billion. GM's bankruptcy filing declared assets of $82 billion and liabilities of $172 billion. On the same day Chrysler's sale of assets to Italian Fiat SpA was approved by bankruptcy court.

May 13. The U.S. Treasury in a two-page letter to Congress outlined plans to regulate the over- the-counter (OTC) derivatives market, in order to quantify and regulate risks that led to the global financial crisis. According to Treasury Secretary Tim Geithner, the CFTC and SEC are reviewing the participation limits in current law to recommend how the Commodity Exchange Act and the securities laws should be amended. Treasury is coordinating with foreign governments to promote the implementation of similar measures to ensure U.S. regulation is not undermined by weaker standards abroad.

May 12. Standard & Poor's (S&P) lowered Mexico's credit rating outlook to negative from stable. Economists are reducing forecasts for real GDP growth in 2009. The central bank now estimates a 3.8%-4.8% annual contraction in 2009. S&P forecasts a 5.5% drop for Mexican real GDP this year. The Mexican economy is hampered by oil and trade. Mexico has long relied on oil revenues which are now falling. International oil prices and domestic production are down. The Constitution keeps the oil industry a state monopoly and the financial weakness of the state oil company, Pemex, has prevented development of deep water reserves in the Gulf of Mexico. Mexico's total trade, imports plus exports, equaled 62% of total Mexican GDP in 2008. Over 85% of Mexico's total trade is with the United States. In the United States, trade accounts for less than 30% of GDP. In the first quarter of 2009, Mexico's exports to the United States fell at a 26% annual rate, less than Canada's exports decline to the United States of 37%.

April 30. Chrysler, the third-largest U.S. vehicle manufacturer, filed for bankruptcy. The firm announced that it would shut four of its U.S. plants, located at Sterling Heights, Michigan; St. Louis, Missouri; Twinsburg, Ohio; and Kenosha, Wisconsin, by the end of 2010. Production at these, and five other U.S. plants (Newark, Delaware, Conner Avenue Detroit, North St. Louis, and its axle plant in Detroit) will be shifted to Canada and Mexico. The U.S. auto industry has been losing jobs for years. In 2008, the industry employed 711,000 people in the United States, down from 1.3 million in 1999. In 2008 U.S. automakers closed 230,000 jobs. Standard & Poor's estimates that even including component manufacturers, the U.S. auto industry accounts for just over 1% of non-farm employment. Outside Mexico, all of Chrysler's North American plants are temporarily closed while Chrysler is reorganized. The new company to emerge is likely to be 20% owned by the Italian firm Fiat, with a majority stake held by the U.S. United Autoworkers Union (UAW). Chrysler is the first bankruptcy filing by a major U.S. auto company since Studebaker in 1933. In Mexico, Chrysler is the fourth largest vehicle maker after Volkswagen, General Motors and Nissan. Chrysler claims that Mexican production may be unaffected. In the first quarter of 2009, total output of 33,998 units was 51% less than the same period of 2008. Mexico's total automobile production fell 41% annually in the first quarter of 2009, to 291,800 units.

May 7. The government's "stress tests" indicated that ten of the largest U.S. banks would have to raise a combined $74.6 billion in capital to cushion themselves against economic under- performance.

May 5. The European Commission lowered its growth forecast for the European Union to -4% in 2009 and -0.1% in 2010.

May 4. The International Monetary Fund approved a 24-month $17.1 billion Stand-By Arrangement for Romania. The total international financial support package will amount to $26.4 billion, with the European Union providing $6.6 billion, the World Bank $1.3 billion, and the European Bank for Reconstruction and Development, the European Investment Bank, and the International Finance Corporation a combined $1.3 billion.

April 30. Chrysler announced merger with Fiat and filed for bankruptcy. Separately, the Financial Accounting Standards Board changed the mark-to-market accounting rule to give banks more discretion in reporting value of assets.

April 28. Swine flu epidemic hits Mexican economy.

April 22. The International Monetary Fund projected global economic activity to contract by 1.3% in 2009 with a slow recovery (1.9% growth) in 2010. Overall, the advanced economies are forecast to contract by 3.8% in 2009, with the U.S. economy shrinking by 2.8%.

April 21. The IMF estimated that banks and other financial institutions faced aggregate losses of $4.05 trillion in the value of their holdings as a result of the crisis. Of that amount, $2.7 trillion is from loans and assets originating in the United States, the fund said. That estimate is up from $2.2 trillion in the fund's interim report in January, and $1.4 trillion last October.

April 14. The IMF granted Poland a $20.5 billion credit line using a facility intended to backstop countries with sound economic policies that have been caught short by the global financial crisis. On April 1, Mexico said that it was tapping the new credit line for $47 billion.

April 2. At the **G-20 London Summit**, leaders of the world's largest economies agreed to tackle the global financial crisis with measures worth $1.1 trillion including $750 billion more for the International Monetary Fund, $250 billion to boost global trade, and $100 billion for multilateral development banks. They also agreed on establishing a new Financial Stability Board to work with the IMF to ensure cooperation across borders; closer regulation of banks, hedge funds, and credit rating agencies; and a crackdown on tax havens, but they could only agree on additional stimulus measures through IMF and multilateral development bank lending and not through country stimulus packages. The leaders reiterated their commitment to resist protectionism and promote global trade and investment.

April 1. The U.S. Conference Board's Consumer Confidence Index inched 0.7 of a point higher in March, virtually unchanged from the 42-year low reached in February. The present situation index has fallen from a cyclical peak of 138.3 in July 2007 to 21.5 this month. Its record low was 15.8 in December 1982, when the unemployment rate stood at a post-war high of 10.8%.

April 1. Japan's economy shrank 3.3%, or by 12.7% in annual terms. This marked the deepest contraction in the economy since the first quarter of 1974, when the global economy was reacting to the oil shock, and the second-biggest decline in growth in the post-war era.

Japan has experienced a record decline in exports. Total exports fell 13.9% in quarterly comparisons and by a stunning 45.0% in annual terms. These declines were mirrored by the Bank of Japan's quarterly business confidence survey, or tankan. The tankan results for the first quarter of 2009's headline Diffusion Index (DI) of business conditions for large manufacturing companies dropped to a reading of -58 in the three months through March from the -24 results recorded in the December quarter. The DI surveys respondents' business conditions expectations over the next three to six months. The reading for the first quarter was the worst on record.

April 1. Mexico's President Felipe Calderón claimed yesterday that his country was willing to take up a new credit line from the International Monetary Fund (IMF). He confirmed that government finances were "in order", allowing the country to boost central bank reserves via a new IMF borrowing of some US$30–40 billion as soon as this week. The IMF has failed to attract any borrower for a US$100-million loan offering last year. Potential borrowers may be concerned over conditionality requirements for loans and the negative message sent out when any economy requires IMF financing. The new Flexible Credit Line (FCL), launched recently by the IMF to attract developing nations, offers eligible countries easy access to large loans. Countries will be able to either immediately draw funds from the FCL, or keep it as an easily accessibly pool of finance.

March 31. The **Organization for Economic Cooperation and Development** (OECD) in a new survey reports worsening economic prospects. It is now expected that the global recession will worsen by an average **GDP contraction** of 4.3% in the OECD area in 2009 before a policy- induced recovery gradually builds strength through 2010. **International trade** is forecast to fall by more than 13% in 2009 and world economic activity will shrink by 2.7%. Specific forecasts include: U.S.: -4% in 2009 and 0% in 2010; Japan: -6.6% in 2009 and -0.5% in 2010; Eurozone: - 4.1% in 2009 and -0.3% in 2010. Brazil's GDP is expected to decline by 0.3% in 2009 while Russia's is projected to fall 5.6%. Growth in India will ease to 4.3% in 2009 and in China to 6.3%. By the end of 2010 **unemployment** rates across OECD nations may reach 10.1% from 7.5% in the first quarter of 2009. The unemployed in the 30 advanced OECD countries would increase by about 25 million, the largest and most rapid growth in OECD unemployment in the post-war period.

March 31. U.S. housing prices continue to fall. The Standard & Poor's S&P/Case-Shiller 20-City Composite Index fell 19.0% annually in January 2009, the fastest on record. High inventories and foreclosures continued to drive down prices. All 20 cities covered in the survey showed a decrease in prices, with 9 of the 20 areas showing rates of annual decline of over 20%.

As of January 2009, average home prices are at similar levels to what they were in the third quarter of 2003. From their peaks in mid-2006, the 10-City Composite is down 30.2% and the 20- City Composite is down 29.1%.

March 31. The **World Trade Organization** (WTO) predicted that the volume of global **merchandise trade** would **shrink by 9%** this year. This will be the first fall in trade flows since 1982. Between 1990 and 2006 trade volumes grew by more than 6% a year, easily outstripping the growth rate of world output, which was about 3%. Now the global economic machine has gone into reverse: output is declining and trade is shrinking faster.

March 30. The central banks of China and Argentina reached an agreement for a 70 billion yuan/U.S. $10 billion currency swap for three years, the sixth such swap China has concluded with emerging economies including South Korea, Hong Kong, Indonesia, Belarus and Malaysia. The move may provide capital to these emerging markets and may in the long-term promote the Chinese yuan's international role. For Argentina, these moves may help to offset challenges in securing foreign exchange financing.

March 24. The Executive Board of the International Monetary Fund (IMF) approved a major overhaul of the IMF's lending framework, including the creation of a new **Flexible Credit Line** (FCL). The changes to the IMF's lending framework include:

- modernizing IMF conditionality for all borrowers,
- introducing a new Flexible Credit Line,
- enhancing the flexibility of the Fund's traditional stand-by arrangement,
- doubling normal access limits for nonconcessional resources,
- simplifying cost and maturity structures, and
- eliminating certain seldom-used facilities.

"These reforms represent a significant change in the way the Fund can help its member countries—which is especially needed at this time of global crisis," said IMF Managing Director Dominique Strauss-Kahn. "More flexibility in our lending along with streamlined conditionality will help us respond effectively to the various needs of members. This, in turn, will help them to weather the crisis and return to sustainable growth."

March 23. The U.S. Treasury released the details of its **Public Private Partnership Investment** Program to address the challenge of legacy toxic assets (mortgages and securities backed by loans) being carried by the financial system. The Treasury and the Federal Deposit Insurance Corporation with funding from the TARP and private capital are to purchase eligible assets worth about $500 billion with the potential to expand the program to $1 trillion.

March 20. The European Union announced additional support for the IMF's lending capacity in the form of a loan to the IMF totaling €75 billion, about US$100 billion.. The EU's common strategy is released. It focuses on regulating hedge funds, private equity, credit derivatives and credit rating agencies, and vowed to crack down on tax havens.

March 19. The **U.S. Federal Reserve** announced a plan to purchase **longer-term Treasury securities**. The Fed is now trying not just to influence the spread between private interest rates and Treasuries (through its mortgage-backed securities purchases, for example), but also to pull down the entire spectrum of interest rates by driving down the rate on benchmark Treasuries. Key points of yesterday's Fed announcement include:

The federal funds rate, with a current target range of 0.0%–0.25%, is likely to remain exceptionally low for "an extended period." Last month, the Fed said the low rate would apply "for some time."

The Fed will purchase:

up to an additional US$750 billion of agency mortgage-backed securities, for a total of US$1.25 trillion, and

up to an additional US$100 billion of agency debt for a total of up to US$200 billion.

It followed the central banks of the United Kingdom and Japan by announcing its intention to purchase longer-term Treasury securities (up to US$300 billion worth) over the next six months.

It has launched its Term Asset-Backed Securities Loan Facility (TALF) program to support credit for households and small businesses, and may expand that program to other lending.

The Fed anticipates that fiscal and monetary stimulus, plus policies aimed at stabilizing the financial sector, will contribute to a gradual resumption of growth—although it has not said when.

This announcement caused the 10-year Treasury yield to fall from just over 2.9% to under 2.6%. Mortgage rates should follow Treasury yields down and spark another refinancing wave. Economists question whether lower rates will revive home purchases as well as refinancing.

March 18. The Federal Reserve announced that it would buy approximately $1.2 trillion in government bonds and mortgage-related securities in order to lower borrowing costs for home mortgages and other types of loans.

March 11. Chinese total exports experienced their biggest fall on record in February declining 25.7% on the year in February, to US$64.9 billion. Imports also declined 24.1% on the year, And China's trade surplus shrank to a three-year low of US$4.84 billion from US$39.1 billion in January. For the first two months of the year combined, exports fell 21.1% from the same period of 2008. Trade contracted despite investment being supported by the recent rapid expansion of credit and by the release of funds under the government's four trillion yuan/US$580 billion fiscal stimulus package.

March 10. Finance Minister Najib Razak announced a large **Malaysian fiscal stimulus** package. The 60 billion ringgit/US$ 16.3 billion package is the government's second supplementary budget, after the initial 7 billion ringgit stimulus already implemented. The package equals 9.0% of gross domestic product (GDP).

March 10. Philippines' exports experienced a record contraction in January as global demand continued to decline. Official data showed that total exports fell 41% year-on-year to US$2.49 billion. In December, exports contracted by a revised 40.3% in annual terms. Shipments of electronics, which account for more than half of total exports, almost halved, shrinking 48.4% in annual terms to US$1.35 billion.

March 10. United Kingdom industrial production suffered the largest annual drop since January 1981 in January. Manufacturing output plunged by 2.9% month on month and 12.8% year on year in January 2009, according to the Office for National Statistics (ONS). This followed a drop of 1.9% monthly in December and marked the eleventh successive monthly decline in manufacturing output.

March 10. China's official registered **unemployment** rate hit a three-year high of 4.2% in 2008. Although during the post-Asian Financial Crisis slowdown, between 1979 and 1982, unemployment was mostly concentrated in the state sector, this time the private sector has experienced worse unemployment, with migrant labor being fired first, with no social programs for relief. The number of business failures is estimated to be 7.5% of the country's Small and Medium sized Enterprises (SMEs), or nearly 500,000 firms.

February 24. U.S. President Barack Obama used his first **address** to a joint session of Congress to outline how the economic recovery can work. He outlined the rationale behind the economic stimulus and the financial sector rescue plans, conceding costs and risks, but warning of the greater danger of inaction. President Obama promised to reduce the federal budget deficit by half by the end of his first term. On the same day, U.S. Federal Reserve Chairman Ben Bernanke testified to Congress that if the financial system is stabilized soon, the recession will end in 2009 and the economy will grow in 2010.

February 24. The **Latvian government fell** over fiscal adjustment measures that are required for Latvia to comply with the IMF-led rescue program terms. This caused Standard & Poor's (S&P) to reduce its sovereign rating for Latvia from BBB- to BB+. S&P has thus cut the Baltic State to junk bond status. Latvia's ratings among various rating institutions currently vary significantly, from BB+ to BBB+.

February 23. The **Dow Jones** Industrial Average lost 3.4% to close at 7113.78, its **lowest level in 12 years**, and just under half the high it reached 16 months ago. Banking stocks led the index down, and losses were experienced in most sectors. The U.S. market declines have influenced international declines as well. Japan's Nikkei 225 ended down 1.5%, Australia's S&P/ASX 200 was off by 0.6%, Taiwan's Taiex lost 1.1%, and China's Shanghai Composite fell 4.6%. Equities are wiping huge amounts off the market value of companies and investments including pensions worldwide.

February 23. The **Chilean** Finance Ministry announced that the Central Bank of Chile will conduct U.S. dollar auctions in March 2009, to finance a US$3 billion **stimulus plan** announced by President Michelle Bachelet in January. US$1 billion will be directed into fiscal spending transactions. These resources will be drawn from the country's sovereign wealth fund, which currently holds around US$20.11 billion.

February 20. Several **Netherlands local and provincial council**s have announced that they are planning to launch local **stimulus packages** to combat the country's economic crisis. The Dutch government is planning to invest €94 million in the local economy and infrastructure projects, including new street lighting and an upgrade of the sewage network. Rotterdam is planning to launch further measures to augment the €200 million package announced in January for the construction industry. Amsterdam plans to invest €200 million in its construction industry, while Utrecht is still exploring options.

February 18. The **German** government agreed on a **revised bank bailout** plan. The first version, from October 2008, cost 480 billion euro/U.S. $603.7 billion, has not delivered appropriate results. The new text must be ratified by parliament before taking effect. To ensure the stability of the German financial sector the new plan considers three factors. Expropriation would be a last resort only. Acceleration of state holdings of bank shares, changes to current stock corporation regulations are proposed. The stabilization fund for the financial markets would increase its debt guarantee time period.

February 17. President Obama signed a **US$787 billion economic stimulus bill**, 111th Congress bill H.R. 1, following House and Senate final votes on the conference report on February 13. H.R. 1, the **American Recovery and Reinvestment Act of 2009** (ARRA), was signed into law as **P.L. 111-5**. The ARRA was enacted as the fiscal centerpiece of a set of wide-ranging policy efforts designed to stabilize the financial sector and the macro-economy. These efforts also included stimulus from the Economic Stimulus Act of 2008 and Troubled Asset Relief Program, among other initiatives. Originally projected to provide $787 billion in stimulus, the Congressional Budget Office (CBO) in 2010 estimated the ten-year costs of the ARRA at $862 billion. As passed, the stimulus package included some $575 billion in government spending and $212 billion in tax cuts.

February 17. U.S. automakers General Motors Corp. and Chrysler LLC submitted recovery plans to the U.S. government requesting $21.6 billion more in loans to enable their recovery.

February 17. Eastern Europe's deepening recession is putting pressure on those **West European bank**s with local **subsidiaries**, Moody's Investors Service reports. The countries with the deepest fiscal deficits—the Baltic states, Bulgaria, Croatia, Hungary and Romania—have the highest external vulnerability. Moody's says Kazakhstan, Russia and Ukraine are also under pressure despite low public external debt. The Austrian banking system is the most exposed; banks there and in Belgium, France, Germany, Italy and Sweden account for 84% of total West European claims. Exposure is heavily concentrated among certain banking groups: Raiffeisen, Erste, Societe Generale, UniCredit and KBC. Modern banking has just emerged in Eastern Europe. Eastern subsidiaries are more vulnerable in times of stress, with deteriorating asset quality and vulnerable liquidity positions. EU member countries have failed to coordinate national stimulus programs, and there appears to be no willingness to finance large cross-border rescue packages.

February 16. Russian President Dmitry Medvedev **replaced** the **governors** of Pskov, Orel and Voronezh, as well as the Nenets Autonomous Region. The terminations suggest that the Kremlin is using the economic crisis as an excuse for getting rid of governors with whom the federal leadership was already unhappy. As local development levels and production profiles vary greatly, the crisis is having diverse effects on Russia's regions. Russian economic activity as a whole may suffer substantially in the crisis, but inequality across Russian regions may be reduced.

February 16. The **Japanese economy contracted** by 3.3% quarterly in December, the Cabinet Office reported on preliminary figures. At an annual rate, GDP fell by 12.7%, and is now performing at its worst since 1974.

February 16. In preparation for the **London Leaders' summit in April**, world leaders are drafting responses to the global financial crisis. The extent to which they agree on the causes of the crisis will be critical to policies proposed. Broad consensus on key features of the financial crisis now includes:

Maturity. It emerged from a market-led process of change that spanned around 30 years, not two or three, and culminated in the long boom that began in the early 1990s.

Regulatory failure. For many reasons, neither regulation nor regulators policed these processes.

Opacity. A major contributory factor was the complexity and opacity of the activities and the balance sheets of major financial institutions.

Credit boom. The boom resulted from countries' competitive deregulation of financial markets over some 30 years.

How these ingredients interacted to cause the crisis remains under debate. The G20 are likely to promote global measures that address both the underlying causes and more immediate responses.

February 14. Finance ministers and central bank governors of the Group of Seven (**G7**) industrialized nations **met** in Rome to discuss the financial crisis and economic slowdown. In order to prevent a resurgence of protectionism, the G7 communique pledged members to do all they could to combat recession without distorting free trade.

February 13. The **U.S. federal government's** monthly **budget** statement reported a deficit of US $83.8 billion in January 2009, compared with a US $17.8-billion surplus a year earlier. Both higher outlays and falling tax receipts led to the deficit. The deficit for the first four months of the 2009 fiscal year ballooned to a record US$569 billion. The Troubled Asset Relief Program (TARP) added about US$42 billion to the deficit in January, bringing TARP spending so far this fiscal year to US$284 billion.

February 13. Eurozone GDP declined by 1.5% quarterly and 1.2% annually in the fourth quarter of 2008, the sharpest contraction since the bloc came into being in January 1999.

February 12. Ukraine's Finance Minister Viktor Pynzenuk **resigned**; Fitch downgraded its long-term foreign and local currency issuer rating from "B+" to "B"; and an International Monetary Fund (IMF) mission left Ukraine last week. The IMF, which has not concluded its US $1.9 billion part of the Ukrainian aid package, called for immediate and serious crisis management. The IMF mission announced last week that a successful implementation of the financial rescue for the country is in jeopardy.

February 12. The **Irish** government reported a 7-billion-euro (US$9 billion) **bank rescue plan** for two of the country's largest banks, the Allied Irish Bank and the Bank of Ireland. Each bank will receive 3.5 billion euro in recapitalization funds. The government attached conditions including preference shares that the government will obtain, with a fixed annual dividend of 8%, partial control over the appointment of the banks' directors, and executive pay reductions with no bonuses.

February 12. China's State Council **approved a stimulus plan** yesterday for the shipbuilding industry, urging banks to expand trade finance for the export of vessels, and extending fiscal and financial support for domestic buyers of long-range ships until 2012. The government will also encourage industry restructuring, and force the replacement of outdated ships. The funds will facilitate shipping research and technology. Mergers and acquisitions will be encouraged for industry consolidation. This is the latest Chinese industry stimulus plan, following support for textiles, automotive, steel, and machinery industries over the past few weeks.

February 12. Chinalco, the Aluminum Corporation of China, announced an investment of US$19.5 billion in Australian mining group **Rio Tinto**. This investment is China's largest-ever overseas purchase. Chinalco will buy $7.2-billion worth of convertible bonds as well as Rio Tinto assets worth $12.3 billion. Rio Tinto assumed substantial debt in its purchase of Canadian aluminum maker Alcan in 2007.

February 12. The **Swiss** government presented a **second economic stimulus plan** worth 700 million Swiss francs (US$603 million). The funds are directed at infrastructure (390 million francs), regions (100 million francs), environment and energy (80 million francs), research (50 million francs), renovation of state buildings (40 million francs), and the tourism sector (12 million francs). The first rescue package worth some 900 million francs launched in November did not have its desired effectiveness.

February 12. Kuwait's Sovereign Wealth Fund lost 15% in 2008. The emirate's sovereign wealth fund lost nine billion dinars (US$30.9 billion) in 2008 as a result of the global economic downturn. One example of losses was the US$5-billion capital injection into Citibank and Merrill Lynch in 2008, which fell to US$2.2 billion before returning to its current value of US$2.8 billion. These figures come days after the government unveiled a US$5.14-billion stimulus package which will be funded by the country's foreign-exchange reserves, as well as the Kuwait Investment Authority.

February 12. Australian legislature **rejected fiscal stimulus package** as Australian unemployment climbed to two-year high. The US$28 billion package failed over environmentalists' objections.

February 5. The Bank of **England**'s Monetary Policy Committee **reduced** its key **interest rate** by 50 basis points from 1.50% to 1.00%. Interest rates are now at their lowest level since the Bank of England was founded in 1694.

February 3. British Prime Minister Gordon Brown and **Chinese** Premier Wen Jiabao said that **coordination** was necessary in order to avert the global financial crisis, at the end of Premier Wen's five-day tour of Europe. Prime Minister Brown said that the United Kingdom is planning to double annual exports within the coming 18 months, from £5 billion to £10 billion. He stressed that the United Kingdom will benefit from China's recent stimulus packages, particularly the aerospace, hi-tech manufacturing, education, pharmaceuticals, and low-carbon technologies industries. **China and the European Union** (EU) have agreed to hold summit talks soon to increase **economic cooperation.**

February 3. Chinese President Hu Jintao will travel to Mali, Senegal, Tanzania, Mauritius, and Saudi Arabia from February 10 to February 17, 2009. Despite the global economic downturn the Chinese government is **increasing investment in Africa** and the Middle East. Chinese-African trade has been increasing by an average of 30% per year, almost reaching US$107 billion in 2008.

February 3. China will give **Senegal** several **cooperation** projects, including a museum, a theater, a children's hospital, and repair of sports stadiums worth some 80 million yuan or U.S. $11.5 million. This brings the total of pledged Chinese investments to Senegal in 2009 to US$117.3 million, including projects for power services, transport equipment and information technology infrastructure.

February 2. The government of **Kazakhstan** announced **nationalization** of two **banks**, BTA Bank, the nation's largest bank, and Alliance Bank, the nations third-largest bank. The government reported it is considering a possible sale of half of its stake in BTA Bank to Russia's Sberbank. The Kazakh government now owns 78.1% of BTA Bank.

February 2. A survey conducted jointly by the **Afghan** government and the United Nations forecast that **opium production** in Afghanistan will **decline** for the second consecutive year in 2009. The report estimates that the total area of poppy fields under cultivation declined to 378,950 acres, a 19% decline from the previous year. The survey also indicated that poppy cultivation in the main producing regions of the south and the southwest fell for the first time in five years. The decline was largely attributable to recent sharp falls in global prices for opiates following saturation of the market and the negative impact of drought. Farmers had also shifted production to staple grains after global prices surged in the first half of 2008. The survey indicates that prices for dry opium tumbled 25% in 2008 while wheat and rice prices rose 49% and 26% respectively. Afghanistan accounts for 90% of the world's supply of opium with proceeds from trafficking providing a main source of income for insurgents in the border regions with Pakistan.

February 2. Ireland average **prices** for **housing** declined by 9.1% in 2008 compared with a fall of 7.3% in 2007. Also, Moody's Ratings Services revised its sovereign outlook for Ireland to negative from stable on the basis of mounting fiscal pressures, economic deterioration, and the government's potentially damaging exposure to the banking sector. This follows a similar revision from Standard & Poor's in January.

January 30. The **U.S.** Bureau of Economic Analysis (BEA) announced that preliminary real gross domestic product (**GDP**)—the output of goods and services produced by labor and property located in the United States – for 2008 rose 1.3%, down from 2.0% in 2007. Real GDP decreased at an annual rate of 3.8 percent in the fourth quarter of 2008, the largest decline since the first quarter of 1982.

January 30. South Korea reported that **industrial output fell** 9.6% in December. Total output tumbled by 18.6% in annual terms compared with the 14.0% decline in November, which was the second-largest decrease in production since the series began in 1970.

January 30. Finland reported that **industrial output** declined by 15.6% year-on-year in December, after falling by a revised rate of more than 9.0% in November. Production decreased in all main industrial sectors. Also, the Finnish government announced an increase in government expenditure of 1.2 billion euro to support the flagging economy. Additional funds are to be allocated to construction, renovation and transport infrastructure projects.

January 29-February 1. The **World Economic Forum** (WEF) met in Davos, Switzerland. Chinese Premier Wen Jiabao and Russian Premier Vladimir Putin blamed the U.S.-led financial system for the global financial crisis. European Central Bank (ECB) President Jean-Claude Trichet noted the ECB is drafting guidelines for European governments' establishment of "bad banks" to consolidate toxic assets.

January 29. Thailand's parliament approved a $3.35 billion stimulus package aimed at boosting its economy battered by months of street protests. Final approval was expected in February.

January 28. The International Monetary Fund (IMF) revised its forecast for world economic growth down to 0.5% for 2009. This would be the lowest level of growth since World War II and down by 1.7 percentage points since the IMF forecast in November 2008. The IMF indicated that despite wide-ranging policy actions by governments and central banks, financial markets are still under stress and the global economy is taking a turn for the worse. The IMF urged governments to take decisive action to restore financial sector health (by providing liquidity and capital and helping to dispose of problem assets) and to provide macroeconomic stimulus (both monetary and fiscal) to support sagging demand.

January 28. Canada announced a $32 billion stimulus package that included infrastructure spending and tax cuts.

January 28. The U.S. House of Representatives passed the American Recovery and Reinvestment Act of 2009 (H.R. 1, Obey). The cost of the bill was estimated at $819 billion.

January 26. Australia announced a $2.6 billion stimulus package.

January 22. Malaysia announced it is preparing a second economic stimulus package to fend off the threat of recession. Singapore unveiled a $13.7 billion stimulus package.

January 21. The Philippines announced a $633 million increase to bring its stimulus program to $6.9 billion.

January 15. The U.S. **Senate** voted to **release** the second half of the Treasury's Troubled Assets Recovery Package (**TARP**) to stabilize the U.S. financial system, granting President-elect Barack Obama authority to spend $350 billion to revive credit markets and help homeowners avoid foreclosure. The Treasury Department announced it would fund a rescue of Bank of America which guarantees $118 billion in troubled assets.

January 6. Chile announced a $4 billion stimulus package.

January 1. Belarus devalued its national **currency**, the Belarusian ruble, by over 20%. The National Bank announced that it will tie its currency immediately to a basket of three currencies—the U.S. dollar, the euro and the Russian ruble.

2008

December 31. The International Monetary Fund (**IMF**) gave tentative approval to **Belarus** for a US$2.5 billion 15 month Stand By Arrangement. Final approval will be decided by the IMF executive board in January.

December 30. South Korea reported that the **industrial output** index declined by 14.1% annually and by 10.7% monthly. The monthly contraction was the largest in 21 years. The slump in production is closely tied with the sharp reverse in exports, which fell by 18.3%.

December 30. Monetary Union Pact approved by **Gulf Cooperation Council (GCC)**—Bahrain, Kuwait, Qatar, Saudi Arabia, and the United Arab Emirates. Representatives from five of the six members of the GCC approved a draft accord for a monetary union yesterday at a summit in Muscat. GCC finance ministers did not agree on the ultimate location of the future central bank. The draft accord prepares for the creation of a monetary council, and the framework for a future monetary union.

December 26. The **Japanese** Ministry of Economy, Trade and Industry released preliminary figures showing that **industrial production** shrank at a record rate and unemployment rose. Total industrial output contracted 8.1% from October to November 2008. This marked the largest decline in industrial production in 55 years.

December 23. Poland's Monetary Policy Council reduced its main **policy rate** by 75 basis points. The Polish main policy rate has been reduced by 1% in two months, and now stands at 5.00%.

December 23. Japanese Cabinet approves record **fiscal plan** for FY2009. The ¥88.5 trillion (US$980.6 billion) fiscal package for FY2009, which begins April 1, 2009, marks a 6.6% increase in spending from initial targets.

December 23. After the IMF submitted a positive review of Iraq's economic reconstruction, the **Paris Club** of sovereign lenders completed the third and final step of **debt forgiveness for Iraq**, reducing Iraq's public external debt with its members by 20% or US$7.8 billion. Most of Iraq's remaining debt consists of official loans from Gulf Arab states and former communist countries, which may be forgiven or discounted if Iraq's economy continues to improve. Under former President Saddam Hussein, Iraq's debt totaled $125 billion.

December 23. New Zealand Real GDP declined 0.4% in quarterly seasonally adjusted terms. This marks the third consecutive quarterly decline in Real GDP. The economy fell into its first recession in more than a decade in the March, 2008. The rate of contraction deepened from the first two quarters of the year during which growth shrank by 0.3% and 0.2% respectively. In annual terms, the economy grew 1.7% in the year through September 2008.

December 23. The central **People's Bank of China** lowered **interest rates** for the fifth time in four months. Benchmark one-year lending and deposit rates were both lowered by 27 basis points to 5.31% and 2.25% respectively. These rates were lowered by their biggest margin in 11 years a month ago, lowered by 108 basis points.

December 22. U.K. Real GDP contracted by 0.6% quarterly in the third quarter of 2008. The Office for National Statistics (ONS) revised the decline in real GDP from its previous estimate of 0.5% quarterly. This marks the first time that the British economy has contracted since the second quarter of 1992. It had stagnated in the second quarter of 2008 and is therefore on the brink of recession, defined as two successive quarters of contracting quarterly GDP. Prior to that, GDP growth had moderated to 0.4% in the first quarter of 2008 from 0.6% in the fourth quarter of 2007 and 0.8% in the third quarter. Annual GDP growth fell to a 16-year low of 0.3% in the third quarter of 2008 from 1.7% in the second quarter and a peak of 3.3% in the second quarter of 2007. Industrial production contracted by 1.4% quarterly, and 2.5% annually in the third quarter, with manufacturing output down by 1.6% quarterly and 2.3% annually. This marks the third successive quarterly decrease in industrial production, meaning that the sector is already in recession.

December 22. Russia reports that **industrial** output growth slowed to 0.6% annual growth in October, then contracted by 8.7% annually in November, the worst monthly report since the economic collapse which followed the ruble crisis of 1998. Critical to Russia's economic slowdown is the unwillingness of Russian banks, which are heavily exposed to foreign currency denominated external debt, to lend.

December 21. Eurostat reports that **Eurozone industrial orders** fell 5.4% monthly in September and 4.7% monthly and 15.1% annually in October.

December 21. Canada reports that its federal government and the province of Ontario will contribute some C$4 billion (US$3.3 billion) to the short-term **automotive rescue** announced by the U.S. administration. The United States will provide US$13.4 billion in emergency loans to General Motors and Chrysler. General Motors is to receive C$3 billion of the Canadian funds, while Chrysler is to receive C$ 1 billion. Ford declines injections. Limits on executive compensation are a requirement for funds.

December 21. Zimbabwe reports its domestic **debt** level increased from Z$1 trillion on August 8 to Z$ 179.6 trillion (US$194 million at the current official inter-bank exchange rate) on September 8. This represents a monthly increase of 17,800%. Interest payments now account for roughly 90% of total debt.

December 19. President Bush announced an **automotive rescue** plan for General Motors Corp. and Chrysler LLC that will make $13.4 billion in federal loans available almost immediately. The money will come from the $700 billion fund set aside to rescue banks and investment firms in October. The government attached several conditions to the three-year loans and set a deadline of March 31 for the automakers to prove they can restructure enough to ensure their survival or recall the loans. As part of the rescue, GM is required to reduce debt by two-thirds via debt-forequity swaps, pay half of the contributions to a retiree health care trust using stock, make union workers' wages competitive with foreign automakers and eliminate the union jobs bank, which pays laid-off workers.

December 19. An international rescue package of 7.5 billion euro (US$ 10.6 billion) for **Latvia** was announced. The IMF reports a 27-month stand by arrangement between Latvia and the IMF, worth 1.7 billion euro (US$2.4 billion). The remainder of the rescue package includes 3.1 billion euro from the European Union (EU), 1.8 billion euro from Nordic countries, 400 million euro from the World Bank, 200 million euro from the Czech Republic, and 100 million euro each from the European Bank of Reconstruction and Development, Estonia and Poland. Latvia nationalized its second largest bank, Parex Bank. Latvia will implement measures to tighten fiscal policy and stabilize its economy.

December 19. The Bank of **Japan** lowered the benchmark **rate** by 20 basis points to 0.3%. This marks the second consecutive monthly cut.

December 18. Turkey reduces **rates** for the second consecutive month. The Central Bank of the Republic of Turkey (CBRT) announced a 125-basis-point cut to their overnight borrowing rate from 16.25% to 15.00%, and their overnight lending rate by 125 basis points, from 18.75% to 17.50%. Turkish interest rates are the highest in Europe, even after the rate cuts.

December 18. Mexican industrial output decreased an annual 2.7% in October, the sixth consecutive monthly decline. More than 80% of Mexico's exports go to the United States.

December 18. Norwegian Central Bank cut its main policy interest **rate** by 175 basis points to 3.0%, the third decrease since October.

December 17. U.S. housing starts plummeted 18.9% in November, to a seasonally adjusted annual rate of 625,000 units. This was a record monthly low.

December 16. The **U.S.** Federal Open Market Committee (FOMC) voted unanimously to lower its target for the **federal funds rate** more than 75 basis points, to a range of 0.0% to 0.25%. Long term bond yields dropped from 2.50% to 2.35%.

December 15. The Bank of **Japan's** tankan survey of **business confidence** fell from minus 3 in the third quarter to minus 24 points in the fourth quarter of the year. The 21 point contraction was the steepest in the index since the oil shocks of the 1970s, and marked the lowest level in the index since 2002.

December 12. Ecuador's President Rafael Correa announced that Ecuador will stop honoring its **external debt**; the country should expect lawsuits from bondholders in the short term. This is not the same as declaring the entire Ecuadorean economy in default.

December 11. 27 European Union (**EU**) governments' leaders approved a 200 billion euro (US$269 billion) **economic stimulus** package. The cost is approximately 1.5% of the EU's total GDP. Member states will pay major shares; supranational EU institutions, such as the European Investment Bank (EIB), will contribute the remaining 30 billion euro.

December 11. Taiwan's central bank cut its leading discount **rate** by three quarters of a percentage point to 2.0%, marking the biggest reduction since 1982. It was also the fifth rate cut in two-and-a-half months.

December 11. The central Bank of **Korea** reduced the seven-day repurchase **rate** by one percentage point to a record low of 3.00%. Interest rates have been reduced by 225 basis points in two months, 100 basis points in October and 125 basis points in November.

December 5. November **U.S. nonfarm employment** loss of 533,000 jobs was the largest in 34 years, compared with the 602,000 decline in December 1974. The U.S. Bureau of Labor Statistics also reported the unemployment rate rose from 6.5 to 6.7 percent. November's drop in payroll employment followed declines of 403,000 in September and 320,000 in October, as revised.

November 25. U.S. real GDP fell 0.5% in the third quarter of 2008. The announcement by the U.S. Bureau of Economic Analysis also reported U.S. second quarter GDP increased 2.8%. BEA attributed the third quarter decline to a contraction in consumer spending and deceleration in exports.

November 24. The U.K. announced a fiscal stimulus package valued at £20 billion (US$30.2 billion) aimed at limiting the length and depth of the apparent U.K. recession. The package included a temporary reduction of value-added tax from 17.5% to 15.0%.

November 24. The IMF Executive Board approved a 23-month Stand-By Arrangement for Pakistan in the amount of $7.6 billion to support the country's economic stabilization program.

November 24. The Central Bank of **Iceland's currency swap arrangement** with Sweden, Norway, and Denmark is extended through December 2009. On the same date, Standard & Poor's Ratings Services, **S&P, reduced** its long-term **Iceland sovereign credit rating** from BBB to BBB-, while maintaining its short-term Iceland sovereign currency rating at A-3.

November 24. The U.S. Treasury, Federal Reserve, and Federal Deposit Insurance Corp. said that they will protect **Citigroup** against certain potential losses and invest an additional $20 billion (on top of the previous $25 billion) in the company. The government is to receive $7 billion in preferred shares in the company.

November 19. The IMF Executive Board agreed to a $2.1 billion loan for Iceland. Following the decision of IMF's Executive Board, Denmark, Finland, Norway, and Sweden agreed to provide an additional $2.5 billion in loans to Iceland.

November 15. At a G-20 (including the G-8, 10 major emerging economies, Australia and the European Union) summit in Washington, the G-20 leaders agreed to continue to take steps to stabilize the global financial system and improve the international regulatory framework.

November 15. Japan announced that it would make $100 billion from its foreign exchange reserves available to the IMF for loans to emerging market economies. This was in addition to $2 billion that Japan is to invest in the World Bank to help recapitalize banks in smaller, emerging market economies. Also, the IMF and **Pakistan** agreed in principle on a $7.6 billion loan package aimed at preventing the nation from defaulting on foreign debt and restoring investor confidence.

November 14. The President's Working Group on Financial Markets (Treasury, Securities and Exchange Commission, Federal Reserve, and the Commodity Futures Trading Commission) announced a series of initiatives to strengthen oversight and the infrastructure of the over-the-counter derivatives market. This included the development of credit default swap central counterparties—clearinghouses between parties that own debt instruments and others willing to insure against defaults.

November 13. The African Development bank conference on the financial crisis ended with a pessimistic outlook for **Sub-Saharan Africa**, due to declines in foreign capital, export markets and commodity-based exports.

November 13. Eurostat declared that **Eurozone** GDP declined by 0.2% in the third quarter of 2008, as well as the second quarter. Since **recession** is defined as two successive quarters of contracting GDP, this means that the Eurozone is technically in recession.

November 12. United States Treasury Secretary Paulson announced a **change** in priorities for the US$700 billion **Troubled Asset Relief Program** (TARP) approved by Congress in early October. The first priority remains to provide direct equity infusions to the financial sector. Roughly US$250 billion has been allocated to this sector. This scope was broadened to include non-banks, particularly insurance companies such as AIG, which provide insurance for credit defaults. Paulson noted that TARP would be used to purchase bank stock, not toxic assets. Paulson's new plan also would provide support for the **asset-backed commercial paper** market, particularly **securitized** auto loans, credit card debt, and student loans. Between August and November 2007 asset-backed commercial paper outstanding contracted by nearly US$400 billion. Paulson rejected suggestions that TARP funds be made available to the U.S. auto industry.

November 12. The Central Bank of **Russia** raised key **interest** rates by 1%. **Swiss** Economics Minister announced the Swiss government would inject 341 million Swiss Francs/US$286.6 million for economic **stimulus**. The State Bank of **Pakistan** raised **interest** rates by 2%, to reduce inflation. It also **injected** 320 billion rupees/US$4 billion into the Pakistan banking system.

November 11. IMF deferred their decision to approve US$2.1 billion loan for **Iceland**. This was the third time the IMF board scheduled then failed to discuss the Iceland proposal.

The tentative Iceland package required Iceland to implement economic stabilization. That economic stabilization was the required trigger for implementation of EU loans to Iceland from Norway, Poland and Sweden. Iceland is reportedly involved in disputes over deposit guarantees with British and Dutch depositors in Icelandic banks.

November 10. The **United States** government announced further aid to **American International Group**, AIG. AIG's September $85 billion loan was reduced to $60 billion; the government bought $40 billion of preferred AIG shares, and $52.5 billion of AIG mortgage securities. The U.S. support of AIG increased from September's $85 billion to $150 billion.

November 9. G-20 meeting of finance ministers and central bank governors in Sao Paulo, **Brazil**, concluded with a communiqué calling for increased role of emerging economies in reform of Bretton Woods financial institutions, including the World Bank and the International Monetary Fund.

November 9. China announced a 4 trillion Yuan/U.S. $587 billion **domestic stimulus package**. primarily aimed at infrastructure, housing, agriculture, health care, and social welfare spending. This program represents 16% of China's 2007 GDP, and roughly equals total Chinese central and local government outlays in 2006.

November 8. Latvian government took over **Parex Bank**, the second-largest bank in Latvia.

November 7. Iceland's President Grimsson reportedly offered the use of the former U.S. Air Force **base at Keflavik** to Russia. The United States departed Keflavik in 2006.

November 7. United States October **employment** report revealed a decline of 240,000 jobs in October, and September job losses revised from 159,000 to 284,000. The U.S. unemployment rate rose from 6.1% to 6.5%, a 14-year high.

November 7. Moody's sovereign rating for **Hungary** is reduced from A2 to A3. Despite IMF assistance, financial instability may require "severe macroeconomic and financial adjustment." **Moody's** reduced its ratings of **Latvia** from A3 to A2, before the Latvian statistical office announced Latvian **GDP fell** at a 4.2% annual rate in the third quarter of 2008. Moody's also announced an outlook reduction for **Estonia and Lithuania**.

November 6. IMF approved SDR 10.5 billion/U.S. $15.7 billion Stand-By Arrangement for **Hungary**. U.S. $6.3 billion is to be immediately available.

November 6. International Monetary Fund announced its updated *World Economic Outlook*. Main findings include that "global activity is slowing quickly", and "prospects for global growth have deteriorated over the past month." The IMF now projects **global GDP growth** for 2009 at 2.2%, 3/4 of a percentage point lower than projections announced in October, 2008. It projects **U.S. GDP growth** at 1.4% in 2008 and -0.7% in 2009.

November 6. The **European Central Bank**, ECB, reduced its key **interest rate** from 3.75% to 3.25%. In two months the ECB has reduced this rate from 4.25% to 3.25%. The **Danish Central Bank** lowered its key lending rate from 5.5% to 5%. The **Czech National Bank** reduced its interest rate from 3.5% to 2.75%. In **South Korea**, the Bank of Korea reduced its key interest rate from 4.25% to 4%. During October the Bank of Korea reduced its rate from 5.25% to 4.25%.

November 4. United States Institute of Supply Management's **manufacturing index** fell 4.6 points in October to 38.9, after previously falling in September. The export orders component of the manufacturing index fell 11 points in October to 41, following a drop of 5 points in September. 41 is the lowest level in this **export index** in 20 years. Exports have been the strongest sector in U.S. manufacturing during the past year.

November 4. Australia. Reserve Bank of Australia lowered its overnight **cash rate** by 75 basis points to 5.25%, the lowest Australian rate since March 2005.

November 4. Indian Prime Minister Manmohan Singh established a **Cabinet-level committee** to evaluate the effect of the financial crisis on India's economy and industries. This follows the **November 2 Indian and Pakistani Central banks'** actions to boost liquidity. India cut its short-term lending rate by 50 basis points to 7.5% and reduced its cash reserve ratio by 100 basis points to 5.5%.

November 4. Chilean President Michelle Bachelet announced a U.S. $1.15 billion **stimulus** package to boost the housing market and channel credit into small and medium businesses.

November 3. IMF announced agreement with **Kyrgyzstan** on arrangement under the Exogenous Shocks Facility to provide at least U.S. $60 million. The agreement requires the approval of the IMF Executive Board to become final.

November 3. Russian Prime Minister Vladimir Putin reported measures to support the real economy. The measures will include temporary preferences for domestic producers for state procurement contracts, subsidizing interest rates for loans intended to modernize production; and tariff protection for a number of industries such as automobiles and agriculture. The new policy aims to support exporters.

October 31. Three of the six **Gulf Cooperation Council**, GCC, countries, **Bahrain, Kuwait and Saudi Arabian central banks** reduced **interest rates** to follow the actions of the U.S. Federal Reserve and other central banks.

October 31. Kazakhstan government will make **capital injections** into its **top four banks**, Halyk Bank, Kazkommertsbank, Alliance Bank and BTA Bank.

October 31. The U.S. Commerce Department reported that **consumer spending** fell 0.3% in September after remaining flat in the previous month. On a year-to-year basis, spending was down 0.4%, the first such drop since the recession of 1991. Consumer spending has not grown since June.

October 30. The U.S. Bureau of Economic Analysis reported that **U.S. real gross domestic product** decreased 0.3 per cent in the third quarter of 2008 after increasing 2.8 per cent in the second quarter of 2008.

October 29. The **U.S. Federal Reserve** lowered its target for the federal funds rate 50 basis points to 1 per cent. It also approved a 50 basis point decrease in the discount rate to 1.25 per cent. The Federal Reserve also announced establishment of temporary reciprocal currency arrangements, or swap lines, with the Banco Central do Brasil, the Banco de Mexico, the Bank of Korea, the Monetary Authority of Singapore, and the Reserve Bank of New Zealand. Swap lines are designed to help improve liquidity conditions in global financial markets.

October 29. IMF approved the creation of a **Short-Term Liquidity Facility**, established to support countries with strong policies which face temporary liquidity problems.

October 28. The IMF, the European Union, and the World Bank announced a joint financing package for **Hungary** totaling $25.1 billion to bolster its economy. The IMF is to lend Hungary $15.7 billion, the EU $8.1 billion, and the World Bank $1.3 billion.

October 28. The U.S. Conference Board said that its **consumer confidence** index has dropped to an all-time low, from 61.4 in September to 38 in October.

October 27. Iceland's **Kaupthing Bank** became the first European borrower to default on yen- denominated bonds issued in Japan (samurai bonds).

October 26. The IMF announced it is set to lend **Ukraine** $16.5 Billion.

October 24. IMF announced an outline agreement with **Iceland** to lend the country $2.1 billion to support an economic recovery program to help it restore confidence in its banking system and stabilize its currency.

October 23. President Bush called for the **G-20** leaders to meet on November 15 in Washington, DC to deal with the global financial crisis.

October 22. Pakistan sought help from the IMF to meet balance of payments difficulties and to avoid a possible economic meltdown amid high fuel prices, dwindling foreign investment and soaring militant violence.

G-20. The Group of 20 Finance Ministers and Central Bank Governors from industrial and emerging-market countries is to meet in Sao Paulo, Brazil on November 8-9, 2008, to discuss key issues related to global economic stability.

October 20. The **Netherlands** agreed to inject €10 billion ($13.4 billion) into **ING Groep** NV, a global banking and insurance company. The investment is to take the form of nonvoting preferred shares with no maturity date (ING can repay the money on its own schedule and will have the right to buy the shares back at 150% of the issue price or convert them into ordinary shares in three years). The government is to take two seats on ING's supervisory board; ING's executive-board members are to forgo 2008 bonuses; and ING said it would not pay a dividend for the rest of 2008.

October 20. Sweden proposed a financial stability plan, which includes a 1.5 trillion Swedish kronor ($206 billion) bank guarantee, to combat the impact of the economic crisis.

October 20. The U.N.'s **International Labor Organization** projects that the global financial crisis could add at least 20 million people to the **world's unemployed**, bringing the total to 210 million by the end of 2009.

October 19. South Korea announced that it would guarantee up to $100 billion in foreign debt held by its banks and would pump $30 billion more into its banking sector.

October 18. President Bush, President Nicolas Sarkozy of France, and the president of the European Commission issued a joint statement saying they agreed to "reach out to other world leaders" to propose an **international summit meeting** to be held soon after the U.S. presidential election, with the possibility of more gatherings after that. The Europeans had been pressing for a meeting of the Group of 8 industrialized nations, but President Bush went one step further, calling for a broader global conference that would include "developed and developing nations"—among them China and India.

October 17. The **Swiss** government said it would take a 9% stake ($5.36 billion) in **UBS**, one of the country's leading banks, and set up a $60 billion fund to absorb the bank's troubled assets. UBS had already written off $40 billion of its $80 billion in "toxic American securities." The Swiss central bank was to take over $31 billion of the bank's American assets (much of it in the form of debt linked to subprime and Alt-A mortgages, and securities linked to commercial real estate and student loans).

October 15. The **G8** leaders (Canada, France, Germany, Italy, Japan, Russia, the United Kingdom and the United States, and the European Commission) stated that they were united in their commitment to resolve the current crisis, strengthen financial institutions, restore confidence in the financial system, and provide a sound economic footing for citizens and businesses. They stated that changes to the regulatory and institutional regimes for the world's financial sectors are needed and that they look forward to a leaders' meeting with key countries at an appropriate time in the near future to adopt an agenda for reforms to meet the challenges of the 21st century.

October 14. In coordination with European monetary authorities, **the U.S. Treasury, Federal Reserve, and Federal Deposit Insurance Corporation** announced a **plan to invest up to $250 billion** in preferred securities of **nine major U.S. banks** (including **Citigroup, Bank of America, Wells Fargo, Goldman Sachs and JPMorgan Chase**). The FDIC also became able to temporarily guarantee the senior debt and deposits in non-interest bearing deposit transaction accounts (used mainly by businesses for daily operations).[254]

October 13. U.K. Government provided $60 billion and took a 60% stake in **Royal Bank of Scotland** and 40% in **Lloyds TSB** and **HBOS**.

October 12-13. Several European countries (**Germany, France, Italy, Austria, Netherlands, Portugal, Spain, and Norway**) announced **rescue plans** for their countries worth as much as $2.7 trillion. The plans were largely consistent with a U.K. model that includes concerted action, recapitalization, state ownership, government debt guarantees (the largest component of the plans), and improved regulations.

October 8. In a coordinated effort, the **U.S. Federal Reserve**, the **European Central Bank**, the **Bank of England** and the **central banks of Canada and Sweden** all reduced **primary lending** rates by a half percentage point. **Switzerland** also cut its benchmark rate, while the **Bank of Japan** endorsed the moves without changing its rates. The **Chinese central bank** also reduced its key interest rate and lowered bank reserve requirements. The Federal Reserve's benchmark short-term rate stood at 1.5% and the European Central Bank's at 3.75%.

October 5. The **German** government moved to guarantee all private savings accounts and arranged a bailout for **Hypo Real Estate**, a German lender. A week earlier, **Fortis**, a large banking and insurance company based in Belgium but active across much of Europe, had received €11.2 billion ($8.2 billion) from the governments of the Netherlands, Belgium and Luxembourg. On October 3, the Dutch government seized its Dutch operations and on October 5, the Belgian government helped to arrange for **BNP-Paribas**, the French bank, to take over what was left of the company.

October 3. **U.S. House of Representatives** passes 110th Congress bill H.R. 1424, Financial Institutions Rescue bill, clearing it for Presidential signing or veto. **President signs bill into law, P.L. 110-343,** the **Emergency Economic Stabilization Act of 2008**, sometimes referred to as the Troubled Assets Relief Program, TARP. The new bill's title includes its purpose:

> "A bill to provide authority for the Federal Government to purchase and insure certain types of troubled assets for the purposes of providing stability to and preventing disruption in the economy and financial system and protecting taxpayers ... "

October 3. Britain's Financial Services Authority said it had raised the amount guaranteed in savings accounts to £50,000 ($88,390) from £35,000. **Greece** also stated that it would guarantee savings accounts regardless of the amount.

October 3. Wells Fargo Bank announced a takeover of **Wachovia Corp**, the fourth-largest U.S. bank. (Previously, Citibank had agreed to take over Wachovia.)

October 1. U.S. Senate passed H.R. 1424, amended, Financial Institutions Rescue bill.

September/October. On September 30, **Iceland**'s government took a 75% share of **Glitnir**, Iceland's third-largest bank, by injecting €600 million ($850 million) into the bank. The following week, it took control of **Landsbanki** and soon after placed Iceland's largest bank, **Kaupthing**, into receivership as well.

September 26. Washington Mutual became the largest thrift failure with $307 billion in assets. **JPMorgan Chase** agreed to pay $1.9 billion for the banking operations but did not take ownership of the holding company.

September 22. Ireland increased the statutory limit for the deposit guarantee scheme for banks and building societies from €20,000 ($26,000) to €100,000 ($130,000) per depositor per institution.

September 21. The **Federal Reserve** approved the transformation of **Goldman Sachs** and **Morgan Stanley** into bank holding companies from investment banks in order to increase oversight and allow them to access the Federal Reserve's discount (loan) window.

September 18. Treasury Secretary Paulson announced a **$700 billion economic stabilization proposal** that would allow the government to buy toxic assets from the nation's biggest banks, a move aimed at shoring up balance sheets and restoring confidence within the financial system. An amended bill to accomplish this was passed by Congress on October 3.

September 16. The **Federal Reserve** came to the assistance of **American International Group, AIG**, an insurance giant on the verge of failure because of its exposure to exotic securities known as credit default swaps, in an $85 billion deal (later increased to $123 billion).

September 15. Lehman Brothers bankruptcy at $639 billion is the largest in the history of the United States.

September 14. Bank of America said it will buy **Merrill Lynch** for $50 billion.

September 7. U.S. Treasury announced that it was taking over **Fannie Mae** and **Freddie Mac,** two government-sponsored enterprises that bought securitized mortgage debt.

August 12. According to Bloomberg, **losses** at the **top 100 banks** in the world from the U.S. subprime crisis and the ensuing credit crunch exceeded $500 billion as write downs spread to more asset types.

May 4. Finance ministers of **13 Asian nations** agreed to set up a foreign exchange pool of at least $80 billion to be used in the event of another regional financial crisis. **China, Japan** and **South Korea** are to provide 80% of the funds with the rest coming from the 10 members of ASEAN.

March. The **Federal Reserve** staved off a **Bear Stearns** bankruptcy by assuming $30 billion in liabilities and engineering a sale of Bear Sterns to **JPMorgan Chase** for a price that was less than the worth of Bear's Manhattan office building.

February 17. The **British** government decided to "temporarily" nationalize the struggling housing lender, **Northern Rock**. A previous government loan of $47 billion had proven ineffective in helping the company to recover.

January. Swiss banking giant **UBS** reported more than $18 billion in writedowns due to exposure to U.S. real estate market. **Bank of America** acquired **Countrywide Financial**, the largest mortgage lender in the United States.

2007

July/August. German banks with bad investments in U.S. real estate are caught up in the evolving crisis, These include **IKB Deutsche Industriebank, Sachsen LB** (Saxony State Bank) and **BayernLB** (Bavaria State Bank).

July 18. Two battered **hedge funds** worth an estimated $1.5 billion at the end of 2006 were almost entirely worthless. They had been managed by **Bear Stearns** and were invested heavily in subprime mortgages.

July 12. The **Federal Deposit Insurance Corp**. took control of the $32 billion **IndyMac Bank (Pasadena, CA)** in what regulators called the second-largest bank failure in U.S. history.

March/April. New Century Financial corporation stopped making new loans as the practice of giving high risk mortgage loans to people with bad credit histories becomes a problem. The **International Monetary Fund** warned of risks to global financial markets from weakened US home mortgage market.

Appendix B. Stimulus Packages Announced by Governments

Date Announced	Country	$Billion	Status, Package Contents
17-Feb-09	United States	787.00	Infrastructure technology, tax cuts, education, transfers to states, energy, nutrition, health, unemployment benefits. Budget in deficit.
4-Feb-09	Canada	32.00	Two-year program. Infrastructure, tax relief, aid for sectors in peril. Government to run an estimated $1.1 billion budget deficit in 2008 and $52 billion deficit in 2009.
7-Jan-09	Mexico	54.00	Infrastructure, a freeze on gasoline prices, reducing electricity rates, help for poor families to replace old appliances, construction of low-income housing and an oil refinery, rural development, increase government purchases from small- and medium-sized companies. Paid for by taxes, oil revenues, and borrowing.
12-Dec-08	European Union	39.00	Total package of $256 billion called for states to increase budgets by $217 billion and for the EU to provide $39 billion to fund cross-border projects including clean energy and upgraded telecommunications architecture.
13-Jan-09	Germany	65.00	Infrastructure, tax cuts, child bonus, increase in some social benefits, $3,250 incentive for trading in cars more than nine years old for a new or slightly used car.
24-Nov-08	United Kingdom	29.60	Proposed plan includes a 2.5% cut in the value added tax for 13 months, a postponement of corporate tax increases, government guarantees for loans to small and midsize businesses, spending on public works, including public housing and energy efficiency. Plan includes an increase in income taxes on those making more than $225,000 and increase National Insurance contribution for all but the lowest income workers.
5-Nov-08	France	33.00	Public sector investments (road and rail construction, refurbishment and improving ports and river infrastructure, building and renovating universities, research centers, prisons, courts, and monuments) and loans for carmakers. Does not include the previously planned $15 billion in credits and tax breaks on investments by companies in 2009.
16-Nov-08	Italy	52.00	Awaiting final parliamentary approval. Three year program. Measures to spur consumer credit, provide loans to companies, and rebuild infrastructure. February 6, announced a $2.56 billion stimulus package that was part of the three-year program that includes payments of up to $1,950 for trading in an old car for a new, less polluting one and 20% tax deductions for purchases of appliances and furniture.
22-Nov-08	Netherlands	7.50	Tax deduction to companies that make large investments, funds to companies that hire temporary workers, and creation of a program to find jobs for the unemployed.
11-Dec-08	Belgium	2.60	Increase in unemployment benefits, lowering of the value added tax on construction, abolishing taxes on energy, energy checks for families, faster payments of invoices by the government, faster government investment in railroads and buildings, lowering of employer's fiscal contributions.
27-Nov-08	Spain	14.30	Public works, help for automobile industry, environmental projects, research and development, restoring residential and military housing, and funds to support the sick.
14-Jan-09	Portugal	2.89	Funds to be provided to medium and small-sized businesses, money for infrastructure, particularly schools, and investment in technological improvement.
20-Nov-08	Israel	5.40	Public works to include desalination plants, doubling railway routes, adding R&D funding, increasing export credits, cutting assorted taxes, and aid packages for employers to hire new workers.

1-Dec-08	Switzerland	0.59	Public works spending on flood defense, natural disaster and energy-efficiency projects.
5-Dec-08	Sweden	2.70	Public infrastructure and investment in human capital, including job training, vocational workshops, and workplace restructuring.; extension of social benefits to part-time workers.
26-Jan-09	Norway	2.88	Investment in construction, infrastructure, and renovation of state-owned buildings, tax breaks for companies.
20-Nov-08	Russia	20.00	Cut in the corporate profit tax rate, a new depreciation mechanism for businesses, to be funded by Russia's foreign exchange reserves and rainy day fund.
3-Dec-08	Egypt	8.51	Infrastructure, Industrial Development Authority, Export Development Fund, investment funds for small- and medium-sized enterprises, funds for industrial modernization, training, technology transfer centers, export promotion, land development
10-Nov-08	China	586.00	Low-income housing, electricity, water, rural infrastructure, projects aimed at environmental protection and technological innovation, tax deduction for capital spending by companies, and spending for health care and social welfare.
13-Dec-08	Japan	250.00	Increase in government spending, funds to stabilize the financial system (prop up troubled banks and ease a credit crunch by purchasing commercial paper), tax cuts for homeowners and companies that build or purchase new factories and equipment, and grants to local government.
6-Apr-09	Japan	146.00	Increasing safety net for non-regular workers, support for small businesses, revitalizing regional economies, promoting green car purchases, promoting solar power and nursing and medical services.
3-Nov-08	South Korea	14.64	$11 billion for infrastructure (including roads, universities, schools, and hospitals; funds for small- and medium-business, fishermen, and families with low income) and tax cuts. Includes an October 2008 stimulus package of $3.64 billion to provide support for the construction industry.
9-Feb-09	South Korea	37.87	The government announced its intention to invest $37.87 billion over the next four years in eco-friendly projects including the construction of dams; "green" transportation networks such as low-carbon emitting railways, bicycle roads, and other public transportation systems; and expand existing forest areas.
16-Dec-08	Vietnam	6.00	Tax cuts, spending on infrastructure, housing, schools, and hospitals.
28-Jan-09	Indonesia	6.32	(Proposed) Tax incentives for companies and individuals, cuts in fuel and electricity prices, spending on infrastructure.
21-Jan-09	Philippines	7.01	Stimulus package wrapped into the current budget. More spending on infrastructure, agriculture, education, and health, cash for poor households, and tax cuts. Partial funding by borrowing from government corporations and from the nation's social security system.
29-Jan-09	Thailand	3.35	Cash for low earners, tax cuts, expanded free education, subsidies for transport and utilities.
22-Jan-09	Singapore	13.70	Personal income tax rebate; cut in maximum corporate tax rate; subsidies for employee wages; training; cash handouts to low-income workers; increase in public sector hiring; assuming 80% of the risk on private bank loans; boosting aid to welfare recipients, government pensioners, and students; invest in infrastructure.

(Continued)

Date Announced	Country	$Billion	Status, Package Contents
30-Nov-08	Malaysia	1.93	High impact infrastructure projects including roads, schools, and housing. Government budget in deficit. Expect a second, larger stimulus package in February or March 2009.
8-Dec-08	India	4.00	Stimulus package includes $70 million to finance exports of textiles and handicrafts; value added tax rate cut at different levels and across products. Public works spending includes funding for various sectors, including: housing, automobile, infrastructure, power, and medium and small industries. In addition, import duties on naptha was revoked, export duty on iron ore was removed, levy on exports of iron were reduced.
28-Nov-08	Taiwan	15.60	Shopping vouchers of $108 each for all citizens, construction projects to be carried out over four years include expanding metro systems, rebuilding bridges and classrooms, improving, railway and sewage systems, and renew urban areas.
31-Dec-08	Sri Lanka	0.14	Cuts in prices for diesel, kerosene, and furnace oil; lifting of surcharge on electricity, incentive for exporters not to retrench workers, lifting of tax on rubber exports, and subsidies for tea farmers.
26-Jan-09	Australia	35.2	$7 billion stimulus package in October 2008 was cash handouts to low income earners and pensioners. January's $28.2 billion package includes infrastructure, schools and housing, and cash payments to low- and middle-income earners. Budget is in deficit.
7-Jan-09	Mexico	54.00	Infrastructure, a freeze on gasoline prices, reducing electricity rates, help for poor families to replace old appliances, construction of low-income housing and an oil refinery, rural development, increase government purchases from small- and medium-sized companies. Paid for by taxes, oil revenues, and borrowing.
23-Dec-08	Brazil	5.00	Program established in 2007 to continue to 2010. Tax cuts (exempt capital goods producers from the industrial and welfare taxes, increase the value of personal computers exempted from taxes) and rebates. Funded by reducing the government's budget surplus.
5-Dec-08	Argentina	3.80	Low-cost loans to farmers, automakers, or other exporters.
6-Jan-09	Chile	4.00	Infrastructure, subsidies for copper producer, lower employer contributions for small- and medium-sized companies, and income tax rebates. Funded from copper windfall earnings saved in sovereign wealth funds and by issuing bonds.

Source: Congressional Research from various news articles and government press releases.
Notes: Currency conversions to U.S. dollars were either already done in the news articles or by CRS using current exchange rates.

APPENDIX C. COMPARISON OF SELECTED FINANCIAL REGULATORY REFORM PROPOSALS[255]

This appendix provides a comparison, in graphic form, of selected proposals for regulatory reform that have been put forward in the wake of the global financial crisis. Seven such proposals are covered in the table below. They are, in chronological order:

U.S. Department of the Treasury, *Blueprint for a Modernized Financial Regulatory Structure*, March 2008. (This study was completed under Secretary Henry Paulson, during the Bush Administration.)

Counterparty Risk Management Policy Group (CRMPG), *Containing Systemic Risk: The Road to Reform*, Aug. 6, 2008. (The CRMPG, a group of commercial and investment bankers, began this study at the suggestion of the President's Working Group on Financial Markets. Its focus is on market participants, rather than regulators.)

Congressional Oversight Panel (COP), *Special Report on Regulatory Reform: Modernizing the American Financial Regulatory System: Recommendations for Improving Oversight, Protecting Consumers, and Ensuring Stability*, January 2009. (The COP was created by the Emergency Economic Stabilization Act of 2008 (P.L. 110-343) to oversee the Troubled Asset Relief Program.)

Group of Thirty, *Financial Reform: A Framework for Financial Stability*, January 15, 2009. (The Group of Thirty is a private, nonprofit body composed of senior representatives of the private and public sectors and academia, which aims to deepen understanding of international economic and financial issues.)

Group of 20 (G-20), *G-20 Working Group on Enhancing Sound Regulation and Strengthening Transparency: Final Report (Draft)*, February 2009. (The G-20 is made up of the finance ministers and central bank governors of 19 countries: Argentina, Australia, Brazil, Canada, China, France, Germany, India, Indonesia, Italy, Japan, Mexico, Russia, Saudi Arabia, South Africa, South Korea, Turkey, the U.K., and the United States, and also the European Union.)

Financial Services Authority (FSA), *The Turner Review: A Regulatory Response to the Global Banking Crisis*, March 2009. (The FSA is the UK regulatory agency with jurisdiction over banking, securities, insurance, and derivatives. Adair Turner has been FSA chairman since September 2008.)

U.S. Department of the Treasury, *Financial Regulatory Reform: A New Foundation*, June 2009. (Treasury has released draft legislative language containing many of these recommendations.)

The table below lists a number of specific recommendations contained in the above reports and studies, and indicates by an "X" which ones contain each recommendation. The absence of an "X" does not necessarily mean that the authors of the report oppose the recommendation—each study has its own scope and focus. In some cases, studies identify issues as needing further study; in others, an issue may be identified as a problem contributing to the financial crisis without a specific recommendation for reform being made. (In neither of these cases would an "X" appear in the table.)

(An "X" indicates that a report includes the recommendation at the left)

Recommendation	Treasury (2009)	FSA	G-20	Group of 30	COP	CRMPG	Treasury (2008)
Systemic Risk							
Create (or designate) a single regulator with responsibility over all systemically-important financial institutions, regardless of their legal form.	X				X		X
All systemically-important financial institutions should be subject to an appropriate degree of regulation.	X	X	X	X	X		X
The systemic risk regulator should have prompt corrective action powers with regard to failing systemically-important firms.	X				X		X
Firms' internal risk controls should be made more robust and should take systemic risk into account. Corporate boards should assume more responsibility for their firms' risk management practices.		X		X		X	
Systemically-important banks should be restricted in certain risky activities, such as affiliation with non-financial firms, proprietary trading, etc.		X		X	X		
Financial institutions' use of stress testing should be more rigorous.	X		X	X		X	
Regulation of critical payment systems should be strengthened.	X						X
International monitoring for systemic risk should be enhanced, and a more formal mechanism should be created.	X	X	X	X	X		
Capital Standards							
Large complex systemically-important financial institutions should be subject to more stringent capital regulation than other firms.	X		X		X		X
Minimum capital standards should be raised throughout the banking system, or for all financial institutions.	X	X	X	X	X		
Capital standards should be adjusted to avoid procyclicality,		X	X	X	X	X	
that is, firms should be required to build up capital during good times, and be allowed to hold less capital during cyclical contractions.							

Regulators' and firms' capital decisions should make greater provision against liquidity risk.	X	X	X	X	X	X	
Hedge Funds and Other Private Pools of Capital							
Hedge funds should be required to register with the Securities and Exchange Commission (SEC) or other national securities regulator.	X		X	X	X		X
Systemically-important hedge funds should be subject to prudential regulation.	X		X	X	X		X
Hedge funds should provide information on a confidential basis to regulators about their strategies and positions.	X	X	X		X		X
Over-the-Counter (OTC) Derivatives							
Credit default swaps should be processed through a regulated centralized counterparty (CCP) or clearing house.	X	X	X	X	X	X	
All standardized OTC derivatives should be processed through a regulated CCP or clearing house.	X				X		
OTC derivatives dealers should subject strong regime.	X						
Non-standard (or customized) OTC derivatives should be reported to a central trade repository or to a regulator.	X				X		
Resolution Authority for Non-Bank Financial Institutions							
To avoid disorderly liquidations, a government agency should have authority to take over a failing, systemically-important non-bank institution, and place it in conservatorship or receivership, outside the bankruptcy system.	X			X			
Money Market Funds							
SEC (or other national regulator) should impose limits on risk-taking to make money market funds less vulnerable to runs.	X			X			
Funds that offer bank-like services should be chartered as special purpose banks, insured, and regulated.				X			
Compensation Structures in Financial Firms							
Pay practices should discourage excessive risk-taking, via incentives for fostering long-term stability rather than maximizing annual performance bonuses.		X	X		X	X	

Regulators should consider compensation structures when assessing firms' risk management practices.			X				
Credit Rating Agencies							
Credit rating agencies (CRAs) should be registered and regulated with the appropriate government agency.	X	X	X		X		
CRAs should be held ccount-accountable for accuracy of ratings, through after the-fact audits or evaluations.				X	X		
The rating process for complex financial instruments, as structured securitized products, should be more transparent, or such instruments subject to additional mandatory risk disclosures.	X	X				X	
CRA revenues (especially when securities issuers pay for ratings) be subject to oversight, greater disclosure, or limits.	X			X	X		
Accounting Standards							
Fair value, or mark-to-market, accounting standards should be modified to reduce their procyclical impact.			X	X			
Current rules for accounting consolidation (specifying when assets and liabilities may be held off the balance sheet) should be replaced by a principles-based standard reflecting the concepts of control and risk exposure.						X	
Other Regulatory Structure Issues							
There should be a single banking regulator for prudential supervision.				X			X
There should be single regulator for consumer products.	X				X		X
Financial regulators should play a greater role in macroeconomic policy-making.		X	X				
Insurance companies should be chartered and regulated at the federal level.				X			X
Government-sponsored enterprises—a clear line should be drawn between public and private firms.				X			
Minimum international standards—a regulatory floor—should apply in all countries, including tax havens and offshore banking centers.	X	X		X	X		

Source: Prepared by CRS.

APPENDIX D. SUMMARY OF POLICY TARGETS AND OPTIONS

This appendix lists the major problems raised by the crisis, the targets of policy, and the policies already being taken or possibly to take by various entities in response to the global financial crisis. The length and breadth of the list indicates the extent that the financial crisis has required diverse and draconian action. Policies or actions not yet taken or are being considered are marked by a "?" in the table. Many of these items are discussed in later sections of this report and are addressed in separate CRS reports.

Table D-1. Problems, Targets of Policy, and Actions Taken or Possibly to Take in Response to the Global Financial Crisis

Problem	Targets of Policy	Actions Taken or Possibly To Take
Containing the Contagion and Restoring Market Operations		
Bankruptcy of financial institutions	Financial institution, Financial sector	• Capital injection through loans or stock purchases—Increase capital requirements • Takeover of company by • government or other company • Allow to go bankrupt
Excess toxic debt	Capital base of debt holding institution	• Write-off of debt by holding institution • Purchase of toxic debt through Public Private Partnership Investment Program government at a discount (March 23, 2009, Treasury announcement) • Ease mark-to-market accounting requirements (April 2, 2009, Financial Accounting Standards Board) • Restructure mortgages • Nationalize debt holding institutions?
Credit market freeze	Lending institutions	• Coordinated lowering of interest rates by central banks/Federal Reserve • Guarantee short-term, uncollateralized business lending • Capital injection through loans or stock purchases
Consumer runs on deposits in banks and money market funds	Banks Brokerage houses	• Guarantee bank deposits • Guarantee money market accounts • Buy underlying money market securities to cover redemptions

Table D-1. (Continued)

Problem	Targets of Policy	Actions Taken or Possibly To Take
Containing the Contagion and Restoring Market Operations		
Declining stock markets	Investors Short sellers	• Temporary ban on short sales of stock • Government purchases of stock?
Global recession, rising unemployment, decreasing tax revenues, declining exports	National governments	• Stimulative monetary and fiscal policies • Increased lending by International • Financial Institutions (April 2009 G-20 declaration to increase IMF funding) • Trade policy? • Support for unemployed • Cash for Clunkers rebates for buying new cars with better gas mileage (June 2009)
Coping with Long-Term, Systemic Problems		
Poor underwriting standards Overly high ratings of collateralized debt obligations by rating companies Lack of transparency in ratings	Credit rating agencies Bundlers of collateralized debt obligations Corporate leveraged lenders	• More transparency in factors behind credit ratings and better models to assess risk? • Regulation of Credit Rating Agencies (April 2, 2009 London Summit) • Changes to the IOSCO Code of Conduct for Credit Rating Agencies? • Strengthen oversight of lenders? • Strengthen disclosure requirements to make information more • easily accessible and usable?
Incentive distortions for originators of mortgages (no penalty for mortgage defaults due to faulty lending practices)	Mortgage originators Fannie Mae/Freddie Mac All participants in the originate-to-distribute chain	• Require loan originators and bundlers to provide initial and ongoing information on the quality and performance of securitized assets or to retain a 5% interest in the security (June 17 Treasury Plan) • Strengthened oversight of mortgage originators (June 17 Treasury Plan) • Penalties for malfeasance by originators?
Shortcomings in risk management practices Severe underestimation of risks in the tails of default distributions and insufficient regard for systemic risk	Investors Banks, securities companies Regulatory agencies	• More prudent oversight of capital, liquidity, and risk management? • Raise capital requirements for complex structured credit products and to account for

Risk models that encourage pro-cyclical risk taking		liquidity risk (June 17 Treasury Plan) • Strengthen authorities' responsiveness to risk? • Set stricter capital and liquidity buffers for financial institutions (June 17 Treasury Plan)
Banks had weak controls over off-balance sheet risks Regulators are "stove piped." Do not deal adequately with large complex financial institutions	Bank structured investment vehicles Bank sponsored conduits Regulatory agencies Financial intermediaries engaged in a combination of banking, securities, futures, or insurance	• —Strengthen accounting and regulatory practices? • —Raise capital requirements for off-balance sheet nvestment vehicles? • —create an independent agency to monitor systemic risk (March 20 and June 17, 2009 Treasury Announcements and plans) • Create a Financial Services Oversight Council or other organization to improve interagency coordination and cooperation (June 17,2009 Treasury plan)
Hedge funds and private equity are largely unregulated Information on Credit Default Swaps not public	Regulatory agencies	• extend regulation and oversight to hedge funds and private equity (April 2, 2009, London Summit, June 17, 2009 Treasury Plan) • create clearing ounterparty for credit default swaps (March 26, 2009 Treasury Announcement)
Consumers being victimized" in credit card, mortgage, and other financial markets	Bank regulatory agencies	• create a Consumer Financial Protection Agency (June 17, 2009 Treasury Plan)
Problems for International Policy		
Lack of consistency in regulations among nations and need for new regulations to cope with new risks and exposures	National regulatory and oversight authorities Bank for International Settlements International Monetary Fund Financial Stability Board (Financial Stability Forum)	• Implement G-20 Action Plan (November 15, 2008 G-20 Summit) • Implement Basel II (Bank for International Settlements' capital and other requirements for banks) (in process by countries) — Bretton Woods II agreement? • Greater role for the Financial Stability Board/Forum and International Monetary Fund (April 2, 2009 London Summit, June 17 Treasury Plan)
		• Establish colleges of national supervisors to oversee financial sectors across boundaries (November 15, 2008 G-20 Summit)
Countries unable to cope with financial crisis	IMF, Development Banks National monetary authorities and governments	• Increased resources for the IMF and World Bank (April 2, 2009 London Summit) (H.R. 2346, provided for increase in quota and loans to the IMF) • Loans and swaps by capital surplus countries • Creation of long-term international liquidity pools to purchase assets?

Table D-1. (Continued)

Problem	Targets of Policy	Actions Taken or Possibly To Take
Containing the Contagion and Restoring Market Operations		
Countries slow to recognize emerging problems in financial systems	National monetary and banking authorities Governments IMF Regional organizations	• Increased IMF and Financial Stability Board/Forum macroprudential/systemic oversight, surveillance and consultations (April 2, 2009 London Summit, June 17 Treasury Plan) • Build more resilience into the system? • Increase reporting requirements? • Establish colleges of national • supervisors to oversee financial sectors across national borders (Nov. 15, 2008, G-20 Summit)
Lack of political support to implement changes in policy	National political leaders	• G-20 international summit meetings —Bilateral and plurilateral meetings and events

Source: Congressional Research Service

Notes: In the Actions to Take column, a "?" indicates that the action or policy has been proposed but is still in development or not yet taken.

APPENDIX E. BRITISH, U.S., AND EUROPEAN CENTRAL BANK OPERATIONS, APRIL TO MID-OCTOBER 2008

	Bank of England	Federal Reserve	European Central Bank	Coordinated Central Bank Announcements
May	Announced that expanded three-month long-term repos would be maintained in June and July.	Expanded size of Term Auction Facility (TAF). Extended collateral of Term Securities Lending Facility (TSLF).		Expansion of agreements between Federal Reserve and European Central Bank.
July		Introduced 84-day TAF. Primary Dealer Credit Facility (PDCF) and TSLF extended to January 2009. Authorized the auction of options for primary dealers to borrow Treasury securities from the TSLF.	Announced that it would conduct operations under the 84-day TAF to provide US dollars to uropean Central Bank counterparties. Announced that supplementary three-month longer-term refinancing operations (LTROs) would be renewed in August and September.	

September	Announced that expanded three-month long-term repos would be maintained in September and October. Announced long-term repo operations to be held monthly. Extended drawdown period for Special Liquidity Scheme 9SLS).	Expanded collateral of PDCF. Expanded size and collateral of TSLF. Announced provision of loans to banks to finance purchase of high quality asset-backed commercial paper from money market mutual funds.	Announced six-month LTROs would be renewed in October, and three-month LTROs would be renewed in November and December. Conducted Special Term Refinancing Operation.	Expansion of agreement between Federal Reserve and European Central Bank. Establishment of swap agreements between Federal Reserve and the Bank of England, subsequently expanded. Bank of England and European Central Bank, in conjunction with the Federal Reserve, announced operation to lend U.S. dollars for one week, subsequently extended to scheduled weekly operations.
October	Extended collateral for one-week U.S. dollar repos and for three-month long-term repos. Extended collateral of all extended-collateral sterling long-term repos, U.S. dollar repo operations, and the SLS to include bank-guaranteed debt under the UK Government bank debt guarantee scheme. Announced Operations Standing Facilities and a Discount Window Facility, which together replace existing Standing Facilities.	Announced payment of interest on required and excess reserve balances. Increased size of TAFs. Announced creation of the Commercial paper Funding Facility.	Increased size of six-month supplementary LTROs. Announced a reduction in the spread of standing facilities from 200 basis points to 100 basis points around the interest rate on the main refinancing operation. Introduced swap agreements with the Swiss National Bank.	Announced schedules for TAFs and Forward TAFs for auctions of U.S. dollar liquidity during the fourth quarter. European Central and Bank of England announced tenders of U.S. dollar funding at 7-day, 28-day, 84-day maturities at fixed interest rates for full allotment. Swap agreements increased to accommodate required level of funding.

Source: *Financial Stability Report*, October 2008, the Bank of England. p. 18.

End Notes

[1] For a more complete list of major developments and actions, see **Appendix A**.
[2] Prepared by Dick K. Nanto, Specialist in Industry and Trade, Foreign Affairs, Defense, and Trade Division.
[3] IHS Global Insight Inc., *IHS Global Insight Report: World (Country Intelligence)*, January 13, 2010.
[4] A moral hazard is created if a government rescue of private companies encourages those companies and others to engage in comparable risky behavior in the future, since the perception arises that they will again be rescued if necessary and not have to carry the full burden of their losses.
[5] International Monetary Fund, *2009 Global Financial Stability Report: Responding to the Financial Crisis and Measuring systemic Risks*, Summary Version, Washington, DC, April 2009, p. 1ff.
[6] See Jochen Andritzky, John Kiff, Laura Kodres, Pamela Madrid, and Andrea Maechler, *Policies to Mitigate Procyclicality*, International Monetary Fund, IMF Staff Position Note SPN/09/09, Washington, DC, May 7, 2009.
[7] See, for example, Friedman, George and Peter Zeihan. "The United States, Europe and Bretton Woods II." A Strafor Geopolitical Intelligence Report, October 20, 2008.
[8] Also see the section entitled Regulatory and Financial Market Reform in this report.
[9] CRS Report RL34730, *Troubled Asset Relief Program: Legislation and Treasury Implementation*, by Baird Webel and Edward V. Murphy.
[10] CRS Report R40537, *American Recovery and Reinvestment Act of 2009 (P.L. 111-5): Summary and Legislative History*, by Clinton T. Brass et al.
[11] For analysis and recommendations by the International Monetary Fund, see "Global Financial Stability Report, Financial Stress and Deleveraging, Macro-Financial Implications and Policy," October 2008. 246 p.
[12] For information on Basel II, see CRS Report RL34485, *Basel II in the United States: Progress Toward a Workable Framework*, by Walter W. Eubanks.
[13] Now called the Financial Stability Board. For recommendations by the Financial Stability Forum, see "Report of the Financial Stability Forum on Enhancing Market and Institutional Resilience, Follow-up on Implementation," October 10, 2008. 39 p.
[14] U.S. Department of the Treasury, *Financial Regulatory Reform: A New Foundation: Rebuilding Financial Supervision and Regulation*, Washington, DC, June 2009, 85 p.
[15] The following countries and territories are represented on the Financial Stability Board: Argentina, Australia, Brazil, China, Canada, France, Germany, Hong Kong SAR, India, Indonesia, Italy, Japan, Korea, Mexico, the Netherlands, Russia, Saudi Arabia, Singapore, South Africa, Spain, Switzerland, Turkey, the United Kingdom, and the United States. The following institutions, standard-setting bodies and other groupings are also members of the FSB: the Bank for International Settlements, European Central Bank, European Commission, International Monetary Fund, Organisation for Economic Co-operation and Development, World Bank, Basel Committee on Banking Supervision, International Accounting Standards Board, International Association of Insurance Supervisors, International Organization of Securities Commissions, Committee on the Global Financial System, and Committee on Payment and Settlement Systems.
[16] In addition to the mandate of the Financial Stability Forum (to assess vulnerabilities affecting the financial system, identify and oversee action needed to address them, and promote coordination and information exchange among authorities responsible for financial stability), the Financial Stability Board is to (1) monitor and advise on market developments and their implications for regulatory policy; (2) advise on and monitor best practice in meeting regulatory standards; (3) undertake joint strategic reviews of the policy development work of the international standard setting bodies to ensure their work is timely, coordinated, focused on priorities and addressing gaps; (4) set guidelines for and support the establishment of supervisory colleges; (5) manage contingency planning for cross-border crisis management, particularly with respect to systemically important firms; and (6) collaborate with the IMF to conduct Early Warning Exercises.
[17] An SDR is a Special Drawing Right, a type of international currency created by the IMF that can be converted into a national currency for use. One SDR currently is worth about $1.55 dollars.
[18] Title I of proposed legislation, Financial Services Oversight Council Act of 2009, submitted by Treasury; see http://www.financialstability.gov/docs/regulatoryreform/07222009/titleI.pdf.
[19] Title II of proposed legislation, "Bank Holding Company Modernization Act of 2009, submitted by Treasury; see http://www.financialstability.gov/docs/regulatoryreform/07222009/titleII.pdf.
[20] Title VI of proposed legislation submitted by Treasury; see http://www.financialstability.gov/docs/regulatory reform/ 07222009/titleVI.pdf.
[21] Title III of proposed legislation, Federal Depository Institutions Supervision and Regulation Improvements Act of 2009, submitted by Treasury; see http://www.financialstability.gov/docs/regulatoryreform/title-III_Natl-Bank-Supervisor_072309.pdf.
[22] Title III of proposed legislation, "Federal Depository Institutions Supervision and Regulation Improvements Act of 2009," submitted by Treasury, see http://www.financialstability.gov/docs/regulatoryreform/title-III_Natl-BankSupervisor_072309.pdf.

[23] Title IV of proposed legislation, Private Fund Investment Advisers Registration Act of 2009, submitted by Treasury, see http://www.treas.gov/press/releases/reports/title%20iv%20reg%20advisers%20priv%20funds%207%2015%2009%20fnl.pdf.

[24] Title IX, Subtitle C of proposed legislation, "Investor Protection Act of 2009, Subtitle C—Improvements to the Regulation of Credit Rating Agencies," submitted by Treasury; see http://www.financialstability.gov/docs/regulatoryreform/titleIX_subtC.pdf and Subtitle E—Improvements to the Asset-Backed Securitization Process; see http://www.financialstability.gov/docs/regulatoryreform/07222009/titleIX.pdf.

[25] Title VII of proposed legislation, "Over-the-Counter Derivatives Markets Act of 2009," submitted by Treasury, see http://www.financialstability.gov/docs/regulatoryreform/titleVII.pdf.

[26] Title VIII of proposed legislation, "Payment, Clearing, and Settlement Supervision Act of 2009," submitted by Treasury; see http://www.financialstability.gov/docs/regulatoryreform/title-VIII_payments_072209.pdf. Title IX, Subtitle D, "Investor Protection Act of 2009,".Subtitle D—Executive Compensation, submitted by Treasury; see http://www.treas.gov/press/releases/docs/tg_218IX.pdf.

[27] Title X of proposed legislation, "Consumer Financial Protection Agency Act of 2009," submitted by Treasury; see http://www.financialstability.gov/docs/regulatoryreform/title-III_Natl-Bank-Supervisor_072309.pdf and Title XI, Improvements to the Federal Trade Commission Act," submitted by Treasury; see http://www.financialstability.gov/docs/TITLE-XI.pdf.

[28] Title IX of proposed legislation, "Investor Protection Act of 2009," submitted by Treasury; see http://www.treas.gov/press/releases/docs/tg205071009.pdf.

[29] Title X of proposed legislation, "Consumer Financial Protection Agency Act of 2009," submitted by Treasury; see http://www.financialstability.gov/docs/regulatoryreform/title-III_Natl-Bank-Supervisor_072309.pdf and Title XI, Improvements to the Federal Trade Commission Act," submitted by Treasury; see http://www.financialstability.gov/docs/TITLE-XI.pdf.

[30] Title XII of proposed legislation, "Resolution Authority for Large, Interconnected Financial Companies Act of 2009", submitted by Treasury; see http://www.financialstability.gov/docs/regulatoryreform/title-XII_resolutionauthority_072309.pdf.

[31] Title XII of proposed legislation, "Additional Improvements for Financial Crisis Management," submitted by Treasury; see http://www.financialstability.gov/docs/regulatoryreform/07222009/titleXIII.pdf.

[32] Title V of proposed legislation, "Office of National Insurance Act of 2009," submitted by Treasury, see http://www.financialstability.gov/docs/regulatoryreform/07222009/title%20V%20Ofc%20Natl%20Ins%207-22-2009%20fnl.pdf.

[33] For discussion, see CRS Report R40417, *Macroprudential Oversight: Monitoring Systemic Risk in the Financial System*, by Darryl E. Getter. CRS Report R40877, *Financial Regulatory Reform: Systemic Risk and the Federal Reserve*, by Marc Labonte.

[34] See CRS Report R40526, *Insolvencies of "Systemically Significant Financial Companies" (SSFCs): Proposal for Federal Deposit Insurance Corporation (FDIC) Resolution*, by M. Maureen Murphy. CRS Report R40843, *Bank Failures and the Federal Deposit Insurance Corporation*, by Darryl E. Getter.

[35] The White House, Office of the Press Secretary, *Remarks by the President on Financial Reform*, Speechs & Remarks, January 21, 2010.

[36] Dan Burrows, "Volcker Urges Lawmakers to End Era of 'Too Big to Fail'," *Daily Finance (Internet edition)*, February 2, 2010.

[37] Paul Volker, "How to Reform Our Finacial System," *The New York Times*, January 31, 2010, Internet edition.

[38] See CRS Report R40613, *Credit Rating Agencies and Their Regulation*, by Gary Shorter and Michael V. Seitzinger.

[39] See CRS Report R40646, *Derivatives Regulation in the 111th Congress*, by Mark Jickling and Rena S. Miller.

[40] CRS Report RL34730, *Troubled Asset Relief Program: Legislation and Treasury Implementation*, by Baird Webel and Edward V. Murphy. CRS Report R40224, *Troubled Asset Relief Program and Foreclosures*, by N. Eric Weiss et al.

[41] CRS Report R40210, *Preserving Homeownership: Foreclosure Prevention Initiatives*, by Katie Jones. CRS Report R40498, *Overview of the Securities Act of 1933 as Applied to Private Label Mortgage-Backed Securities*, by Kathleen Ann Ruane. CRS Report RL33879, *Housing Issues in the 110th Congress*, coordinated by Libby Perl.

[42] CRS Report R40696, *Financial Regulatory Reform: Analysis of the Consumer Financial Protection Agency (CFPA) as Proposed by the Obama Administration and H.R. 4173 (Formerly H.R. 3126)*, by David H. Carpenter and Mark Jickling. CRS Report R40857, *Consumer Financial Protection by Federal Agencies*, by Mark Jickling.

[43] The reports are at http://tarptracker.org/cop.

[44] CRS Report RS22583, *Executive Compensation: SEC Regulations and Congressional Proposals*, by Michael V. Seitzinger.

[45] For summary, see: Senate Committee on Banking, Housing, and Urban Affair, Restoring American Financial Stability—Committee Print, c. 2009. http://banking.senate.gov/public/_files/FinancialReformSummaryFC11189.pdf.

[46] See CRS Report RL34412, *Containing Financial Crisis*, by Mark Jickling.
[47] See Board of Governors of the Federal Reserve System, *Federal Reserve Press Release*, March 18, 2009. U.S. Department of the Treasury, *U.S. Treasury and Federal Reserve Board Announce Launch of Term Asset-Backed Securities Loan Facility (TALF)*, Press Release tg-45, March 3, 2009. CRS Report RL3 1416, *Monetary Aggregates: Their Use in the Conduct of Monetary Policy*, by Marc Labonte.
[48] Eric S. Rosengren, *Addressing the Credit Crisis and Restructuring the Financial Regulatory System: Lessons from Japan*, Federal Reserve Bank of Boston, Paper given at the Institute of International Bankers Annual Washington Conference, Boston, MA, March 2, 2009.
[49] Thomas F. Cooley, "Swedish Banking Lessons," *Forbes.com*, January 28, 209.
[50] For details, see CRS Report RL34730, *Troubled Asset Relief Program: Legislation and Treasury Implementation*, by Baird Webel and Edward V. Murphy
[51] U.S. Department of the Treasury, *Treasury Department Releases Details on the Public Private Partnership Investment Program*, Press Release tg-65, March 23, 2009.
[52] For details, see CRS Report RL34427, *Financial Turmoil: Federal Reserve Policy Responses*, by Marc Labonte. "The Fed's Trillion," *The Washington Post*, May 5, 2009, p. A14.
[53] Norma Cohen, "OECD Sees Strongest Outlook since 2007," *Financial Times*, June 24, 2009, FT.com.
[54] Matthew Saltmarsh, "Euro Zone Officially Out of Recession," *The New York Times*, November 14, 2009, p. Internet edition.
[55] Camilla Anderson, *IMF Spells Out Need for Global Fiscal Stimulus*, International Monetary Fund, IMF Survey Magazine: Interview, Washington, DC, December 28, 2008.
[56] David Saha and Jakob von Weizsäcker, *Estimating the size of the European stimulus packages for 2009*, Brugel, JVW/ DS, 12 December 2008.
[57] Charles Freedman, Michael Kumhof, Douglas Laxton, and Jaewoo Lee, *The Case for Global Fiscal Stimulus*, International Monetary Fund, IMF Staff Position Note SPN/09/03, March 6, 2009.
[58] Steven Pearlstein, "Asia, Europe Find Their Supply Chains Yanked. Beware the Backlash," *The Washington Post*, February 20, 2009, pp. D1, D3.
[59] International Monetary Fund, *IMF Financial Activities—Update June 18, 2009*, Washington, DC, June 18, 2009, http://www.imf.org/external/np/tre/activity/2009/061809.htm.
[60] The Bretton Woods Agreements in 1944 established the basic rules for commercial and financial relations among the world's major industrial states and also established what has become the World Bank and International Monetary Fund.
[61] Information on the London G-20 Summit is available at http://www.londonsummit.gov.uk/en/.
[62] For details, see http://www.pittsburghsummit.gov/.
[63] Group of Twenty Nations. "London Summit – Leaders' Statement," 2 April 2009 http://www.londonsummit.gov.uk/ resources/en/PDF/final-communique
[64] Friedman, George and Peter Zeihan. "The United States, Europe and Bretton Woods II." A Strafor Geopolitical Intelligence Report, October 20, 2008.
[65] See CRS Report R40496, *The Global Financial Crisis: Foreign and Trade Policy Effects*, coordinated by Dick K. Nanto.
[66] Dennis C. Blair, *Annual Threat Assessment of the Intelligence Community for the Senate Select Committee on Intelligence*, Director of National Intelligence, Washington, DC, February 12, 2009. See also, U.S. Senate, Committee on Foreign Relations, "Foreign Policy Implications Of The Global Economic Crisis," Roundtable before the Committee On Foreign Relations, February 11, 2009.
[67] Johnston, Tim. "Asia Nations Join to Prop Up Prices," *Washington Post*, November 1, 2008, p. A10. "Record Fall in NZ Commodity Price Gauge," *The National Business Review*, November 5, 2008.
[68] Joby Warrick, "Experts See Security Risks in Downturn, Global Financial Crisis May Fuel Instability and Weaken U.S. Defenses," *Washington Post*, November 15, 2008. P. A01. Bokhari, Farhan, "Pakistan's War On Terror Hits Roadblock, Global Economic Crisis Prompts Military To Consider Spending Cutbacks," CBS News (online version), October 28, 2008.
[69] David M. Herszenhorn and Sheryl G. Stolberg, "Health Plan Opponents Make Their Voices Heard," *The New York Times*, August 4, 2009, p. A12.
[70] World Trade Organization, Director-General, *Report to the TPRB from the Director-General on the Financial and Economic Crisis and Trade-Related Developments*, Report No. WT/TPR/OV/W/2, July 15, 2009.
[71] Simon J. Evenett, Editor, *The Unrelenting Pressure of Protectionism: The 3rd GTA Report*, Centre for Economic Policy Research, Global Trade Alert, London, December 10, 2009, 21-23.
[72] World Trade Organization, Director-General, *Report to the TPRB from the Director-General on the Financial and Economic Crisis and Trade-Related Developments*, Report No. WT/TPR/OV/W/2, July 15, 2009, p. 60.
[73] H.R. 1 (P.L. 111-5) Sec. 1605 provides that none of the funds appropriated or otherwise made available by the act may be used for a project for the construction, alteration, maintenance, or repair of a public building or public work unless all of the iron, steel, and manufactured goods used in the project are produced in the United States provided that such action would not be inconsistent with the public interest, such products are not produced in the United States, and would not increase the cost of the overall project by more than 25%:

[74] "Europe Warns against 'Buy American' Clause," *Spiegel Online International*, February 3, 2009, Internet edition.
[75] For details, see CRS Report RL343 14, *China's Holdings of U.S. Securities: Implications for the U.S. Economy*, by Wayne M. Morrison and Marc Labonte.
[76] For details, see CRS Report RL343 14, *China's Holdings of U.S. Securities: Implications for the U.S. Economy*, by Wayne M. Morrison and Marc Labonte.
[77] The G-7 includes Canada, France, Germany, Italy, Japan, United Kingdom, and the United States. The G-8 is the G-7 plus Russia. The G-20 adds Argentina, Australia, Brazil, China, India, Indonesia, Mexico, Saudi Arabia, South Africa, South Korea, and Turkey. See: CRS Report R40977, *The G-20 and International Economic Cooperation: Background and Implications for Congress*, by Rebecca M. Nelson.
[78] Pew Research Center, *Confidence in Obama Lifts U.S. Image Around the World*, A Pew Global Attitudes Project, Washington, DC, July 23, 2009, http://pewglobal.org/reports/display.php?ReportID=264.
[79] See CRS Report R40417, *Macroprudential Oversight: Monitoring Systemic Risk in the Financial System*, by Darryl E. Getter.
[80] See CRS Report R40578, *The Global Financial Crisis: Increasing IMF Resources and the Role of Congress*, by Jonathan E. Sanford and Martin A. Weiss.
[81] White House, Office of the Secretary, *Below is a statement from the President upon signing H.R. 2346 on June 24, 2009:*, Washington, DC, June 26, 2009, http://www.whitehouse.gov/the_press_office/Statement-from-the-Presidentupon-signing-HR-2346/.
[82] Progress on these items as of mid-March 2009 is summarized in: U.K. Chair of the G20, *Progress Report on the Immediate Actions of the Washington Action Plan*, Annex to the G20 Finance Ministers' and Central Bank Governors' Communique - 14 March, London, March 14, 2009.
[83] Prepared by Dick K. Nanto, Specialist in Industry and Trade, Foreign Affairs, Defense, and Trade Division.
[84] Edmund Conway, "WEF 2009: Global crisis 'has destroyed 40pc of world wealth'," *Telegraph.co.uk*, January 29, 2009, Internet edition.
[85] For example, see CRS Report RL34485, *Basel II in the United States: Progress Toward a Workable Framework*, by Walter W. Eubanks.
[86] Leslie Scism, "S&P Gauges Bond Loss Potential on Mortgages," *The Wall Street Journal*, November 9, 2009, p. C1.
[87] Lucas Papademos, "*Strengthening macro-prudential supervision in Europe*," Speech by Lucas Papademos, Vice President of the ECB, Brussels, Belgium, March 24, 2009.
[88] See CRS Report R40417, *Macroprudential Oversight: Monitoring Systemic Risk in the Financial System*, by Darryl E. Getter.
[89] See CRS Report R40249, *Who Regulates Whom? An Overview of U.S. Financial Supervision*, by Mark Jickling and Edward V. Murphy
[90] Squam Lake Working Group on Financial Regulation, *A Systemic Regulator for Financial Markets*, Council on Foreign Relations, Center for Geoeconomic Studies, Working Paper, May 2009, p. 2.
[91] Lorenzo Bini Smaghi, "Lorenzo Bini Smaghi: Going forward – regulation and supervision after the financial turmoil," Bank for International Settlements, *BIS Review*, 77, 2009.
[92] For an analysis of global production networks, see CRS Report R40167, *Globalized Supply Chains and U.S. Policy*, by Dick K. Nanto.
[93] CRS Report RS22583, Executive Compensation: *SEC Regulations and Congressional Proposals*, by Michael V. Seitzinger.
[94] Prepared by Dick K. Nanto. See also, CRS Report RL34730, Troubled Asset Relief Program: *Legislation and Treasury Implementation*, by Baird Webel and Edward V. Murphy.
[95] For a review of past financial crises, see Luc Laeven and Fabian Valencia. "Systemic Banking Crises: A New Database," International Monetary Fund Working Paper WP/08/224, October 2008. 80p.
[96] Gelpern, Anna. "Emergency Rules," *The Record* (Bergen-Hackensack, NJ), September 26, 2008.
[97] From 2005-2007, the U.S. current account deficit (balance of trade, services, and unilateral transfers) was a total of $2.2 trillion.
[98] Reuters. Factbox—Global foreign exchange reserves. October 12, 2008.
[99] See CRS Report RL34336, *Sovereign Wealth Funds: Background and Policy Issues for Congress*, by Martin A. Weiss.
[100] See U.S. Joint Economic Committee, "Chinese FX Interventions Caused international Imbalances, Contributed to U.S. Housing Bubble," by Robert O'Quinn. March 2008.
[101] For further analysis, see CRS Report RL34412, *Containing Financial Crisis*, by Mark Jickling, U.S. Joint Economic Committee, "The U.S. Housing Bubble and the Global Financial Crisis: Vulnerabilities of the Alternative Financial System," by Robert O'Quinn. June 2008.
[102] Fannie Mae (Federal National Mortgage Association) is a government-sponsored enterprise (GSE) chartered by Congress in 1968 as a private shareholder-owned company with a mission to provide liquidity and stability to the U.S. housing and mortgage markets. It operates in the U.S. secondary mortgage market and funds its mortgage investments primarily by issuing debt securities in the domestic and international capital markets. Freddie Mac (Federal Home Loan Mortgage Corp) is a stockholder-owned GSE chartered by Congress in

1970 as a competitor to Fannie Mae. It also operates in the secondary mortgage market. It purchases, guarantees, and securitizes mortgages to form mortgage-backed securities. For an analysis of Fannie Mae and Freddie Mac's role in the subprime crisis, see David Goldstein and Kevin G. Hall, "Private sector loans, not Fannie or Freddie, triggered crisis," McClatchy Newspapers, October 12, 2008.

[103] A credit default swap is a credit derivative contract in which one party (protection buyer) pays a periodic fee to another party (protection seller) in return for compensation for default (or similar credit event) by a reference entity. The reference entity is not a party to the credit default swap. It is not necessary for the protection buyer to suffer an actual loss to be eligible for compensation if a credit event occurs. The protection buyer gives up the risk of default by the reference entity, and takes on the risk of simultaneous default by both the protection seller and the reference credit. The protection seller takes on the default risk of the reference entity, similar to the risk of a direct loan to the reference entity. See CRS Report RS22932, *Credit Default Swaps: Frequently Asked Questions*, by Edward V. Murphy and Rena S. Miller.

[104] Notional value is the face value of bonds and loans on which participants have written protection. World GDP is from World Bank. Development Indicators.

[105] International Swaps and Derivatives Association, ISDA Applauds $25 Trn Reductions in CDS Notionals, Industry Efforts to Improve CDS Operations. News Release, October 27, 2008.

[106] For information on the International Swaps and Derivatives Association, see http://www.isda.org. In 2008, credit derivatives had collateralized exposure of 74%. See ISDA, *Margin Survey 2008*. Collateral calls have been a major factor in the financial difficulties of AIG insurance.

[107] Thomas M. Anderson, "Best Ways to Invest in BRICs," Kiplinger.com, October 18, 2007.

[108] For these and other indicators of the crisis in credit, see http://www.nytimes.com/interactive/2008/10/08/business/economy/2008 1008-credit-chart-graphic.html.

[109] Prepared by Martin A. Weiss, Specialist in International Trade and Finance, Foreign Affairs, Defense, and Trade Division.

[110] Mark Scott, "Economic Problems Threaten Central and Eastern Europe," *Business Week*, October 17, 2008.

[111] Information on ongoing IMF negotiations is available at http://www.imf.org.

[112] International Monetary Fund, "IMF Executive Board Approves Stand-by Arrangement for Pakistan." Press Release No. 08/303, November 24, 2008.

[113] Reinhart, Carmen and Calvo, Guillermo (2000): When Capital Inflows Come to a Sudden Stop: Consequences and Policy Options. Published in: in Peter Kenen and Alexandre Swoboda, eds. Reforming the International Monetary and Financial System (Washington DC: International Monetary Fund, 2000) (2000): pp. 175-20 1.

[114] "New paradigm changes currency rules," *Oxford Analytica*, January 17, 2008.

[115] See CRS Report RL34336, *Sovereign Wealth Funds: Background and Policy Issues for Congress*, by Martin A. Weiss.

[116] Cigdem Akin and M. Ayhan Kose, "Changing Nature of North-South Linkages: Stylized Facts and Explanations." International Monetary Fund Working Paper 07/280. Available at http://www.imf.org/external/pubs/ft/wp/2007/ wp07280.pdf.

[117] Joanna Slater and Jon Hilsenrath, "Currency-Price Swings Disrupt Global Markets ," *Wall Street Journal*, October 25, 2008.

[118] Arvind Subramanian , "The Financial Crisis and Emerging Markets," Peterson Institute for International Economics, Realtime Economics Issue Watch, October 24, 2008.

[119] The Group of Ten is made up of eleven industrial countries (Belgium, Canada, France, Germany, Italy, Japan, the Netherlands, Sweden, Switzerland, the United Kingdom, and the United States).

[120] Stephen Jen and Spyros Andreopoulos, "Europe More Exposed to EM Bank Debt than the U.S. or Japan," Morgan Stanley Research Global, October 23, 2008.

[121] Dirk Willem te Velde, "The Global Financial Crisis and Developing Countries," *Overseas Development Institute*, October 2008.

[122] David Roodman, "History Says Financial Crisis Will Suppress Aid," *Center for Global Development*, October 13, 2008.

[123] Prepared by J. F. Hornbeck, Specialist in International Trade and Finance, Foreign Affairs, Defense, and Trade Division.

[124] United Nations. Economic Commission on Latin America and the Caribbean. *Latin America and the Caribbean in the World Economies, 2007. Trends 2008*. Santiago: October 2008. p. 28.

[125] Decoupling generally refers to economic growth trends in one part of the world, usually smaller emerging economies, becoming less dependent (correlated) with trends in other parts of the world, usually developed economies. See Rossi, Vanessa. *Decoupling Debate Will Return: Emergers Dominate in Long Run*. London: Chatham House, 2008. p. 5.

[126] Ocampo, Jose Antonio. The Latin American Boom is Over. *REG Monitor*. November 2, 2008.

[127] International Monetary Fund. *Global Markets Monitor*, June 15, 2009, and Fidler, Stephen. Going South. *Financial Times*. January 9, 2009. p. 7.

[128] International Monetary Fund. *Global Markets Monitor*, September 18, 2009.

[129] Ibid, and International Monetary Fund. Regional Economic Outlook. *Western Hemisphere: Grappling with the Global Financial Crisis*. Washington, D.C. October 2008. pp. 7-10 and IMF. *Global Markets Monitor*, October 1, 2009.

[130] United Nations. Economic Commission on Latin American and the Caribbean. *Economic Survey of Latin America*

[131] Ibid.

[132] Orozco, Manual. *Understanding the Continuing Effect of the Economic Crisis on Remittances to Latin America and the Caribbean*. Inter-American Development Bank. Washington, DC. August 10, 2009.

[133] Board of Governors of the Federal Reserve System. *Federal Reserve Press Release*. October 29, 2008 and *Minutes of the Federal Open Market Committee April 28-29, 2009*.

[134] United Nations, ECLAC, *Economic Survey of Latin America and the Caribbean 2008-2009*, p. 38.

[135] International Monetary Fund. *Regional Economic Outlook – Western Hemisphere: Stronger Fundamentals Pay Off*. Washington, D.C. May 2009. p. 18-22.

[136] Global Outlook. *Mexico*. March 17, 2009 and International Monetary Fund, *Global Markets Monitor*, June 16, 2009.

[137] IHS Global Insight. *Mexico: Economic Recovery Gets Under Way in Mexico*. September 30, 2009.

[138] Ibid., and The Wall Street Journal. *Mexico and Brazil Step In to Fight Currency Declines*, October 24, 2008 and *Latin America Monitor: Mexico*. December 2008.

[139] CRS trade calculations based on U.S. Department of Commerce data. Latin American Newsletters. *Latin American Mexico and NAFTA Report*, March 2009, p. 10 and United Nations. Economic Commission on Latin America and the Caribbean, *Economic Survey of Latin America and the Caribbean, 2008-2009*, p. 38.

[140] Ibid and United Nations. ECLAC. *The Reactions of the Governments of the Americas to the International Crisis: An Overview of Policy Measures up to 31 March 2009*. April 2009.

[141] Latin American Newsletters. *Latin American Mexico and NAFTA Report*, May 2009, p. 8-10 and IHS Global Insight. *Economic Recovery Gets Under Way in Mexico*. September 30, 2009.

[142] Business Monitor International. *Latin American Monitor: Brazil*. September 2009 and International Monetary Fund. *Global Markets Monitor*, September 17, 2009.

[143] Canuto, Otaviano. Emerging Markets and the Systemic Sudden Stop. *RGE Monitor*. November 12, 2008 and Wheatley, Jonathan. Brazilian Economy Is the Real Lure for the Yield-Hungry. *Financial Times*. May 7, 2009.

[144] International Monetary Fund. *Global Markets Monitor*, June 15, 2009 and Business Monitor International. *Latin American Monitor: Brazil*. September 2009.

[145] Business Monitor International. *Latin American Monitor: Brazil*. September 2009.

[146] Business Monitor International. *Latin American Monitor: Brazil*. September 2009, Soliani, Andre and Iuri Dantas. Brazil Freezes 37.2 Billion Reais of 2009 Budget. *Bloomberg Press*. January 27, 2009, and Brazil-U.S. Business Council. *Brazil Bulletin*. September 28, 2009.

[147] United Nations. Economic Commission on Latin American and the Caribbean. *Economic Survey of Latin America and the Caribbean, 2008-2009*. July 2009.

[148] Latin American Newsletters. *Latin American Economy & Business*, January 2009, pp. 10-11, Global Insight. *Argentina*. June 12, 2009, and República Argentina. Instituto Nacional de Estadística y Censos. Utilización de la Capacidad Instalada en la Industria. August 2009.

[149] Benson, Drew and Bill Farles. Argentine Bonds, Stocks Tumble on Pension Fund Takeover Plan. *Bloomberg*. October 21, 2008 and International Monetary Fund. *Global Markets Monitor*. March 17, 2009.

[150] Latin American Monitor. *Latin American Economy and Business*. August 2009.

[151] Global Insight. *Argentina: S&P Lowers Argentina's Rating to B-*. November 3, 2008 and Latin America Weekly Report. *Lula May Accept Argentine Protectionism*. March 12, 2009. p. 8.

[152] International Monetary Fund. Regional Economic Outlook. *Western Hemisphere: Grappling with the Global Financial Crisis*. Washington, DC. October 2008. p. 8, and IMF. *Global Markets Monitor*, October 1, 2009.

[153] Ibid., *Latin American Brazil & Southern Cone Report*, January 2009, p. 10, IMF. *Global Markets Monitor*. March 2, 2009, and United Nations. Economic Commission on Latin American and the Caribbean. *Economic Survey of Latin America and the Caribbean, 2008-2009*. July 2009.

[154] IHS Global Insight. *Argentine Economy Contracts 0.8% in Q2*. October 1, 2009.

[155] Prepared by William H. Cooper, Specialist in International Trade and Finance, Foreign Affairs, Defense, and Trade Division.

[156] Economist Intelligence Unit. November 12, 2009. However, GDP grew modestly in the third quarter causing Finance Minister Kudrin to declare the recession over.

[157] Ibid.

[158] Economist Intelligence Unit. *Country Report–Russia*. October 2008. p. 6

[159] Economist Intelligence Unit. *Country Report—Russia*. June 2009. p. 5.

[160] Ibid. p. 6.

[161] IMF. World Economic Outlook. October 2009.

[162] INS Global Insight. June 3, 2009. Economist Intelligence Unit. *Country Report—Russia*. June 2009. p.7.

[163] Available on Kremlin website http://www.kremlin.ru.

[164] Prepared by James K. Jackson, Specialist in International Trade and Finance, Foreign Affairs, Defense, and Trade Division.

[165] For additional information, see CRS Report R40415, *The Financial Crisis: Impact on and Response by The European Union*, by James K. Jackson.

[166] Pan, Phillip P., Economic Crisis Fuels Unrest in E. Europe, *The Washington Post*, January 26, 2009, p, A1.

[167] *Regional Economic Outlook: Europe*, International Monetary Fund, April, 2008, p. 19-20; and *EU Banking Structures*, European Central Bank, October 2008, p. 26.

[168] Frank, Nathaniel, Brenda Gonzalez-Hermosillo, and Heiko Hesse, *Transmission of Liquidity Shocks: Evidence from the 2007 Subprime Crisis*, IMF Working Paper #WP/08/200, August 2008, the International Monetary Fund.

[169] Flash Estimates for the Fourth Quarter of 2008, Eurostat news release, STAT/09/19, February 13, 2009.

[170] Hilsenrath, Jon, Joellen Perry, and Sudeep Reddy, Central Banks Launch Coordinated Attack; Emergency Rate Cuts Fail to Halt stock Slide; U.S. Treasury Considers Buying Stakes in Banks as Direct Move to Shore Up Capital, the *Wall Street Journal*, October 8, 2008, p. A1.

[171] Castle, Stephen, British Leader Wants Overhaul of Financial System, *The New York Times*, October 16, 2008.

[172] The G-7 consists of Canada, France, Germany, Italy, Japan, the United Kingdom, and the United States.

[173] *Summit of the Euro Area Countries: Declaration on a Concerted European Action Plan of the Euro Area Countries*, European union, October 12, 2008.

[174] *EU Sets up Crisis Unit to Boost Financial Oversight*, Thompson Financial News, October 16, 2008.

[175] *Ibid.*

[176] Bradbury, Adam, EU Eyes Next Step on Clearing, *The Wall Street Journal Europe*, January 7, 2009. p. 21.

[177] Communication From the Commission, From Financial Crisis to Recovery: A European Framework for Action, European Commission, October 29, 2008.

[178] The Lisbon Strategy was adopted by the EU member states at the Lisbon summit of the European Union in March 2001 and then recast in 2005 based on a consensus among EU member states to promote long-term economic growth and development in Europe.

[179] The combination of labor market flexibility and security for workers.

[180] Hall, Ben, George Parker, and Nikki Tait, European Leaders Decide on Deadline for Reform Blueprint, *Financial Times*, November 8, 2008, p. 7.

[181] Benoit, Bernard, Germany Doubles Size of Stimulus, *Financial Times*, January 6, 2009, p. 10; Walker, Marcus, Germany's Big Spending Plans, *The Wall Street Journal Europe*, January 13, 2009, p. 3.

[182] Benoit, Bernard, German Stimulus Offers Job Promise, *Financial Times*, December 16, 2008. p. 1.

[183] Walker, Marcus, Germany Mulls $135 Billion in Rescue Loans, *The Wall Street Journal Europe*, January 8, 2009. p. 1.

[184] Steinbruck, Peer, Germany's Way Out of the Crisis, *The Wall Street Journal*, December 22, 2008.

[185] Parussini, Gabrielle, France to Give Banks Capital, With More Strings Attached, *The Wall Street Journal Europe*, January 16, 2009, p. A17.

[186] Gauthier-Villars, David, Leading News: France Sets Stimulus Plan, *The Wall Street Journal Europe*, December 5, 2008, p. 3.

[187] Hall, Ben, France Gives Renault and Peugeot E.U.R 779m, *Financial Times*, December 16, 2008, p. 4.

[188] Abboud, Leila, France Considers New Measures to Aid Auto Companies, *The Wall Street Journal Europe*, January 15, 2009, p. 4.

[189] *Report*, The High-Level Group on Financial Supervision in the EU, Chaired by Jacques de Larosiere, February 25, 2009.

[190] *Driving European Recovery*, Communication for the Spring European Council, Commission of the European Communities, April 3, 2009.

[191] Level 3 committees represent the third level of the Lamfalussy process the EU uses to implement EU-wide policies. At the third level, national regulators work on coordinating new regulations with other nations. and they may adopt non-binding guidelines or common standards regarding matters not covered by EU legislation, as long as these standards are compatible with the legislation adopted at Level 1 and Level 2.

[192] *A European Economic Recovery Plan*: Communication From the Commission to the European Council, Commission of the European Communities, COM(2008) 800 final, November 26, 2008. The full report is available at http://ec.europa.eu/commission_barroso/president/pdf/Comm_20081126.pdf.

[193] The Market Abuse Directive was adopted by the European Commission in April 2004. The Directive is intended to reinforce market integrity in the EU and contribute to the harmonization of the rules against market abuse and establishing transparency and equal treatment of market participants in such areas as accepted market practices in the context of market manipulation, the definition of inside information relative to derivatives on commodities, and the notification of the relevant authorities of suspicious transactions.

[194] The Bank of England, *Financial Stability Report*, April 2008, p. 10.

[195] Scott, Mark, Is Britain's Stimulus Plan a Wise Move? *Business Week*, November 24, 2008; Werdigier, Julia, Britain Offers $30 Billion Stimulus Plan, *The New York Times*, November 25, 2008.

[196] Falloon, Matt, and Mike Peacock, UK Government to Borrow Record Sums to Revive Economy, *The Washington Post*, November 24, 2008.
[197] *Real Help for Business*, press release, Department for Business, Enterprise and Regulatory Reform, January 14, 2009; Mollenkamp, Carrick, Alistair MacDonald, and Sara Schaefer Munoz, Hurdles rise as U.K. Widens Stimulus Plan, *The Wall Street Journal Europe*, January 14, 2009, p. 1.
[198] Benoit, Bertrand, Tom Braithwaaite, Jimmy Burns, Jean Eaglesham, et. al., Iceland and UK clash on Crisis, *Financial Times*, October 10, 2008, p. 1.
[199] Anderson, Camilla, Iceland Gets Help to Recover From Historic Crisis, *IMF Survey Magazine*, November 19, 2008.
[200] Iceland Raises Key Rate by 6 Percentage Points, *The New York Times*, October 29, 2008.
[201] Jolly, David, Nordic Countries Add $2.5 Billion to Iceland's Bailout, *The New York Times*, November 20, 2008.
[202] Wardell, Jane, Iceland's Financial Crisis Escalates, BusinessWeek, October 9, 2008; Pfanner, Eric, Meltdown of Iceland's Financial system Quickens, *The New York Times*, October 9, 2008.
[203] Portes, Richard, The Shocking Errors Behind Iceland's Meltdown, *Financial Times*, October 13, 2008, p. 15.
[204] Buiter, Willem H., and Anne Sibert, *The Icelandic Banking Crisis and What to Do About it: The Lender of Last Resort Theory of Optimal Currency Areas*. Policy Insight No. 26, Centre for Economic Policy Research, October 2008. p. 2.
[205] Prepared by Ben Dolven, Asia Section Research Manager, Foreign Affairs, Defense, and Trade Division.
[206] An Astonishing Rebound, *The Economist*, August 13, 2009.
[207] Ibid.
[208] Despite Ambivalence, Pakistan May Wrap Deal by Next Week, *The Wall Street Journal*, October 28, 2008.
[209] IMF 'Has Six Days to Save Pakistan,' *Financial Times*, October 28, 2008.
[210] Pakistan Says it will Need Financing Beyond IMF Deal, *The Wall Street Journal*, November 17, 2008.
[211] See, for instance, Jeffrey Sachs, The Best Recipe for Avoiding a Global Recession, *Financial Times*, October 27, 2008.
[212] The moved was announced in a November 14 opinion piece by Japanese Prime Minister Taro Aso, Restoring Financial Stability, printed in *The Wall Street Journal*.
[213] Leaders of Europe and Asia Call for Joint Economic Action, *New York Times*, October 25, 2008.
[214] Chinese Premier Blames Recession on U.S. Actions, *Wall Street Journal*, January 29, 2009.
[215] ASEAN's members are Indonesia, Singapore, Malaysia, Thailand, the Philippines, Brunei, Vietnam, Cambodia, Laos and Burma (Myanmar).
[216] For a fuller discussion of the Chiang Mai Initiative, see East Asian Cooperation, Institute of International Economics, http://www.iie.com/publications/chapters_preview/345/3iie3381.pdf.
[217] Japan, China, S. Korea Eye Financial Stability Forum, *Reuters*, October 20, 2008.
[218] Asian Leaders See Growth Driver, *The Wall Street Journal*, December 15, 2008.
[219] Japan Passes Contentious Stimulus Budget, *Associated Press*, January 27, 2009.
[220] The section on China was prepared by Wayne M. Morrison, Specialist in Asian Trade and Finance, Foreign Affairs, Defense, and Trade Division.
[221] For an overview of the China Investment Corporation, see CRS Report RL34337, *China's Sovereign Wealth Fund*, by Michael F. Martin.
[222] China's holdings of Fannie Mae and Freddie Mac securities are likely to be more substantial, but less risky (compared to other sub-prime securities), especially after these two institutions were placed in conservatorship by the Federal Government in September 2008.
[223] China's economy was already slowing down before the global financial crisis hit. This was in large part the result of government efforts to slow the rate of inflation. China's real GDP growth fell from 13% in 2007 to 9% in 2008. The global financial crisis has sharply diminished economic growth. Thus, the Chinese government has abandoned its anti-inflation policies and instead has sought to stimulate the economy.
[224] *Chinaview*, September 27, 2008.
[225] Global Insight, *Country Intelligence Analysis, China*, October 20, 2008.
[226] China *Xinhua News Agency*, November 12, 2008.
[227] Global Insight, Country Intelligence, China, October 15, 2009.
[228] SOUTH KOREA: Seoul Faces Growth and Liquidity Tests, *Oxford Analytica*, October 8, 2008.
[229] Lee Warns Against Dollar Hoarding, *Korea Times*, October 8, 2008.
[230] See Merrill Lynch, "Asia: Risks Rising", October 3, 2008.
[231] For more information about Pakistan's economic crisis, see CRS Report RS22983, *Pakistan's Capital Crisis: Implications for U.S. Policy*, by Michael F. Martin and K. Alan Kronstadt.
[232] "Pakistan's Zardari to Give Up Powers," *AFP*, September 20, 2008.
[233] Simon Cameron-Moore, "Pakistan Needs $ 10-15 Bln Fast, Says PM's Adviser," *Reuters*, October 21, 2008.
[234] "IMF Okays $7.6 Bln Package for Pakistan: Tareen," *Associated Press of Pakistan*, November 15, 2008.
[235] Jamie Anderson, "Pakistan Turns to IMF for Financial Aid," *Money Times*, November 16, 2008.
[236] "Pakistan Unveils Package for Economic Stability," *Reuters*, September 19, 2008.

[237] Farhan Bokhari, "Pakistan Vows to Target Rich Tax Evaders as IMF Concludes Talks on Vital Loan," *Financial Times*, November 3, 2008.

[238] For an analysis of bubbles, see CRS Report RL33666, *Asset Bubbles: Economic Effects and Policy Options for the Federal Reserve*, by Marc Labonte.

[239] Lanman, Scott and Steve Matthews. "Greenspan Concedes to 'Flaw' in His Market Ideology," *Bloomberg News Service*, October 23, 2008.

[240] Soros, George. *The New Paradigm for Financial Markets: The Credit Crisis of 2008 and What it Means* (PublicAffairs, 2008) p. i. Soros proposes a new paradigm that deals with the relationship between thinking and reality and accounts for misconceptions and misinterpretations.

[241] International Monetary Fund. "The Recent Financial Turmoil—Initial Assessment, Policy Lessons, and Implications for Fund Surveillance," April 9, 2008.

[242] Gerstenzang, James. "Bush will Meet with G-20 After Election," *Los Angeles Times*, October 23, 2008.

[243] G-20, Leaders' Statement: The Pittsburgh Summit, September 25, 2009, http://www.pittsburghsummit.gov/mediacenter/129639.htm.

[244] G-20, *Meeting of Finance Ministers and Central Bank Governors, United Kingdom, 14 March 2009*, Communiqué, March 14, 2009.

[245] Prepared by Dick K. Nanto and Martin A. Weiss. For further information see CRS Report RS22976, *The Global Financial Crisis: The Role of the International Monetary Fund (IMF)*, by Martin A. Weiss.

[246] Lipsky, John. "Global Prospects and Policies," Speech by John Lipsky, First Deputy Managing Director, International Monetary Fund, at the Securities Industries and Financial Markets Association, New York, October 28, 2008. World Bank. "The Unfolding Crisis, Implications for Financial Systems and Their Oversight," October 28, 2008. p. 8.

[247] See CRS Report RS22976, *The Global Financial Crisis: The Role of the International Monetary Fund (IMF)*, by Martin A. Weiss.

[248] Each member country of the IMF is assigned a quota, based broadly on its relative size in the world economy. A member's quota determines its maximum financial commitment to the IMF and its voting power. The U.S. quota of about $58.2 billion is the largest.

[249] IMF Signs $100 Billion Borrowing Agreement with Japan, *IMF Survey Magazine: In the News*, February 13, 2009.

[250] "China Urges World Monetary Systems Diversification," *Dow Jones Newswire*, April 2, 2009, http://www.djnewswires.com/eu.

[251] Timothy R. Homan, "IMF Plans to Issue Bonds to Raise Funds for Lending Programs," *Bloomberg.com*, April 25, 2009.

[252] Bob Davis, "IMF Considers Issuing Bonds to Raise Money," *Wall Street Journal*, February 1, 2009.

[253] Prepared by J. Michael Donnelly, Information Research Specialist, Knowledge Services Group. Opinions are those of the sources and not those of CRS. Source: Various news articles, reports, and blog excerpts. Beginning July 1, 2009, source information is provided.

[254] U.S. Treasury. "Joint Statement by Treasury, Federal Reserve and FDIC." Press Release HP-1206, October 14, 2008.

[255] Prepared by Mark Jickling, Specialist in Financial Economics.

In: Global Economics Crisis and Cooperation
Editor: Jonathan P. Castle

ISBN: 978-1-61761-114-8
© 2010 Nova Science Publishers, Inc.

Chapter 2

THE G-20 AND INTERNATIONAL ECONOMIC COOPERATION: BACKGROUND AND IMPLICATIONS FOR CONGRESS

Rebecca M. Nelson

SUMMARY

Governments discuss and coordinate economic policies using a mix of formal institutions, such as the World Trade Organization (WTO) and International Monetary Fund (IMF), and more informal economic forums, like the Group of Seven, or G-7, and the Group of 20, or G-20. This report focuses on informal economic forums, and, specifically, the role of the G-20 in coordinating governments' responses to the current economic crisis. The members of the G-7 are Canada, France, Germany, Italy, Japan, the United Kingdom, and the United States. The G-20 includes the G-7 members plus Argentina, Australia, Brazil, China, India, Indonesia, Mexico, Russia, Saudi Arabia, South Africa, South Korea, Turkey, and the European Union (EU).

Since the mid-1970s, leaders from the G-7, a small group of developed countries, have gathered annually to discuss and coordinate financial and economic policies. Large emerging-market economies such as China started to have more sway in financial markets in the 1990s, and the Asian Financial Crisis in 1997-1998 showed that emerging markets were too important to exclude from international economic discussions. The G-20 was formed in 1999 as an opportunity for finance ministers and central bank governors from both developed and emerging-market countries to discuss financial issues. The G-20 remained a less prominent forum than the G-7, as it involved meetings among finance ministers while the G-7 sessions also involved summit meetings among heads of governments or heads of state.

With the onset of the current financial crisis, the G-7 leaders decided to convene the G-20 leaders for a meeting, or "summit," to discuss and coordinate policy responses to the crisis. To date, the G-20 leaders have held three summits to coordinate policy responses to the crisis: November 2008 in Washington, DC; April 2009 in London; and September 2009 in Pittsburgh. At the Pittsburgh summit, the G-20 leaders announced that the G-20 would henceforth be the premier forum for international economic coordination, supplanting the G-7's role as such.

The G-20 leaders have made commitments on a variety of issue areas. Implementation of some of these commitments by the United States would require legislation. Issues that are likely to influence future policy debates and/or the legislative agenda include: financial regulatory reform, a new international framework to monitor and coordinate economic policies, voting reform at the IMF and World Bank, increased funding of multilateral development banks (MDBs), elimination of fossil fuel subsidies, concluding a new international agreement to reduce greenhouse gas emissions, concluding the WTO Doha multilateral trade negotiations, and meeting previous commitments on foreign aid.

The shift from the G-7 to the G-20 as the premier forum for international economic coordination may raise issues for international economic coordination in the future. Some suggest the shift will foster cooperation, by increasing the legitimacy of the decisions reached and including countries that are big players in the global economy. Others argue that the shift will hinder efforts at cooperation, because such a large, heterogeneous group of countries will have trouble reaching agreements on key issues. Some say the G-20 meetings should be even larger and more comprehensive, to include poor and small nations in their deliberations. Others say that the existing G-20 is already sufficiently diverse and increasing the size would make it too cumbersome and less effective.

INTRODUCTION

The Group of Twenty, or G-20, is a forum for advancing international economic cooperation among developed and emerging-market countries.[1] Since the G-20 was established in 1999, the G-20 finance ministers and central bank governors have met annually to discuss economic and financial issues. In the wake of the current global financial crisis, the leaders of the developed countries decided to convene the G-20 heads of government or heads of state for a meeting, or "summit," to discuss and coordinate policy responses to the crisis.[2] The summit, held in Washington, DC in November 2008, was the first time this particular group of leaders had gathered to coordinate economic policies. For the past 30 years, economic discussions among advanced economies at the leader level occurred among the Group of Seven (G-7) nations, a much smaller group of developed countries as shown in **Figure 1**.[3]

The G-20 leaders convened for two additional summits, in London in April 2009 and in Pittsburgh in September 2009, to continue discussions on policy responses to the crisis. In each of the three G-20 summits, the G-20 leaders made several policy commitments, and the depth and scope of these commitments have increased over time. In Washington, DC, the commitments were focused on short- and medium-term responses to the crisis, including regulatory reform, expansionary macroeconomic policies, and commitments to free trade. In London, the G-20 leaders reached more substantial agreements on crisis management, including increasing the resources of the International Monetary Fund (IMF) and multilateral development banks (MDBs) by $1.1 trillion. At the Pittsburgh summit, the G-20 pledged commitments on a diverse set of issue areas, including changes in the relative voting power of member countries at the IMF and World Bank, creating a new framework to correct global imbalances, taking new steps to address food security issues, and eliminating fossil fuel subsidies.

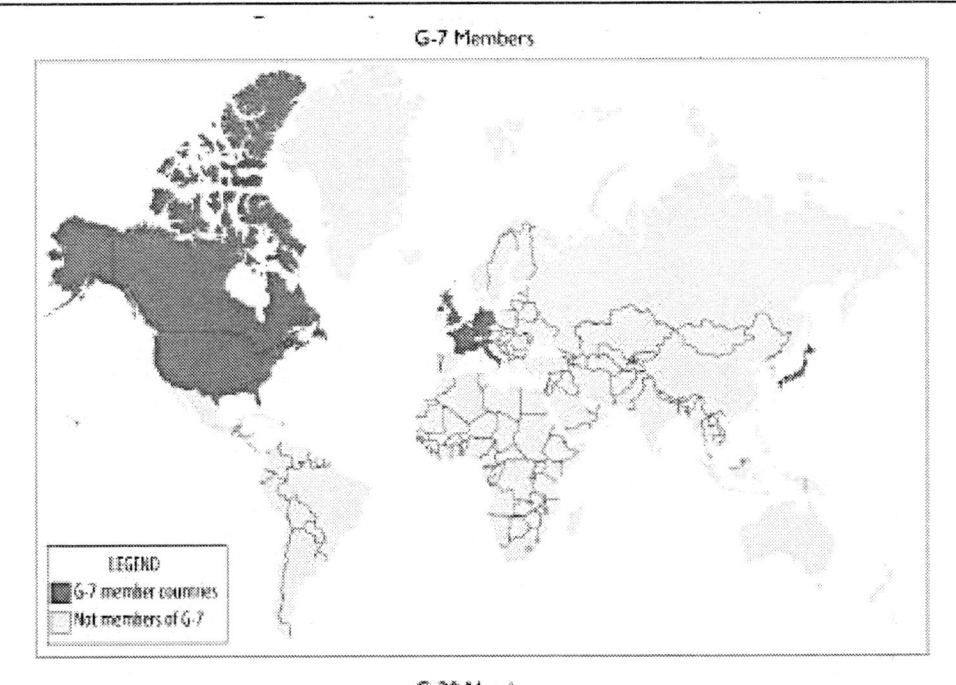

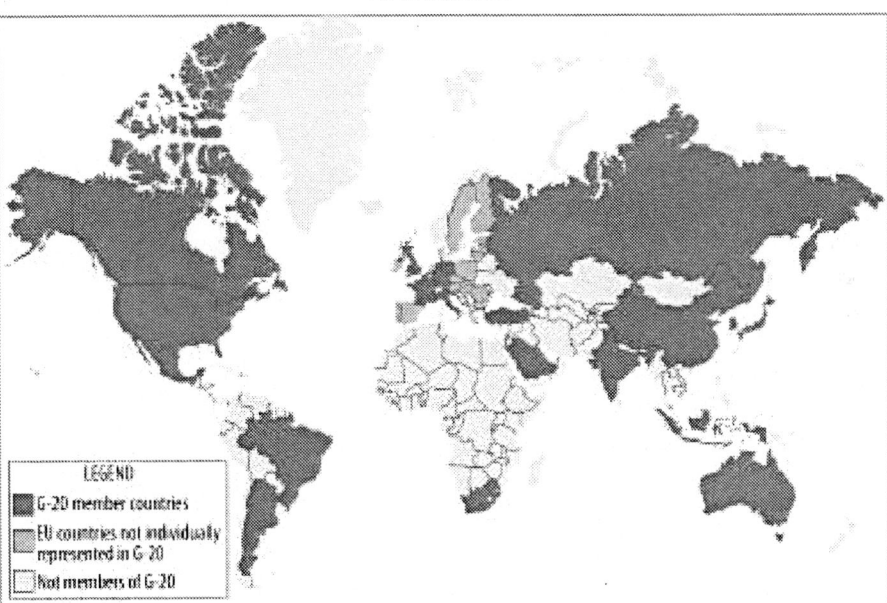

Source: G-20 website, http://www.g20.org
Notes: The European Union (EU) is a member of the G-20. Pink (for color copies) or medium gray (for blackand-white copies) indicate members of the European Union (EU) that are not individually represented in the G20.

Figure 1. Expansion of the G-7 to the G-20

Additionally, the G-20 leaders announced at the Pittsburgh summit that, henceforth, the G-20 would be the premier forum for international economic cooperation, displacing the G-7's long-standing status as the primary forum for coordinating international economic policies. G-20 discussions are not to cover international relations and foreign policy issues, though this may change in future years. For these issues, the Group of Eight, or G-8 (the G-7 members plus Russia) will likely continue to be the principal forum, though more consultation with other countries is also likely. The transition from the G-7 to the G-20 for economic issues may have a substantial impact on international economic coordination in the future. Some argue that the transition will foster greater cooperation, while others contend these goals could be hindered.

Congressional interest in the G-20 is, at the least, two-fold. First, implementing many of the commitments made by the Administration at the G-20 summits to date would require reform of U.S. laws and regulations. As a consequence, the agreements reached by the G-20 leaders may influence policy debates and the legislative agenda. Second, the transition from the G-7 to the G-20 may impact U.S. coordination with other countries on international economic issues in the future. To provide oversight of U.S. participation in international economic forums, it is important to highlight the issues raised by the shift from the G-7 to the G-20.

This report addresses the following key issues:

- Context on the emergence of the G-20 as the premier forum for international economic coordination;
- Background on how the G-20 operates, including where and when the G-20 meets and how the G-20 reaches decisions;
- An overview of the three G-20 summits and analysis of how they have evolved;
- Major G-20 commitments that are likely to shape the policy agenda moving forward; and
- Broader issues raised by the shift from the G-7 to the G-20.

THE RISE OF THE G-20 AS THE PREMIER FORUM FOR INTERNATIONAL ECONOMIC COOPERATION

Economic Coordination in Formal Institutions and Informal Forums

Since World War II, governments have created and used formal international institutions and more informal forums to discuss economic policies. As economic integration has increased over the past 30 years, however, international economic policy coordination has become even more active and significant. Globalization may bring economic benefits, but it also means that a country's economy is increasingly affected by the economic policy decisions of other governments. These effects are not always positive. For example, a country's exports may decline should another country devalue its currency or restrict imports to attempt to reverse a trade deficit or protect domestic industries. Instead of countries unilaterally implementing these "beggar-thyneighbor" policies, some say they may be better off coordinating to refrain from such negative outcomes. Another reason countries may want to coordinate policies is that some economic policies, like fiscal stimulus, are more effective in open economies when countries implement them together.

Governments use a mix of formal international institutions and international economic forums to coordinate economic policies. Formal institutions, such as the International Monetary Fund (IMF), the Organization for Economic Co-operation and Development (OECD), the World Bank, and the World Trade Organization (WTO), are typically formed by an official international agreement and have a permanent office with staff performing ongoing tasks. Governments have also relied on more informal forums for economic discussions, such as the G-7 and the Paris Club.[4] These economic forums do not have formal rules or a permanent staff. This report focuses on informal forums, particularly the G-20.[5]

1970s – 1990s: Developed Countries Dominate Financial Discussions

Prior to the current global financial crisis, international economic discussions at the top leadership level primarily took place among a small group of developed industrialized countries. Beginning in the mid-1970s, leaders from a group of five developed countries—France, Germany, Japan, the United Kingdom, and the United States—began to meet annually to discuss international economic challenges, including the oil shocks and the collapse of the Bretton Woods system of fixed exchange rates. This group, called the Group of Five, or G-5, was broadened to include Canada and Italy, and the Group of Seven, or G-7, formally superseded the G-5 in the mid-1980s. In 1998, Russia also joined, creating the G-8.[6] Russia does not usually participate in discussions on international economic policy, which continued to occur mainly at the G-7 level. Meetings among finance ministers and central bank governors typically precede the summit meetings.

Macroeconomic policies discussed in the G-7 context include exchange rates, balance of payments, globalization, trade, and economic relations with developing countries. One of the most significant agreements reached by the G-7 was at the first summit in Rambouillet, France, in 1975. The G-7 leaders agreed to a new monetary system to replace the system of fixed exchange rates that unraveled in the early 1970s and set the stage for amending the IMF Articles of Agreement to allow floating exchange rates.[7] Examples of other significant agreements reached by the G-7 are the Plaza Agreement in 1985 and the Louvre Accord in 1987. The Plaza Agreement aimed to depreciate the U.S. dollar in relation to German Deutsche mark and the Japanese yen, and the Louvre Accord aimed to halt the continued decline of the U.S. dollar. Over time, the G-7's and, subsequently the G-8's, focus on macroeconomic policy coordination expanded to include a variety of other global and transnational issues, such as the environment, crime, drugs, AIDS, and terrorism.

1990s – 2008: Emerging Markets Gain Greater Influence

Expanding the G-7 to the G-20 is a significant shift in how international economic coordination has been organized for the past three decades. At the same time, the impetus for this shift has been building as emerging-market countries have become more active in the international economy.

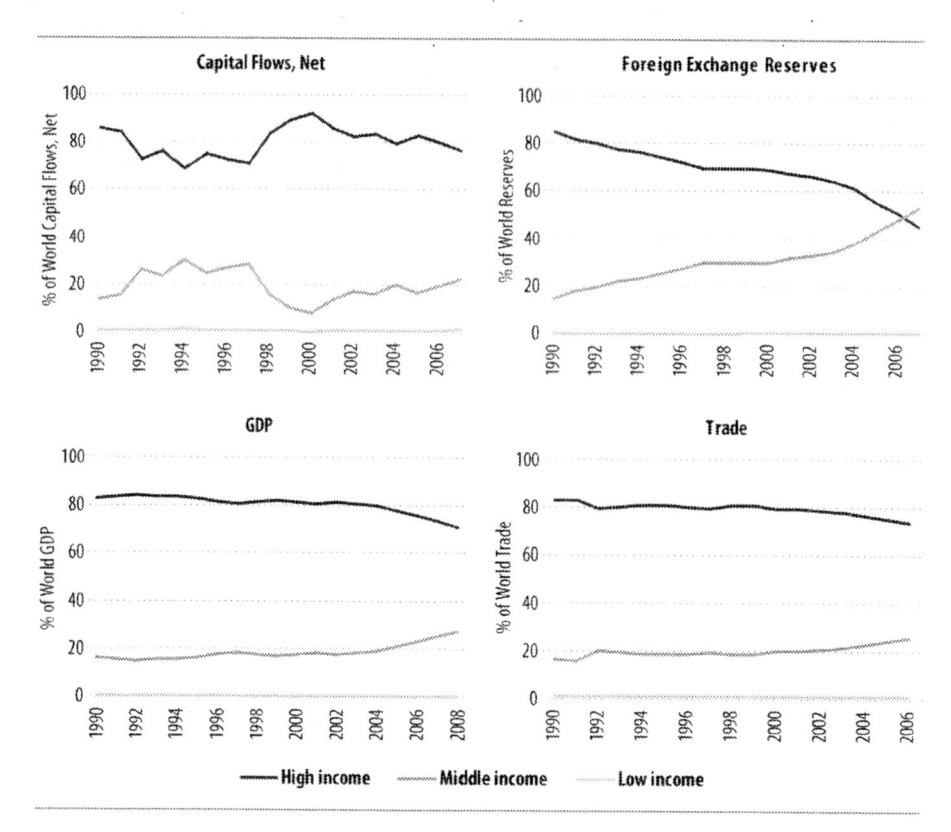

Source: World Bank World Development Indicators. Capital includes portfolio investment and foreign direct investment.

Figure 2. Increasing Role of Emerging-Market Countries in the International Economy

Consider **Figure 2**, which examines the proportion of world capital flows (net), foreign exchange reserves, GDP, and trade held by high-, middle-, and low-income countries. In the early 1990s, middle income countries (roughly equivalent to emerging-market countries) started receiving a much larger proportion of the world's capital flows, including portfolio investment and foreign direct investment. Their share dropped during the Asian financial crisis in the late 1990s, but has slowly been rising since 2000. Likewise, middle-income countries' share of world foreign exchange reserves has been steadily on the rise since the 1990s. In recent years, the reserve holdings of middle-income countries has become larger than the reserve holdings of high-income countries. Middle-income countries' share of world GDP and world trade was largely stagnant in the 1990s but has started to increase over the past decade.

Although middle-income countries, or emerging-market countries, have become more active in the international economy, particularly in financial markets starting in 1990, this was not reflected in the international financial architecture until the Asian financial crisis in 1997-1998. The Asian financial crisis in 1997-1998 demonstrated that problems in the financial markets of emerging- market countries can have serious spillover effects on financial markets in developed countries, making emerging markets too important to exclude from discussions on economic and financial issues. The Group of 22, or G-22, was established as a temporary forum for finance ministers and central bank governors from both advanced industrialized and emerging-market countries to discuss the Asian Financial Crisis.[8] The G-22 met twice in 1998, and was superseded by the Group of 33, or G-33, to discuss international financial stability and the international financial stability forum.[9] The G-33 was also a temporary forum that met twice in 1999.

Including emerging-market countries in economic discussions proved to be fruitful, and the G-20 was established in late 1999 as a permanent international economic forum for developed and emerging-market countries. However, the G-20 was a secondary forum to the G-7 and G-8; the G-20 convened finance ministers and central bank governors, while the G-8 also convened leaders in addition to finance ministers.

Emerging markets were also granted more sway in international economic discussions when the G-8 partly opened its door to them in 2005.[10] The United Kingdom's Prime Minister Tony Blair invited five emerging economies–China, Brazil, India, Mexico, and South Africa–to participate in its discussions but not as full participants (the "G-8 +5"). The presence of emerging-market countries gave them some input in the meetings but they were clearly not treated as full G-8 members. Brazil's finance minister is reported to have complained that developing nations were invited to G-8 meetings "only to take part in the coffee breaks."[11]

2008 – Present: Emerging Markets Get a Seat at the Table

It is only with the outbreak of the current financial crisis in fall 2008 that emerging markets have been invited as full participants to international economic discussions at the highest level. There are different explanations for why the shift from the G-7 to the G-20 occurred. Some emphasize a recognition by the leaders of developed countries that emerging markets have become sizable players in the international economy and are simply "too important to bar from the room."[12]

Others suggest that the transition from the G-7 to the G-20 was driven by the negotiating strategies of European and U.S. leaders. It is reported that that France's president, Nicolas Sarkozy, and Britain's prime minister, Gordon Brown, pushed for a G-20 summit, rather than a G8 summit, to discuss the economic crisis in order to dilute perceived U.S. dominance over the forum, as well as to "show up America and strut their stuff on the international stage."[13]

Likewise, it is reported that President George W. Bush also preferred a G-20 summit in order to balance the strong European presence in the G-8 meetings.[14] Some attribute the G-20's staying power to the political difficulties of reverting back to the G-7 after having convened the G-20.

HOW THE G-20 OPERATES

Frequency of Meetings

The G-8 and G-20 heads-of-state meetings, or summits, are the focal points of the G-8 and G-20 discussions and where the forums' key decisions are announced. However, various lower-level officials meet frequently before the summits to begin negotiations and after the summits to discuss the logistical and technical details of implementing the agreements announced at the summits.

Prior to the current global financial crisis, the G-20 finance ministers and central bank governors have met once a year since the G-20 was established in 1999. The annual meeting of G-20 finance ministers and central bank governors has been preceded by extensive preparation to provide them with up-to-date analysis and insights and to better inform their consideration of policy challenges and options. This includes two deputies meetings each year as well as extensive technical work, including an array of workshops, reports, and case studies on specific subjects.

As economic discussions at the leader level transition from the G-7 to the G-20, it is expected that the G-20 schedule will mimic the G-7's schedule in the past. The G-7 leaders, and Russia, have met annually, and the G-7 finance ministers and central bank governors have met at least semiannually, and as frequently as four times a year, to monitor developments in the world economy and assess economic policies. The G-20 leaders are scheduled to meet twice in 2010, June 2010 in Canada and November 2010 in South Korea. Starting in 2011, the G-20 expects to hold summits on an annual basis.

At various points in time, usually at the request of the G-8 leaders, the G-7 or G-8 ministers of development, education, employment and labor, energy, ministers, global information and society, health, justice, science, and trade have also occasionally convened to discuss pertinent issues. The G-20 has already, for example, called on the G-20 employment and labor ministers to meet in 2010 to discuss the problem of unemployment.

In addition to the summits and various ministerial meetings, there are also meetings among the leaders' personal representatives, known as "sherpas."[15] Sherpas meet several times a year to prepare for the forthcoming summit, attend the formal summit meetings with the leaders, and hold several follow-up meetings. The sherpa team for each country typically includes a lead sherpa and two "sous-sherpas": a finance sous-sherpa and a foreign affairs sous-sherpa.[16] The foreign affairs sous-sherpa covers issues outside the purview of finance, such as trade and the environment.

Finally, a variety of task forces, working groups, and expert groups have been established by the G-8 leaders or G-7 finance ministers over the years as well to support the work of the G-8 and the G-7. Examples include the Financial Action Task Force (FATF), the Financial Stability Forum (FSF), the Counter-Terrorism Action Group, and the Global Fund to Fight AIDS, Tuberculosis, and Malaria, and the G-8 Renewable Energy Task Force.

U.S. Representation

Because the G-20 began as a forum for finance ministers and central bank governors, the Treasury Department and the Federal Reserve have traditionally been the primary U.S. agencies involved in the G-20 meetings. As the G-20 has replaced the G-7 on finance issues, the Treasury Department has taken the lead on the G-20 meetings. However, the Treasury Department works closely with other agencies throughout the G-20 process. In addition to the Federal Reserve, the Treasury Department also coordinates with the State Department, the U.S. Agency for International Development, and, increasingly, the Department of Energy to coordinate G-20 issues. The White House, particularly through the National Security Council and the U.S. Trade Representative, is also heavily involved in the G-20 planning process.

The U.S. sherpa for the G-20 is the Deputy National Security Advisor for International Economic Affairs, a position currently held by Mike Froman. The U.S. sous-sherpa for finance issues is the Under Secretary of International Affairs at the Treasury Department, who also represents the U.S. at G-20 meetings at the level of deputy finance minister. Lael Brainard has been designated for this position subject to confirmation by the Senate. The Senate Finance Committee held her confirmation hearing in November 2009 and while a vote on her confirmation has not yet been scheduled, it is anticipated that it will occur soon. Finally, the U.S. sous-sherpa for foreign affairs issues is the Under Secretary for Economic, Energy, and Agricultural Affairs at the State Department. Robert D. Hormats currently holds this position.

Location of Meetings and Attendees

Unlike formal international institutions, such as the United Nations and the World Bank, the G-20 does not have a permanent headquarters or staff. Instead, each year, a G-20 member country serves as the chair of the G-20. The chair hosts the highest level meetings, which before the crisis was among finance ministers but moving forward will be the leaders' summit meetings. The chair also establishes a temporary office that is responsible for the group's secretarial, clerical, and administrative affairs, known as the temporary "secretariat." The secretariat also coordinates the G-20's various meetings for the duration of its term as chair and typically posts details of the G-20's meetings and work program on the G-20's website.[17]

The chair rotates among members and is selected from a different region each year. Table 1 lists the previous and current chairs of the G-20, as well as the member country slotted to chair in 2010 (South Korea) and 2011 (France). The United States has never officially chaired the G-20, although the United States has hosted two of the three G-20 summits held to date.

In addition to the G-20 members, Spain and the Netherlands have also attended, as observers, the three G-20 summits to date. Several regional organizations and international organizations have also attended the G-20 summits. For example, official participants at the London summit included the leaders of the G-20 member countries as well as representatives from the following organizations:

- the European Commission
- the European Council
- the Association of Southeast Asian Nations (ASEAN)
- the Financial Stability Board (FSB, formerly the Financial Stability Forum, FSF)
- the International Monetary Fund (IMF)
- the New Partnership for Africa's Development (NEPAD)
- the United Nations
- the World Bank
- the World Trade Organization[18]

Table 1. Chairs of the G-20, 1999-2011

Year	Country
1999-2001	Canada
2002	India
2003	Mexico
2004	Germany
2005	China
2006	Australia
2007	South Africa
2008	Brazil
2009	United Kingdom
2010	South Korea
2011	France

Source: G-20 website, http://www.g20.org.

Agreements

All agreements, comments, recommendations, and policy reforms reached by the G-20 finance ministers and central bankers, as well as by G-20 leaders, are done so by consensus. There is no formal voting system as in some formal international economic institutions, like the IMF. Participation in the G-20 meetings is restricted to members and not open to the public. After each meeting, however, the G-20 publishes online the agreements reached among members, typically as communiqués or declarations.[19] The G-20 does not have a way to enforce implementation of the agreements reached by the G-20 at the national level; the G-20 has no formal enforcement mechanism and the commitments are non-binding. This contrasts with, for example, the World Trade Organization (WTO), which does have formal enforcement mechanisms in place.[20] However, according to the participants, each G-20 meeting reviews the agreements and commitments reached at prior meetings.

OVERVIEW OF THE G-20 SUMMITS

The G-20 has been at the forefront of coordinating responses to the economic crisis. As mentioned previously, the G-20 has held three summits since the onset of the financial crisis: Washington, DC in November 2008, London in April 2009, and Pittsburgh in September 2009. These summits are generally preceded by meetings of finance ministers and other chief economic officials. The G-20 has two summits scheduled for 2010: Canada in June 2010 and South Korea in November 2010. Starting in 2011, the G-20 leaders are expected to convene on an annual basis, though meetings at a financial minister level are likely to occur more often.

After each summit, the G-20 leaders issue a declaration or communiqué detailing the agreements reached among the members.[21] The types of agreements reached at the G-20 summits have evolved as the crisis has transitioned from economic free-fall to signs of recovery and as the G-20 has solidified as a forum for international economic cooperation at the leader level. With each subsequent summit, the G-20's commitments have become more specific, extended over longer time horizons, covered more issue areas, and emphasized greater participation of emerging- market countries in the international financial architecture.

Washington, DC, November 2008

The Washington, DC summit focused on immediate crisis management. The G-20 pledged to pursue extensive regulatory reforms, including the creation of new international regulatory standards and national level reforms. The G-20 also pledged to use expansionary macroeconomic policies, both fiscal and monetary, to stimulate aggregate demand and encourage economic growth, or at least keep things from getting worse. Finally, the G-20 committed to refrain from protectionist trade policies.

London, April 2009

The London summit occurred several months after the Washington, DC summit, but the G-20 leaders were still in crisis management mode. The G-20 leaders reiterated many of the commitments from the Washington, DC summit and also reached agreement on more specific and far-reaching policy responses to the crisis. One of the biggest commitments from the London summit was the pledge to increase funding for the IMF and the MDBs by $1.1 trillion, including tripling of the IMF's lending capacity.[22] The G-20 leaders also pledged $5 trillion in fiscal stimulus spending over the next two years and to create the Financial Stability Board (F SB) as the successor to the Financial Stability Forum (F SF) to coordinate and monitor progress on regulatory reforms. The G-20 also emphasized their commitment to concluding the World Trade Organization (WTO) Doha Round of multilateral trade negotiations, which have stalled since 2001, and honoring their foreign aid commitments. Reforming the international financial institutions (IFIs) to increase the representation of emerging-market countries was discussed, but no real specific commitments were put forth.

Pittsburgh, September 2009

The Pittsburgh summit occurred as the global recession was bottoming out, although unemployment was generally still rising in developed countries. The tone of the Pittsburgh communiqué reflects a sense of accomplishment with the G-20's response to address the crisis, while recognizing more work was needed. The G-20 leaders announced the creation of a new framework to coordinate and monitor national economic policies in order to correct the current global imbalances and prevent such imbalances from occurring in the future. The G-20 also announced more specific plans to increase the representation of emerging-market countries at the IMF and World Bank, as well as specific commitments on a host of new policy areas, including economic development and the environment.

Protests at G-20 Summits

Each of the three G-20 summits have attracted protesters. The protesters tend to come from a mix of broad movements, including environmentalists, trade unions, socialist organizations, faith-based groups, anti-war camps, and anarchists.[23] At the Pittsburgh summit, for example, thousands of protestors gathered in the streets, holding signs with slogans such as "We Say No To Corporate Greed" and "G20=Death By Capitalism."[24] The protests have primarily been peaceful, although at times tensions between the police and protesters have escalated. In Pittsburgh, protestors began throwing rocks,[25] police used pepper gas against a group of students,[26] and several protestors were arrested.[27]

ISSUES ON THE HORIZON

The major G-20 commitments that are likely to influence the policy agenda in the near future are described and analyzed in greater detail below.

Regulatory Reform

Some argue that a major cause of the current global financial crisis was the failure of policymakers to adequately regulate financial markets both domestically and globally. Consequently, proposals for regulatory reform have been central components of each of the three G-20 summits to date. The proposals have generally emphasized the need for new international regulatory standards and the implementation of regulatory reforms at the national level. Examples of the reforms proposed include:

- Creating new global accounting standards,
- Expanding the transparency of complex financial instruments,
- Strengthening and harmonizing capital standards,
- Reassessing banker compensation,
- Regulating all systemically important financial institutions,
- Regulating credit rating agencies, and
- Fighting illicit financial activity.

At the G-20 summit held in Pittsburgh, the G-20 leaders announced several deadlines for some key regulatory reforms. These include:

- Developing new standards for bank capital by end-20 10,
- Implementing new capital standards by end-2012,
- Strengthened regulation of over-the-counter derivatives markets by end-2012,
- Addressing cross-border resolutions and systemically important financial institutions by end-2010,
- Converging on new global accounting standards by June 2011,
- Implementing countermeasures against tax havens from March 2010, and

- Initiating a peer review process of non-cooperative jurisdictions (NCJs) by February 2010.

As noted earlier, the G-20 leaders also announced the creation of the FSB as a successor to the FSF. The FSF was founded in 1999, the wake of the Asian financial crisis, to promote international financial stability. The new FSB has a larger membership, including the major emerging-market countries, and a stronger mandate to coordinate and monitor progress in strengthening financial regulation. Secretary of Treasury Tim Geithner considers that, in effect, the FSB will be the fourth pillar in the architecture of international cooperation along with the IMF, the World Bank, and the WTO.[28]

The FSB is currently undertaking a project to compare national implementation of regulatory reforms and identify cross-country differences and any need for policy actions to address them. As the FSB itself acknowledges, the FSB can develop coherent policy proposals and monitor progress on implementation, but "only national authorities can assure implementation that is effective and consistent across borders."[29] In the FSB's analysis to date, the FSB finds that while regulatory reforms are well underway, they are far from complete.[30] Given the G-20's commitments on regulatory reform in the Pittsburgh summit and the FSB's project to assess the status of national implementation of regulatory reforms, regulatory reform is likely to be a key issue moving ahead and major legislation has been introduced by key committees.

A New Framework to Coordinate and Monitor Economic Policies

Some believe that the United States' external deficit and China's external surplus contributed to an unstable imbalance in the world financial system. In order to correct this imbalance, and promote compatible national economic policies in the future, the G-20 announced a new "Framework for Strong, Sustainable and Balanced Growth."[31] The Framework would operate in three stages. First, the G-20 members would agree on shared policy objectives, updated as economic conditions evolve. Second, each G-20 member would agree to establish national, medium-term policy frameworks, and the G-20 members would work in conjunction with the IMF to assess the collective implications of national policy frameworks for global growth and financial stability. Third, the G-20 members would, based on the results of the peer review process, consider and agree to actions that are necessary to meet the common objectives.

If the peer review process, or "cooperative process of mutual assessment," reveals policies that are not consistent with the G-20's shared policy objectives, the only mechanism currently available for inducing policy change is the threat of "naming and shaming." This has worked to some extent for the G-7 economic process, but it has worked less well in international organizations. Some question, then, whether the new G-20 Framework will be different than IMF surveillance.[32] The IMF has the responsibility to monitor the international monetary system and the economic and financial policies of individual IMF member countries. In recent years, it has also monitored broader global and regional trends. Under its surveillance programs, the IMF can point to weaknesses in an economy but does not have authority to enforce policy changes to address those weaknesses. Countries that do not need to borrow from the IMF have often shrugged off its advice. It is not clear under the current framework for the G-20 how the mutual assessments will translate into policy actions by participating countries on particular key issues such as correcting global imbalances that may require increasing savings in the United States or increasing spending in China.

That said, even if the G-20 Framework is in practice similar to IMF surveillance, the G-20 Framework would raise the profile of monitoring economic policies to the leader level and would emphasize the importance of multilateral surveillance. It is also worth noting that "naming and shaming" has at times been an effective strategy for inducing reform. For example, the Financial Action Task Force on Money Laundering (FAFT)'s blacklist of non-cooperative countries and entities was effective in bringing about reforms on anti-money-laundering efforts.

Developing countries are publicly supportive of the Framework, but *The Economist* reports that they are uneasy about formalizing a realignment of global imbalances.[33] *The Economist* speculates that developing countries' public support for the Framework is driven by suspicions that the policy reforms suggested by the mutual assessments will be difficult to enforce.[34] Moreover, some worry that efforts to address the problem of international financial imbalances without simultaneous efforts to address the conditions which caused the imbalances to occur might have unsatisfactory results.

Increasing the Representation of Emerging Markets in International Financial Institutions (IFIs)

There has been frustration among emerging-market countries that the IMF and the World Bank have not been reformed to reflect their increased weight in the world economy. The G-20 pledged a shift of at least 5% of the IMF quota share (which impacts voting power) from over-represented countries to under-represented countries by January 2011.[35] The G-20 leaders also committed to increase at least 3% of the voting power for developing and transition countries at the World Bank. Although the G-20 leaders agreed to this voting reform in the abstract, it has yet to be decided exactly which countries would lose or gain voting rights. Taking voting power away from countries is politically sensitive, and negotiations over the specifics of voting reform are expected to be difficult, particularly with European countries who are likely to lose voting shares in the reforms.[36] The United States, by contrast, is unlikely to lose voting power in the negotiations, as the United States is actually an under-represented country at the IMF. The United States chose to allow its proportional share to decline in recent decades, partly to make room for new members and partly to lower its financial obligation.

To date, voting reform at the IMF has garnered more attention than the World Bank. Which countries, more specifically, are over- and under-represented at the IMF? There is general agreement that each IMF member's quota should broadly reflect its relative size in the world economy.[37] One way to gauge which countries are over- and under-represented at the IMF is to compare a country's share of world GDP with its IMF quota share.[38] By this metric, countries with quota shares that are larger than their share of world GDP may be considered to be overrepresented at the IMF. For example, because Saudi Arabia's quota share in the IMF is 2.93% but its share of world GDP is only 0.71%, Saudi Arabia may be considered to be over-represented. Another example is Belgium, whose quota share is 1.93% even though its share of world GDP is only 0.59%.

By contrast, countries may be considered to be under-represented at the IMF when their quota share is smaller than their share of world GDP. The United States is generally considered to be under-represented at the IMF, with a quota share of 17.67% but 21.82% of world GDP. **Figure 3** shows examples of countries that are over- and under-represented at the IMF.[39]

The G-20 leaders also pledged that the heads and senior leadership of the international financial institutions should be appointed through an "open, transparent, and merit-based selection process." This may affect the 60-year-old unwritten convention that the Managing Director of the IMF is selected by Western European countries and the President of the World Bank is selected by the United States. However, the wording in the G-20 statement is vague and to date there is no consensus within the U.S. government or internationally on how this would be implemented in practice.

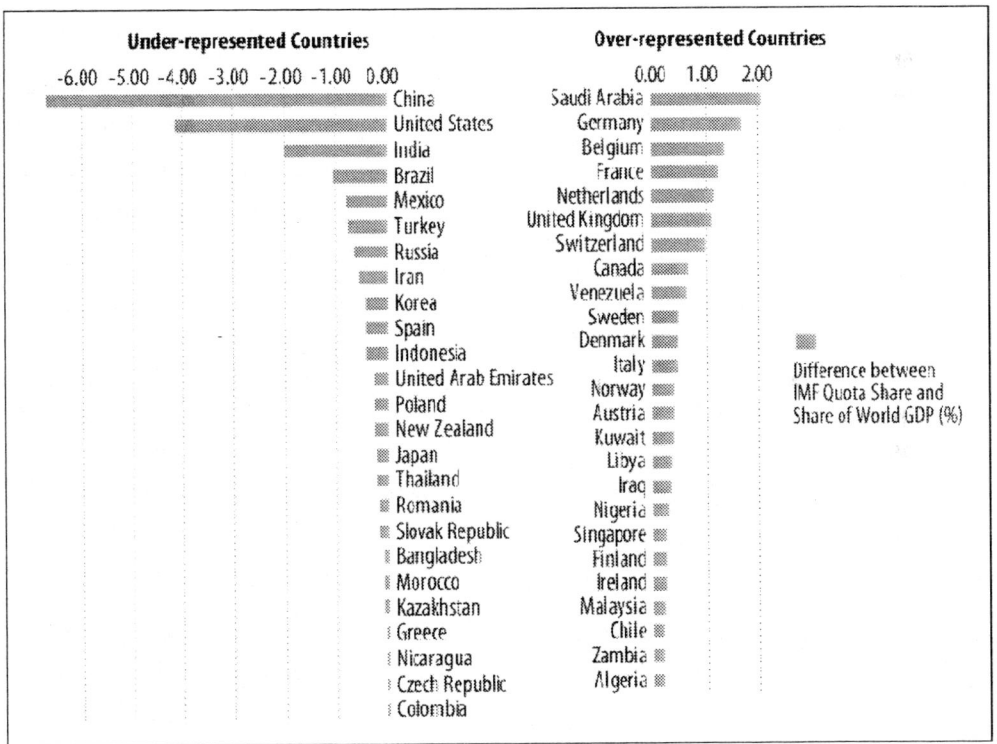

Source: Data used in calculations from "Updated IMF Quota Day – September 2009," International Monetary Fund, September 23, 2009. Available at http://www.imf.org/external/np/fin/quotas

Notes: 25 IMF members with the smallest and largest differences between IMF quota share and share of world GDP. GDP is adjusted for purchasing power parity (PPP).

Figure 3. Examples of Country Representation at the IMF

Increased Funding of the Multilateral Development Banks (MDBs)

As the current financial crisis spread internationally during 2008 and 2009, more and more countries turned to the IMF and the World Bank for loans. IMF lending almost doubled from $17.1 billion to $32.54 billion between October and December 2008. Expecting a greater demand for IMF loans in the future, the G-20 leaders agreed at the London summit to triple the Fund's lending capacity to $750 billion as part of a larger $1.1 trillion package to increase IFI funding.[40] Specifically, the leaders agreed to increase the resources of the New Arrangements to Borrow (NAB), a supplemental fund that bolsters IMF resources, by up to $500 billion. To fulfill this commitment, Congress approved the extension of a $100 billion loan to the NAB in May 2009, included in the FY2009 Spring Supplemental Appropriations for Overseas Contingency Operations (P.L. 111-32). In the end, total new commitments to the NAB are greater than $500 billion, more than originally expected.[41]

At the G-20 summit in Pittsburgh, the G-20 turned their attention to the lending capacity of the multilateral development banks (MDBs). Proposals have been made in all the MDBs in the past year suggesting that substantial increases in their capital stock are needed. There are two general reasons why the MDBs are requesting general capital increases. First, demand for loans is high. The current crisis and the resulting shrinkage in private capital flows is creating a large gap in the external financing needs for developing countries. The World Bank estimates this gap is between $350 billion and $635 billion for 2009 alone, and is expected to continue in 2010 and beyond.[42] Second, it has been noted that the Inter-American Development Bank (IDB)'s request for a general capital increase comes on the heels of a loss of nearly $1.9 billion in 2008.[43]

An overview of these MDB proposals for capital increases are provided below:

- **International Bank for Reconstruction and Development (IBRD), a facility of the World Bank**:[44] According to a report prepared by the bank's staff, the IBRD needs a capital increase in the range of $2.8 billion and $8.7 billion.[45] The IBRD's current capital base is $190 billion.[46]
- **International Finance Corporation (IFC), a facility of the World Bank:**[47] According to a staff report, the IFC needs a capital increase of $1.8 billion to $2.4 billion.[48] The IFC's current capital base is $16 billion.[49]
- **African Development Bank (AfDB):** In June 2009, the Board of Governors of the AfDB began consideration of a proposal to triple the institution's capital base to $100 billion.[50]
- **Asian Development Bank (AsDB):** On May 12, 2009, the Board of Governors of the AsDB agreed to triple the Bank's capital base, from $55 billion to $165 billion.[51] Under the terms of the plan, each country will be eligible to subscribe shares totaling 200% of its current subscription by the end of 2010.
- **European Bank for Reconstruction and Development (EBRD):** The President of the EBRD has recommended to member countries that the institution's capital base be increased by 50% from €20 million to €30 million.[52] In dollars, this is approximately an increase from $30 million to $45 million.

- **Inter-American Development Bank (IDB):** In March 2009, a commission appointed by President Luis Alberto Moreno of the IDB proposed that the financial base of the institution should be tripled through a new capital increase of up to $180 billion.[53]

The proposals are in the preliminary stages, and the Treasury Department is currently analyzing the capital needs of the different MDBs to see if any capital increase is warranted, and if so, how much it should be. The G-20 leaders have called on their finance ministers to consider how mechanisms such as temporary callable and contingent capital could be used to increase MDB lending in times of crisis. The current hope is to conclude negotiations on commitments for any general capital increases by Spring 2010. If the United States agrees to participate in a capital increase for any of the MDBs, it is anticipated that this would be included in the FY20 12 budget. There is also strong indication that donors would require that a capital increase of any of the MDBs would be accompanied by reforms of the MDBs.

In the view of many, the need and size of any MDB capital increases would depend on the availability of private funds. Prior to the current global financial crisis, in 2007, net capital inflows to emerging markets were at a historic peak of $1,252 billion in 2007.[54] Capital flows began slowing in 2008 and fell to $349 billion in 2009. Capital flows to emerging markets are forecasted to rebound to $672 billion in 2010. There are some important differences among regions, as shown in **Figure 4**. Capital has returned to emerging markets in Latin America and Asia more quickly than to emerging markets in Eastern Europe, Africa, and the Middle East.

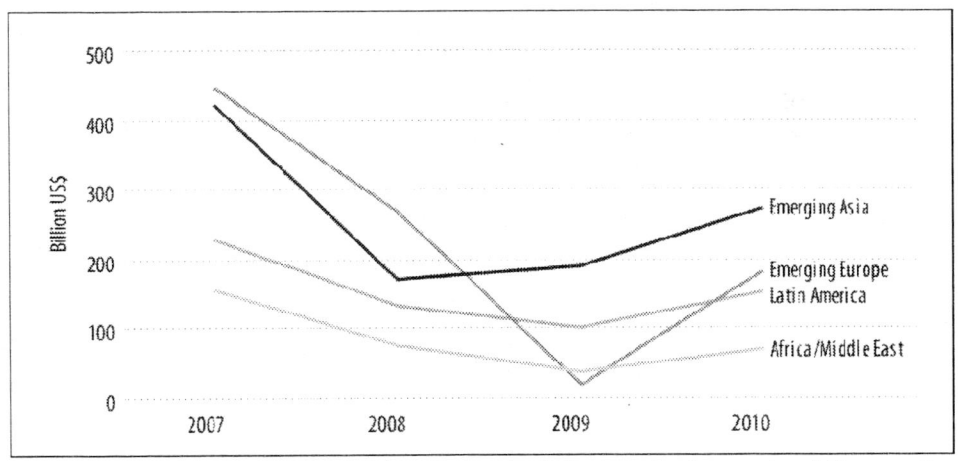

Source: "Capital Flows to Emerging Market Economies," *Institute for International Finance*, October 3, 2009.

Notes: Data for 2009 and 2010 are forecasts. Emerging Europe includes Bulgaria, Czech Republic, Hungary, Poland, Romania, Russia, Turkey, and Ukraine. Latin America emerging markets include Argentina, Brazil, Chile, Poland, Ecuador, Mexico, Peru, and Venezuela. Emerging Asia includes China, India, Indonesia, Malaysia, Philippines, South Korea, and Thailand. Africa/Middle East emerging markets include Egypt, Lebanon, Morocco, Nigeria, Saudi Arabia, South Africa, and UAE.

Figure 4. Net Capital Inflows to Emerging Market Economies, by Region

The new lending capacity generated by new increases in the capital base of the MDBs would not be available to support expanded lending until at least 2012. It cannot be determined at this time whether private flows will have returned to the 2007 levels by that time and whether new loans or guarantees by the MDBs would be needed to attract or enhance such private flows. Also, it is not clear whether the high level of inflows seen before the crisis were sustainable or whether their size actually contributed to the severity of the crisis in some instances when the flow precipitously declined. Overall, however, the resurgence of capital flows to emerging markets raises questions about the need for permanent capital increases, and, if reform fatigue sets in, it is unclear how much momentum this issue will have going forward.

Official Development Assistance

Concern about the toll of the current global financial crisis on low-income countries has been a central feature at the G-20 summits. The G-20 leaders have reaffirmed their resolve to meet the Millennium Development Goals (MDGs) and the foreign aid commitments to Africa put forth at the 2005 G-8 summit in Gleneagles, Scotland.[55] The G-20 also pledged to take new steps to increase access to food, fuel, and finance among the world's poorest. Specifically, the G-20 leaders called on the World Bank to develop the new trust fund to support the new Food Security Initiative for low-income countries that was announced in the summer of 2009. The G-20 also pledged, on a voluntary basis, to increase funding for programs to bring clean and affordable energy to the poorest, such as by providing funding for the Scaling Up Renewable Energy Program and the Energy for the Poor Initiative. The G-20 agreed to support the safe and sound spread of new modes of financial service delivery capable of reaching the poor, building on the example of micro finance. The G-20 also pledged to launch a "G-20 SME [small and medium-sized enterprise] Finance Challenge," which is a call to the private sector to put forward its best proposals for how public finance can maximize the deployment of private finance on a sustainable basis.

There is general concern that pledges to meet existing aid commitments may fall short. The MDG Gap Task Force, created by the Secretary-General of the United Nations to monitor progress on reaching the MDGs, has expressed concern that foreign aid may fall due to the crisis at a time when aid needs to increase in order to reach the MDGs.[56] Additionally, the MDG Gap Task Force is concerned that the distribution of aid is skewed to a just a couple of countries, specifically Iraq and Afghanistan.

Whether the G-8 will meet the targets for aid to Africa, as promised in Gleneagles, is also in question. According to the organization ONE, which monitors aid commitments and disbursements to Africa, this is primarily caused by shortfalls from a few G-8 members, particularly Italy and France.[57] Other G-8 members, including Canada, Japan, and the United States, are on track to meet their G-8 Gleneagles commitments to Africa.[58]

Given the difficulty in meeting existing aid commitments, it is unclear as to what extent the G-20 members will take the steps necessary to implement the new programs aimed at increasing access to food, fuel, and finance in low-income countries. Some have pointed out that details of the new plans are sparse, contributing to questions about their implementation.[59]

A Green Recovery

As the current financial crisis has begun to seemingly bottom out, the G-20 leaders have turned to other issues, including the environment. The G-20 leaders have committed to eliminating fossil fuel subsidies over the medium-term and reach an agreement on reducing greenhouse gas emissions at the U.N. Climate Change conference in Copenhagen in December 2009.[60]

Support for the ban on fossil fuel subsidies comes from the Obama Administration, who pushed for the G-20 commitment in Pittsburgh.[61] It is estimated that the removal of fossil fuel subsidies by 2020 would reduce greenhouse gas emissions by 10% in 2050, and it is reported that the President views the elimination of fossil fuel subsidies as a "down payment" on the international goal of reducing greenhouse gas emissions by 50% from 1990 levels by 2050.[62]

In addition to the environmental benefits, eliminating fossil fuel subsidies may also even out the large price swings that have characterized the oil markets in recent years.[63] With fossil fuel subsidies, increases in the price of oil are not necessarily passed on to consumers. This means that demand for oil can continue to rise even as oil prices increase and in fact further contribute to the price increase, leading to large upswings in the price of oil. Stabilizing oil prices may prove important as the current financial crisis has led to what some see as under-investment in the energy sector, such as energy companies drilling fewer oil and gas wells. Under-investment in the energy sector may lead to higher energy prices, particularly for oil and electricity, in a few years.[64] Additionally, elimination of fossil fuel subsidies may ease the budget deficit problems of many countries.

Eliminating fossil fuel subsidies may prove difficult. Governments in low-and middle-income countries, who spend $310 billion a year on fossil fuel subsidies compared to the $20-30 billion spent annually by developed countries, may be reluctant for political reasons to eliminate these subsidies.[65] In 2008, cuts in subsidies in Egypt, India, and Indonesia resulted in street protests and political upheaval.[66] Eliminating fossil fuel subsidies in rich countries may also face obstacles. The Environmental Law Institute, a think-tank, estimates that the United States spent $72 billion on fossil-fuel subsidies between 2002 and 2008.[67] Elimination of fossil fuel subsidies would require Congressional approval, and it is expected that the oil industry would strongly oppose such legislation.[68]

Reaching an agreement on reducing greenhouse gas emissions, as a successor to the Kyoto Protocol, at the United Nations Framework Convention on Climate Change (UNFCCC) in Copenhagen in December 2009 may also face difficulties.[69] Some economists estimate that a new international agreement to reduce greenhouse gas emissions would cost $100 billion a year by 2020, and it is not clear who would foot the bill.[70] Developing countries susceptible to adverse effects of climate change have also expressed concerns that the size of the cuts in greenhouse gas emissions being discussed are not big enough. Developed countries want more concrete promises from developing countries, and even among developed countries there are disagreements about how much emissions should be cut by.

Preparatory talks held in Bangkok in October 2009 have resulted in leaders downplaying expectations, suggesting that the December 2009 summit will merely lay the groundwork for negotiations in 2010.[71] In mid-November, President Barack Obama conceded at the Asia Pacific Economic Co-operation (APEC) summit in Singapore that it was unlikely that a new agreement on greenhouse gas emissions would be reached at the December summit in

Copenhagen.[72] However, it is reported that President Obama intends to tell delegates at the conference that the United States is committed to reducing its greenhouse gas emissions in the range of 17% below 2005 levels by 2020 and 83% by 2050.[73] The 17% reduction is consistent with the legislation passed by the House in June 2009 (H.R. 2454). The Senate has not passed legislation on greenhouse gas emissions; equivalent legislation is pending in the Senate.

Conclude WTO Doha Round of Multilateral Trade Negotiations

The G-20 leaders have also pledged to conclude the WTO Doha Round of multilateral trade negotiations in 2010. Doha negotiations have been stalled since 2001 due to differences among the United States, the European Union, and developing countries on major issues including agriculture, industrial tariffs, non-tariff barriers, and services.[74]

To date, there appears to be a disconnect between the pledges of the G-20 leaders and the lack of specific negotiations on the ground to meet this goal. It is not evident that WTO members have made progress in resolving the stalemate over the Doha negotiations, and the G-20 pledge to get the Doha Round back on track by next year is viewed by many as unlikely to be met.[75] Confidence might be enhanced if the G-20 discussed the basic controversies deadlocking the Doha negotiations rather than just announcing their intent to reach agreement.

This skepticism surrounding Doha is underscored by the fact that G-20 members by and large have not refrained from protectionist trade policies in the face of the current global financial crisis. Data from Global Trade Alert (GTA), an independent and privately funded organization, indicate that G-20 members have implemented a total of 139 policies that almost certainly discriminate against foreign commercial interests between November 2008 and October 2009.[76] The scope of these measures are also fairly substantial, affecting on average 12 sectors and 77 trading partners. Furthermore, there are an additional 194 policies that the G-20 countries have implemented or announced that are likely or almost certainly discriminatory against foreign commercial interests. A report by the World Bank reports similar movements toward protectionist trade policies, but notes that these measures are believed to have had only marginal effects on trade.[77] Overall, the protectionist backlash appears to have been much lower than during the Great Depression in the 1930s.

IMPLICATIONS OF THE TRANSITION FROM THE G-7 TO THE G-20

Will the Transition to the G-20 Help or Hinder Economic Cooperation?

Fundamental questions for U.S. foreign economic policy are whether the shift from the G-7 to the G-20 will help or hinder efforts at international economic cooperation, and how it might affect US interests. Some argue that the shift will foster international economic cooperation. Including a broader membership, it is argued, will give greater legitimacy to the agreements reached by the G-20, since they are not just decided by the "rich club" of countries. Likewise, emerging-market countries, especially China and India, are big players in international financial markets, and it is argued that they should be included in international financial discussions. Additionally, expanding the G-7 to the G-20 may help the G-7 gain favor with large emerging-market countries, which could facilitate cooperation in non-economic areas such as climate change.

Others argue expanding the G-7 to the G-20 will weaken or undermine efforts at international economic cooperation. The G-20 countries are a heterogeneous group of countries with different political and economic philosophies. Including such a large, heterogeneous group of countries in the same forum, some argue, will limit the scope of the agreements reached, or the ability to reach agreements at all. In the same vein, some argue that record of implementation of the agreements reached by the G-20 will be worse than the implementation record of the G-7. G-20 emerging- market countries look a lot different than G-20 developed countries on a number of factors that could impact implementation, including rule of law, government effectiveness, and control of corruption, as shown in **Figure 5**. Of course, agreement among a homogeneous group of advanced industrial democracies may not much help resolve world problems if other countries do not participate.

Still others argue that international economic coordination will be no different under the G-20 than it was under the G-7. One rationale is that emerging-market countries have been de facto participants in the G-7 for several years and their views had already been incorporated in the G-7. An alternative rationale is that, in practice, the G-7 will dominate the G-20 negotiations and emerging-markets will have less influence over the discussions.

It is worth nothing that some of these views are not necessarily mutually exclusive. It is possible to imagine, for example, a situation where the G-20 makes fewer commitments than the G-7, but the commitments that the G-20 does reach are seen as more legitimate than those reached by the G-7.

Is the G-20 the Right Group of Countries?

When the developed countries decided to include emerging markets in discussions on policy responses to the crisis, the G-20 was an expedient choice because it was a well established group that encompassed the G-7 and several large emerging-market countries. The G-20 members were selected by the G-7 when the G-20 was formed in 1999, and the decision on which countries to include reflected a need for broad geographic representation and systemic economic importance.[78] The membership of the G-20 has not changed since its establishment.

Some argue that the G-20 was the right choice for expanding the G-7, because the G-20 represents two-thirds of the world's population, 90% of world GDP, and 80% of world trade.[79] A mix of policymakers and academics have long advocated replacing the G-7 by the G-20, or at least making the G-20 a more prominent economic forum.[80]

Others have reservations with respect to whether the G-20 is the right group of developed and emerging-market countries. With the developed countries, there are concerns that European interests are still over-represented in the G-20, with Europeans taking up five of the 20 slots (Germany, France, Italy, the United Kingdom, and the European Union). This problem is exacerbated by Spain and the Netherlands, who have gained attendance to all three G-20 summits even though they are not official members. That said, some maintain that, based on economic weight, Spain is a more justified member of the G-20 than Italy.

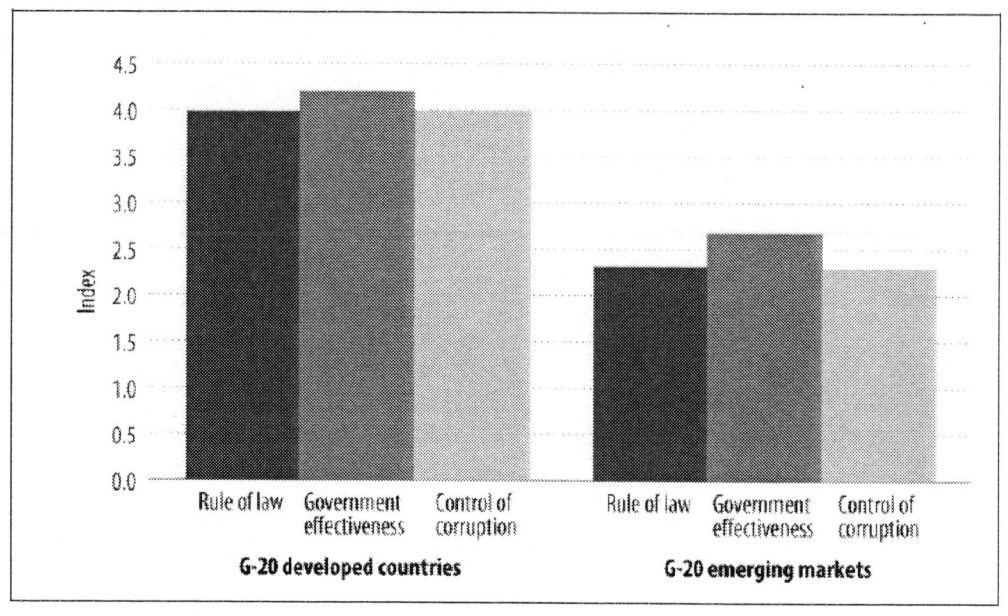

Source: Daniel Kaufmann, Aart Kraay and Massimo Mastruzzi, "Governance Matters VIII: Governance Indicators for 1996-2008," *World Bank Policy Research*, June 2009.

Notes: Data on a five point scale (re-scaled from 0 to 5), where higher scores correspond to better outcomes. G-20 developed countries include Australia, Canada, France, Germany, Italy, Japan, the United Kingdom, and the United States. G-20 emerging-market countries include Argentina, Brazil, China, India, Indonesia, Mexico, Russia, Saudi Arabia, South Africa, South Korea, and Turkey. Governance indicators are calculated by Kaufman, Kraay, and Masturzzi using a large number of individual data sources, including surveys of firms and individuals as well as the assessments of commercial risk rating agencies, non-governmental organizations, and a number of multilateral aid agencies and other public sector organizations. "Rule of law" captures perceptions of the extent to which agents have confidence in and abide by the rules of society, and in particular the quality of contract enforcement, property rights, the police, and the courts, as well as the likelihood of crime and violence. "Government effectiveness" captures perceptions of the quality of public services, the quality of the civil service and the degree of its independence from political pressures, the quality of policy formulation and implementation, and the credibility of the government's commitment to such policies. "Control of corruption" captures perceptions of the extent to which public power is exercised for private gain, including both petty and grand forms of corruption, as well as capture of the state by elites and private interests.

Figure 5. Selected Governance Indicators for the G-20 Developed and Emerging-Market Countries

There are also questions about the selection of large emerging-market countries. Some argue that several emerging markets are not included in the forum, but should be based on their economic and political importance. Poland, Thailand, Egypt, and Pakistan are typically cited as examples.[81] **Table 2** shows that there are 13 countries that are not members of the G-20 but whose economies are as large as other G-20 members. It is unlikely that any current members of the G-20 would resign or could be pushed out in order to allow new countries to join. One issue that may confront the G-20 in the future is how to balance, on one hand, fair representation in the forum and, on the other hand, keeping the size of the forum manageable.

Table 2. World's Largest Countries and Entities, by GDP
2008 data, billions of U.S. dollars

Rank	G-20 Members	Non G-20 Members	GDP
1.	European Union		$18,493
2.	United States		14,195
3.	Japan		4,867
4.	China		3,942
5.	Germany		3,653
6.	France		2,843
7.	United Kingdom		2,833
8.	Italy		2,330
9.	Russia		1,699
10.		Spain	1,623
11.	Brazil		1,621
12.	Canada		1,571
13.	India		1,233
14.	Australia		1,047
15.	South Korea		999
16.	Mexico		950
17.		Netherlands	863
18.	Turkey		748
19.		Belgium	507
20.		Sweden	503
21.	Indonesia		488
22.		Switzerland	473
23.	Saudi Arabia		464
24.		Norway	459
25.		Poland	451
26.		Austria	419
27.		Taiwan	409
28.		Iran	364
29.		Greece	362
30.		Denmark	349
31.		Venezuela	335
32.	Argentina		324
33.	South Africa		296

Source: IMF World Economic Outlook.
Notes: The European Union (EU) includes 27 countries.

Beyond the Current Crisis: What Will the G-20's Focus Be?

As the G-20 summits have progressed, the scope of discussions has broadened to include a diverse set of issues, ranging from IFI reform to food security to climate change. Some have suggested that the G-20's agenda has become too ambitious.[82] When the crisis does wind down, it is not yet clear whether the G-20's focus will return to more traditional economic policy coordination (such as exchange rates and trade) or if the new policy items on the G-20's Pittsburgh agenda will become the primary focus of the forum.

In addition, it is still to be seen how the G-20 will fit in with existing international institutions. Much of the London and Pittsburgh G-20 communiqués is devoted to reiterating commitments made in other venues, such as the WTO (for trade) and the United Nations (for climate change, for example). On one hand, the G-20's focus at the leader level on trade and climate change may provide the jolt necessary to make progress on international negotiations that have stalled for years. Likewise, the G-20 may facilitate trade-offs among major concerns that would not be possible in issue-specific forums. On the other hand, the G-20 may find it difficult to make progress on policy areas that have proven so difficult to get traction on in the past. The G-7 often made decisions which were then taken to the IFIs for implementation, and it is not clear whether the G-20 will have the same leadership capacity.

Finally, it is worth noting that it has been only in the most recent summit that global imbalances have been explicitly addressed in the G-20 communiqués. This is partly due to the fact that correcting imbalances was not an immediate way to "stop the bleeding," but it is also partly due to the fact that global imbalances are politically sensitive. For the reasons discussed above, there is some skepticism that the G-20's proposal to correct global imbalances will carry much weight.[83] China is hinting it will be strengthening its currency, the renminbi, which would help correct global imbalances,[84] although these signals have been mixed. To the extent that further action would be needed, policymakers may need to find other forums, institutions, or bilateral discussions to address these issues. The issue of imbalances has, for example, been acknowledged in bilateral discussions between the United States and China in the "U.S.-China Strategic and Economic Dialogue" (or "S&ED"), although this has not translated into concrete steps or plans of action on this issue. Other countries might be seriously affected by the consequence of bilateral deals, however, and this might complicate settlement of related issues affecting more countries in other contexts.

ACKNOWLEDGMENTS

Susan Chesser assisted with research on G-20 protests; Pat McClaughry helped create the maps; and Amber Wilhelm assisted with preparation of the graphs.

End Notes

[1] The G-20 includes Argentina, Australia, Brazil, Canada, China, France, Germany, India, Indonesia, Italy, Japan, Mexico, Russia, Saudi Arabia, South Africa, South Korea, Turkey, United Kingdom, and the United States, as well as the European Union (EU). Spain and the Netherlands have also been invited to participate as observers. The G-20's website is http://www.g20.org. The University of Toronto G-20 Research Group is also a good

source of information; their website is http://www.g20.utoronto.ca/. The G-20 discussed in this report should not be confused with the coalition of developing countries in the World Trade Organization (WTO) formed in 2003, also referred to as the G-20.

[2] For more on the current global financial crisis, see: CRS Report RL34742, *The Global Financial Crisis: Analysis and Policy Implications*, coordinated by Dick K. Nanto.

[3] The G-7 includes Canada, France, Germany, Italy, Japan, the United Kingdom, and the United States. Russia has joined the G-7 meetings at the leader level (summits) as a full participant since 1998, forming the Group of Eight (G-8). With a smaller economy than the G-7 members, Russia does not usually participate in international economic discussions, however, which continued primarily at the G-7 level. For example, Russia is not included in the G-7 meetings at the finance minister level.

[4] The Paris Club is an informal group of developed countries. The group provides financial services such as debt restructuring and debt relief to indebted developing countries.

[5] For more information about formal international institutions, see, for example: CRS Report R40578, *The Global Financial Crisis: Increasing IMF Resources and the Role of Congress*, by Jonathan E. Sanford and Martin A. Weiss and CRS Report RL32060, *World Trade Organization Negotiations: The Doha Development Agenda*, by Ian F. Fergusson.

[6] While the EU is not an official member of the G-7 or G-8, the EU has participated in meetings since 1977. The EU is represented by the president of the European Commission and the president of the European Council. The EU does not hold leadership positions within the G-8 or host summits.

[7] Nicholas Bayne, "Reforming the International Financial Architecture: The G7 Summit's Successes and Shortcomings," July 2001, http://www.g8.utoronto.ca/conferences/2001/rome/bayneRev.pdf.

[8] The members of the G-22 are the G-8 members plus Argentina, Australia, Brazil, China, Hong Kong, India, Indonesia, Malaysia, Mexico, Poland, Singapore, South Africa, South Korea, and Thailand.

[9] The members of the G-33 are the G-8 members plus Argentina, Australia, Belgium, Brazil, Chile, China, Côte d'Ivoire, Egypt, Hong Kong, India, Indonesia, South Korea, Malaysia, Mexico, Morocco, the Netherlands, Poland, Saudi Arabia, Singapore, South Africa, Spain, Sweden, Switzerland, Thailand, and Turkey.

[10] Emerging markets had been sporadically invited to a few G-8 summit dinners and events as early as 1989, but their participation was very minor compared to 2005 onwards. See Peter I. Hajnal, *The G8 System and the G20* (Ashgate, 2007), pp. 47-49.

[11] Jonathan Wheatley, "G20 Calls for Expanded Role to Combat Economic Turmoil," *Financial Times*, November 10, 2009.

[12] "After the Fall," *The Economist*, November 15, 2009.

[13] "Not a Bad Weekend's Work," *The Economist*, November 16, 2008.

[14] Ibid.

[15] The term "sherpa" is a play on words. Typically, sherpas refer to local people, typically men, in Nepal who are employed as guides for mountaineering expeditions in the Himalayas. Recall that meetings held among leaders are called "summits," which also refers to the highest point of a mountain.

[16] The term "sous-sherpa" is also a play on words, referencing the French term "sous-chef" for under-chef or an assistant to a master chef.

[17] http://www.g20.org

[18] Jenilee Guebert, *Plans for the Third G20 Summit: Pittsburgh 2009*, G20 Research Group, University of Toronto, August 18, 2009, pp. 44-45, http://www.g20.utoronto.ca/g20plans/g20leaders090818.pdf.

[19] http://www.g20.org

[20] E.g., see: CRS Report RS20088, *Dispute Settlement in the World Trade Organization (WTO): An Overview*, by Jeanne J. Grimmett.

[21] The G-20 communiqués are posted online at http://www.g20.org/pub_communiques.aspx.

[22] For more on the $1.1 trillion package to increase IFI and MDB resources, and the requisite congressional authorizations, see: CRS Report R40578, *The Global Financial Crisis: Increasing IMF Resources and the Role of Congress*, by Jonathan E. Sanford and Martin A. Weiss.

[23] Carl Prine, "An Overview of Protests Expected in Pittsburgh for G-20," *Pittsburgh Tribune-Review*, September 20, 2009.

[24] Michelle Nichols, "Protesters, Police Clash After G20 in Pittsburgh," *Reuters*, September 25, 2009.

[25] Daniel Lovering and Michael Rubinkam, "G-20 March Turns Chaotic as Police, Protesters Clash on Streets of Pittsburgh," *AP Newswire (Government Feed)*, September 24, 2009.

[26] Michelle Nichols, "Protesters, Police Clash After G20 in Pittsburgh," *Reuters*, September 25, 2009.

[27] Dennis B. Roddy and Michael A. Fuoco, "Protests Lead to 19 Arrests Across City," *Pittsburgh Post-Gazette*, September 25, 2009.

[28] Treasury Department, "Press Briefing by Treasury Secretary Tim Geithner on the G20 Meeting Pittsburgh Convention Center," press release, September 24, 2009, http://www.treas.gov/press/releases/tg405.htm.

[29] Ibid., pp. 13.

[30] Financial Stability Board. Improving Financial Regulation: Report of the Financial Stability Board to the G20 Leaders. September 25, 2009.

[31] http://www.g20.org/Documents/pittsburgh_summit_leaders_statement_250909.pdf.

[32] E.g., see Chris Giles, "Three-Stage Plan for Growth," *Financial Times*, September 26, 2009 and Chris Giles, "Spot the Difference," *Financial Times*, September 23, 2009.

[33] "Regaining their Balance," *The Economist*, September 26, 2009.

[34] Ibid.

[35] IMF quotas determine a country's maximum financial commitment to the IMF and its voting power, and has bearing on its access to IMF financing.

[36] "Money, Votes and Politics," *The Economist*, October 7, 2009.

[37] E.g., see "IMF Quotas," International Monetary Fund, October 31, 2009. Available at http://www.imf.org/external/np/exr/facts/quotas. Also see "Quota Reform at the G-20," Reserve Bank of Australia, February 2006. Available at http://www.treasury.gov.au/documents/1102/HTML/docshell.asp?URL=G20_Quota_Reform.htm.

[38] GDP used in this section is adjusted for purchasing power parity (PPP). GDP adjusted for PPP means that GDP is adjusted to account for differences in prices across countries. Others argue that market-based GDP, unadjusted for PPP, should be used. In the current IMF quota formula, GDP is a weighted average of market-based and PPP GDP, at 60% and 40% respectively. Using market-based GDP does produce slightly different rankings; Figures 3 and 4 are intended as examples and should not be taken as definitive rank orders of under- and over-represented countries.

[39] These are examples; see fn. 55.

[40] For more information, see: CRS Report R40578, *The Global Financial Crisis: Increasing IMF Resources and the Role of Congress*, by Jonathan E. Sanford and Martin A. Weiss.

[41] International Monetary Fund, *Bolstering the IMF's Lending Capacity*, November 5, 2009, http://www.imf.org/external/np/exr/faq/contribution.htm.

[42] World Bank, *Review of IBRD and IFC Financial Capacities: Working with Partners to Support Global Development*, October 5, 2009.

[43] Daniel Bases and Javier Mozzo, "IADB Should Increase Capital by $150-$180 Billion," *Reuters*, March 29, 2009.

[44] The International Bank for Reconstruction and Development (IBRD) is one of two World Bank facilities that lend directly to governments to finance projects and programs. The other facility is the International Development Association (IDA). The IBRD provides middle-income developing countries with loans at near-market rates using funds raised by the World Bank on the international capital markets. While many of these countries can borrow on the international capital markets, and are increasingly doing so, some seek loans from the World Bank to gain access to World Bank technical assistance and advisory services, as well as the prestige and legitimacy that come with World Bank-backed projects. IDA was established in 1960, 16 years after the creation of the IBRD, due to concerns that low- income countries could not afford to borrow at the near-market rate terms offered by the IBRD. Consequently, IDA provides concessional loans and grants to poor countries funded by contributions from donors and transfers from the IBRD.

[45] World Bank, *Review of IBRD and IFC Financial Capacities: Working with Partners to Support Global Development*, September 29, 2009.

[46] Japan Credit Rating Agency, Ltd., Affirms AAA Ratings on International Bank for Reconstruction and Development; Outlook Stable, April 25, 2008,
http://www.jcr.co.jp/english/top_cont/rat_info04.php?no=08i007&PHPSESSID=f809554a5fc99e428fcfd7a0cf5ec7dd.

[47] The IFC was established in 1956 and promotes sustainable private sector development by financing private sector projects and companies in the developing world, helping private companies in the developing world mobilize financing international financial markets, and providing advice and technical assistance to businesses and governments.

[48] World Bank, *Review of IBRD and IFC Financial Capacities: Working with Partners to Support Global Development*, September 29, 2009.

[49] IFC, *IFC 2009 Financials, Projects, and Portfolio*, 2009, p. 4, http://www.ifc.org/if cext/annualreport.nsf/AttachmentsByTitle/AR2009_Volume2/$FILE/AR2009_Volume2.pdf.

[50] "African Development Bank Seeks Additional Capital-Treasurer," *Reuters Africa*, September 23, 2009.

[51] The formal proposal may be found at Asian Development Bank. *Information on Subscription for the Fifth General Capital Increase*. May 2009. See http://www.adb.org/Documents/Brochures/Fifth-General-Capital-Increase/generalcapital-increase.pdf.

[52] "EBRD Seeks 50% Increase in Capital," *Financial Times*, September 28, 2009.

[53] Joshua Goodman and Helen Murphy, " IDB Seeking Up to $180 Bln in Capital to Boost Loans (Update2)," *Bloomberg*, March 29, 2009.

[54] Data for this section is from "Capital Flows To Emerging Market Economies," *Institute for International Finance*, October 3, 2009.

[55] The Millennium Development Goals are a series of eight development goals, ranging from halving extreme poverty to halting the spread of HIV/AIDS, to be reached by 2015. The Millennium Development Goals were

agreed to by world leaders at the United Nations Headquarters in New York in 2000. In order to help reach the Millennium Development Goals, leaders at the G-8 summit in Gleneagles, Scotland in 2005, committed to doubling aid to Africa by 2010. This is agreement is often referred to as the "Gleneagles commitments." Russia did not commit to raising aid to Africa, leading some to refer to the Gleneagles commitments as made by the G-7. For more on U.S. foreign aid see: CRS Report R40213, *Foreign Aid: An Introduction to U.S. Programs and Policy*, by Curt Tarnoff and Marian Leonardo Lawson.

[56] Millennium Development Goal (MDG) Gap Task Force, *Strengthening the Global Partnership for Development in a Time of Crisis*, 2009.

[57] ONE, *The Data Report 2009: Monitoring the G8 Promise to Africa*, May 19, 2009.

[58] Ibid.

[59] See e.g., "G20 asks World Bank to set up agriculture fund," *Reuters*, September 25, 2009.

[60] For more information, see: CRS Report R40910, *Status of the Copenhagen Climate Change Negotiations*, by Jane A. Leggett and Richard K. Lattanzio.

[61] Ben Geman, "White House Wants Fuel Subsidy Cuts on G-20 Agenda," *Washington Post*, September 16, 2009.

[62] "Fossilised Policy," *The Economist*, October 1, 2009.

[63] "No Free Lunch: The G-20's Case Against Fossil-Fuel Subsidies," *Wall Street Journal*, September 25, 2009.

[64] International Energy Agency, *World Energy Outlook 2009*, November 10, 2009.

[65] "Fossilised Policy," *The Economist*, October 1, 2009.

[66] Ibid.

[67] Environmental Law Institute, *Estimating U.S. Government Subsidies to Energy Sources: 2002 -2008*, September 2009.

[68] "Fossilised Policy," *The Economist*, October 1, 2009.

[69] The Koyoto Protocol is a 1997 climate change agreement that set greenhouse gas emissions targets for industrialized countries. It was never ratified by the United States.

[70] "United Nations Framework Convention on Climate Change," *New York Times*, accessed October 21, 2009.

[71] "Bangkok Blues," *The Economist*, October 15, 2009.

[72] Edward Luce, Kevin Brown, and Fiona Harvey, et al., "Obama Damps Climate Hopes," *Financial Times*, November 16, 2009.

[73] John M. Broder, "Obama to Go to Copenhagen with Emissions Target ," *New York Times*, November 25, 2009.

[74] For more on the Doha negotiations, see: CRS Report RL32060, *World Trade Organization Negotiations: The Doha Development Agenda*, by Ian F. Fergusson.

[75] E.g., see "Regaining Their Balance," *The Economist*, 26 September 2009.

[76] http://www.globaltradealert.org/ Accessed October 20, 2009. GTA is coordinated by the Centre for Economic Policy Research (CEPR) and has been cited extensively in the media, including *The Economist, Forbes, The Financial Times*, and *The Wall Street Journal*.

[77] Elisa Gamberoni and Richard Newfarmer, *Trade Protection: Incipient but Worrisome Trends*, International Trade Department, World Bank, Trade Note #37, March 2, 2009. http://siteresources. worldbank.org/ NEWS/ Resources/Trade_Note_37.pdf.

[78] Brookings, *The G-20 (Group of 20)*, http://www.brookings.edu/reports/2009/~/media

[79] Arvind Panagariya, *The G-20 Summit and Global Trade: Restore Credit and Resist Protectionism*, Brookings, March 14, 2009. Trade data includes intra-EU trade.

[80] For an overview of these proposals, see Peter I. Hajnal, *The G8 System and the G20* (Ashgate, 2007), ch. 12.

[81] "G20 Gains Stature But is Overambitious," *Oxford Analytica*, September 28, 2009.

[82] Ibid.

[83] E.g., see Nouriel Roubini, "A Balanced Global Diet," *New York Times*, October 28, 2009.

[84] Geoff Dyer, "Chinese Hint at Stronger Renminbi," *Financial Times*, November 12, 2009.

In: Global Economics Crisis and Cooperation
Editor: Jonathan P. Castle

ISBN: 978-1-61761-114-8
© 2010 Nova Science Publishers, Inc.

Chapter 3

LIMITING CENTRAL GOVERNMENT BUDGET DEFICITS: INTERNATIONAL EXPERIENCES

James K. Jackson

SUMMARY

The global financial crisis and economic recession spurred national governments to boost fiscal expenditures to stimulate economic growth and to provide capital injections to support their financial sectors. Government measures included asset purchases, direct lending through national treasuries, and government-backed guarantees for financial sector liabilities. The severity and global nature of the economic recession raised the rate of unemployment, increased the cost of stabilizing the financial sector, and limited the number of policy options that were available to national leaders. In turn, the financial crisis negatively affected economic output and contributed to the severity of the economic recession. As a result, the surge in fiscal spending, combined with a loss of revenue, has caused government deficit spending to rise sharply when measured as a share of gross domestic product (GDP) and increased the overall level of public debt. Recent forecasts indicate that should the current economic rebound take hold, budget deficits on the whole likely will stabilize, but are not expected to fall appreciably for some time.

The sharp rise in deficit spending is prompting policymakers to assess various strategies for winding down their stimulus measures and to curtail capital injections without disrupting the nascent economic recovery. This report focuses on how major developed and emerging-market country governments, particularly the G-20 and Organization for Economic Cooperation and Development (OECD) countries, limit their fiscal deficits. Financial markets support government efforts to reduce deficit spending, because they are concerned over the long-term impact of the budget deficits. At the same time, they are concerned that the loss of spending will slow down the economic recovery and they doubt the conviction of some governments to impose austere budgets in the face of public opposition. Some central governments are examining such measures as budget rules, or fiscal consolidation, as a way to trim spending and reduce the overall size of their central government debt. Budget rules can be applied in a number of ways, including limiting central government budget deficits to a determined percentage of GDP. To the extent that fiscal consolidation lowers the market rate of interest, such efforts could improve a government's budget position by lowering borrowing costs and stimulating economic growth. Other strategies include authorizing independent public institutions to spearhead fiscal consolidation efforts and developing medium-term budgetary frameworks for fiscal planning. Fiscal consolidation efforts, however, generally require policymakers to weigh the effects of various policy trade-offs, including the trade-off between adopting stringent, but enforceable, rules-based programs, compared with more flexible, but less effective, principles-based programs that offer policymakers some discretion in applying punitive measures.

OVERVIEW AND BACKGROUND

In its recent economic outlook,[1] the International Monetary Fund (IMF) indicated that fiscal balances, or the annual budget balance, of the economically advanced G-20[2] countries weakened by 6 percentage points of GDP between 2007 and 2009, rising from 1.9% to 7.9% of GDP. The largest impact on the fiscal balances of the advanced G-20 countries was projected to occur in 2009 and 2010. Also, the forecast indicates that government debt, or the accumulated amount of government deficits, among the advanced G-20 countries will rise on average by 14.5% of GDP by the end of 2009, compared with 2007, as indicated in **Table 1**.[3] This forecast is considered by the IMF to represent the middle of the range of estimates, and it is based on the assumption that the economic recovery will continue at the pace experienced in mid-2009. In the same forecast, the annual budget deficits for the emerging G-20 countries were projected to widen on average from a surplus of 0.2% of GDP in 2007 to a deficit of 3.2% of GDP in 2009, while government debt was expected to remain at a constant share of GDP. For European governments, the rise in government budget deficits and the increase in the total amount of government debt is undermining their efforts to reduce the size of their annual central government budget deficits. These estimates for the growth in government debt could change, depending on the success governments have in liquidating at favorable prices the assets they acquired during the financial crisis, the timing and strength of the economic recovery, and the extent of any payout on official guarantees.

The magnitude and pervasive nature of the government deficits is unsettling international capital markets. In general, public sector debts are rising relative to national gross domestic product (GDP), the broadest measure of a nation's economic output. The international markets also have become increasingly wary of rising government deficits due to an increased perception of risk. In particular, these perceived risks are viewed as being especially high in Europe where financial institutions are exposed to economic troubles in Greece, Portugal, and Spain. According to the Bank for International Settlements (BIS) the euro area banks hold more than 70% of the outstanding public sector debt of Greece.[4] Furthermore, the uneven pace of the economic recovery is adding to perceptions of risk.

Table 1. Fiscal Balance and Government Debt of G-20 Countries
(expressed as a percent of national GDP)

Country	Fiscal Balance 2007	2008	2009	2010	2014	Government Gross Debt 2007	2008	2009	2010	2014
Argentina	-2.3%	-0.5%	-3.6%	-2.3%	-0.4%	65.9%	49.2%	38.6%	33.7%	23.5%
Australia	1.6	1.7	1.8	1.7	1.7	8.9	8.1	7.9	7.2	4.2
Brazil	-2.2	-1.1	-1.3	-1.2	-0.6	67.7	65.4	64.7	62.9	54.1
Canada	1.4	0.5	-1.5	-1.9	2.1	64.2	60.8	63.0	62.6	46.5
China	0.9	-0.1	-2.0	-2.0	-0.5	20.2	17.9	22.2	23.4	18.6
France	-2.7	-3.3	-5.5	-6.3	-2.7	63.9	66.1	72.3	77.1	79.4
Germany	-0.2	-0.1	-3.3	-4.6	0.1	65.0	68.7	76.1	80.1	77.2
India	-5.2	-7.8	-8.5	-7.4	-4.5	80.5	80.6	82.7	82.9	71.6
Indonesia	-1.2	0.1	-2.6	-2.0	-1.6	35.0	32.5	31.8	31.3	28.3
Italy	-1.6	-2.7	-3.9	-4.3	-4.2	104.1	105.6	109.4	112.4	118.0
Japan	-3.4	-4.7	-7.1	-7.2	-6.4	195.5	202.5	217.0	225.1	222.3
Korea	3.8	1.4	-0.8	-0.8	0.6	32.1	32.8	32.9	33.0	29.3
Mexico	-1.4	-1.7	-2.9	-2.8	-2.3	38.3	39.3	42.1	42.5	42.0
Russia	6.8	5.3	-2.6	-2.0	-3.5	7.3	5.8	6.5	6.5	6.4
Saudi Arabia	15.8	35.0	-1.2	1.7	2.6	18.7	12.9	11.6	9.7	5.8
South Africa	0.9	-0.2	-1.9	-1.7	-0.3	28.5	27.2	27.0	26.7	22.2
Spain	2.2	-3.1	-6.1	-6.0	-2.1	36.2	38.6	48.6	53.8	56.3
Turkey	-2.3	-2.5	-2.3	-2.0	0.3	38.9	38.7	40.4	40.4	29.7
United Kingdom	-2.7	-4.2	-7.2	-8.1	-4.8	44.0	50.4	61.0	68.7	76.2
United States	-2.9	-6.4	-12.0	-8.9	-5.1	63.1	68.7	81.2	90.2	99.5
G-20	-1.1	-2.6	-6.2	-5.3	-3.0	63.5	65.5	72.5	76.7	76.8
Advanced G-20 Countries	-1.9	-4.1	-7.9	-6.8	-3.8	78.8	83.2	93.2	99.8	103.5
Emerging Market G-20 Countries	0.2	-0.1	-3.2	-2.8	NA	37.7	35.7	37.6	37.8	32.0

Source: *The State of Pubic Finances: Outlook and Medium-Term Policies After the 2008 Crash*, the International Monetary Fund, March 6, 2009, Table 6.

Generally, the rising level of public sector debts in most countries do not reflect profligate spending, but reflect measures policymakers adopted to avert a more serious and protracted economic recession. Nevertheless, policymakers and financial markets are especially concerned over the situation in Europe, where some investors view the rising deficits in Portugal, Spain, Greece, and Ireland as increasing the risks for a default and the potential for additional turmoil in the financial markets.[5] In some cases, these countries have borrowed heavily from the European Central Bank (ECB). The ECB requires borrower countries to provide government bonds rated above BBB- as collateral, but that minimum rating is expected to rise to A- by the end of the 2010 and would rule out Greek bonds if rating agencies continue to downgrade the sovereign bonds.

For this and other reasons, the economic conditions of Portugal, Greece, Spain, and Ireland were a key topic at the early February 2010 meeting of G7 finance ministers and the exchange value of the euro has depreciated against the dollar recently amid broader concerns over the impact budget deficits will have on the larger economies in the Eurozone.[6] Such concerns could tighten credit and raise borrowing costs for a broad number of countries. Rather than relying on the International Monetary Fund to provide loans to the four countries in the most immediate danger, the richer economies of the Eurozone, particularly France and Germany, may well step in and provide loans and other assistance to those nations in trouble. Prospects of a default by any member of the Eurozone, however, could severely strain the cohesion of the zone and challenge some aspects of European economic integration.

In addition to the IMF's projections, the latest Economic Outlook[7] by the Organization for Economic Cooperation and Development (OECD) also projects an economic recovery to begin in 2010. The OECD estimates, however, that economic performance among OECD countries on average after 2010 will be below that experienced in the period prior to the financial crisis. According to the OECD, most developed countries will continue to face severe imbalances within their economies, including low levels of output, low levels of private investment, high rates of unemployment (including a higher rate of permanent unemployment), low inflation, and large central government deficits. As OECD economists have noted,[8] economic downturns that follow a banking crisis typically last longer and involve greater losses in economic output and a greater deterioration in the fiscal balances of central governments than economic recessions not associated with a banking crisis. In most of the cases studied by OECD economists, the banking crises usually involved a single country or a small group of countries. As a result, those countries were able to export their way out of their economic recession. In the current environment, however, one could argue that few of the large number of countries that are concurrently experiencing an economic recession likely will succeed in exporting their way to an economic recovery.

IMPACT ON CENTRAL GOVERNMENT BUDGETS

The current financial and economic crises have worsened the financial position of the central government budgets of the G-20 countries, although the impact of the crises has varied by country. The two crises are affecting the balance sheets of the central governments in three broad areas. First, governments adopted a broad range of special measures to support the financial system. Second, policymakers adopted discretionary fiscal stimulus measures to spur economic growth in order to stem the effects of the sharp drop in economic activity. Third, most economies experienced a loss in tax revenue and a surge in non-discretionary spending, referred to as automatic stabilizers, including such activities as unemployment insurance, that rise without direct legislative authorization. As a result of these factors, the financial crisis has undermined the effectiveness of budget rules as government budgets are affected by large or prolonged internal or external shocks.

Table 2 displays the combination of these three spending activities on the overall balance of G-20 countries. The data indicate that over the 2009-2010 period, the overall fiscal balance for the United States is expected to fall from -5.9% to -8.9% of GDP as automatic stabilizers kick in and as discretionary policy actions, in the form of deficit spending, increase. Additionally, the data indicate that the U.S. budget balance is being affected almost equally by automatic stabilizers, discretionary fiscal policy actions, and by other actions, including extraordinary measures, that were taken to shore up the financial sector. In comparison, Saudi Arabia and Russia experienced a double-digit deterioration in their budget balances as their government budgets shifted from running a surplus to being in deficit, due in large part to the drop in oil revenues as the price of oil fell during the economic recession. Saudi Arabia also adopted other discretionary fiscal measures that contributed to its budget deficit. Great Britain, as is the case with other G-20 members, adopted discretionary spending measures. Those measures, however, were less a factor in driving up its budget deficits than spending associated with automatic stabilizers.

Table 2. Overall Central Government Budget Balances, Automatic Stabilizers and Discretionary Measures of G-20 Countries (as a percent of GDP)

	Overall Balance				Average Annual Change in 2008-2010 compared to 2007			
	2007	2008	2009	2010	Overall Balance	Automatic Stabilizers	Discretionary Measures	Other
Argentina	-2.3	-0.5	-3.6	-2.3	0.2	-0.6	-0.4	1.2
Australia	1.6	0.1	-2.2	-2.8	-3.3	-1.7	-1.5	0.0
Brazil	-2.2	-1.5	-1.0	-0.8	1.1	-0.7	-0.2	2.0
Canada	1.4	0.4	-3.2	-3.7	-3.6	-1.8	-0.9	-0.9
China	0.9	-0.3	-3.6	-3.6	-3.4	-0.6	-2.1	-0.7
France	-2.7	-3.1	-6.0	-6.2	-2.5	-2.4	-0.4	0.3
Germany	-0.2	-0.1	-4.0	-5.2	-3.0	-1.6	-1.1	-0.2
India	-5.2	-8.4	-10	-8.6	-3.8	-0.4	-0.4	-3.0
Indonesia	-1.2	0.1	-2.5	-2.1	-0.3	-0.1	-0.6	0.5
Italy	-1.5	-2.7	-4.8	-5.2	-2.7	-2.6	-0.1	0.0
Japan	-3.4	-5.0	-8.1	-8.3	-3.7	-2.2	-0.7	-0.9
Korea	3.8	1.2	-2.2	-3.2	-5.1	-1.5	-1.6	-2.1
Mexico	-1.4	-1.9	-3.2	-2.9	-1.3	-1.3	-0.5	0.6
Russia	6.8	4.2	-5.2	-5.1	-8.8	-1.4	-1.3	-6.1
Saudi Arabia	15.8	35.5	-8.3	-6.5	-8.9	-0.5	-3.1	-5.4
South Africa	0.9	-0.1	-2.7	-3.4	-3.0	-0.6	-1.0	-1.5
Turkey	-2.1	-3.0	-4.2	-3.3	-1.4	-2.1	0.0	0.7
United Kingdom	-2.7	-5.5	-9.5	-11.0	-6.0	-2.5	-0.5	-2.9
United States	-2.9	-5.9	-7.7	-8.9	-4.6	-1.6	-1.6	-1.4
G-20 PPP GDP-weighted average	-1.1	-2.6	-5.9	-6.3	-3.8	-1.4	-1.2	-1.2
Memo-randum item: EU G-20	-1.6	-2.7	-6.0	-6.9	-3.5	-2.2	-0.6	-0.7

Source: *Global Economic Policies and Prospects*, IMF Staff Note for the Group of Twenty Meeting, March 13-14, 2009, the International Monetary Fund.

Notes: PPP stands for purchasing power parity, or the data have been adjusted to account for exchange rates. The three spending areas are: 1) automatic stabilizers, or those governments payments that are ratcheted up automatically as the rate of economic growth slows (unemployment insurance, for instance); 2) discretionary measures, or macroeconomic policy actions that were taken specifically to address the economic downturn; 3) other expenditures, such as fiscal expenditures to shore up distressed banks; and 4) the overall balance, or the combination of the three effects. Negative numbers indicate deficit spending as a percent of GDP.

Table 3. Size and Timing of Fiscal Packages (Change in central government budget balances by component and period)

	2008-2010 net effect on fiscal balance			Distribution over the period		
	Spending	Tax revenue	Total	2008	2009	2010
	Percent of 2008 GDP			Percent of total net effect		
Australia	-4.1%	-1.3%	-5.4%	13.0%	54.0%	33.0%
Austria	-0.4	-0.8	-1.2	0.0	79.0	21.0
Belgium	-1.1	-0.3	-1.4	0.0	51.0	49.0
Canada	-1.7	-2.4	-4.1	12.0	41.0	47.0
Czech Republic	-0.3	-2.5	-2.8	0.0	56.0	44.0
Denmark	-2.6	-0.7	-3.3	0.0	33.0	67.0
Finland	-0.5	-2.7	-3.2	0.0	47.0	53.0
France	-0.6	-0.2	-0.7	0.0	68.0	32.0
Germany	-1.6	-1.6	-3.2	0.0	48.0	52.0
Greece	0.0	0.8	0.8	0.0	100.0	NA
Hungary	7.5	0.2	7.7	0.0	51.0	49.0
Iceland	1.6	5.7	7.3	0.0	28.0	72.0
Ireland	2.2	6.0	8.3	6.0	39.0	55.0
Italy	-0.3	0.3	0	0.0	15.0	85.0
Japan	-4.2	-0.5	-4.7	2.0	74.0	25.0
Korea	-3.2	-2.8	-6.1	17.0	62.0	21.0
Luxembourg	-1.6	-2.3	-3.9	0.0	65.0	35.0
Mexico	-1.2	-0.4	-1.6	0.0	100.0	NA
Netherlands	-0.9	-1.6	-2.5	0.0	49.0	51.0
New Zealand	0.3	-4.1	-3.7	6.0	54.0	40.0
Norway	-0.9	-0.3	-1.2	0.0	100.0	NA
Poland	-0.8	-0.4	-1.2	0.0	70.0	30.0
Portugal	..	..	-0.8	0.0	100.0	0.0
Slovak Republic	-0.7	-0.7	-1.3	0.0	41.0	59.0
Spain	-2.2	-1.7	-3.9	32.0	44.0	23.0
Sweden	-1.7	-1.7	-3.3	0.0	43.0	57.0
Switzerland	-0.3	-0.2	-0.5	0.0	68.0	32.0
Turkey	-2.9	-1.5	-4.4	17.0	46.0	37.0
United Kingdom	-0.4	-1.5	-1.9	11.0	85.0	4.0
United States	-2.4	-3.2	-5.6	21.0	37.0	42.0
Major seven	-2.1	-2	-4.1	15.0	47.0	38.0
OECD average	-0.9	-0.9	-1.7	12.0	60.0	28.0

Source: Official Packages Across OECD Countries: Overview and Country Details, Organization for Economic Cooperation and Development, March 31, 2009.

The OECD also has estimated the impact of spending increases and the loss of tax revenue on the budget balances of major economies that are associated with the fiscal stimulus packages that the developed economies adopted, as indicated in **Table 3.** On average, a decrease in tax revenue and an increase in spending due to the stimulus packages adopted by the developed countries in 2008 to counter the economic recession and the financial crisis are expected to have a relatively equal impact on the budget balances of the developed countries. For the United States, the loss in tax revenue is expected to have a larger negative impact on the budget balance than the negative effect associated with a higher level of spending. The OECD estimates indicate that the economic recovery that began in 2009 will stem the continued deterioration in budget balances in 2010, but that it likely will not be a strong enough recovery to turn around the budget balances in most of the larger economies.

This continued erosion in budget balances through 2010 is raising concerns among some policymakers who contend that the budget deficits will undermine market confidence in their governments. As a result of these concerns, some analysts argue that capital markets will grow reluctant to finance the budget deficits without greater compensation in the form of higher returns, which would add to the overall cost of the deficits. In a recent report, however, the IMF concluded that a rise in the level of the central government's debt, by itself, does not necessarily have a major adverse impact on a government's solvency and, therefore, on financial markets. Nevertheless, the IMF cautions that the rise in government debt represents an important challenge that should not be ignored. The IMF contends that the source of the rise in government debt is a factor in market confidence. According to the IMF, the current rise in government deficits for most countries does not represent an explosive upward path in spending, but represents targeted and necessary policy responses to the financial and economic crises. A rise in government debt that is directed at stemming an economic recession or a financial crisis does not necessarily undermine market confidence as long as governments can undertake credible programs to reduce spending once the crisis has been averted. With some notable exceptions such as Greece, the rise in spending generally is not viewed as representing profligate spending by central governments, but is attributed to measures to address the financial crisis, including spending on social programs that rise without overt discretionary actions. Such automatic stabilizers have an especially large impact on the spending of governments within the European Union, where the government sector accounts for a larger share of total GDP.

FISCAL CONSOLIDATION: COUNTRY EFFORTS

Since 1990, numerous national governments in developed countries have undertaken fiscal consolidation efforts, often by adopting a budgetary rule that restricts the size of the annual amount of the government budget deficit to a certain percentage of GDP. The reasons for fiscal consolidations are as varied as the governments themselves. Most often, policymakers are motivated to reduce the government's budget deficit due to a variety of concerns. These include: the rising pressure on public finances of aging populations; the cost of financing a rising amount of debt; the impact on price inflation; the crowding out of private investment; and the reputation and credibility of the government and its economic policies in the financial markets. **Table 4** details fourteen instances between 1990 and 2005 identified by the IMF in which governments in developed countries undertook fiscal consolidation. As is indicated, these efforts generally were initiated for a short period of time and were designed to meet a specific objective. The details provided by the IMF include the political and macroeconomic environment in which the fiscal consolidation occurred and the condition of the central governments' budget. In a number of cases, budget consolidation can be associated with a change in governments in which the budget deficit was an issue in the preceding election.

The IMF concluded that successful fiscal consolidation efforts generally were accompanied by a supportive domestic and international environment, including, but not limited to, periods of sustained positive economic growth among trading partners. While fiscal consolidation generally tends to reduce the overall rate of growth in an economy in the short run due to the drop in the central government's contribution to GDP growth, the IMF authors concluded that: 1) this negative effect was not as pronounced as had been indicated in previous studies; 2) that in some cases fiscal consolidation had a positive impact on the rate of economic growth; and 3) that the long-term impact on economic growth from a reduction in central government spending depended on a range of factors, including the strength of private domestic demand.[9]

To reduce the size of the government's deficit spending, policymakers have a number of options. These options include reducing current spending, increasing current revenue, reducing capital spending, or some combination of spending reductions and revenue increases. While the record on the economic effects of these various approaches to fiscal consolidation is mixed, a study by the OECD concluded that "spending restraint (notably with respect to government consumption and transfers) is more likely to generate lasting fiscal consolidation and better economic performance" than revenue enhancements.[10] Despite this general result, the OECD study also concluded that the experiences of OECD countries was that revenue increases "accounted for a larger fraction of the total reduction,"[11] than did reductions in government spending. In addition, the study concluded that three-fourths of the episodes involved a combination of cuts in government expenditures and increases in government revenues. Reductions in capital spending generally played a small role in such fiscal consolidation efforts, according to the OECD study.

Table 4. Fiscal Consolidation Efforts in Selected Developed Countries

Episode	Political Background	Macroeconomic Background	Government Finances
Canada, 1994–97	Majority federal government elected in 1993 to address fiscal issues; similar election result in 1994-95 in the two largest provinces.	Recovery from recession; low inflation; high output gap and unemployment; exchange rate depreciation; improving current account balance.	Sizable deficit and debt stock; large share of debt held at short term and by nonresidents; high tax-to-GDP ratio; expending entitlements; sub-federal fiscal issues.
Denmark, 2004–05	The ruling center-right coalition entered the second half of its term with a diminishing voter support.	Continued economic slowdown (since 2001) characterized by gradually rising unemployment.	A moderate level of public debt (of about 50% of GDP), a near-balanced budget.

Table 4.(Continued)

Episode	Political Background	Macroeconomic Background	Government Finances
Finland, 1998	Both the coalition elected in 1991 and the grand coalition elected in 1995 had a clear mandate for EMU membership.	Gradual consolidation (from 1992) started at the time of deep recession characterized by high output gap, rising unemployment, low inflation, and depreciating exchange rate. By 1998 the economy had recovered and enjoyed a growth rate well above the EU average.	High deficit and medium-level but rapidly increasing debt, high tax-to-GDP ratio and expanding entitlement programs.
France, 1996–97	The president brought forward parliamentary elections by one year to ensure that the new government had a clear mandate for fiscal consolidation and that domestic elections did not interfere with the pre-EMU meeting of the European Council in early 1998.	The consolidation was launched against the background of a slow recovery from a recession, characterized by relatively high unemployment, low inflation, and exchange rate depreciation.	The expansionary policy in response to the 1993 recession left France with a large fiscal deficit and a medium-level but rapidly rising public debt, falling short of the EMU criteria.
Germany, 2003–05	The coalition led by the Social-Democratic Party narrowly won the elections in September 2002. The comprehensive reform plan (Agenda 2010) was unveiled in March 2003.	Three years of static output, high nemployment, concerns about possible deflation, heavy losses in the financial sector.	Fiscal deficit widened to about 3.7% of GDP in 2002, with public debt hovering around 60% of GDP.
Ireland, 2003–04	The coalition government enjoyed a strong parliamentary majority since 2002. In addition, there were few differences of views within the coalition.	After a decade of strong growth, economic activity (excluding profits of multinationals) decelerated markedly in 2002 and remained subdued in 2003.	Relatively low level of public debt (below 35% of GDP), a near-balanced budget, a relatively low tax-to-GDP ratio.
Italy, 1997	The consolidation was preceded by the electoral reforms at both the central and regional levels, which resulted in more stable governments with longer political horizons.	The consolidation attempt was launched during the time when growth turned negative in late 1996 - early 1997 after strong performance in 1995, and the return of the recession of the early 1990s was perceived as likely Inflation was declining but the unemployment remained high.	Very high debt (of over 115% of GDP in 1997), rising in spite of fiscal consolidation attempts since early 1990s.

Table 4.(Continued)

Episode	Political Background	Macroeconomic Background	Government Finances
Japan, 2004	Ruling coalition since 2000. In 2004, the positions of the ruling party in both houses of parliament shrank as the government's approval rating hit the low of 36 percent (compared to 70–90% in 2001), partly due to the passage of pension reforms.	Gradual economic recovery since mid-2002, with contributions from both exports and domestic demand, characterized by gradually declining unemployment and easing of deflation.	A decade of high fiscal deficits (about 8 percent of GDP in 2003) led to a rapid accumulation of public debt, which reached 160% of GDP. The revenue-to-GDP ratio remained below 30%, while social security outlays kept rising.
Netherlands, 2004–05	As a result of early elections in January 2003, center-right coalition government took office.	There had been a significant downturn in activity since 2000. During the two years, growth averaged barely 0.2%, with unemployment rising. Activity began to pick up in 2004 and growth was projected at about 1% in 2004 and 1¾% in 2005. The authorities had the challenge of nurturing the emerging recovery while ensuring fiscal sustainability.	There had been a sharp deterioration in the fiscal position with the 3 percent Maastricht deficit ceiling breached in 2003. The general government balance worsened by almost 5½ percentage points during the first three years of the decade, as a result of the 2001 tax reform, increases in health care and education spending, and a higher deficit of local governments (reaching 0.6 percent of GDP).
New Zealand, 2003	Competitive political environment, with the opposition calling on the ruling Labor Party to introduce more tax cuts and improve the quality of health and education services. However, the September 2005 elections did not lead to any significant relaxation of fiscal policy and the incumbent party was re-elected with a confirmed mandate for continued fiscal consolidation.	Solid and accelerating economic growth, narrowing current account deficit, unemployment at a 16-year low.	A slight budget surplus and a moderate level of public debt (of about 40% of GDP), which exceeded, however, the government's long-term target of 30% of GDP.

Table 4.(Continued)

Episode	Political Background	Macroeconomic Background	Government Finances
Spain, 1996–97	Elected in March 1996, the coalition government had a mandate for fiscal consolidation.	A relatively rapid economic recovery after the recession that culminated in a negative growth in 1993. While economic activity was on the rise and inflation gradually subsided, high unemployment (at above 20% of labor force) proved to be persistent.	Public finances have gradually deteriorated since 1988 with annual fiscal deficits exceeding 7% of GDP in 1995. Public debt has rapidly risen to over 70% of GDP.
Sweden, 1994–98	The Social Democrat minority government launched fiscal consolidation following the 1994 general elections.	The deepest recession since the 1930s, accompanied by high inflation, quickly rising unemployment, exchange rate depreciation and associated improvement in the current account balance.	Fiscal deficit exploded to over 12% of GDP as a result of the cyclical downturn and the underfinanced tax reform of 1990–91, with public debt reaching 80% of GDP.
United Kingdom, 1995–98	The popularity of the conservative party by the middle of the term was low. After 18 years of being in opposition, the Labor Party won elections in May 1997 with an overwhelming majority in Parliament. The new government confirmed the course of fiscal consolidation and introduced a number of new policy reforms, including transferring the responsibility for setting interest rates from the Treasury to the Bank of England.	Three successive years of solid economic growth, led by private consumption. Unemployment was falling rapidly, while inflation remained relatively low.	Public sector fiscal deficit increased to over 7 percent of GDP by 1994, the debt-to-GDP ratio was on the rise and already exceeded the target level of 40% by about 8 percentage points.
United States, 1994	New Democratic President took over in January 1993. The Congress was also Democratic and there was expectation of an initiative to reduce debt.	Economic activity had been weak for some time, and unemployment was rising.	The federal government fiscal situation had been deteriorating at a sharp pace. The deficit was almost 5% of GDP. In nominal terms federal debt had quadrupled over 1980–92 and the debt ratio was projected to continue rising at a high rate.

Source: Kumar, Manmohan S., Daniel Leigh, and Alexander Plekhanov, *Fiscal Adjustments: Determinants and Macroeconomic Consequences,* International Monetary Fund, IMF Working Paper WP/07/178, July 1007, p. 10-11.

BUDGET RULES

One approach developed countries have used to address government budget deficits has been to adopt some type of a budget rule. A study by the OECD on fiscal consolidation concluded that most developed countries have at some time adopted budget rules that restrict the amount of deficit spending to a specified percent of GDP and that constrain the overall level of the central government's debt, as indicated in **Table 5**.[12] One common feature of these rules is that most of them were applied for a relatively short period of time. In contrast, members of the European Union (EU), which account for half of the total number of developed countries, have adopted both short-term, country-specific budget rules, and long-term EU-wide budget rules.

In general, the OECD concluded after observing fiscal consolidation efforts among OECD countries since 1990 that the more successful of these efforts combined rules to balance the budget with requirements to reduce expenditures. The study argues that no one rule fits all countries and all circumstances, but that successful programs of consolidation seem to have some common features. These features include rules that are simple to manage, while incorporating enough flexibility, or discretion, to respond to downturns in the business cycles. The OECD study also observed that budget rules that rely on reducing expenditures generally have been more successful. By focusing on expenditures, the rules were more successful because: 1) they were not reliant on cyclically volatile revenues; 2) they were designed to let economic stabilizers work during a downturn; and 3) they saved windfall gains during an upturn. The data in **Table 5** also indicate if the budget rules include provisions for dealing with windfall surpluses and a "Golden Rule" provision. A golden rule provision requires that the central government's current expenditures match its current revenues, exclusive of capital investments.

BUDGET RULES IN EUROPE: THE STABILITY AND GROWTH PACT

In contrast to the short-term, country-specific budget rules most OECD countries have adopted at various times to address rising central government budget deficits, the members of the EU also operate within the requirements of the Stability and Growth Pact, which was adopted in 1997. EU members decided that, due to the disparate performance and composition of their economies, it was necessary to adopt a fiscal rule in lieu of relying on market forces to coordinate their economic policies. The Pact consists of preventive measures that include monitoring the fiscal policies of the members by the European Commission and the European Council so that fiscal discipline is maintained and enforced in the Economic and Monetary Union (EMU). The Pact also includes corrective measures that provide for fines for countries that fail over a number of years to meet the Pact's requirements. The European Union comprises the largest single bloc of countries that collectively have applied a long-term set of rules. These rules require the members to apply corrective measures to reduce their annual budget deficits and to reduce the overall level of their government debt if the annual deficits or the overall amount of debt exceed certain prescribed percentages of GDP. Since the Stability and Growth Pact was adopted, however, it has not always been applied consistently, which eventually led the EU to amend the Pact.

The basic elements of the Stability and Growth Pact did not originate with the Pact itself, but were part of the original Maastricht Treaty that served as the founding document for the present-day EU. The budget rules are based on Articles 99 and 104 of the Treaty, and related decisions, including the excessive deficit procedure protocol. Article 99 of the Treaty requires the members to "regard their economic policies as a matter of common concern." They also are required to coordinate their economic policies in order to have "similar economic performance." Article 104 requires EU members to "avoid excessive government deficits." EU members are expected to follow established guidelines regarding the ratio of the government deficit relative to GDP and the ratio of government debt to gross domestic product. The Protocol on Excessive Deficit Procedure established the specific guidelines that are applied under Article 104. Under this protocol, EU members are expected to have an annual budget deficit no greater than 3% of GDP at market prices and government debt no more than an amount equivalent to 60% of GDP. The number of member states with a fiscal deficit above 3% of GDP increased from two in 2007 to twenty in 2010.[13]

Table 5. Fiscal Rules Being Applied in Developed Countries

Country	Name and date	Budget target	Expenditure target	Rule to deal with windfall revenues	Golden rule
Australia	Charter of Budget Honesty (1998)	yes	no	no	no
Austria	Stability and Growth Pact (1997)	yes	no	no	no
	Domestic Stability Pact (2000)				
Belgium	Stability and Growth Pact (1997)	yes	no	yes	no
	National budget rule (2000)				
Canada	Debt repayment plan (1998)	yes	no	yes	no
Czech republic	Stability and Growth Pact (2004)	yes	yes	no	no
	Law on budgetary rules (2004)				
Denmark	Medium term fiscal strategy (1998)	yes	yes	no	no
Finland	Stability and Growth Pact (1997)	yes	yes	no	no
	Spending limits (1991, revised in 1995 and 1998)				
France	Stability and Growth Pact (1997)	yes	yes	Since 2006	no
	Central Government Expenditure Ceiling (1998)				
Germany	Stability and Growth Pact (1997)	yes	yes	no	yes
	Domestic Stability Pact (2002)				

Table 5. (Continued)

Country	Name and date	Budget target	Expenditure target	Rule to deal with windfall revenues	Golden rule
Greece	Stability and Growth Pact (1997)	yes	no	no	no
Hungary	Stability and Growth Pact (2004)	yes	no	no	no
Ireland	Stability and Growth Pact (1997)	yes	no	no	no
Italy	Stability and Growth Pact (1997)	yes	yes	no	no
	Nominal ceiling on expenditure growth (2002)				
Japan	Cabinet decision on the Medium Term Fiscal Perspective (2002)	yes	yes	no	no
Luxembourg	Stability and Growth Pact (1997)	yes	no	no	no
	Coalition agreement on expenditure ceiling (1999, 2004)				
Mexico	Budget and Fiscal Responsibility Law (2006)	yes	no	yes	no
Netherlands	Stability and Growth Pact (1997)	yes	yes	yes	no
	Coalition agreement on multiyear expenditure targets (1994, revised in 2003)				
New Zealand	Fiscal Responsibility Act (1994)	yes	yes	no	no
Norway	Fiscal Stability Guidelines (2001)	yes	no	yes	no
Poland	Stability and Growth Pact (2004)	yes	no	no	no
	Act on Public Finance (1999)				
Portugal	Stability and Growth Pact (1997)	yes	no	no	no
Slovak Republic	Stability and Growth Pact (2004)	yes	no	no	no
Spain	Stability and Growth Pact (1997)	yes	no	no	no
	Fiscal Stability Law (2004)				
Sweden	Fiscal Budget Act (1996, revised in 1999)	yes	yes	no	no
Switzerland	Debt containment rule (2001, but in force since 2003)	yes	yes	yes	no
United Kingdom	Code for Fiscal Stability (1998)	yes	no	no	yes

Source: Guichard, Stephanie, Mike Kennedy, Eckhard Wurzel, and Christophe Andre, *What Promotes Fiscal Consolidation: OECD Country Experiences*, Organization for Economic Cooperation and Development [EC/WKP(2007) 13], 2007.

Notes: The Golden Rule generally restricts central governments from borrowing to fund current spending. Borrowing to fund investments generally is exempted from the budget rules. Essentially, the rule attempts to equate current spending with current revenues.

All of the members of the EU are expected to meet the requirement of the budget rules. Nevertheless, the rules are of especial importance to the group of countries known as the euro area, because the members have adopted the euro as their common currency. Typically, countries have a set of economic policy tools available to them to manage their economies. These macroeconomic policy tools generally include such monetary and fiscal policy measures as control over the nation's money supply, adjustments in tax rates, and control over government spending. In addition, nations have tools to affect the international exchange value of their currency. By adopting a common currency, however, the euro area countries ceded control of their currency to the European Central Bank. Consequently, the euro area countries agreed that the loss of the exchange rate tool meant that they would need to make greater efforts to control their government spending and their government budgets in order to restrain inflationary pressures and to promote similar economic performance among countries that have widely disparate economies. As a result, the euro area countries adopted budget rules as a component of their common policy approach.

As the Pact took effect in 1999, EU members began criticizing the rules-based approach of the Pact for being too stringent and they questioned whether the rules could be enforced. In 2003, the weaknesses of the Pact were exposed when the European Council voted not to apply the punitive procedures under the Excessive Deficit Procedure to France and Germany, which had experienced rising levels of government debt. Some EU members argued that the Pact focused too heavily on the rules-based percentage guidelines associated with the Pact without regard for the circumstances under which a government's level of debt or its deficit spending may rise, for instance as a result of a temporary increase in government spending to counter an economic downturn.[14]

The EU experience with the Pact demonstrates the policy tradeoffs that generally are involved in adopting such programs. In order to have a fiscal consolidation program be effective, the program needs to have stringent rules and penalties for violating the rules. At the same time, the current economic recession and financial crisis have demonstrated that policymakers need some flexibility and discretion in implementing budget rules in order to adjust the policy mix and generally to respond to differences in economic conditions. A fiscal deficit during periods of economic recession or very slow growth, for instance, likely would require a different policy prescription than one that arises during periods of strong economic growth when revues would be high and payments made through automatic stabilizers would be low.

In 2005, the EU members adopted a number of changes to the Stability and Growth Pact. These changes shifted the enforcement of the Pact from a rules-based regime to one based more on a set of principles with more latitude for discretion in enforcing the corrective requirements. In the area of prevention, the modified Pact provides for each EU member to develop its own medium-term objectives to bring its deficit spending and its debt level into compliance based on the unique economic conditions of each member. The modified Pact also relaxes the annual deficit targets as Members move their budget balances into compliance and the Pact factors in the effects of cyclical economic activity. The corrective measures also were modified in a number of important ways. The changes allow Members to avoid the corrective measures if their annual fiscal deficit is above 3% of GDP if they can demonstrate that the deficit is caused by "exceptional and temporary" circumstances. In addition, members can argue that their budget deficit should be exempt from the penalties of the Excessive Deficit Procedure if they can demonstrate that the deficit is the result of "other relevant factors." Among the other relevant factors that are listed as fiscal expenditures are: 1) officially sponsored research and development; 2) European policy goals; 3) support for international objectives; 4) capital expenditure programs; 5) pension reform; 6) fiscal consolidation programs; and 7) high contributions to EU-wide initiatives.

In 2008 as the financial crisis was unfolding, EU members were asked to provide a fiscal stimulus to their economies in ways that would comply with the Stability and Growth Pact. These efforts were part of a $256 billion Economic Recovery Plan[15] proposed by the European Commission to fund cross-border projects, including investments in clean energy and upgraded telecommunications infrastructure. In order to comply with the Stability and Growth Pact, the EU asked its members to make their fiscal stimulus plans timely, temporary, and targeted, so they would not have a permanent impact on tax rates or on spending commitments beyond that necessary to counter the effects of the two crises. As a result, each EU member was asked to contribute an amount equivalent to 1.5% of their GDP to boost consumer demand. In addition, members were tasked to invest in such capital projects as energy efficient equipment in order to create jobs and to save energy, invest in environmentally clean technologies to convert such sectors as construction and automobiles to low-carbon sectors, and to invest in infrastructure and communications. This plan also proposed official support measures to increase the rate of employment and to focus investments on such high technology sectors as telecommunications and environmentally safe technologies.

CONCLUSIONS

Financial markets and policymakers are growing increasingly concerned over the high level of deficit spending and the growing amount of government debt among a large number of advanced and developing economies. Unlike previous bouts with rising government deficits in developing countries, most of the current increase in government spending does not reflect out of control spending, but represents a calculated response to a severe economic downturn and a global financial crisis. In general, the two crises have affected the balance sheets of the central governments in three broad areas: 1) special fiscal measures to address the financial crisis; 2) discretionary fiscal stimulus measures to spur economic growth; and 3) a surge in non- discretionary spending and a loss of tax revenue. As a result of these factors, the financial crisis has undermined the effectiveness of budget rules as government budgets are affected by large or prolonged internal or external shocks. Most estimates indicate that such deficits will stabilize in 2010, but will not decline appreciably for some time after that. On balance, losses in tax revenue and an increase in spending associated with fiscal stimulus measures to counter the economic recession and the financial crisis are expected to have a relatively equal negative impact on the budget balances of the developed countries.

One approach most developed countries have used to address government budget deficits has been to adopt a budget rule. In general, most developed countries have at some time adopted budget rules to restrict the amount of deficit spending to a specified percent of GDP and to constrain the overall level of the central government's debt. One common feature of these rules, however, is that most of them were applied for a relatively short period of time. In contrast, members of the EU have adopted both short-term, country-specific budget rules, and long-term EU-wide budget rules. Academic studies seem to indicate that the more successful budget efforts combined rules to balance the budget with requirements to reduce expenditures. In developing such budget rules, policymakers are caught between designing rules that are enforceable, but inflexible, versus rules that are flexible and responsive to discretion, but less enforceable.

For national policymakers, the rising budget deficits and nascent economic recovery present a challenging policy mix. Various governments have budget rules in place to limit the budget deficits, but the necessity of continuing to provide stimulus to their economies to keep the recovery on track has put these budget rules on hold. For policymakers, the challenge is to unwind the fiscal stimulus measures that were adopted to prop up the financial sector and boost economic growth without short-circuiting the economic recovery. The strength of the economic recovery will determine the extent to which these dual policy goals are in conflict. A faster pace recovery will reduce the size of the government's budget deficits, which should work to ease the concerns of financial markets. Over the short-term, however, financial markets have displayed increased weariness over the magnitude and the pervasive nature of the deficits, especially in Europe. This could result in tighter credit and higher interest rates for all market participants. Investors are particularly concerned over the exploding government debts and public unrest in Spain, Greece, Portugal, and Ireland. Eventually, the wealthier economies of Europe, particularly France and Germany, may feel compelled to step in and provide financial assistance to the four struggling economies. This incident may well provide one more challenge to European economic integration.

End Notes

[1] *World Economic Outlook*, International Monetary Fund, October 2009.
[2] Members of the G-20 are: Argentina, Australia, Brazil, Canada, China, France, Germany, India, Indonesia, Italy, Japan, Mexico, Russia, Saudi Arabia, South Africa, South Korea, Turkey, the United Kingdom, the United States, and the European Union.
[3] *The State of Public Finances: Outlook and Medium-Term Policies After the 2008 Crisis*, International Monetary Fund, March 6, 2009.
[4] *BIS Quarterly Review*, The Bank for International Settlements, March 2010, p.1.
[5] Faiola, Anthony, Debt Concerns Weigh on Europe, *The Washington Post*, February 6, 2010, p. A1.
[6] The sixteen members of the Eurozone are: Austria, Belgium, Cyprus, Finland, France, Germany, Greece, Ireland, Italy, Luxembourg, Malta, Netherlands, Portugal, Slovakia, Slovenia, and Spain.
[7] *OECD Economic Outlook*, Organization for Economic Cooperation and Development, June 2009, p. 212.
[8] Haugh, David, Patrice Ollivaud, and David Turner, *The Macroeconomic Consequences of Banking Crises in OECD Countries*, Organization for Economic Cooperation and Development, March 6, 2009.
[9] Kumar, Manmohan S., Daniel Leigh, and Alexander Plekhanov, *Fiscal Adjustments: Determinants and Macroeconomic Consequences*, International Monetary Fund, IMF Working Paper WP/07/178, July 1007, p. 22.
[10] Guichard, Stephanie, Mike Kennedy, Echkard Wursel, and Christophe Andre, *What Promotes Fiscal Consolidation: OECD Country Experiences*, the Organization for Economic Cooperation and Development, Working Paper No. 553, May 28, 2007, p. 7.
[11] Ibid., p. 10.
[12] Guichard, Stephanie, Mike Kennedy, Echkard Wursel, and Christophe Andre, *What Promotes Fiscal Consolidation: OECD Country Experiences*, Organization for Economic Cooperation and Development, May 28, 2007.

[13] Public Finances in the EMU 2009, p. 30.
[14] Beetsma, Roel M.W.J., and Xavier Debrun, *Implementing the Stability and Growth Pact: Enforcement and Procedural Flexibility*, IMF Working Paper WP/05/59, International Monetary Fund, March 2005.
[15] *A European Economic Recovery Plan*: Communication From the Commission to the European Council, Commission of the European Communities, COM(2008) 800 final, November 26, 2008. The full report is available at: http://ec.europa.eu/commission_barroso/president/pdf/Comm_20081126.pdf

In: Global Economics Crisis and Cooperation
Editor: Jonathan P. Castle

ISBN: 978-1-61761-114-8
© 2010 Nova Science Publishers, Inc.

Chapter 4

THE GLOBAL ECONOMIC CRISIS: IMPACT ON SUB-SAHARAN AFRICA AND GLOBAL POLICY RESPONSES

Alexis Arieff, Martin A. Weiss and Vivian C. Jones

SUMMARY

Sub-Saharan Africa has been strongly affected by the global recession, despite initial optimism that the global financial system would have few spillover effects on the continent. The International Monetary Fund (IMF) estimated in 2009 that average economic growth in Africa would slow to 1%, from an annual average of over 6% to 1% over the previous five years, before rebounding to 4% in 2010. As a region, Africa is not thought to have undergone a recession in 2009. However, most African countries are thought to require high rates of economic growth in order to outpace population growth and make progress in alleviating poverty.

The mechanisms through which the crisis has affected Africa include a contraction in global trade and a related collapse in primary commodity exports, on which many countries are dependent. Foreign investment and migrant worker remittances are also expected to decrease significantly, and some analysts predict cuts in foreign aid in the medium term if the crisis persists. Africa's most powerful economies have proven particularly vulnerable to the downturn: South Africa has experienced a recession for the first time in nearly two decades, and Nigeria and Angola have reported revenue shortfalls due to the fall in global oil prices. Several countries seen as having solid macroeconomic governance, notably Botswana, have sought international financial assistance to cope with the impact of the crisis. At the same time, a number of low-income African countries are projected to experience relatively robust growth in 2009 and 2010, leading some economists to talk of Africa's underlying economic resilience.

The 111th Congress has monitored the impact of the global economic crisis worldwide. The Supplemental Appropriations Act, 2009 (P.L. 111-32), provided $255.6 million for assistance to vulnerable populations in developing countries affected by the crisis. While an initial House report indicated several countries, including five in Africa, should receive priority consideration, the subsequent conference report did not specify recipients. In August 2009, the Obama Administration notified Congress that four African countries—Ghana, Liberia, Tanzania, and Zambia—would benefit from the funds appropriated in the supplemental. More broadly, U.S. policy responses to the impact of the crisis overseas have focused on supporting the policies of multilateral organizations, including the IMF, the World Bank, and the African Development Bank (AfDB). These organizations have increased their lending commitments and created new facilities to help mitigate the impact of the global crisis on emerging market and developing countries worldwide.

This report analyzes Africa's vulnerability to the global crisis and potential implications for economic growth, poverty alleviation, fiscal balances, and political stability. The report describes channels through which the crisis is affecting Africa, and provides information on international efforts to address the impact, including U.S. policies and those of multilateral institutions in which the United States plays a major role. For further background and analysis, see CRS Report RL34742, *The Global Financial Crisis: Analysis and Policy Implications*, coordinated by Dick K. Nanto.

RECENT DEVELOPMENTS

Amid signs that the global economy is emerging from the worldwide recession of late 2008 and 2009, African economies appear to be recovering from the crisis with the potential to significantly increase growth rates in the coming year. IMF Director Dominique Strauss-Kahn stated in March 2010 that African economies were recovering faster than expected from the global downturn.[1] Africa's apparent economic resilience can be explained by a variety of complex factors. Many African governments, particularly those of resource-rich and middle-income countries, lessened the economic blow of the recession by implementing economic stimulus and/or financial sector rescue packages. Sizable assistance by international financial institutions, with U.S. support, also played an important stabilizing role. Still, the drop in economic growth experienced in most African countries in 2008 and 2009 is thought to have significantly negatively affected African countries' ability to make progress in reducing poverty. Moreover, Africa's continued reliance on commodity exports could blunt the expected recovery.[2]

Many investors reportedly view Africa's growth in 2010 as stemming from an expected rise in mining activity following its collapse in late 2008, combined with recent gains in communications infrastructure and political stability.[3] African economies also appear to be benefiting anew from investment and trade with large emerging economies such as China, India, Russia, and Brazil, which appear to have recovered more quickly from the global recession than traditional industrialized nations.[4]

In August 2009, the Obama Administration notified Congress that four African countries— Ghana, Liberia, Tanzania, and Zambia—would benefit from funds appropriated by Congress in 2009 for "assistance for vulnerable populations in developing countries severely affected by the global financial crisis," with various eligibility requirements. A total of $255.6 million in Economic Support Funds (ESF) were appropriated for this "crisis fund" in the Supplemental Appropriations Act, 2009 (P.L. 11 1-32).[5] As of early 2010, $32.5

million had been obligated for programs in Ghana, $25.2 million for Liberia, $37.9 million for Tanzania, and $25 million for Zambia.[6]

Amid signs that the crisis has peaked, policymakers' attention has again shifted toward emphasizing longer-term policies to ensure that growth increases and contributes to broad socioeconomic development. In November 2009, U.N. Secretary-General Ban Ki-moon stated that Africa's future economic prosperity would require industrialization, improved access to global markets, and a "green agricultural revolution."[7] International attention has also focused on stemming Africa's illicit economies, including bribery, theft, money laundering, and trafficking in people, narcotics, and weaponry. A March 2010 study by Global Financial Integrity showed illicit capital outflows from Africa totaled $854 billion between 1970 and 2008, creating a "staggering" negative economic impact.[8]

OVERVIEW

What began as a bursting of the U.S. housing market bubble has ballooned into a global financial and economic crisis, leading to the most severe global recession since the Great Depression of the 1930s. Starting in September 2008, credit flows froze, lender confidence dropped, and economies around the world dipped toward recession. Having begun in industrialized countries, this financial crisis quickly spread to emerging market and developing economies. Investors pulled capital from countries, even those with small levels of perceived risk, and caused values of stocks and domestic currencies to plunge. Slumping exports and commodity prices have added to developing countries' woes. The International Monetary Fund (IMF) estimated that the global economy would contract by 1.1% in 2009, but that it could rebound to 3.1% growth in 2010.[9]

Developing economies may not have played a major role in the onset of the crisis, but they may have less resilient economic systems that can be highly affected by actions in global markets. Most industrialized countries have been able to finance their own rescue packages by borrowing domestically and in international capital markets, but many emerging market and developing economies have insufficient sources of capital and have turned to help from regional development banks, the IMF, the World Bank, and traditional donors such as the Group of Eight (G-8).

Many analysts were initially optimistic that the impact of the global financial crisis on Sub-Saharan Africa (henceforth, "Africa")[10] would be negligible. African economies are among the least exposed to the global financial system of any world region, and African banks hold few of the "toxic assets" that helped spark the crisis.[11] However, as the financial crisis has deepened into a global economic recession, African economies are experiencing strong negative effects due to a contraction in global trade, including reduced demand for African commodity exports, tighter financing conditions overseas, and a drop in foreign direct investment and other capital inflows. Additional revenue streams such as tourism and remittances from African workers abroad are also expected to fall, and foreign aid is predicted to decrease, particularly if the crisis persists.

In its most recent regional economic analysis on Africa, the IMF estimated that average economic growth in Africa would slow from an average of 6.5% per year between 2002 and 2007—a historic high—to 1% in 2009, before recovering to 4% in 2010.[12] The crisis is expected to dampen prospects for reducing African poverty, as at least 7% annual growth is generally considered necessary for outpacing population growth and making significant progress in alleviating the toll of hunger, unemployment, and disease.[13] Anticipated negative growth in some countries, including in Africa's largest economy by far, South Africa, may have further ripple effects for smaller neighboring economies who depend on regional powerhouses for trade, remittances, and employment. Unemployment—already high in all African countries—is expected to rise, with potential implications for political stability.

The Obama Administration has emphasized African economic growth as a foreign policy goal. Secretary of State Hillary Clinton stated in October 2009 that the Administration seeks to "help create the right conditions" for growth through improvements in trade, development and agriculture aid, energy security, public private partnerships, and good governance.[14]

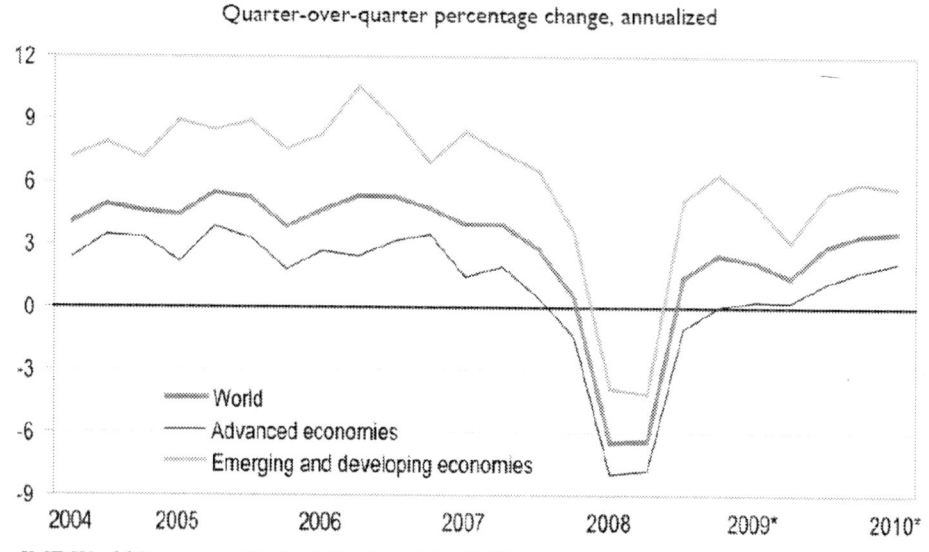

Source: IMF World Economic Outlook Update, July 2009.
Note: Quarter-over-quarter changes in GDP differ from yearly figures.
* In all graphs, 2009 and 2010 figures reflect estimates and projections, respectively.

Figure 1. Global Gross Domestic Product (GDP) Growth

LIMITED AND FAULTY DATA

Infrequent and flawed economic data collection in nearly all African countries has contributed to significant variation in estimates of the economic impact of the crisis. For example, the IMF estimate of 1.5% average growth in 2009 is significantly lower than the Organization for Economic Cooperation and Development (OECD) estimate of 2.8% growth, but higher than the 1% growth predicted by the World Bank and the 1.7% contraction predicted by the Economist Intelligence Unit.[15] Challenges include a lack of data collection capacity on the part of national governments and the difficulties of collecting reliable information in war-torn and infrastructure-poor societies. Given these problems, some analysts rely on unusual indicators such as cell-phone and building material sales, rather than GDP, to probe the health of African economies.

Congressional Interest

The impact of the global economic crisis threatens to undermine long-term U.S. foreign policy goals in Africa, including regional stability, increased trade, the alleviation of poverty and hunger, and socioeconomic development. In August 2009, Congressman Gregory Meeks led a congressional delegation to Africa focusing on the impact of the economic crisis. One participant, Congresswoman Marcia L. Fudge, stated that the delegation

> spent significant time examining the effect of the global economic crisis on local economies. We were especially interested in how the multilateral development banks and the United States supports, particularly the African Development Bank, are helping countries to obtain grants, loans and technical assistance. We also explored the role and impact of the IMF on the region during this period of economic crisis.[16]

While Congress has acted to address the impact of the economic crisis on poor countries, legislators have not specifically targeted this assistance at African countries. The Supplemental Appropriations Act, 2009 (P.L. 111-32), included $255.6 million in Economic Support Funds (ESF) for "assistance for vulnerable populations in developing countries severely affected by the global financial crisis."[17]

BACKGROUND: AFRICAN ECONOMIES

Trends Prior to the Crisis

The Africa region experienced strong economic growth in recent years, averaging 6.5% per year between 2002 and 2007. Growth was facilitated by macroeconomic reforms and driven by high external demand for primary commodities, notably oil and minerals. Trade was bolstered by steady growth in industrialized countries and explosive growth in emerging economic powerhouses such as China and India. Demand for African commodities drove an investment surge in many countries, with foreign direct investment (FDI) stocks nearly doubling between 2003 and 2007.[18] Net private capital inflows—including FDI, remittances, portfolio flows, and other sources—are thought to have quadrupled between 2000 and 2008.[19] These changes followed decades of post-independence economic stagnation.

While Africa's recent growth was driven by the global commodity boom, many other factors contributed as well. Both net oil exporters and oil importers experienced growth of over 5% between 2004 and 2008 (**Figure 2**), and investment extended beyond traditional foreign interests in extractive industries. The IMF reported in 2008 that Africa's "fast growers are a diverse group, including resource-rich and landlocked countries and resource-poor countries that have not had large gains in their terms of trade."[20] In many countries, productivity increased and domestic investment improved, in part due to remittances from African workers overseas. Domestic demand also grew, notably in telecommunications as mobile phone and internet use spread rapidly. Recent growth has been aided by policy reforms, as many African governments have improved economic governance through better banking regulations, oversight mechanisms, and fiscal restraint, which brought down inflation, encouraged private investment, and instilled greater macroeconomic stability. Some believe international debt relief programs contributed to these trends. The rate of armed conflict has also declined since the start of the decade, making some countries and the region more attractive to foreign investment.

Development Challenges

Despite these positive trends, economic growth has failed to raise incomes sufficiently to trigger significant progress in meeting the Millennium Development Goals (MDGs) and other antipoverty benchmarks.[21] Progress on the MDGs has been slower in Africa than in any other region: according to the World Bank, the rate in Africa of those living on less than $1.25 per day has hovered around 50% since 1981, while the number of poor people, in absolute terms, has nearly doubled, from 200 million in 1981 to 380 million in 2005.[22] Economic development is constrained in many countries by numerous structural factors, including a lack of technological investment in agriculture; limited communications and transportation infrastructure; high population growth; high ratios of foreign debt to national income; and the burden of disease. Many countries rely on external aid to balance their budgets and provide basic services. Unrest and instability continue in many areas, and few states constitute transparent and representative democratic regimes.[23]

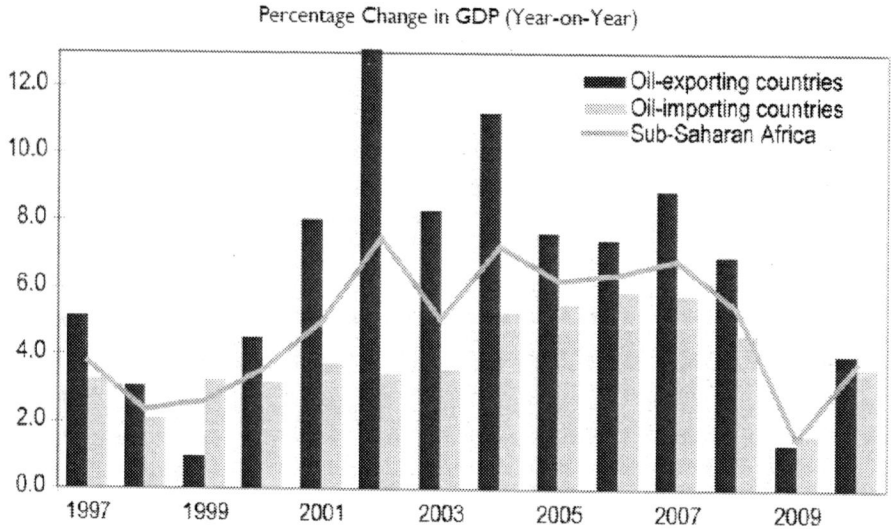

Source: IMF Sub-Saharan Africa Regional Economic Outlook Database, April 2009.
Note: Oil exporting countries are Angola, Cameroon, Chad, Republic of Congo, Equatorial Guinea, Gabon, and Nigeria. All other African countries are net oil importers.

Figure 2. Economic Growth in Africa

African exports are the least diversified of all developing regions.[24] Many African economies remain reliant on primary commodity exports, which has rendered them vulnerable to external shocks. Natural resource extraction, while effective at creating growth and drawing foreign investment, is also associated with high levels of corruption, labor exploitation, environmental degradation, and internal displacement. During recent periods of high resource revenues, oil- and mineral-producing countries failed to use such revenues to further increase productivity, significantly diversify their economies, or improve social services. Simultaneously, windfall profits may have contributed to already endemic corruption in some countries.

Many analysts argue that despite recent economic reforms, growth and development are limited in many African countries by policy choices that restrict competitiveness. According to the World Bank, Africa is the world's second most trade-restrictive region (after South Asia), and African countries have among the world's fewest and weakest services trade liberalization commitments. The region, on average, also displays "the worst rankings in business environment, governance, logistics, and other trade facilitation indicators."[25] Labor productivity is the lowest, on average, of any world region.[26] Due to low levels of regional integration, Africa has consistently had considerably lower rates of intraregional trade than other world regions.[27] Service provision, such as electricity, is severely limited in many countries, impacting individual household consumption as well as the economic feasibility of private firms.

In addition, African economies continue to be affected by the lingering impact of the 2008 food crisis. In 2008, already rising global food prices spiked to record heights, partly due to high oil prices but also to other complex factors.[28] Those most affected by the crisis were impoverished populations in developing countries, many of whom already suffer from chronic hunger.[29] The crisis strained household budgets and compromised individual resilience to further economic hardship. While African oil exporters benefited from higher oil prices, most oil importers ran fiscal deficits as governments subsidized food imports, fertilizer, and other agricultural inputs. The crisis fed high inflation and sparked food riots and political unrest in several countries. The fiscal costs of African policy responses to the crisis doubled between 2007 and 2008, to an average of 1% of GDP, according to the IMF.[30]

Many additionally argue that the broader geopolitical environment poses challenges to Africa's development. Some contend that neocolonial relationships continue to dominate Africa's trade ties, while African countries have a limited voice in international trade regulatory bodies. While oil and mineral exporters face low tariffs overseas, exporters of other commodities, such as cotton or sugar, face much higher export barriers.[31]

How the Crisis Is Affecting Africa

The global recession has affected most African countries through a variety of mechanisms, or channels, including a decline in global trade, a drop in investment, falling remittances from overseas workers, and possible cuts in foreign aid. These channels are largely connected to Africa's "real" economy, rather than its financial sector.[32]

Annual Percentage Change

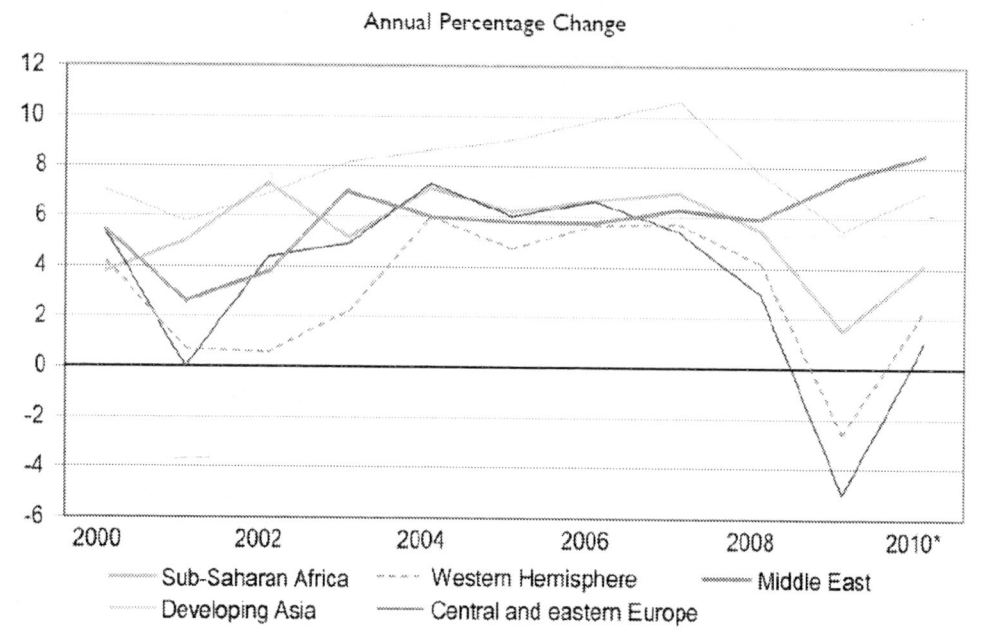

- Sub-Saharan Africa
- Western Hemisphere
- Middle East
- Developing Asia
- Central and eastern Europe

Source: IMF World Economic Outlook, April 2009.

Figure 3. GDP Growth by Region

International Trade

World trade was projected to shrink by 11% in 2009, its first decline since 1982 and reportedly the biggest drop since the mid-1940s.[33] Advanced economies are expected to be the hardest hit, with exports projected to drop by over 13%, but poorer nations are nonetheless expected to see exports fall by over 6%.[34] Since the United States, the European Union, and China cumulatively count for nearly 70% of African trade, African exporters are suffering from the decrease in global demand. For example, total exports to the United States from all 41 countries eligible for trade benefits under the African Growth and Opportunity Act (AGOA) declined by 63% in the first half of 2009, compared to the same period of 2008.[35]

While Africa accounts for less than 2% of global trade, many African economies depend on exports of primary commodities, whose prices on the world market have declined drastically due to the global crisis.[36] The price slump in oil and many mineral commodities, combined with decreased external demand, dealt a severe blow to the region: oil and other mineral fuels represented 68% of African exports to the world by value in 2008; ores, slag and ash about 14%; and precious stones about 4%.[37] African countries are thus exporting less on average, and at lower prices, than a year ago. Investor perceptions of risk have exacerbated the impact of falling commodity prices for resource-rich African countries that are also fragile or post-conflict states. Several other countries depend in part on international tourist arrivals (understood as trade in services), which declined worldwide by about 8% in the first four months of 2009 compared to 2008.[38] Overall, African countries' export exposure to advanced economies—the degree to which economic shifts in developed countries may impact African economies through decreased demand for African exports—has increased in recent years. According to the IMF, on average, a 1-percentage-point decline in world growth (trade-weighted) is associated with a roughly 0.5- percentage-point drop in GDP growth in Africa.[39]

Global trade could drop even further if countries react to the economic crisis by enacting additional trade barriers.[40] African economies face the further risk that the global recession will spark new attempts by developed countries to restrict imports and protect local producers. Some analysts fear that policies aimed at encouraging trade with Africa—such as AGOA, the European Union's "Everything But Arms" program, or the Doha Development Round of the World Trade Organization—could be threatened by political pressures to become more isolationist.[41] The tightening of international credit markets is also expected to render it more difficult for African countries to access trade finance.[42] In prior financial crises, a drop in the availability of trade finance negatively impacted the operations of private firms in developing countries. However, it is unclear whether the current crisis will have a similar impact.[43]

In its October 2009 *Regional Economic Outlook*, the IMF praised African governments for refraining from responding to the crisis with trade restrictions and other policies that could deter future growth.[44] Indeed, the trade picture for Africa is not without its bright spots, particularly for countries that have made recent significant investments in infrastructure and resource development.[45] For example, Burkina Faso's export performance is expected to expand rapidly in 2009-20 10 due to a recovery in the country's cotton sector, combined with a surge in gold exports as four new mines begin full production. Djibouti, a major cargo transportation hub, is also expected to see rapid growth in export volumes as a new shipping terminal in Doraleh (about 4 miles south of Djibouti's existing port) comes online. In Liberia, revitalization of mineral, timber, rubber, and palm oil production is forecasted to drive export growth, with increased exports of coffee and cocoa also contributing. Export growth in Malawi is expected to be boosted by the expansion of a uranium mine in Kayelekera.

Trade with the United States

The value of total U.S. trade with Africa increased by about 29% between 2007 and 2008. After at least three years of continuous growth, however, the value of Africa's exports to the United States decreased in value by about 57% in the first six months of 2009 in comparison to the same period in 2008. U.S. exports to Africa decreased in value by about 9%. The decline in the value of U.S. imports from Africa largely reflects the decline in oil prices from late 2008 through early 2009, as oil and mineral fuels account for about 80% of all U.S. imports from Africa, and 92% of all U.S. imports under AGOA. Petroleum imports did not decrease in volume as dramatically as they did in value. However, decreases in U.S. and global consumption are likely to continue to have a negative effect on most exports from the region.

Trade with China

Because recent growth in Africa was driven in part by commodity exports to China, Africa is particularly vulnerable to fluctuations in China's economic growth. In 2007, China was the destination for some 13% of Africa's exports and the source of roughly 10% of Africa's imports.[46] These figures represent a long trend of increased Chinese trade and commercial ties with Africa, particularly with countries rich in natural resources. China's trade with Africa greatly increased in recent years, reportedly growing to $74 billion in the first eight months of 2008, a 62% increase over the previous year.[47] Even with the impact of the crisis in the second half of 2008, total SinoAfrican trade for the year was reportedly $106.8 billion, a significant increase from 2007.[48] This trade has spurred Chinese investment in large infrastructure projects in Africa, which in some cases are thought to have helped alleviate constraints on economic competitiveness.

Analysts suggest that China is reevaluating some resource extraction agreements, particularly in countries perceived as politically unstable, in light of the global slump.[49] At the same time, recent statistics on China's growth in the first months of 2009 showed robust, if somewhat reduced, economic growth. Furthermore, China's domestic economic stimulus package reportedly relies heavily on infrastructure construction, which has kept demand steady for some primary inputs, such as oil, copper, tin, and lumber.[50] Indeed, while Chinese private-sector engagement with Africa has apparently decreased as a result of the crisis, some Chinese firms and the Chinese government have continued to negotiate economic and resource-acquisition agreements with African countries. Chinese diplomatic outreach to African governments has also continued.[51]

Capital Flows

Capital flows—which include foreign direct investment (FDI), portfolio investment flows, worker remittances, private charity, and foreign aid—are thought to have helped fuel Africa's recent economic growth.[52] Between 2000 and 2007, private capital inflows were the most important source of external finance for the region, growing from an estimated $8.9 billion in 2000 to $54.8 billion in 2007—or 6.5 times global foreign aid of $8.5 billion. FDI peaked in 2008 at $32.6 billion, and accounted for between 2.5% and 5% of annual GDP between 2001 and 2007.[53] At the same time, flows of FDI and portfolio investment are clustered among Africa's oil-exporting economies and South Africa (**Figure 5**), and may have little impact in many African countries.

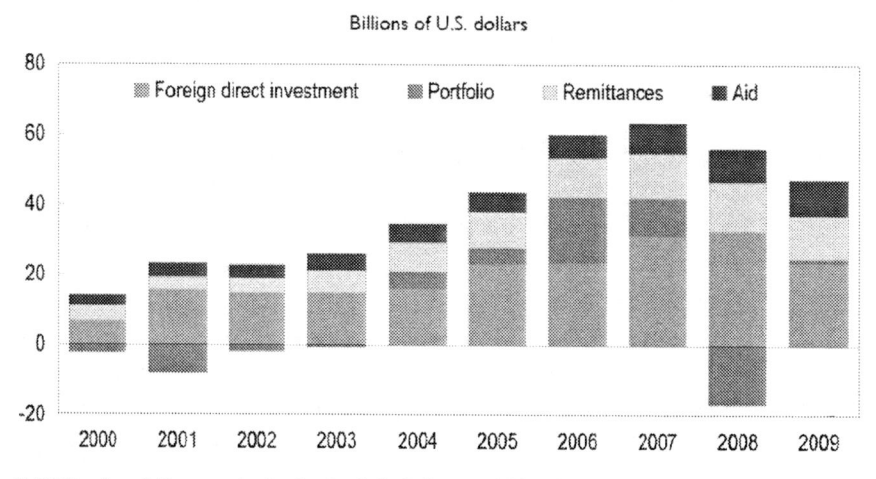

Source: IMF Regional Economic Outlook: Sub-Saharan Africa, April 2009.

Figure 4. Capital Inflows to Africa

The contraction of capital flows to Africa has been sharp. The IMF estimated that FDI in Africa would drop by roughly 26.7% in 2009, compared to 2008 (**Figure 4**). Between the second quarter of 2008 and year's end, Africa saw the sharpest contraction in cross-border lending of all emerging regions—over 50%—compared with less than 20% for emerging market countries in other regions.[54] Portfolio investment flows were initially the most impacted by the crisis, reversing from inflows of $18.7 billion in 2006 to outflows of $16.7 billion in 2008 (**Figure 4**). These outflows have hit Africa's "frontier economies" the hardest as foreign investors fled the region's stock markets for safer, more liquid investments at home.[55] However, limited available research suggests that while portfolio investment declines will have significant impacts on the financial sectors of affected countries, the impact on regional growth is expected to be minimal.[56] FDI remains the largest share of inward capital flows for the region as a whole, and is expected to be a key driver of future growth.

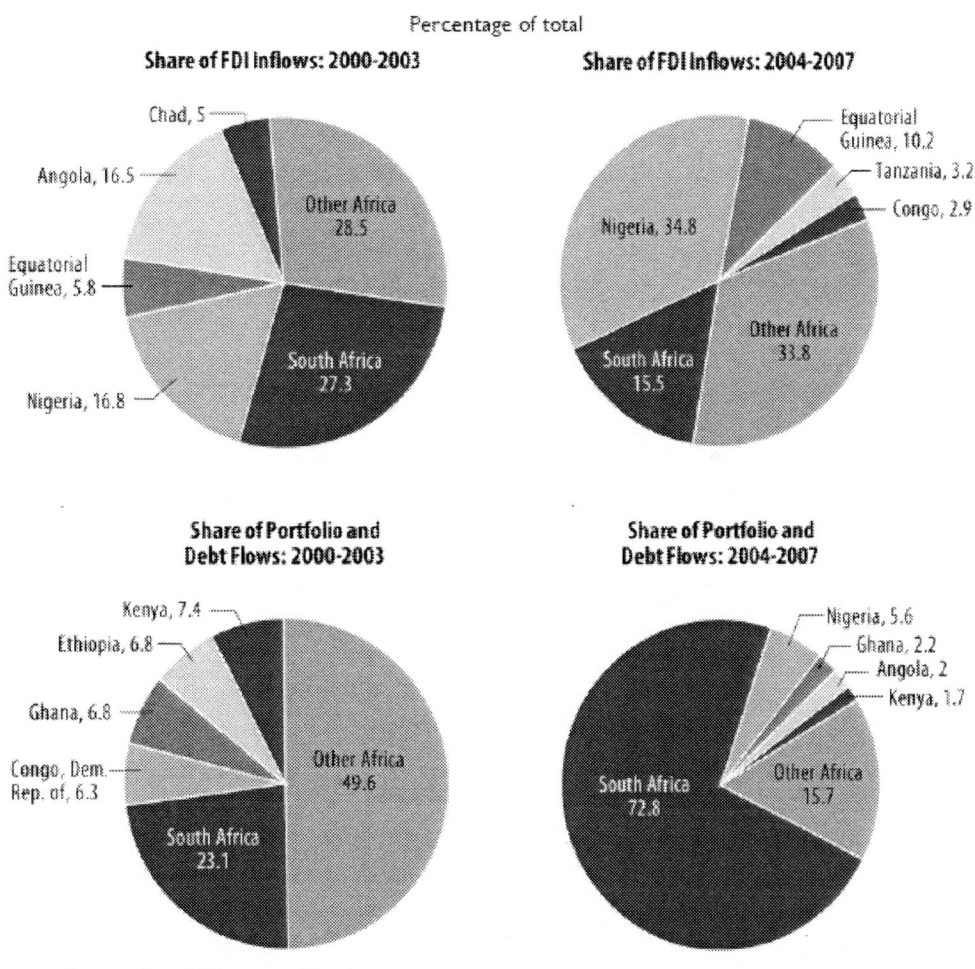

Source: International Monetary Fund.

Figure 5. Top Recipients of Private Capital Flows in Africa

Migrant Remittances

Of all forms of international capital flows, remittances—or monies sent home by foreign workers overseas—are thought to be the most stable, reacting least to international politics or events.[57] While Africa receives smaller amounts of remittances than other regions, their impact is thought to be relatively large compared to the size of African economies and due to the fact that Africa's extractive industries often provide little economic trickle-down into the local economy. Recorded remittances to Africa totaled $18.59 billion in 2007, nearly rivaling foreign aid flows; the actual amount is likely higher, since the region receives a large share through informal transfers and unofficial mechanisms and networks.[58] Within the region, remittances are thought to account for 3.7% of GDP on average, although there is significant variation among countries. Remittances in Lesotho, for example, were reported to be 29% of GDP in 2007, according to the World Bank. By total recorded flows, Nigeria and Kenya receive the highest value of remittances.

Global remittance levels were projected to fall 5-8% in 2009, from an estimated $305 billion in 2008, according to the World Bank. In Africa, remittance levels were projected to fall by 4.4% in 2009; while significant, this is a slightly smaller drop in percentage terms than the worldwide average for low- and middle-income countries.[59] Remittance levels could fall further if continuing economic troubles cause destination countries to tighten immigration restrictions. The long-term implications are difficult to assess, as they depend on complex factors such as the share of unskilled jobs in destination countries and the relative value of local currencies compared to currencies in which remittances are earned.[60]

Foreign Aid

While only a small handful of donors to date—including Italy, France, and Iceland—have reduced bilateral foreign assistance to Africa due to the crisis, the global flow of foreign aid could suffer in the medium term if the global downturn continues.[61] A more significant decline in aid flows, if it occurs, is expected to lag behind other economic indicators due to the long-term planning process in donor countries. Some observers predicted that while aid levels in 2009 and 2010 would be largely unaffected by the crisis, they could drop in 2011 and 2012 as developed countries experience continued fiscal strains and political pressures to balance budgets. Nonetheless, African governments have requested donors to increase aid flows in order to help offset the impact of the crisis on their domestic economies.[62] Analysts continue to debate whether foreign aid has helped or hindered Africa's socioeconomic development in the long run.[63]

Many African economies are vulnerable to a downturn in foreign aid flows, particularly those that are not natural resource exporters; many rely on donors for budget support.[64] Compared to other regions, Africa receives the highest total amount of overseas development assistance (including international debt relief), according to the Organization for Economic Cooperation and Development (OECD).[65] In 2006-2007, Africa received the equivalent of nearly $27.19 billion in bilateral overseas development assistance as defined by the OECD, far greater than the next largest recipient, the Middle East and North Africa, which received $14.03 billion.[66]

Prior Aid Commitments

During the 2005 Group of Eight (G-8) Summit in Gleneagles, Scotland, members pledged to roughly double annual aid to Africa by 2010.[67] Some countries—such as the United States— committed to a dollar-figure increase, while European countries committed to raising the percentage of national income spent on aid to Africa. According to the organization ONE, which monitors aid commitments and disbursements to Africa, the G-8 Gleneagles commitments amount to raising annual overseas development aid to Africa by $21.48 billion (in 2008 dollars) on top of what was already being spent in 2005, by 2010. The commitment by the United States was to raise annual aid to Africa to a total of $8.8 billion.[68]

Most observers believe G-8 aid to Africa will not reach the levels promised at Gleneagles.[69] This may be attributed mainly to shortfalls by France, Italy, and Germany; other G-8 members, including the United States, are believed to be on track to meet their commitments.[70] In addition, reductions in projected national income in donor countries have negatively affected the real value of European commitments based on a percentage of GDP.

IMPLICATIONS OF THE CRISIS IN AFRICA

Economic growth in Africa began to decrease in the second half of 2008, with average growth falling from nearly 7% in 2007 to just under 5.5% in 2008, according to the IMF. African countries with relatively developed financial markets—such as South Africa and Nigeria—were the first to feel the effects of the crisis. The IMF projected average economic growth in Africa would plunge from 6.5% per year between 2002 and 2007 to 1% in 2009. At the same time, average growth rates for the region largely reflect Africa's largest economies, including oil exporters and middle-income countries (of which South Africa is the largest), where the impact of the crisis has been strongest. Median annual economic growth was expected to decelerate from 4.75% on average between 2002 and 2007 to 2.5% in 2009.[71] While some observers argue that merely sustaining positive average growth (as opposed to a recession) means the impact of the crisis on Africa will be relatively minor compared to other regions, others contend that Africa's developing economies require high levels of growth to outpace demographic trends and translate into significant poverty alleviation. For example, per-capita average GDP in Africa was projected to decline by nearly 1% in 2009.[72]

The IMF reported in mid-October that most African economies "nonetheless seem to be responding to this storm better than those of the past," having "generally avoided the major macroeconomic stabilities that followed previous global slowdowns."[73] According to the IMF, Africa is projected to experience an economic recovery in 2010, rebounding to 4% growth on average. Such an outcome would represent a rapid bounce-back compared to sluggish recoveries following previous global recessions.[74] This scenario has led some observers to speak of Africa's underlying economic "resilience," pointing toward robust domestic demand and the lasting effects of macroeconomic reforms.[75] In late September 2009, World Bank President Robert Zoellick stated, "Over time, Africa can also become a pole of growth... Coming out of the crisis, there could be a new opportunity."[76]

Sub-Regional Variations

Regional averages of economic growth are heavily weighted toward Africa's largest economies, and do not necessarily reflect the expected impact of the crisis on any given country. Because South Africa, Nigeria, and Angola represented over 60% of Africa's combined gross domestic product (GDP) in 2008, regional aggregated statistics disproportionately reflect the impact of the crisis on these countries.[77] Nigeria and Angola have been strongly affected because much of their economies depend on oil exports, while South Africa, by far Africa's largest economy, is already experiencing a recession, its first in 17 years.

Middle-income countries (a relatively small category in Africa; see Note, **Figure 6**) and oil exporters are experiencing the strongest negative impact from the global crisis.[78] The impact on middle-income countries is reflected by South Africa, where GDP was projected to decline by 2.25% in 2009, due largely to South Africa's close integration into global financial markets and tight trade links with the rest of the world.[79] South Africa's neighbors are expected to experience negative spill-over effects due to trade, investment, and financial linkages to the regional economic giant. Another example of a middle-income country experiencing economic distress due to the crisis is Botswana, whose economy is highly dependent on diamond exports.[80]

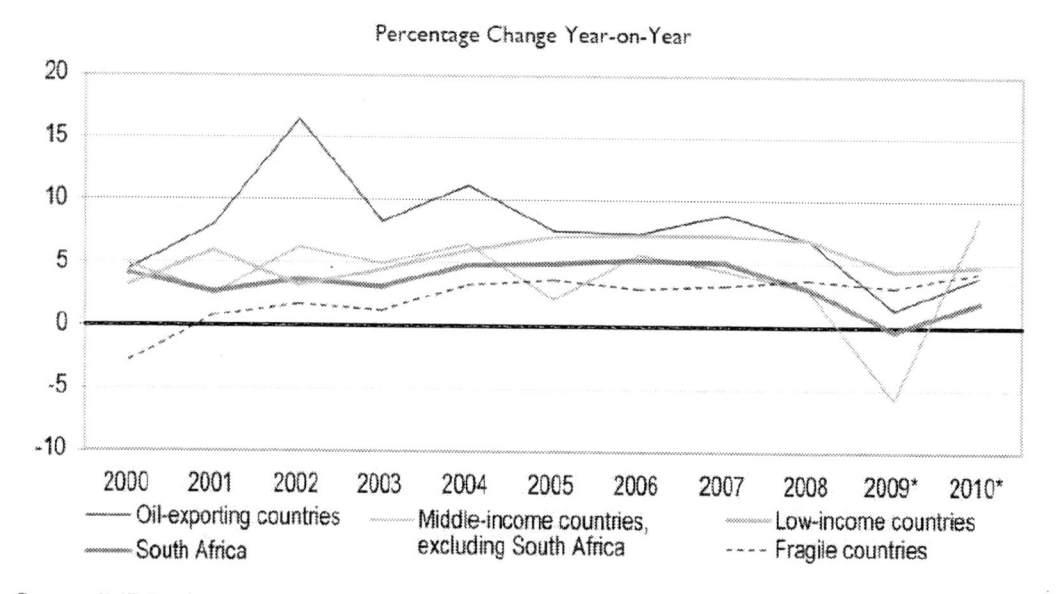

Source: IMF Regional Economic Outlook Database, April 2009.
Notes: Country classifications follow IMF categories. **Oil Exporting Countries**: Angola, Cameroon, Chad, Republic of Congo, Equatorial Guinea, Gabon, and Nigeria. **Middle-Income Countries**: Botswana, Cape Verde, Lesotho, Mauritius, Namibia, Seychelles, South Africa, Swaziland. Low-Income Countries: Benin, Burkina Faso, Ethiopia, Ghana, Kenya, Madagascar, Malawi, Mali, Mozambique, Niger, Rwanda, Senegal, Tanzania, Uganda, Zambia. **Fragile Countries**: Burundi, Central African Republic, Comoros, Democratic Republic of Congo, Côte d'Ivoire, Eritrea, the Gambia, Guinea, Guinea-Bissau, Liberia, São Tomé and Príncipe, Sierra Leone, and Togo. [Growth figures for Zimbabwe and Somalia are not included in most IMF metrics.]

Figure 6. GDP Growth

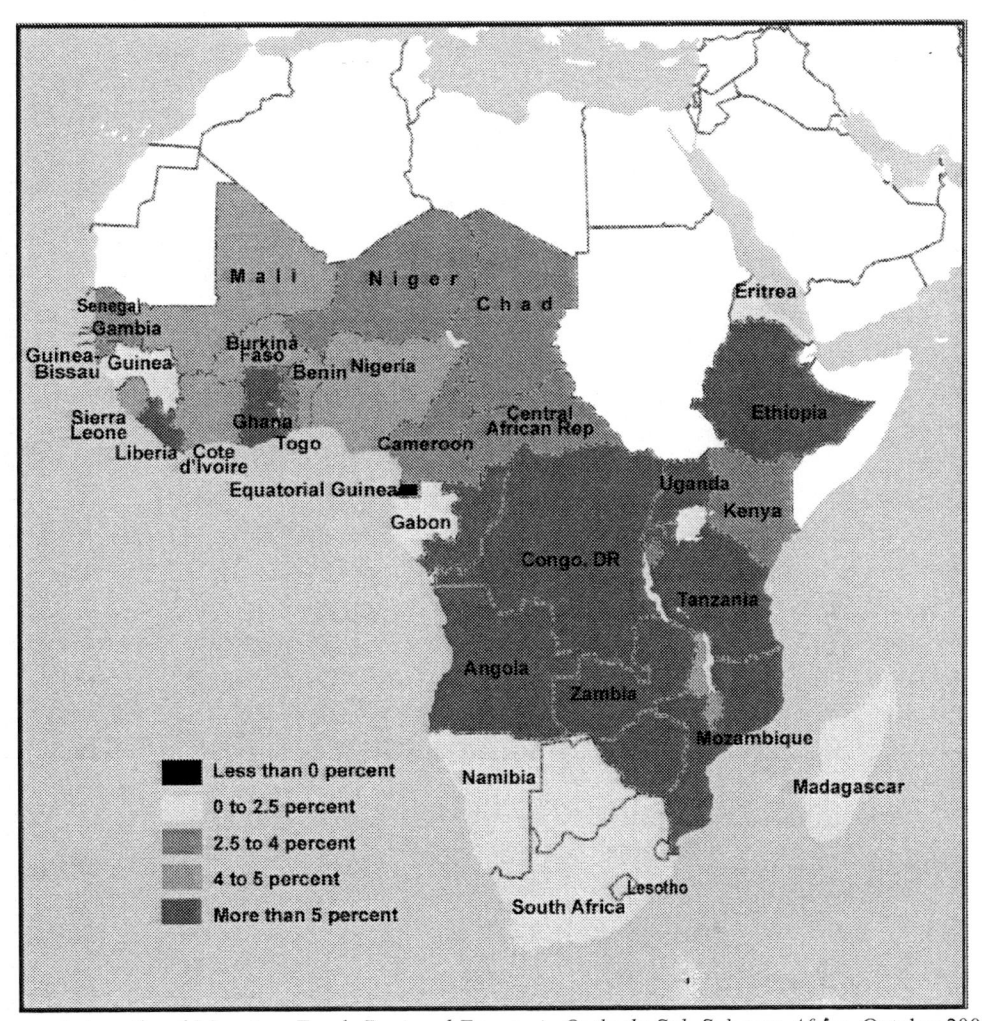

Source: International Monetary Fund, *Regional Economic Outlook: Sub-Saharan Africa*, October 2009

Figure 7. Projected Average Yearly Economic Growth, 2008-2011

On the other hand, many low-income countries that do not rely on oil or mineral exports—such as Ethiopia, Ghana, Rwanda, and Uganda—were projected to experience relatively strong economic growth in 2009, albeit at lower levels than before the crisis. Average GDP in low-income countries is expected to contract by 2.5 percentage points between 2008 and 2009, to relatively strong 4.5% growth.[81] Many of Africa's low-income countries are expected to benefit from positive terms-of-trade movements, as prices of food and fuel imports have fallen. Fragile and post-conflict states, particularly those that rely on primary commodity exports, will be negatively affected by the crisis, but many are also expected to rebound in 2010 if peace and stability gains are consolidated. Idiosyncratic factors unrelated to the global crisis are further expected to exert strong influence in many African countries, including rainfall, declining oil production in some Gulf of Guinea countries, labor strikes, and political instability.

Fiscal and Trade Balances

The economic crisis is already having a deep impact on fiscal and trade balances throughout the region (**Figure 8** and **Figure 9**). In recent years, debt forgiveness and improved fiscal discipline contributed to greater economic stability: between 2004 and 2008, the region's governments maintained a budget surplus of 1.75% on average. During those four years, the surplus in African oil exporters averaged 6.5% of GDP. Fiscal positions have already turned negative due to the crisis: the IMF has projected deficits of 4.75% of GDP in 2009 and 2.72% of GDP in 2010.[82] Fiscal deficits in oil exporters were expected to average over 6% in 2009.

Current account positions—the difference between a nation's total exports of goods, services, and transfers, and its total imports of them—were also expected to decline, from a surplus of 1.22% of GDP in 2008 to a deficit of 6.23% of GDP in 2009.[83] Weakened commodity prices are exacerbating these effects in oil-producing states.

Fiscal deficits reflect both increased government spending aimed at expanding social safety nets and declining government revenues due to decreases in the collection of taxes and royalties on natural resource extraction, customs and tariffs on trade, and taxes and fees on tourist activity and other consumption. While these effects will vary on a country-by-country basis, many countries are expected to have difficulty financing their deficits.[84] Several African governments had planned to raise long-term financing through the issuance of sovereign bonds, as Gabon successfully did in late 2007. Because of the impact of the crisis on global liquidity, these plans have reportedly either been unsuccessful (South Africa), canceled (Ghana), or delayed (Kenya, Nigeria, Tanzania, and Uganda).[85]

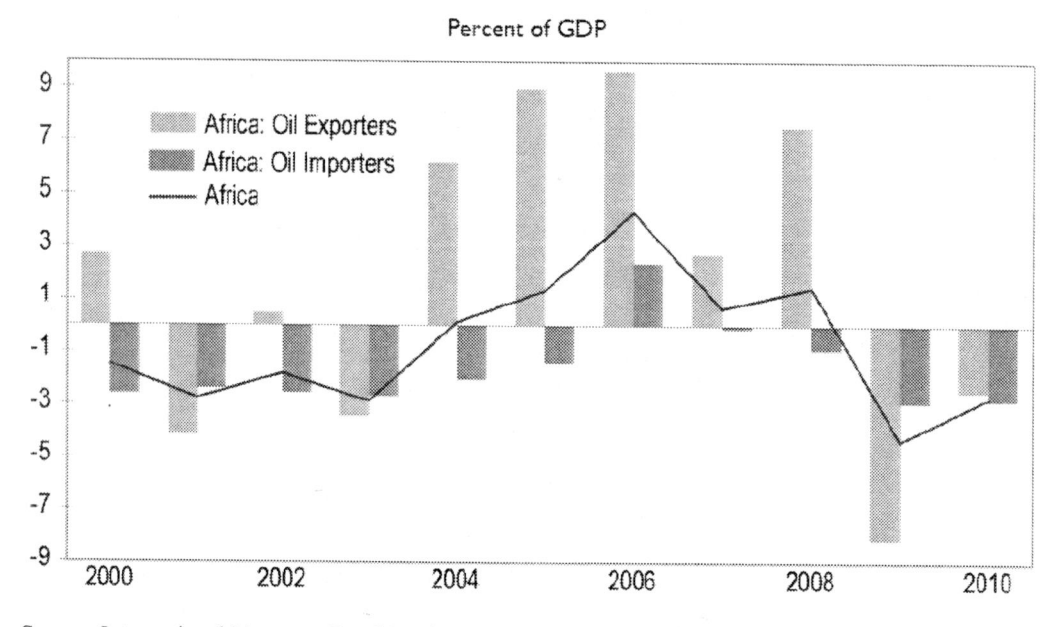

Source: International Monetary Fund Regional Economic Outlook database, April 2009.

Figure 8. Fiscal Balances Percent of GDP.

Percent of GDP

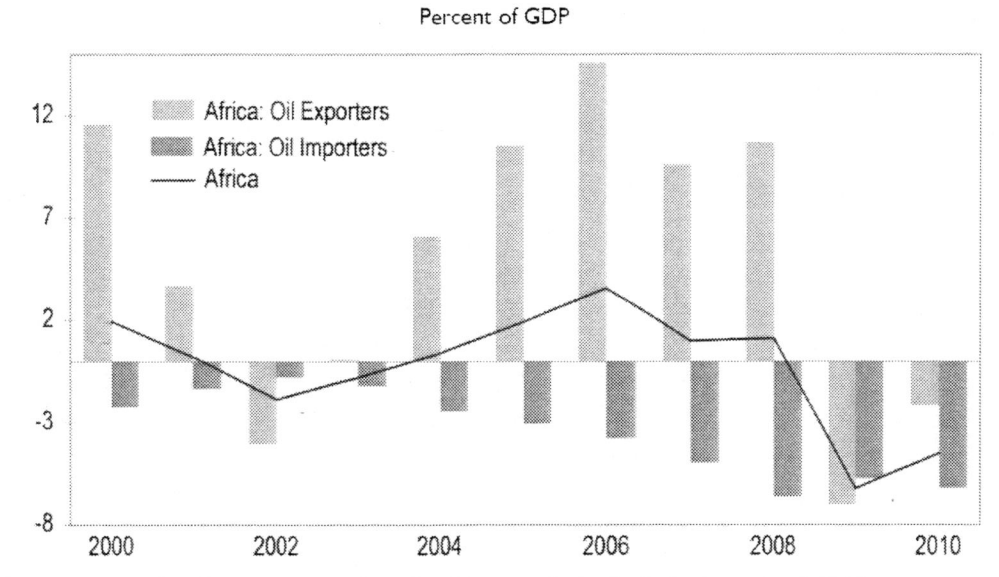

[Chart showing Africa: Oil Exporters, Africa: Oil Importers, and Africa from 2000 to 2010]

Source: International Monetary Fund Regional Economic Outlook database, April 2009.

Figure 9. Current Account Balances

While some oil exporters and middle-income countries have enacted fiscal stimulus packages, the capacity to do so is expected to be restrained in most African countries, even with international assistance. Combined with the difficulty of raising financing and abating investor risk aversion, budgetary pressures have reportedly caused some major infrastructure projects, including government-funded projects and public-private partnerships, to come under strain.

Poverty Reduction

The crisis is expected to set back or reverse efforts to alleviate poverty in Africa, the world's poorest region. Multilateral organizations project that the economic crisis could increase poverty worldwide by at least 45 million people. [86] In Africa, the IMF estimated that the crisis would add 7 million people to the ranks of those living below US$1.25 a day in 2009, and a further 3 million in 2010.[87] Indeed, while average GDP growth in Africa was expected to remain positive in 2009, per capita GDP was expected to contract in many African countries (**Figure 10**).

The impact on poverty in Africa may be further compounded by the effects of the 2008 food crisis, which made many African families more vulnerable to sudden economic shocks, especially as domestic prices for fuel and food remain relatively high in many countries.[88] Many African households teeter just above the international poverty line, and a small impact on average household income could translate into a large jump in poverty as measured by international standards. Additionally, already insufficient social safety nets are expected to be further strained by a reduction in budget allocations for public services as government revenues drop. Some predict that the human costs of the economic crisis will be dire: for example, one World Bank analysis estimates that the crisis will directly cause 30,000-50,000 excess infant deaths in Africa, with most of these additional deaths likely to be poorer children, and overwhelmingly female.[89]

Food Security

The economic crisis is expected to compound existing challenges for African food security. The United Nations estimated last year that the proportion of undernourished people in Africa's population rose to 29% in 2008, compared to 28% in 2004-2006, and that it would rise further in 2009; progress in eradicating hunger had already stalled or reversed in 2008 due to the global food crisis.[90] While inflation declined throughout Africa in the second half of 2008 with the slump in oil and food prices on the world market, global food prices have remained higher than they have been in a decade, nearly double historical levels.[91] Moreover, Africa's insulated markets and factors such as poor transportation infrastructure have limited the pass-through of lower global prices to domestic markets. According to the Food and Agriculture Organization (FAO), food crises persist in at least 20 African countries.[92] While high food prices may serve as an incentive for some crop producers, most analysts believe that they have a net negative effect on Africa's poor.

Political Stability

Many believe fallout from the global economic crisis could have implications for Africa's political stability. The Economist Intelligence Unit recently contended that "as people lose confidence in the ability of government to restore [economic] stability, protests look increasingly likely.... There is growing concern about a possible global pandemic of unrest."[93] This may be particularly pertinent for post-conflict and "fragile" states, where institutions are especially weak, investors wary, and donors under pressure to pare down financial commitments as their own economies suffer.

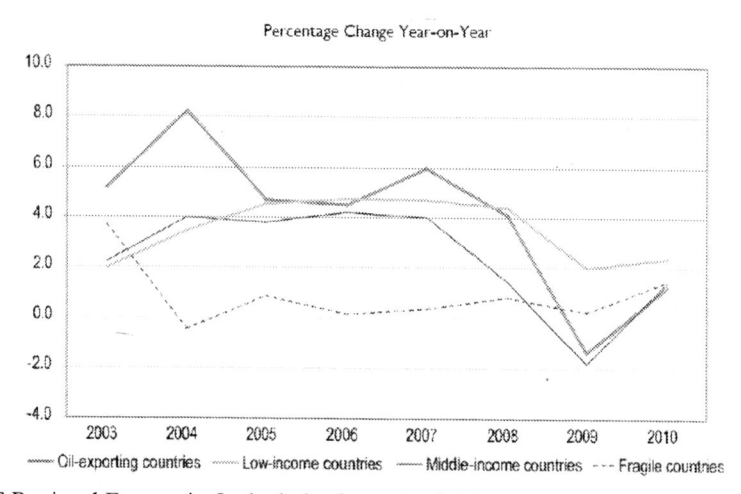

Source: IMF Regional Economic Outlook database, April 2009.

Figure 10. African GDP Per Capita

Analysts' assumptions are based in part on observations from mid-2008, when rising food prices sparked food riots across the continent and were thought to have played a role in political unrest in several countries. As the crisis pushes up the number of impoverished and unemployed individuals, long-standing potential instability may be ignited—particularly if local populations identify their governments as the culprits of economic hardship, if political or military contenders for power use the economic crisis as a weapon against incumbents, or if observation of unrest in neighboring countries acts as a vector of contagion. Tensions from the crisis may exacerbate preexisting sources of instability in many African countries, including ongoing or recently resolved conflicts, fragile institutions, xenophobia, and income inequality. At the same time, widespread economically driven protests such as those seen in 2008 have not been repeated in 2009, and some believe the threat may be overstated.

INTERNATIONAL EFFORTS TO ADDRESS THE IMPACT OF THE CRISIS ON AFRICA

Developed Countries

At the Group of 20 (G-20) summit in London in April 2009, member states agreed to inject $1 trillion into the world economy in order to combat the effects of the global crisis. This included a commitment to support growth in emerging market and developing countries. For example, the G-20 committed to increase lending resources available to the IMF by $250 billion through immediate contributions from some IMF member countries, and to use additional resources from agreed sales of IMF gold to provide $6 billion in additional financing (including concessional lending) for poor countries over the next two to three years. At the same time, some observers contend that "the legitimate concerns of LICs [low-income countries] in general, and Africa in particular, have not featured prominently in international rescue efforts."[94]

At the July 2009 G-8 summit in L'Aquila, Italy, members declared that they were "determined to assist developing countries in coping with the impact of the [economic] crisis" and committed to fulfilling the Gleneagles commitments on aid (discussed earlier) and improving aid effectiveness, and strengthening global initiatives to achieve the MDGs and other anti-poverty goals.[95] Led by the United States, the G-8 agreed to mobilize $20 billion over the next three years for agricultural development assistance in additional to prior commitments of emergency and humanitarian food aid. The United States committed to doubling U.S. agricultural development assistance to more than $1 billion in 2010, providing at least $3.5 billion over the next three years. Significant portions of any increase in agricultural assistance may be directed toward African countries. However, some observers view these pledges as unlikely to be fully upheld.

International Financial Institutions

The World Bank, African Development Bank (AfDB), and the IMF have all stepped up lending to the region since the onset of the financial crisis. These institutions have also reformed several of their existing loan and assistance programs, or created new facilities, to target their efforts to the current crisis. These include, for example, the IMF's Exogenous Shocks Facility, the World Bank's new Financial Crisis Response Fast-Track Facility and Infrastructure Crisis Facility, and the AfDB's new Emergency Liquidity Facility and Trade Finance Initiative. These are aimed at offsetting budget shortfalls, increasing liquidity, and providing financing for infrastructure and trade finance—all of which are considered by many analysts to be crucial to Africa's eventual economic recovery.

The World Bank and the AfDB share a development focus, and provide financing for projects as wide-ranging as heavy infrastructure, education and health policies, financial sector development, and natural resource management. World Bank lending to Africa in its 2009 fiscal year (July 1, 2008-June 30, 2009) was $9.9 billion, up 36% from $7.3 billion in FY2008.[96] The AfDB, according to its president Donald Kabaruka, is on target to commit $11 billion in 2009, doubling its 2008 commitments.[97] Much of this assistance is at highly discounted interest rates.

The World Bank

To ramp up assistance to the World Bank's poorest member countries, World Bank member countries approved the Financial Crisis Response Fast-Track Facility. This facility will allow the Bank to front-load $2 billion of the $42 billion of assistance available under its International Development Association's 2007 financial replenishment (known as IDA-15). A total of 15 African countries had benefitted from front-loading of IDA resources by August 2009. The Democratic Republic of Congo was one of the first countries to take advantage of this new facility, receiving Bank approval for a package totaling $100 million in February 2009.

The World Bank's private sector arm, the International Finance Corporation (IFC), has expanded or launched five new facilities aimed at supporting the private sector in affected emerging market and developing countries worldwide. The IFC expects financing for these new facilities to total roughly $31 billion between 2009 and 2011. The World Bank has also initiated several policies aimed at mitigating the impacts of the crisis on Africa in particular, including scaling up its lending and policy advice with a focus on poverty-reducing activities, safety nets, infrastructure support, and budget support to compensate for the loss in private capital flows. Beneficiary countries of World Bank targeted lending include South Africa, Mauritius, the Democratic Republic of Congo, Comoros, Ghana, Kenya, and Zambia.

In addition, the World Bank's new Infrastructure Crisis Facility (IFC) is making $300 million available to provide top-up financing for viable, privately funded infrastructure projects experiencing financial distress, or which are no longer able to reach financial closure. The Bank is also stepping up knowledge assistance to help countries prepare contingency plans for responding to the crisis. This package of assistance supplements the Bank's $1.2 billion Global Food Crisis Response Program (GFRP), launched in response to the 2008 food crisis. As of January 2009, 10 African countries had received a total of $83 million in GFRP resources to fund seed and fertilizer purchases, safety net programs, and budget support for governments whose fiscal balances were hurt by high fuel costs. The Bank also increased its lending to projects supporting African agriculture, from $800 million in 2008 to $1 billion in 2009. The Bank also plans to expand infrastructure investments through a $45 billion Infrastructure Recovery and Assets Platform (INFRA), about one-third of whose resources will be spent in Africa, depending on country demand.

Billions of Dollars

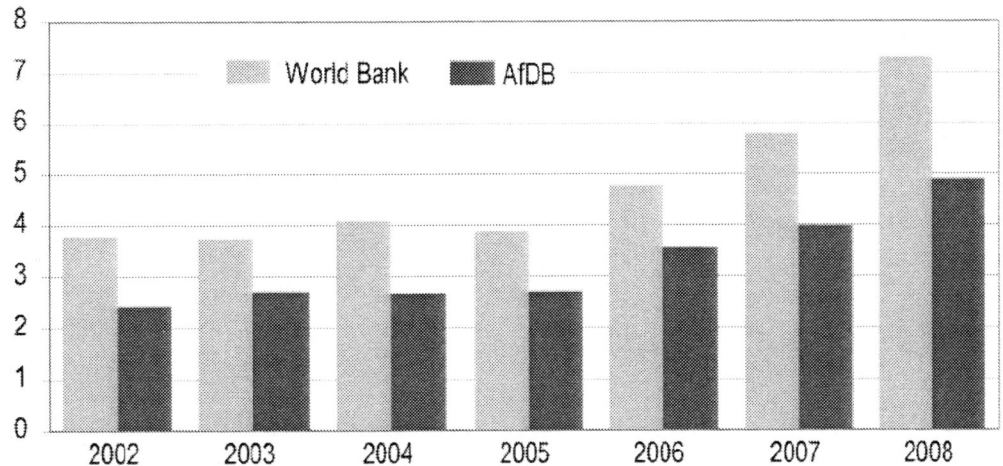

[Bar chart showing World Bank and AfDB commitments from 2002 to 2008. Approximate values:
- 2002: World Bank ~3.8, AfDB ~2.5
- 2003: World Bank ~3.8, AfDB ~2.7
- 2004: World Bank ~4.1, AfDB ~2.7
- 2005: World Bank ~3.9, AfDB ~2.8
- 2006: World Bank ~4.8, AfDB ~3.6
- 2007: World Bank ~5.8, AfDB ~4.0
- 2008: World Bank ~7.3, AfDB ~4.9]

Source: World Bank, African Development Banks.

Figure 11. World Bank and African Development Bank Commitments to Africa

The African Development Bank

The African Development Bank Group (AfDB) announced four new crisis-response initiatives in March 2009: a $1.5 billion Emergency Liquidity Facility (ELF); a $1 billion Trade Finance Initiative (TFI); a framework for accelerated transfer of African Development Fund resources to eligible countries; and enhanced policy advisory support.[98] The newly created ELF aims to provide financing to eligible African beneficiaries to support a broad range of obligations, including underpinning a fiscal stimulus and supporting public-private partnerships at risk. The ELF has a fast-tracked application process, with proposals considered by the AfDB Board within 10 working days.[99] The TFI plans to launch a new line of credit of $500 million designed to enable commercial banks and development institutions in Africa to use Bank resources to support trade financing. Accelerated African Development Fund transfers—concessional loans and grants—are expected to provide budget support and infrastructure financing.[100]

In addition to various ongoing and new projects addressing infrastructure, governance, macroeconomic policy, skills development, humanitarian relief, and other areas, the AfDB has approved several loans in recent months designed primarily to offset the impact of the global economic crisis. The Bank reportedly saw its lending nearly double to $11 billion between mid- 2008 and mid-2009, with funds going largely to budgetary support, trade finance, and infrastructure projects (notably ports and airports in Tunisia, Senegal, and Djibouti, where investors had withdrawn).[101] Recent loans explicitly linked to fallout from the crisis include a $1.5 billion loan for Botswana designed to help address a budget deficit estimated at 13.5% of GDP, the first such loan to Botswana from the AfDB in 17 years (June 2009); and a $97.18 million grant to the Democratic Republic of Congo to finance the country's Emergency Program to Mitigate the Impacts of the International Financial Crisis (May 2009).[102]

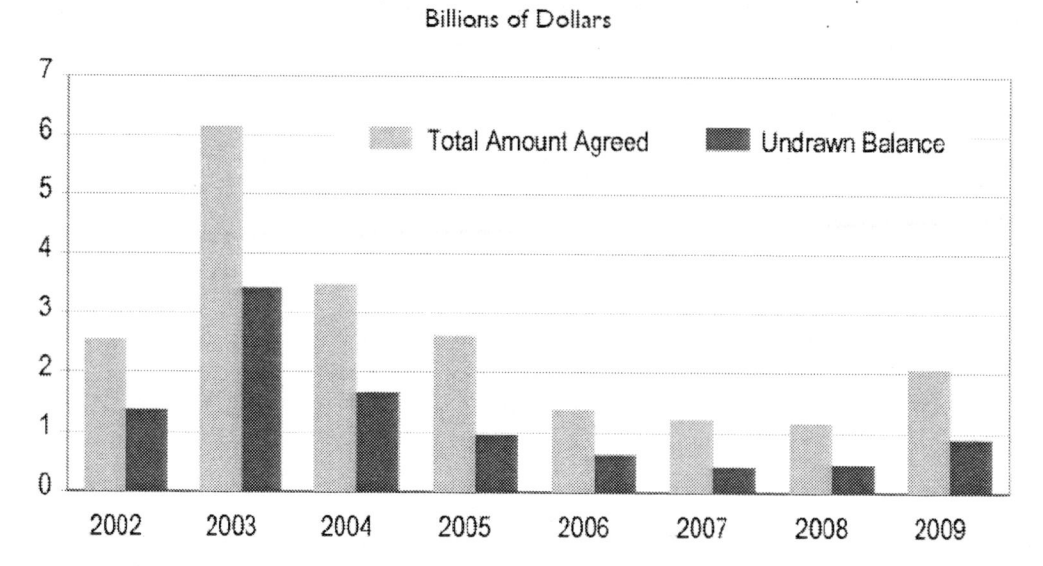

Source: International Monetary Fund.
Notes: Amounts are the total amount of outstanding PRGF and ESF loans to African countries at the end of April for each year.

Figure 12. IMF Concessional Loans to Africa

The International Monetary Fund

Unlike the AfDB and the World Bank, which fund specific development projects, the IMF provides loans to help countries that cannot meet their international payments and are unable to borrow money from other governments or raise capital on the financial markets at affordable terms. The IMF is often called the international lender of last resort.[103] The Fund is increasing its financial assistance to Africa in response to the crisis, doubling "access limits"—the ceiling amount that countries may borrow—for low-income countries. IMF lending to low-income countries in response to the economic crisis is expected to reach $8 billion by the end of 2010.[104]

In Africa, new IMF lending commitments from January to mid-July 2009 were $2.7 billion, an increase from $1.1 billion in 2008.[105] The amount of IMF credit available to the region fell sharply following implementation of the Multilateral Debt Relief Initiative (MDRI) agreed on at the June 2005 G-8 summit in Gleneagles, Scotland; the total amount of IMF credit available to African countries totals about $4.7 billion, $2 billion of which remains undrawn. Cote D'Ivoire ($581 million) and Zambia ($342 million) have the largest loan programs in the region.[106] With the exception of one loan (to Gabon), all IMF financial assistance to Africa is provided through the IMF 's concessional lending facilities, the Poverty Reduction and Growth Facility (PRGF) and the Exogenous Shocks Facility (ESF).[107]

The IMF has also accelerated long-standing efforts to revamp its lending and policy support programs for African borrowers and other low-income countries. Among recent reforms, the creation of $250 billion worth of IMF special drawing rights (SDRs) and their equi-proportional (all countries receive an amount relative to their IMF quota share) allocation to all member countries is of particular interest, as is the approval of a second SDR allocation (around $33.9 billion) specifically for under-represented countries, many in

Africa.[108] African countries are expected to receive around $11 billion in SDRs from the two allocations, which will be helpful for countries in the region that have seen their foreign exchange reserves drop sharply in an effort to avoid defaulting on their foreign financial obligations.[109]

African Governments

African governments established a Committee of Ten African Finance Ministers and Central and Regional Bank Governors (C-10) at an AfDB-organized meeting in Tunis in November 2008. Finance ministers and central bank governors have met several times since then to discuss the impact of the crisis and possible policy responses. Some countries have set up economic monitoring units and deployed limited fiscal and monetary resources. Steps taken by some African governments have reportedly included fiscal stimulus packages (e.g. Mauritius, South Africa), targeted assistance to certain sectors (Nigeria, Uganda), expansionary monetary policy (Botswana, Namibia, South Africa), and bond financing of public expenditures (Cape Verde, Kenya).[110]

Nevertheless, most African governments have little capacity to fund policy interventions to address the crisis. Effective economic governance continues to be lacking in many countries, and responses are projected to be restrained by the relative unavailability of foreign reserves, insufficient budgetary margins for enacting fiscal stimulus packages, and restrictions on incurring further external debt in countries that have benefited from international debt relief. While multilateral institutions have urged African governments to focus spending on social security nets and infrastructure projects—which have the potential to stimulate the economy while addressing some of the long-term obstacles to economic growth—regional expenditures on infrastructure fell far short of World Bank recommendations even before the crisis hit.[111] Some believe high levels of corruption could additionally impede the effectiveness of government responses to the crisis.

OUTLOOK AND ISSUES FOR CONGRESS

There is strong congressional interest in African socioeconomic development and regional stability. Congressional interest in fostering U.S. economic ties with African countries is evidenced in recent hearings, such as that held in June 2009 by the House Committee on Energy and Commerce, Subcommittee on Commerce, Trade, and Consumer Protection and the House Committee on Foreign Affairs, Subcommittee on Africa and Global Health, on "U.S.-Africa Trade Relations: Creating a Platform for Economic Growth"; in pending legislation, such as H.Con.Res. 128, "Expressing the sense of Congress that Africa is of significant strategic, political, economic, and humanitarian importance to the United States" (referred to the House Foreign Affairs Committee in May 2009); and in existing laws and programs such as the African Growth and Opportunity Act (AGOA). A consideration of the impact of the crisis may affect bilateral and regional aid levels and programs, U.S. trade policy toward Africa, and analyses of regional and country-level political trends, among other areas.

The U.S. government has announced several new policies to aid developing countries affected by the crisis, though it has not, to date, formulated a policy specifically aimed at addressing the impact on Africa. The Supplemental Appropriations Act, 2009 (P.L. 111-32, passed into law on June 24, 2009), includes $255.6 million in Economic Support Funds (ESF) for "assistance for vulnerable populations in developing countries severely affected by the global financial crisis," with certain eligibility criteria. However, while an initial House report on the legislation provided that five African countries—Ghana, Liberia, Mozambique, Tanzania, and Zambia—should "receive priority consideration," along with several other countries outside the region, the subsequent conference report did not include such specifications.[112] In July 2009, the Obama Administration noted the impact of the economic crisis on developing countries in announcing its commitment to double U.S. agricultural development assistance to more than $1 billion in 2010, and to provide at least $3.5 billion over the next three years.[113] The initiative is global, not uniquely focused on Africa, though the Administration cited the U.S. Comprehensive Africa Agriculture Development Program (CAADP) as a "model."[114]

U.S. responses to date have focused on support for multilateral lending and grant initiatives. Moving forward, this may include increased financial support to the international financial institutions to which African countries are expected to apply for economic support during the crisis. In the 2009 Supplemental (P.L. 111-32), Congress approved U.S. participation in a range of measures designed to increase the amount of financial assistance the IMF may provide to its member states in the wake of the economic crisis.[115] The AfDB has also requested an increase in financing by the G-20.[116] Relevant legislation includes S. 955, the African Development Fund Replenishment Act of 2009.

End Notes

[1] Agence France-Presse, "IMF Sees Faster African Recovery from Economic Slump," March 7, 2010.
[2] Reuters, "World Bank Sees African Economies Rebounding in 2010," March 18, 2010.
[3] Reuters, "Davos Special Report: Africa Rising," January 26, 2010.
[4] Reuters, "Brazil, Others Squeeze China in Scramble for Africa," November 4, 2009.
[5] Title XI, Section 1105, "Global Financial Crisis."
[6] State Department response to CRS query, April 6, 2010.
[7] U.N. News, "Industrialization Will Help Africa Fully Join World Economy, Says Ban," November 20, 2009.
[8] Global Financial Integrity, *Illicit Financial Outflows from Africa: Hidden Resource for Development*, March 2010.
[9] IMF, *World Economic Outlook Update*, July 8, 2009.
[10] This report uses the terms Africa and Sub-Saharan Africa interchangeably, comprising the region as defined by the International Monetary Fund except where otherwise indicated.
[11] Only one country in the region, South Africa, is considered by the IMF to be an "emerging market economy," possessing a full range of financial institutions that are integrated with the global economy (such as subsidiaries of foreign-owned banks and insurance companies, asset management funds, pension funds, etc).
[12] IMF, *Regional Economic Outlook: Sub-Saharan Africa*, October 2009.
[13] African Development Bank (AfDB), *Impact of the Crisis on African Economies—Sustaining Growth and Poverty Reduction: African Perspectives and Recommendations to the G20*, March 21, 2009.
[14] U.S. Department of State, "Secretary of State Clinton Delivers Remarks at the Corporate Council on Africa's Seventh Biennial US-Africa Business Summit," October 1, 2009.
[15] IMF, *Regional Economic Outlook: Sub-Saharan Africa*, April 2009; OECD/African Development Bank (AfDB), *African Economic Outlook*, May 2009; World Bank, *Global Development Finance: Charting a Global Recovery*, June 2009; Economist Intelligence Unit (EIU), *Global Outlook*, August 2009. Some of the differences in these estimates may be attributable to variances in country lists and in the timing of analysis.
[16] Congressional Record – House, page H9477, "Congressional Black Caucus," September 14, 2009.

[17] Title XI, Section 1105, "Global Financial Crisis." The eligibility criteria outlined in the conference report are that countries must have a 2007 per capita Gross National Income of $3,705 or less; have experienced a contraction in predicted growth rates of 2% or more since 2007; and demonstrate consistent improvement on the democracy and governance indicators as measured by the Millennium Challenge Corporation 2009 Country Scorebook.

[18] U.N. Conference on Trade and Development (UNCTAD) data, cited in World Economic Forum, *Africa Competitiveness Report*, June 10, 2009.

[19] Oxford Analytica, "Africa: Economic growth is strong but constrained," May 15, 2008.

[20] IMF, *Regional Economic Outlook: Sub-Saharan Africa*, October 2008.

[21] The Millennium Development Goals are, broadly, to achieve the following by 2015: (1) Reduce by half the level of extreme poverty and hunger; (2) Achieve universal primary education; (3) Eliminate gender disparity in primary and secondary education preferably by 2005, and at all levels by 2015; (4) Reduce by two thirds the mortality rate among children under five; (5) Reduce by three quarters the maternal mortality ratio; (6) Halt and begin to reverse the spread of HIV/AIDS, and the incidence of malaria and other major diseases; (7) Integrate the principles of sustainable development into country policies and programs, reverse the loss of environmental resources, reduce by half the proportion of people without sustainable access to safe drinking water and basic sanitation, and achieve significant improvement in lives of at least 100 million slum dwellers by 2020; and (8) Develop a global partnership for development. See United Nations, "Millennium Development Goals," at http://www.un.org/millenniumgoals/.

[22] United Nations, *The Millennium Development Goals Report 2009*; United Nations, *Africa and the Millennium Development Goals: 2007 Update*; World Bank, "Overview: Understanding, Measuring, and Overcoming Poverty."

[23] See, for example, Freedom House, *Freedom in Sub-Saharan Africa 2009*.

[24] World Bank, *World Trade Indicators 2008*. Despite diversification efforts in many mid- and low-income African countries, South Africa remains the most diversified economy on the continent.

[25] World Bank, *World Trade Indicators 2008*, p. 72. See also Alberto Portugal-Perez and John S. Wilson, "Trade Costs in Africa: Barriers and Opportunities for Reform," World Bank Development Research Group, September 2008; World Bank, *Doing Business Report 2009*; World Economic Forum, *Africa Competitiveness Report*, June 10, 2009; and Economist Intelligence Unit, "Sub-Saharan Africa Economy: Outstripped," September 8, 2009.

[26] United Nations, *The Millennium Development Goals Report 2009*.

[27] U.N. Conference on Trade and Development (UNCTAD), *Economic Development in Africa: Strengthening Regional Economic Integration for Africa's Development*, June 25, 2009.

[28] See e.g. Food and Agriculture Organization (FAO), *The State of Food Insecurity in the World*, 2008.

[29] CRS Report R40 127, *The Impact of Food Insecurity and Hunger on Global Health: Issues for Congress*, by Tiaji Salaam-Blyther and Charles E. Hanrahan.

[30] IMF, *Regional Economic Outlook Sub-Saharan Africa*, April 2009.

[31] World Bank, *World Trade Indicators 2008*.

[32] A notable exception is South Africa, where the financial sector spillover from the global crisis has been a major factor behind an ongoing recession.

[33] IMF, *World Economic Outlook*, April 2009; Todd Moss, Center for Global Development, *How the Economic Crisis is Hurting Africa—And What To Do About It*, May 2009; Moin Siddiqi, "How to Improve Africa's Trade Performance," *African Business*, July 1, 2009.

[34] IMF, *World Economic Outlook*, April 2009.

[35] Data available at http://www.agoa.info. The African Growth and Opportunity Act is a U.S. trade preference program, begun in 2000 (P.L. 106-200, as amended), that provides certain goods from Sub-Saharan Africa duty-free access to the U.S. market. AGOA extends preferential treatment to imports from eligible countries that are pursuing market reform measures. See CRS Report RL3 1772, *U.S. Trade and Investment Relationship with Sub-Saharan Africa: The African Growth and Opportunity Act*, by Vivian C. Jones, for further background.

[36] Statement of Florizelle B. Liser, Assistant U.S. Trade Representative for Africa, before the House hearing on "U.S.- Africa Trade Relations: Creating a Platform for Economic Growth," June 24, 2009.

[37] Trade statistics are based on CRS calculations using the Global Trade Atlas Navigator database and the U.S. International Trade Commission Trade Dataweb. Oil and mineral fuels account for about 80% of all U.S. imports from Sub-Saharan Africa, and 92% of all U.S. imports under the African Growth and Opportunity Act (AGOA).

[38] U.N. World Tourism Organization, "World Tourism in the Face of the Global Economic Crisis," May 12, 2009.

[39] IMF, *Regional Economic Outlook Sub-Saharan Africa*, April 2009; see also Paulo Drummond and Gustavo Ramirez, "Spillovers From the Rest of the World into Sub-Saharan African Countries," IMF Working Paper, 2009.

[40] Moin Siddiqi, "How to Improve Africa's Trade Performance," *African Business*, July 1, 2009.

[41] E.g. Todd Moss, Center for Global Development, *How the Economic Crisis is Hurting Africa—And What To Do About It*, May 2009.

[42] "Trade finance" refers to the role of banks, institutions, and private corporations in facilitating the movement of merchandise in global trade. See, e.g., Thomas Dorsey, "Trade Finance Stumbles," *Finance and Development*, March 2009.

[43] John Humphrey, "Trade Financing: Is it a barrier to Africa's exports?," *Vox*, April 28, 2009.

[44] IMF, *Regional Economic Outlook: Sub-Saharan Africa*, October 2009.

[45] Examples drawn from country reports by the Economist Intelligence Unit (EIU).

[46] U.S. Department of Commerce, International Trade Administration, *U.S.-African Trade Profile*, July 2009.

[47] Oxford Analytica, "Africa: Positive Economic Outlook Belies Fragility," May 23, 2005, and "Africa: Growth to Suffer Despite Insulated Banks," October 15, 2008.

[48] Reuters, "Factbox—China's Growing Business in Africa," February 12, 2009.

[49] E.g. Lydia Polgreen, "As Chinese Investment in Africa Drops, Hope Sinks," *The New York Times*, March 25, 2009; Oxford Analytica, "China/Africa: Ties Should Weather Global Downturn," June 10, 2009.

[50] Standard Bank, *Implications of the Financial Crisis on Sino-African Relations*, June 30, 2009.

[51] See CRS Report RL34620, *Comparing Global Influence: China's and U.S. Diplomacy, Foreign Aid, Trade, and Investment in the Developing World*, coordinated by Thomas Lum.

[52] *Foreign direct investment* reflects direct investments in productive assets, such as factories, mines, and land, by a company incorporated in a foreign country. It does not include foreign investment in stock markets. *Portfolio investment* is a more passive form of investment that includes holding equity securities and debt securities in the form of bonds and notes, money market instruments, and financial derivatives such as options. See also the *International Monetary Fund Balance of Payments Manual*, available at http://www.imf.org/external/pubs/ft/bopman/bopman.pdf.

[53] IMF Sub-Saharan Africa Economic Outlook database, April 2009.

[54] Razia Khan, "Africa: Financing the Future," *Standard Chartered Global Focus*, May 14, 2009.

[55] The term "frontier economies" refers to economies that are smaller and less developed than emerging markets, but which investors believe have significant growth potential. In Africa, the IMF considers the following countries to constitute frontier economies: Botswana, Cape Verde, Ghana, Kenya, Mauritius, Mozambique, Namibia, Nigeria, Seychelles, Tanzania, Uganda, and Zambia. There are some signs that investor interest in African frontier economies has rebounded since April 2009; see Reuters, "Africa Attracts $1 Billion in Fund Flows This Year," August 3, 2009.

[56] José Brambila Macias and Isabella Massa, "The Global Financial Crisis and Sub-Saharan Afirca: The effects of slowing private capital inflows on growth," Overseas Development Institute Working Paper 304, June 2009.

[57] E.g. Dilip Ratha, "Workers Remittances: An Important Source of Development Finance," *Global Development Finance 2003: Striving for Stability in Development Finance*, World Bank, 2003.

[58] World Bank "Migration and Remittances" data.

[59] Dilip Ratha and Sanket Mohapatra, *World Bank Revised Outlook for Remittance Flows 2009-2011*, March 23, 2009.

[60] See EIU, "Going With the Flow," July 1, 2009 and "Africa Economy: Remittances Flows Ebb," July 23, 2009.

[61] In the case of France, reductions in the total amount of bilateral aid are partly due to the fact that aid commitments are tied in many cases to France's GDP; as GDP has been revised downward due to the crisis, so have aid flows.

[62] AfDB/Committee of African Finance Ministers and Central Bank Governors Established to Monitor the Crisis, *Impact of the Crisis on African Economies—Sustaining Growth and Poverty Reduction: African Perspectives and Recommendations to the G20*, March 21, 2009.

[63] See, among many, ONE, *Guiding Principles for Aid Reform in The United States*, available at http://www.one.org/c/us/policybrief/765/; Jeffrey Sachs, *The End of Poverty: Economic Possibilities for Our Time* (Penguin: 2006); William Easterly, *The White Man's Burden: Why the West's Efforts to Aid the Rest Have Done So Much Ill and So Little Good* (Penguin: 2006); and Oxfam, *Smart Development: Why U.S. Foreign Aid Demands Major Reform*, February 2008. See also CRS Report RL32489, *Africa: Development Issues and Policy Options*, by Raymond W. Copson.

[64] IMF, *Regional Economic Outlook: Sub-Saharan Africa*, October 2008. The IMF notes at the same time that "fears that large increases in aid may also undermine exports are 'difficult to prove, but difficult to dismiss'" (p. 3).

[65] Overseas development aid may include debt relief, budgetary support, and funding for specific types of development projects, among others. If debt relief is not counted, Africa's aid-dependency compared to other regions has varied recent years.

[66] OECD Factbook 2009: Economic, Environmental and Social Statistics.

[67] G-8 members made this commitment on behalf of members of the Development Assistance Committee (DAC), a sub-organization of the Organization for Economic Co-operation and Development (OECD) responsible for development issues and development policies. Russia did not commit to raising aid to Africa, leading some to refer to the Gleneagles commitments as made by the G-7.

[68] ONE, *The Data Report 2009: Monitoring the G8 Promise to Africa*, May 19, 2009.
[69] OECD, *2009 DAC Report on Aid Predictability*; United Nations, *Millennium Development Goal 8: Strengthening the Global Partnership in a Time of Crisis*, 2009.
[70] ONE, *The Data Report 2009: Monitoring the G8 Promise to Africa*, May 19, 2009.
[71] IMF, *Regional Economic Outlook: Sub-Saharan Africa*, October 2009.
[72] Ibid.
[73] Ibid: 3.
[74] Ibid. Previously, African Development Bank President Donald Kaberuka has expressed concern that international credit shortages and investors' risk aversion could cause African countries to recover more slowly from the crisis than those of other regions. AFP, "Africa to Lag Recovery From Crisis: African Development Bank," April 26, 2009.
[75] Remarks by Dr. Henry G. Broadman, Managing Director of the Albright Group LLC, at the School of Advanced International Studies (SAIS), Washington DC, September 23, 2009.
[76] Robert B. Zoellick, "After the Crisis?" Remarks delivered at the School of Advanced International Studies, Washington DC, September 28, 2009.
[77] CRS calculation based on IMF World Economic Outlook data, April 2009.
[78] According to the IMF, GDP growth in oil-exporting countries is expected to decline by 6.5 percentage points in 2009 relative to the 2004-2008 average, and by 7 percentage points on average in middle-income countries. IMF, *Regional Economic Outlook*, October 2009.
[79] Ibid.
[80] Considered to be one of Africa's most stable and best-governed economies, Botswana received a record $1.5 billion loan from the African Development Bank (AfDB) in June 2009, designed to cover a budget gap estimated at 13.5% of GDP due to the collapse in world diamond prices. Diamonds are thought to account for roughly two-thirds of Botswana's total exports and 28% of GDP. It was the first time in 17 years that Botswana had applied for an AfDB loan; it has previously served as a contributor to the AfDB's concessional loan facility, the African Development Fund. AfDB, "AfDB Approves US$1.5 Billion Budget Support for Botswana to Help Country Cope with the Financial Crisis," June 2, 2009; U.S. State Department, "Background Note: Botswana," August 2009.
[81] IMF, *Regional Economic Outlook: Sub-Saharan Africa*, October 2009. According to the IMF, low-income countries in Africa are expected to fare better in the crisis than those in other regions. See also Todd Moss, Center for Global Development, *How the Economic Crisis is Hurting Africa—And What To Do About It*, May 2009.
[82] IMF, *Regional Economic Outlook: Sub-Saharan Africa*, October 2009.
[83] IMF, *Regional Economic Outlook: Sub-Saharan Africa*, April 2009.
[84] Reuters, "Factbox—Five Risks to Watch in Africa," October 1, 2009. See also Andrew Berg et al, "Fiscal Policy in Sub-Saharan Africa in Response to the Impact of the Global Crisis" (IMF Staff Position Note), May 14, 2009.
[85] AfDB/Committee of African Finance Ministers and Central Bank Governors Established to Monitor the Crisis, *Impact of the Crisis on African Economies—Sustaining Growth and Poverty Reduction: African Perspectives and Recommendations to the G20*, March 21, 2009.
[86] For the purpose of global aggregation and comparison, the World Bank measures global poverty according to reference lines set at $1.25 and $2 per day (2005 Purchasing Power Parity terms). World Bank, "Overview: Understanding, Measuring, and Overcoming Poverty," online at http://go.worldbank.org/RQBDCTUXW0; World Bank/International Bank for Reconstruction and Development, *Swimming Against the Tide: How developing countries are coping with the global crisis*, March 2009; Africa Progress Panel, *An Agenda for Progress at a Time of Global Crisis: A Call for African Leadership*, June 10, 2009; Inter-Press Service (IPS), "Continent 'Not Badly Hit' Despite 16 Million More Poor," June 11, 2009.
[87] IMF, *Regional Economic Outlook: Sub-Saharan Africa*, October 2009.
[88] In some countries, depreciating exchange rates are putting additional upward pressures on prices, including food imports. IMF, *Regional Economic Outlook: Sub-Saharan Africa*, April 2009.
[89] Jed Friedman and Norbert Schady, World Bank, *How Many More Infants Are Likely to Die in Africa as a Result of the Global Financial Crisis?* August 2009.
[90] United Nations, *The Millennium Development Goals Report 2009*.
[91] IMF, *Regional Economic Outlook: Sub-Saharan Africa*, April 2009; Reuters, "World Food Prices Stabilize, No Drop in Sight—WFP" August 7, 2009.
[92] Africa Progress Panel, *An Agenda for Progress at a Time of Global Crisis: A Call for African Leadership*, June 10, 2009.
[93] EIU, "Sub-Saharan Africa Politics: Submerging Markets," April 14, 2009. See also Amnesty International, "Economic crisis reveals deeper human rights problems," May 28, 2009; and U.N. Integrated Regional Information Networks (IRIN), "Africa: Helping Fragile States Survive Financial Crisis," May 14, 2009.
[94] Africa Progress Panel, *An Agenda for Progress at a Time of Global Crisis: A Call for African Leadership*, June 10, 2009.

[95] G-8 Declaration, "Responsible Leadership for a Sustainable Future," L'Aquila, Italy, July 2009.

[96] "World Bank Group Support to Crisis-Hit Countries at Record High," World Bank, July 1, 2009.

[97] Reuters, "AfDB Sees Commitments Almost Doubling to $11 Bln," August 5, 2009.

[98] AfDB, "AfDB Response to Financial Crisis Economic Impact," March 5, 2009. The African Development Fund (AfDF) is a concessional lending/grant making facility for low-income African member countries. There are currently 38 AfDF borrower countries. The AfDF is primarily financed by 24 non-regional countries including the United States, Canada, and several European and Asian countries. See CRS Report RS22690, *The African Development Bank Group*, by Martin A. Weiss.

[99] AfDB, "Emergency Liquidity Facility (ELF)," at http://www.afdb.org/en/projects-operations/financial-products/emergency-financing/.

[100] AfDB, "AfDB Response to Financial Crisis Economic Impact," March 5, 2009.

[101] AfDB, "Africa: AfDB Seeks Resources Increase From G20," September 22, 2009.

[102] AfDB, "AfDB Approves US$1.5 Billion Budget Support for Botswana to Help Country Cope with the Financial Crisis," June 2, 2009; and AfDB, "AfDB Grants US$97 Million Budget Support to DRC to Mitigate Impacts of Financial Crisis." The latter grant is expected to help strengthen the foreign reserves of the Central Bank of Congo, increase the availability of essential imports, and assist the government in meeting key benchmarks for reaching the IMF-led Heavily Indebted Poor Countries (HIPC) completion point in 2009, paying state employee salaries, and making regular utility payments for public entities, among other goals.

[103] CRS Report RL32364, *The International Monetary Fund: Organization, Functions, and Role in the International Economy*, by Jonathan E. Sanford and Martin A. Weiss.

[104] CRS Report R40578, *The Global Financial Crisis: Increasing IMF Resources and the Role of Congress*, by Jonathan E. Sanford and Martin A. Weiss.

[105] IMF, "The IMF Response to the Global Financial Crisis: Meeting the Needs of Low-Income Countries," July 29, 2009.

[106] CRS Report RS22534, *The Multilateral Debt Relief Initiative*, by Martin A. Weiss.

[107] PRGF loans are intended to help low-income countries address balance of payments concerns, such as those created by the financial crisis. Unlike IMF assistance to more developed economies, however, PRGF loans are provided at concessional (i.e. below market) interest rates. The ESF is intended to provide countries with quicker and easier access to assistance to help them cope with economic shocks that have a negative impact on their economy but are beyond their governments' control. Conditionality is focused on steps needed to adjust to the economic shock, with less attention to the structural adjustment measures more commonly associated with SBA, EFF and PRGF assistance. In September 2008, access was made more flexible and the earlier requirement that countries must have PRGF in place was dropped.

[108] The First Amendment to the IMF Articles of Agreement, which went into effect in 1969, authorized the IMF to create a new international reserve asset that could be used to supplement IMF member country's foreign exchange reserves. SDRs are not a global reserve currency. However, they can be exchanged for hard convertible currency among IMF member nations.

[109] Joe Bavier, "Sub-Saharan Africa to Receive $10 Bln in SDRs-IMF," Reuters, May 25, 2009. See also Alex Sienaert, "IFI Support to Africa – A Closer Look," Standard Chartered, July 20, 2009.

[110] Africa Progress Panel, *An Agenda for Progress at a Time of Global Crisis: A Call for African Leadership*, June 10, 2009; AfDB/Committee of African Finance Ministers and Central Bank Governors Established to Monitor the Crisis, *Impact of the Crisis on African Economies—Sustaining Growth and Poverty Reduction: African Perspectives and Recommendations to the G20*, March 21, 2009.

[111] Oxford Analytica, "Policy Options Limited for Managing Downturn," June 15, 2009.

[112] H.Rept. 111-105, May 12, 2009; H.Rept. 111-151, June 11, 2009.

[113] White House, "Africa: Food Security - Investing in Agricultural Development to Reduce Hunger and Poverty," July 10, 2009.

[114] See CRS Report R40127, *The Impact of Food Insecurity and Hunger on Global Health: Issues for Congress*, by Tiaji Salaam-Blyther and Charles E. Hanrahan (Appendix E), for background on the CAADP.

[115] CRS Report R40578, *The Global Financial Crisis: Increasing IMF Resources and the Role of Congress*, by Jonathan E. Sanford and Martin A. Weiss.

[116] AfDB, "Africa: AfDB Seeks Resources Increase From G20," September 22, 2009; Reuters, "Resources Running Out: African Development Bank Chief," October 7, 2009.

INDEX

A

abuse, 7, 10, 169
accountability, 6, 8, 52, 71, 72, 126
accounting, 16, 30, 45, 73, 115, 128, 157, 158, 159, 184
accounting standards, 16, 73, 157, 184
acquisitions, 13, 109, 135
adjustment, 42, 93, 132, 144
advisory body, 48
aerospace, 136
agencies, 5, 6, 7, 8, 24, 25, 29, 30, 44, 49, 53, 72, 73, 76, 112, 123, 128, 130, 159, 160, 180, 184, 194
aggregate demand, 43, 183
aggregation, 245
aging population, 207
agricultural sector, 45
agriculture, 65, 102, 143, 145, 152, 192, 200, 222, 224, 238
AIDS, 177, 180
Air Force, 143
airports, 239
American Recovery and Reinvestment Act, vii, 1, 6, 11, 77, 125, 133, 137, 162
Angola, ix, 219, 224, 232
annual rate, 40, 50, 78, 84, 111, 113, 114, 127, 134, 137, 141, 144
antidumping, 20
anxiety, 31
appetite, 107
arbitrage, 29
Argentina, viii, 20, 27, 35, 41, 42, 45, 46, 76, 93, 130, 153, 154, 163, 165, 168, 173, 189, 194, 195, 198, 203, 205, 217
armed conflict, 224
ASEAN, 62, 149, 170, 181
assessment, 46, 70, 88, 97, 185

Association of Southeast Asian Nations, 62, 181
Attorney General, 104
audits, 11, 91, 156
authenticity, 96
authorities, 9, 10, 19, 22, 25, 26, 31, 55, 103, 118, 147, 159, 160, 163, 169, 185, 210
authors, 37, 154, 208
automobiles, 126, 145, 216
automotive sector, 114

B

background, 209, 220, 243, 246
backlash, 192
Bahrain, 138, 145
bail, 86, 105, 108, 121
balance of payments, 36, 62, 74, 75, 120, 146, 177, 246
balance sheet, vii, 1, 13, 25, 27, 41, 44, 60, 73, 86, 134, 148, 157, 159, 204, 216
balanced budget, 123, 208, 209
bank debt, 39, 162
bank failure, 76, 149
Bank of England, 53, 57, 136, 147, 161, 162, 169
bankers, 6, 100, 110, 120
banking industry, 57, 67, 76
banking sector, 35, 57, 59, 137, 146
bankruptcy, 4, 18, 19, 24, 25, 28, 30, 34, 43, 76, 80, 84, 97, 98, 105, 106, 112, 114, 119, 121, 127, 128, 148, 149, 156
bargaining, 102
barriers, 19, 73, 111, 192, 225, 227
basic services, 126, 224
basis points, 41, 44, 46, 96, 136, 138, 139, 140, 141, 144, 145, 162
BBB, 132, 142, 203
beef, 18
benchmarks, 224, 246

246   Index

bias, 96
bilateral aid, 244
blame, 21
bleeding, 196
board members, 104, 146
bondholders, 3, 79, 119, 141
bonds, 24, 46, 76, 93, 102, 108, 116, 131, 135, 145, 153, 166, 203, 234, 244
borrowers, 21, 62, 87, 92, 113, 116, 129, 130, 240
breakdown, 65
Bretton Woods conference, 69
Bretton Woods system, 17, 177
budding, 46
budget allocation, 235
budget cuts, 78
budget deficit, viii, ix, 21, 33, 47, 87, 93, 114, 132, 150, 191, 201, 202, 203, 204, 207, 212, 213, 215, 217, 239
budget surplus, 34, 153, 210, 234
building societies, 57, 148
Bulgaria, 35, 87, 133, 189
business cycle, 5, 16, 73, 212
business environment, 225
buyer, 5, 29, 89, 166

C

candidates, 90
capital expenditure, 216
capital flight, 68
capital flows, 24, 30, 36, 37, 38, 63, 77, 98, 102, 178, 188, 190, 229, 230, 238
capital goods, 153
capital inflow, 38, 41, 93, 189, 221, 223, 228, 244
capital markets, 22, 30, 35, 45, 46, 102, 166, 199, 202, 207, 221
capital outflow, 221
capital projects, 216
capitalism, 19, 69
carbon, 34, 88, 136, 151, 216
category b, 46
CBS, 165
Census, 107
challenges, 18, 19, 23, 44, 70, 73, 97, 110, 124, 130, 147, 177, 180, 225, 236
chaos, 47, 105
chicken, 107
civil service, 194
civil war, 126
clean energy, 33, 55, 71, 150, 216
clients, 29, 54
climate, 21, 71, 83, 88, 100, 191, 193, 196, 200
climate change, 21, 71, 88, 100, 191, 193, 196, 200

closure, 238
coal, 96
cocoa, 227
coffee, 18, 179, 227
collateral, 5, 24, 28, 29, 30, 95, 161, 162, 203
collateral damage, 24
colleges, 55, 160, 163
color, 175
commercial bank, 9, 13, 101, 239
commercial ties, 227
commodity, ix, 4, 13, 23, 26, 36, 40, 41, 43, 44, 45, 50, 75, 96, 98, 114, 142, 219, 220, 221, 223, 224, 226, 227, 233, 234
commodity markets, 26
commodity producers, 96
communication, 30, 86
communist countries, 139
community, 9, 26, 106
compensation, 11, 16, 19, 26, 49, 70, 73, 95, 97, 105, 113, 140, 156, 166, 184, 207
compensation package, 98
competition, 23, 125
competitive markets, 73
competitiveness, 52, 225
complement, 55
complexity, 24, 29, 50, 119, 134
compliance, 16, 75, 215
composition, 71, 212
conference, 62, 69, 104, 133, 142, 146, 191, 192, 220, 242, 243
conflict, 23, 217, 226, 233, 236
Congressional Budget Office, 77, 114, 133
consciousness, 4
consensus, 6, 14, 56, 134, 169, 182, 187
consolidation, ix, 135, 157, 201, 207, 208, 209, 210, 211, 212, 215, 216
Constitution, 127
consulting, 94
consumer demand, 45, 216
consumer goods, 20, 90
consumer protection, 71, 126
consumption, 53, 60, 62, 66, 88, 90, 96, 101, 124, 126, 208, 211, 225, 227, 234
consumption patterns, 101
consumption rates, 62
contingency, 76, 163, 238
continuous data, 84
contract enforcement, 194
controversies, 192
convention, 187
convergence, 72
conviction, ix, 201

coordination, viii, 2, 16, 52, 53, 55, 72, 78, 136, 147, 163, 174, 176, 177, 193, 196
copper, 18, 40, 111, 153, 228
corruption, 124, 193, 194, 224, 241
cost of living, 104
cotton, 225, 227
coup, 79
credit history, 116
credit market, 12, 31, 40, 46, 50, 63, 105, 138, 227
credit rating, 7, 9, 24, 28, 29, 43, 49, 72, 73, 112, 127, 128, 130, 142, 159, 184
creditors, 77, 80, 85, 86, 106
creditworthiness, 50
crime, 177, 194
crisis management, 8, 54, 58, 75, 135, 163, 174, 183
criticism, 62, 94, 119
crowding out, 207
crude oil, 20, 124
cultivation, 136
current account, 27, 30, 35, 36, 60, 63, 67, 70, 166, 208, 210, 211
current account balance, 208, 211
current account deficit, 35, 67, 166, 210
current account surplus, 36, 60, 63
current prices, 83
cycles, 70

D

danger, 90, 132, 204
data collection, 222
database, 31, 84, 234, 235, 236, 243, 244
deaths, 236
debt service, 77
debt servicing, 32
debtors, 103
debts, 47, 51, 67, 79, 86, 87, 93, 202, 203, 217
decoupling, 37, 40
deduction, 150
deflation, 209, 210
delegates, 192
democracy, 243
Democrat, 84, 211
Democratic Party, 63, 91, 104, 209
Democratic Republic of Congo, 232, 238, 239
Denmark, 59, 110, 142, 195, 206, 208, 213
Department of Commerce, 167, 244
Department of Energy, 180
deposit accounts, 58
deposits, 2, 9, 11, 12, 58, 59, 101, 102, 113, 121, 147, 158
depreciation, 20, 33, 59, 93, 151, 209, 211
depression, 81

deregulation, 19, 27, 134
destination, 227, 230
devaluation, 87
developed countries, viii, 35, 37, 40, 75, 173, 174, 177, 178, 179, 183, 191, 193, 194, 198, 204, 207, 212, 216, 226, 227, 230
developed nations, 102
developing nations, vii, 1, 6, 21, 61, 129, 146, 179
development assistance, 23, 73, 230, 237, 242
development banks, 2, 4, 7, 15, 22, 71, 72, 75, 76, 128, 174, 188, 221, 223
diamonds, 114
diffusion, 105
diplomacy, 21, 22
direct investment, 77, 116, 244
directors, 56, 95, 104, 135
disaster, 3, 151
disbursement, 90, 112
disclosure, 27, 72, 73, 119, 157, 159
discretionary policy, 204
dislocation, 23, 25, 78
displacement, 225
disposition, 58
distortions, 46, 159
distress, 55, 92, 232
diversification, 119, 243
diversity, 55, 71
doctors, 11
domestic demand, 47, 90, 104, 118, 120, 124, 208, 231
domestic investment, 60, 223
domestic markets, 236
dominance, 179
donors, 68, 189, 199, 221, 230, 236
draft, 3, 12, 95, 138, 154
drawing, 224
drinking water, 243
drought, 111, 136
drug trafficking, 72
drugs, 177
dumping, 20, 21, 107
duty-free access, 243

E

early warning, 6, 17, 22, 54, 74
earnings, 5, 77, 88, 113, 153
economic activity, 4, 23, 24, 31, 43, 48, 49, 50, 82, 111, 115, 120, 128, 129, 134, 204, 209, 211, 215
Economic and Monetary Union, 212
economic change, 35
economic competitiveness, 228

economic cooperation, 71, 74, 136, 174, 175, 183, 192, 193
economic crisis, viii, 4, 10, 18, 46, 48, 67, 90, 98, 133, 146, 170, 173, 179, 182, 219, 221, 223, 227, 234, 235, 236, 237, 239, 240, 242
economic development, 70, 183
economic downturn, 23, 42, 47, 48, 49, 50, 52, 53, 96, 112, 114, 117, 122, 124, 135, 136, 204, 205, 215, 216
economic fundamentals, 22, 40, 41, 43, 59, 70, 78
economic growth rate, 14, 30, 34
economic indicator, 35, 230
economic institutions, 182
economic integration, 49, 176, 204, 217
economic performance, 204, 208, 213, 215
economic policy, 3, 41, 48, 53, 68, 103, 176, 177, 192, 196, 215
economic problem, 18, 40, 68, 87
economic reform, 225
economic reforms, 225
economic systems, 221
economic transformation, 59
economic welfare, 40
election, 63, 146, 208
electricity, 33, 65, 68, 109, 126, 150, 151, 152, 191, 225
eligibility criteria, 242, 243
eligible countries, 129, 239, 243
Emergency Economic Stabilization Act, 148, 153
employees, 53, 95, 97, 105
employment, 43, 44, 64, 74, 82, 85, 98, 106, 117, 118, 127, 141, 143, 180, 216, 222
energy efficiency, 33, 57, 71, 88, 150
energy markets, 71
enforcement, vii, 1, 16, 24, 69, 182, 215
engineering, 149
environmental degradation, 225
environmental protection, 33, 151
environmental resources, 243
epidemic, 128
equilibrium, 69
equipment, 34, 136, 151, 216
equities, 6, 27, 30, 31, 44, 50
equity, 2, 5, 8, 9, 19, 24, 26, 56, 58, 71, 77, 88, 100, 103, 113, 121, 130, 142, 160, 244
equity market, 24
erosion, 207
euro adoption, 112
European Investment Bank, 79, 128, 141
European policy, 216
exchange rate, 32, 34, 42, 46, 58, 70, 90, 94, 112, 119, 140, 153, 177, 196, 205, 208, 209, 211, 215, 245
expenditures, viii, 4, 47, 50, 118, 201, 205, 212, 216, 217, 241
expertise, 26, 74, 75
exploitation, 88, 225
export promotion, 151
export subsidies, 20
exporter, 18, 86, 109
export-led growth, 36
exposure, 15, 39, 40, 50, 63, 64, 92, 95, 137, 148, 149, 157, 166, 226
external financing, 40, 188
external shocks, 204, 216, 224
extraction, 224, 228, 234
extreme poverty, 200, 243
extremist movements, 18

F

factories, 34, 83, 103, 110, 114, 120, 151, 244
fairness, 7
faith, 184
family income, 41
farmers, 152, 153
FDI inflow, 77
fears, 50, 93, 244
federal funds, 13, 131, 141, 145
Federal Reserve Board, 17, 91, 101, 164
Federal Trade Commission Act, 163
feelings, 21
financial capital, 5
financial development, 22, 69, 74
financial distress, 62, 238
financial instability, 42, 144
financial oversight, 51, 62
financial providers, 11
financial regulation, 3, 12, 24, 26, 69, 71, 82, 100, 106, 119, 185
financial resources, 76
Financial Services Authority, 148, 154
financial shocks, 50
financial stability, 7, 26, 54, 55, 56, 62, 70, 71, 146, 163, 179, 185
financial support, 15, 67, 75, 124, 128, 135, 242
Finland, 40, 59, 137, 142, 206, 209, 213, 217
First Amendment, 246
fiscal deficit, viii, 43, 78, 90, 112, 133, 201, 209, 210, 211, 213, 215, 225
fiscal policy, 47, 90, 140, 204, 210, 215
fish, 84, 111
fishing, 124
fixed exchange rates, 177
flexibility, 70, 75, 130, 169, 212, 215
flight, vii, 1, 13, 30, 39, 41, 68

floating exchange rates, 177
flooding, 94, 125
fluctuations, 65, 227
food prices, 225, 236, 237
footwear, 111
forecasting, 3, 43, 47
foreclosure, 10, 87, 92, 138
foreign affairs, 180, 181
foreign aid, ix, 40, 174, 183, 190, 200, 219, 221, 225, 228, 230
foreign assistance, 23, 40, 230
foreign banks, 101
foreign capital flows, 37
foreign direct investment, 64, 116, 178, 221, 223, 228
foreign exchange, 27, 30, 33, 36, 63, 112, 130, 142, 149, 151, 166, 178, 241, 246
foreign investment, 35, 38, 42, 45, 146, 224, 244
foreign policy, 4, 23, 176, 222, 223
formula, 71, 199
Fourth Amendment, 112
fraud, 10, 72, 95
Fraud Enforcement and Recovery Act, 10
free trade, 134, 174
FSB, 17, 71, 100, 163, 185
fuel efficiency, 108
funding, 6, 16, 22, 49, 57, 61, 71, 72, 79, 84, 120, 125, 130, 151, 152, 158, 162, 174, 183, 188, 190, 244

G

general election, 211
global climate change, 88
global demand, 41, 44, 111, 118, 131, 226
global economy, 3, 24, 37, 40, 61, 73, 79, 89, 90, 101, 103, 104, 106, 110, 117, 129, 137, 174, 220, 221, 242
global markets, 45, 221
global trade, ix, 7, 15, 37, 48, 72, 75, 120, 128, 219, 221, 225, 226, 244
globalization, 30, 102, 177
goods and services, 26, 47, 114, 124, 137
governance, ix, 11, 16, 22, 52, 54, 69, 71, 72, 73, 97, 100, 219, 222, 223, 225, 239, 241, 243
government budget, ix, 53, 57, 74, 202, 204, 206, 207, 212, 215, 216
government expenditure, 6, 15, 111, 137, 208
government intervention, 19
government revenues, vii, 1, 4, 208, 234, 235
government securities, 13, 27, 32
government spending, 15, 34, 42, 45, 57, 78, 87, 90, 111, 133, 151, 208, 215, 216, 234

greenhouse gas emissions, 88, 174, 191, 200
gross domestic product, viii, 3, 15, 29, 50, 87, 93, 97, 102, 111, 114, 115, 124, 131, 137, 145, 201, 202, 213, 232
growth rate, 14, 35, 37, 47, 70, 130, 209, 220, 231, 243
guardian, 116
guidance, 73, 89
guidelines, 24, 110, 137, 163, 169, 213, 215

H

hard currency, 27, 112
harmonization, 169
headquarters, 181
health insurance, 81
hedging, 16, 24, 43
height, 81
HIPC, 246
HIV, 200, 243
HIV/AIDS, 200, 243
holding company, 7, 86, 148
homeowners, 34, 87, 116, 138, 151
host, 16, 55, 183, 198
household income, 107, 235
hub, 227
hue, 5
human capital, 151
human development, 71
human rights, 245

I

ideals, 48
ideology, 69
image, 21
imbalances, 2, 3, 6, 24, 70, 86, 99, 103, 174, 183, 186, 196, 204
immigration, 230
impacts, 18, 186, 229, 238
imported products, 20
imports, 4, 19, 20, 21, 41, 43, 46, 47, 64, 94, 105, 109, 111, 112, 117, 118, 123, 124, 127, 176, 225, 227, 233, 234, 243, 245, 246
impulses, 117
incidence, 68, 243
inclusion, 21, 52
income inequality, 237
income tax, 11, 33, 58, 111, 150, 152, 153
income transfers, 47
incumbents, 237
independence, 124, 194, 223
industrial democracies, 193

industrial sectors, 137
industrialization, 221
industrialized countries, vii, 1, 4, 23, 35, 37, 39, 40, 87, 177, 200, 221, 223
inequality, 134
inertia, 4
inflation, 30, 45, 50, 67, 74, 82, 93, 97, 103, 107, 110, 115, 143, 170, 204, 207, 208, 209, 211, 224, 225, 236
information exchange, 163
information technology, 20, 136
initiation, 20
injections, viii, 3, 12, 19, 21, 140, 145, 201
INS, 47, 168
instinct, 26, 30
institutional change, 3
insulation, 63
integration, 25, 232
interagency coordination, 159
Inter-American Development Bank, 42, 43, 76, 167, 188, 189
interbank market, 50
interdependence, 37, 49
interference, 45, 91
intermediaries, 25, 159
International Bank for Reconstruction and Development, 188, 199, 245
International Development Association (IDA), 77, 197, 199
international financial institutions, 4, 7, 15, 68, 71, 72, 124, 183, 187, 220, 242
International Financial Institutions, 16, 73, 186, 237
international relations, 176
international standards, 16, 17, 157, 235
international trade, 26, 30, 59, 105, 225
intervention, vii, 1, 4, 12, 19, 41, 46, 56, 96
investment bank, 13, 63, 76, 101, 148, 153
investment capital, 21, 27
invisible hand, 26
iron, 18, 20, 96, 109, 152, 165

J

job creation, 85
job training, 151
jobless, 81, 82, 121
jurisdiction, 79, 154

K

kerosene, 152

L

labor force, 54, 211
labor markets, 118
lack of confidence, 41, 91
landlocked countries, 223
layoffs, 122
leadership, 18, 21, 44, 51, 62, 71, 101, 119, 134, 177, 187, 196, 198
legislation, 2, 7, 11, 55, 79, 85, 88, 92, 103, 107, 114, 126, 163, 164, 169, 174, 185, 191, 192, 241, 242
legislative proposals, 56
lender of last resort, 22, 59, 69, 74, 97, 240
liquidity, 3, 17, 42, 43, 45, 50, 56, 57, 59, 60, 63, 76, 85, 95, 112, 118, 124, 133, 137, 144, 145, 155, 159, 160, 162, 166, 234, 238
lobbying, 4, 85, 114, 115
local government, 34, 81, 143, 151, 210
logistics, 225
lower prices, 5, 226

M

machinery, 46, 111, 135
macroeconomic environment, 208
macroeconomic policies, 3, 27, 52, 70, 99, 174, 183
macroeconomic policy, 124, 157, 177, 205, 215, 239
macroprudential analysis, 25
majority, 57, 89, 104, 113, 118, 127, 209, 211
malaria, 243
malfeasance, 159
management, 19, 54, 79, 88, 104, 120, 126, 242
mandates, 16, 73
mania, 100
manipulation, 72, 169
manufactured goods, 20, 165
manufacturing, 82, 88, 98, 110, 114, 117, 120, 122, 129, 132, 136, 139, 144
manufacturing companies, 129
market access, 102
market discipline, 69
market economy, 242
market segment, 24, 26
market share, 126
marketing, 56, 116
marketplace, 6, 8, 31
meat, 111
media, 65, 200
median, 101, 103, 107
mediation, 55
medium of exchange, 5
membership, 16, 72, 73, 74, 124, 185, 192, 193, 209

merchandise, 20, 130, 244
mergers, 13
metallurgy, 45
metals, 110
migrant workers, 23, 64
migration, 23
militancy, 68
military, 21, 22, 23, 68, 125, 126, 151, 237
military aid, 23
misconceptions, 170
mobile phone, 223
modernization, 151
momentum, 110, 190
monetary policy, 4, 11, 13, 31, 42, 45, 82, 91, 96, 97, 117, 241
monetary union, 138
money laundering, 221
money supply, 12, 31, 215
monopoly, 127
moral hazard, 2, 4, 9, 25, 76, 78, 105, 162
morale, 95
mortality rate, 243
mortgage-backed securities, 43, 50, 112, 131
multidimensional, 37
multilateral aid, 194
multinational corporations, 6
multinational firms, 25
multiples, 75
muscles, 110

N

naming, 185, 186
narcotics, 221
national borders, 51, 56, 58, 71, 160
national debt, 6, 11
national income, 77, 224, 231
national policy, 185, 217
national security, 20
National Security Council, 181
nationalism, 19
natural disasters, 75
natural gas, 48, 109
natural resource management, 238
natural resources, 40, 227
negative equity, 92
negative outcomes, 176
negotiating, 68, 79, 179
neoliberalism, 19
nuclear program, 124
nursing, 34, 151
nutrition, 33, 150

O

obstacles, 106, 191, 241
Office of Management and Budget, 114
Official Development Assistance, 190
oil production, 233
oil revenues, 18, 33, 127, 150, 152, 204
oil sands, 109
opacity, 134
open markets, 19
openness, 71
opiates, 136
opinion polls, 78
opportunities, 20, 50, 108
optimism, ix, 219
ores, 226
Organization for Economic Cooperation and Development, viii, 14, 24, 103, 105, 129, 201, 204, 206, 214, 217, 222, 230
output gap, 208, 209
output index, 138
outreach, 228
oversight, vii, 1, 2, 4, 6, 8, 9, 11, 16, 19, 22, 24, 26, 27, 49, 54, 55, 56, 69, 71, 72, 84, 91, 95, 112, 142, 148, 157, 159, 160, 176, 223
ownership, 19, 51, 79, 118, 119, 147, 148

P

pain, 86
palm oil, 227
pandemic, 236
paradigm, 69, 167, 170
patriotism, 67
payroll, 82, 98, 141
peer review, 185
penalties, 215
pension reforms, 210
pensioners, 34, 152
performance, 44, 47, 50, 56, 78, 128, 156, 159, 209, 212, 227
performance indicator, 47
permission, iv
permit, 51
personal computers, 34, 153
pharmaceuticals, 136
plants, 114, 119, 127, 151
police, 81, 85, 184, 194
policy choice, 45, 225
policy instruments, 52
policy makers, 27
policy options, viii, 8, 201
policy rate, 85, 138

policy reform, 40, 182, 186, 211, 223
policy responses, viii, 20, 40, 42, 173, 174, 183, 193, 207, 225, 241
political instability, 49, 61, 126, 233
political leaders, 18, 62, 160
political party, 104
politics, 104, 230
pools, 7, 88, 160
poor performance, 83
population growth, ix, 219, 221, 224
portfolio, 5, 41, 43, 85, 86, 101, 178, 223, 228, 229
portfolio investment, 178, 228, 229
ports, 20, 33, 150, 239
Portugal, 78, 147, 151, 202, 203, 206, 214, 217, 243
poultry, 125
poverty, ix, 4, 23, 70, 88, 107, 124, 126, 219, 220, 221, 223, 231, 235, 237, 238, 245
poverty alleviation, 220, 231
poverty line, 235
poverty reduction, 4, 126
precedent, 78, 87, 109
preferential treatment, 243
presidency, 110
prestige, 199
prevention, 10, 87, 92, 215
price changes, 75
price index, 118, 122
price stability, 70
prisons, 33, 150
private banks, 45
private firms, 49, 157, 225, 227
private investment, 88, 93, 204, 207, 224
private sector investment, 45
probability, 29
probability distribution, 29
probe, 104, 222
procurement, 145
producers, 19, 21, 34, 125, 145, 153, 227, 236
production capacity, 21, 89, 106
production networks, 166
productivity growth, 117
profit, 33, 62, 64, 81, 89, 151
profit margin, 64
profitability, 19, 114
project, 47, 83, 94, 108, 165, 185, 235
properties, 92
property rights, 194
property taxes, 111
prosperity, 70, 97, 104, 221
protectionism, 19, 20, 21, 72, 73, 106, 128, 134
prototype, 108
provincial councils, 133
public debt, viii, 46, 90, 201, 208, 209, 210, 211

public expenditures, 241
public finance, 43, 45, 90, 126, 190, 207
public housing, 33, 57, 150
public interest, 165
public investment, 54
public policy, 105
public sector, 42, 152, 153, 194, 202, 203
public service, 194, 235
public support, 9, 27, 186
public-private partnerships, 235, 239
pumps, 89
purchasing power, 187, 199, 205
purchasing power parity, 187, 199, 205

Q

query, 242
questioning, 19, 40
quotas, 46, 71, 112, 187, 199

R

radicalism, 18
rainfall, 233
rash, 116
rating agencies, 24, 29, 112, 156, 159, 194, 203
raw materials, 94, 125
reading, 104, 105, 110, 129
real assets, 18
real estate, 11, 50, 64, 66, 79, 96, 147, 149
real time, 53
reality, 4, 56, 170
recall, 140
recognition, 46, 179
recommendations, iv, 6, 16, 17, 22, 54, 55, 56, 69, 73, 74, 154, 162, 163, 182, 241
reconstruction, 65, 139
recovery plan, 133
reforms, 7, 8, 16, 49, 52, 59, 68, 69, 73, 90, 97, 99, 109, 113, 130, 147, 183, 184, 185, 186, 189, 209, 223, 231, 240
refugees, 83
regional economies, 34, 83, 151
regional integration, 225
regulatory bodies, 225
regulatory framework, 25, 142
regulatory oversight, 71
reinsurance, 48
relative size, 171, 186
relaxation, 210
relief, 20, 33, 61, 124, 132, 150, 198, 224, 230, 239, 241, 244

remittances, ix, 23, 40, 41, 43, 219, 221, 222, 223, 225, 228, 230
renewable energy, 71
repair, 136, 165
replacement, 135
repo, 161, 162
reputation, 80, 207
reserve currency, 104, 119, 246
reserves, 5, 21, 27, 30, 33, 36, 37, 43, 44, 59, 60, 61, 62, 63, 67, 97, 108, 109, 112, 120, 127, 129, 135, 142, 151, 166, 178, 241, 246
resilience, ix, 26, 118, 160, 219, 220, 225, 231
resistance, 102
resolution, 12, 13, 21, 69
resources, 7, 15, 19, 23, 58, 60, 75, 93, 98, 109, 112, 120, 130, 132, 160, 165, 174, 188, 198, 237, 238, 239, 241
respect, 9, 45, 73, 101, 120, 163, 193, 208
responsiveness, 159
restructuring, 13, 28, 51, 79, 84, 86, 89, 92, 135, 151, 198
retail, 56, 94, 98
retirement, 11
revaluation, 94
revenue, viii, ix, 41, 42, 201, 204, 206, 207, 208, 210, 216, 219, 221
rights, iv, 3, 21, 56, 100, 186
risk assessment, 25
risk aversion, 235, 245
risk factors, 40
risk management, 56, 72, 73, 154, 156, 159
risk perception, 50
risk-taking, 11, 16, 73, 156
rubber, 18, 152, 227
ruble, 47, 138, 139
rule of law, 73, 193
rural development, 33, 150, 152

S

safe haven, 41
sanctions, 57, 124
saturation, 136
savings, 3, 53, 56, 62, 63, 99, 103, 147, 148, 186
savings account, 147, 148
savings rate, 53
scaling, 238
schema, 16
SDRs, 7, 22, 71, 112, 125, 240, 246
sea level, 83
secondary education, 243
Secretary of Defense, 23
Secretary of the Treasury, 11

Securities Exchange Act, 9
seed, 238
sewage, 34, 133, 152
shame, 116
shape, 90, 97, 100, 176
shareholders, 8, 11, 12, 54, 59, 106
shipbuilding, 135
shock, 27, 41, 75, 105, 129, 246
shock therapy, 105
shortage, 68
short-term interest rate, 45, 63
Sierra Leone, 232
signals, 124, 196
signs, 6, 59, 60, 61, 64, 85, 104, 106, 147, 182, 184, 220, 221, 244
single currency, 78
slag, 226
small businesses, 2, 34, 58, 67, 131, 151
social benefits, 33, 150, 151
social programs, 41, 42, 45, 132, 207
social safety nets, 43, 70, 112, 234, 235
social security, 90, 152, 210, 241
social services, 225
social welfare, 34, 143, 151
solidarity, 48
Somalia, 232
sovereignty, 22, 54, 69
space, 24
special drawing rights, 240
specifications, 242
speculation, 81
speech, 64, 81, 90, 102
spillover effects, ix, 178, 219
spillovers, 74
stabilization, 4, 36, 41, 58, 122, 126, 133, 141, 143, 148
stabilizers, 6, 15, 53, 118, 204, 205, 207, 212, 215
standard of living, 47
State Department, 180, 181, 242, 245
state intervention, 90
state-owned banks, 45, 47, 63, 94
state-owned enterprises, 63
statistics, 14, 45, 92, 106, 123, 228, 232, 243
steel, 20, 109, 125, 135, 165
stock exchange, 59
stock markets, 30, 66, 158, 229, 244
stock value, 30
storms, 115
strategy, 36, 94, 105, 109, 112, 117, 130, 186, 213
structural adjustment, 246
structural reforms, 70, 124
subprime loans, vii
sub-Saharan Africa, 126

subsidy, 20, 107
substitutes, 47
supervision, 6, 7, 8, 9, 25, 27, 48, 49, 51, 54, 55, 56, 58, 62, 70, 72, 74, 118, 157, 166
supervisor, 53
supervisors, 6, 52, 54, 55, 73, 160
surging, 84
surplus, 45, 90, 94, 111, 131, 134, 160, 185, 202, 204, 234
surveillance, 74, 97, 160, 185, 186
survey, 102, 104, 110, 113, 120, 122, 129, 136, 141
survival, 140
suspects, 109
sustainability, 43, 60, 70, 210
sustainable development, 102, 243
sustainable growth, 48, 71, 130
systemic risk, 2, 5, 6, 7, 8, 9, 12, 16, 22, 24, 25, 73, 85, 88, 91, 95, 126, 154, 155, 159

T

takeover, 59, 148
tariff, 20, 105, 145, 192
tax breaks, 33, 118, 150, 151
tax cuts, 15, 33, 34, 42, 53, 57, 81, 133, 137, 150, 151, 152, 210
tax deduction, 33, 34, 150, 151
tax evasion, 68, 103
tax increase, 33, 57, 123, 150
tax rates, 215, 216
tax reform, 210, 211
tax system, 68
taxation, 68
technical assistance, 74, 199, 223
technology transfer, 151
teeth, 110
telecommunications, 33, 55, 111, 150, 216, 223
tensions, 46, 78, 184
territory, 79, 117
terrorism, 18, 58, 72, 177
testing, 17, 155
textiles, 20, 45, 46, 111, 135, 152
theft, 221
threats, 95
thrifts, 11
time allocation, 112
time frame, 17, 124
tin, 228
Title I, 163
tourism, 76, 135, 221
tracks, 22, 108
trade agreement, 20, 106, 111
trade benefits, 226

trade deficit, 124, 176
trade liberalization, 225
trade policy, 241
trade preference, 243
trade union, 184
trade-off, ix, 196, 202
trading partner, 20, 108, 109, 192, 208
trading partners, 20, 108, 109, 192, 208
traditions, 55
training, 43, 74, 151, 152
traits, 98
tranches, 5
transactions, 6, 25, 42, 45, 60, 116, 132, 169
transformation, 88, 148
transparency, 7, 16, 26, 49, 52, 56, 71, 72, 73, 126, 159, 169, 184
transport, 65, 94, 109, 126, 136, 137, 152
transportation, 34, 151, 224, 227, 236
transportation infrastructure, 224, 236
trends, 40, 77, 83, 167, 185, 224, 231, 241
trial, 87, 95, 116
tsunami, 69

U

U.S. Bureau of Labor Statistics, 84, 98, 121, 141
U.S. Department of the Treasury, 153, 154, 163, 164
U.S. economy, 23, 40, 42, 85, 103, 113, 122, 128
U.S. history, 149
U.S. policy, 6, 220
U.S. Treasury, 13, 17, 21, 27, 32, 62, 107, 115, 118, 126, 127, 130, 142, 147, 149, 164, 168, 171
unemployment insurance, 6, 15, 45, 81, 204, 205
unemployment rate, 44, 67, 82, 92, 98, 121, 124, 129, 132, 141, 143
uniform, 35
unions, 11
unique features, 3
universe, 100
universities, 33, 34, 150, 151
uranium, 109, 227
urban areas, 34, 83, 152

V

value added tax, 20, 33, 57, 150, 152
vector, 237
vegetables, 111
vehicles, 45, 73, 74, 79, 111, 114, 115, 117, 124, 125, 159
vein, 193
venture capital, 88
vessels, 124, 135

veto, 21, 147
victims, 83
violence, 68, 124, 146, 194
volatility, 40
voting, 3, 100, 171, 174, 182, 186, 199
vouchers, 34, 152
vulnerability, 38, 39, 133, 220

W

wages, 53, 140, 152
weakness, 54, 94, 101, 106, 127
wealth, 6, 18, 24, 27, 36, 38, 63, 75, 81, 102, 115, 120, 132, 135, 153, 166
welfare, 33, 34, 152, 153
wells, 191
wholesale, 50
withdrawal, 3, 85
wool, 109

workers, 33, 34, 43, 58, 81, 85, 103, 109, 117, 119, 121, 124, 140, 150, 151, 152, 169, 221, 223, 225, 230
working groups, 180
workplace, 151
World Trade Organization, viii, 3, 19, 46, 69, 73, 99, 102, 105, 107, 125, 130, 165, 173, 177, 181, 182, 183, 197, 198, 200, 227
World War I, 114, 137, 176
worry, 60, 186
wrongdoing, 57

X

xenophobia, 237

Y

yuan, 94, 108, 109, 121, 130, 131, 136